BOOKLEGGERS AND SMUTHOUNDS

BOOKLEGGERS
AND
SMUTHOUNDS

THE TRADE IN EROTICA, 1920–1940

JAY A. GERTZMAN

UNIVERSITY OF PENNSYLVANIA PRESS · Philadelphia

10 9 8 7 6 5 4 3 2 1

Published by
University of Pennsylvania Press
Philadelphia, Pennsylvania 19104-4011

Library of Congress Cataloging-in-Publication Data

Gertzman, Jay A.
   Bookleggers and smuthounds : the trade in erotica, 1920–1940 /
Jay A. Gertzman.
      p.   cm.
   Includes bibliographical references and index.
   ISBN 0-8122-3493-6 (alk. paper)
   1. Erotica — United States.   2. Pornography — United States.
I.Title.
HQ472.U6G47   1999
363.4′7′0973 — dc21   99-12229
                                                                CIP

Frontispiece: Curious books, excited readers: detail from an advertisement for Boccaccio's *Decameron Tales,* offered by mail order from the Franklin Publishing Company. From *College Life,* Feb. 1931, 6.

To Arnold, Chris, and Cliff

Contents

Introduction

Many of the men and women who began careers in printing, publishing, and distributing erotic literature in the 1920s and 1930s have passed away or are quite elderly. Once, snarl words were used legally to stigmatize such individuals and their products. The federal antiobscenity statutes, lobbied through Congress by Anthony Comstock in 1873 and enforced just as powerfully half a century later, called their wares "obscene, lewd, lascivious, indecent, filthy, or vile." Comstock, and his supporters and successors, applied the same epithets to the dealers. But sometimes (and, despite their assertions, often incidentally), the dealers' work helped liberate the popular imagination and furthered democratic principles of freedom of speech and action. Hard-driving entrepreneurs, these bookmen and bookwomen catered to American needs in a society where sexual repression and prurience were commonplace. This book commemorates their work, their life experiences, and their contributions to contemporary culture.

The business of distributing erotica has changed dramatically since the 1920s and 1930s. The same can be said of sexual taboos. They still exist, however, and challenges made to taboos by commercial enterprises such as publishing, filmmaking, and bookselling continue to provoke moral indignation. Erotica dealers' careers and personal tensions in the social context of the interwar period can teach us a great deal about how both repressing and trading upon sexual curiosity affect moralists and merchants. *Bookleggers and Smuthounds* presents information gathered in part from personal interviews and archival collections. This supplements, and in some cases corrects, existing secondary sources. In reviewing the body of material, I have become convinced that publishers of erotica and the moralists who attacked them during the early twentieth century had (as they continue to have) a subtle symbiotic relationship. As savvy businesspeople, erotica distributors necessarily appealed to prurient fascination. As they invited their clients to indulge curiosities that kept intact the association of sex with obscenity and shameful silence, the blunt fact of their existence provided antivice crusaders with the public enemy they needed to show how fascination with sex was indeed a moral offense exploited by people with contempt for purity.

Documenting what those who sold erotica did fills in a missing chapter in early twentieth-century American publishing history, supplying detailed information on the kind of literary censorship practiced at the time and on its motives. By "erotica" I mean all sexually explicit material whose dissemination was subject to dispute during the interwar period, ranging from writing that seems innocuous now, but was then thought to border on the obscene, to the blatant below-the-counter cartoons and stories in which the movements of the "two-backed monster" were sketched with the aid of as many four-letter words as possible. I do not do so to suggest that commercially profitable writings about sex are either good or bad, although "prurience" is an important word in seeking to separate sexuality from shame and guilt. Because of the commercial profits resulting, as our popular culture every day exemplifies, from tying sexuality to titillation, shame, and shock, people must decide for themselves the validity of this connection, as well as to what extent sexual behavior should remain private, and experimentation carefully guided. The identification of sex with prurience is important, and can perhaps best be understood if I use the most objective, least value-laden term possible — one that allows readers to separate material "in some sense 'about' sexual activity" (i.e., erotica) from "the subset of erotic presentations and representations that by virtue of their frankness or other offensive or disturbing properties shock or embarrass many people" (i.e., pornography). As Richard A. Posner, court of appeals judge and lucid commentator on law, privacy, and obscenity, warns, "the terms 'erotic,' 'pornographic,' and 'obscene' overlap in confusing ways."[1]

My reason for choosing to use "erotica" and not "pornography" may become clearer by considering the term the International Reform Federation used to stigmatize the sub-rosa cartoons and stories mentioned above. The federation favored "flagitious," possibly because it was more loaded with moral indignation than "pornographic," which was of course pejorative, but could be used by hard-liners, as was "porno," to denote anything from the *Arabian Nights* to Frank Harris's *My Life and Loves*. When so many literary representations of sex are considered morally problematic, one struggles to find the most vigorous terms ranking them from questionable to horrible. Booksellers, critics, and bibliographers addressed this problem by using the term "gallant" for decorously written stories and essays about sexual attraction. Boston's Watch and Ward Society, which considered both birth-control information and *Lady Chatterley's Lover* as egregious, cast a skeptical eye on gallant, or "polite," works, as they termed them. In using the term "erotica" to cover the range of sexually explicit books, then, I am not judging material "in some way about sex" as either positive or negative. Today, both "pornography" and "hard-core" denote vulgarity when used by conservative moralists, as "flagitious" did during the 1920s and 1930s (although that word was not nearly as ubiquitous as "hard-core" is now). Considering sexual writings objectively, without assigning them value, allows the story of what both prosecutors and distributors did with them to take the foreground. Why and how the trade in erotica became a public presence in the interwar period, and what that tells us about the life experiences of people in the business, is the focus of this book.

A final reason for preferring the term "erotica" to "pornography" is that the latter can carry connotations of subversion. In the context of my discussion, the one would be as misleading as the other. Laura Kipnis has recently identified the fear and contempt pornography generates today with its creation and distribution by nonelite individuals and groups oblivious to mainstream moral and aesthetic standards.[2] Pornography, she says, expresses the alienation of those at the bottom of the social scale: it is low-class; it seduces its readers into abandoning their responsibilities and, possibly, makes them see the social order and its moral contradictions from the perspective of the most disenfranchised. For these reasons Kipnis does not dismiss pornography, but posits for it a political power of its own. Although her insights are provocative and valuable, the dealers I discuss had little in common with those Kipnis studied. My subjects offered a wider variety of materials, many of which had literary and social value. That these individuals were regarded as upstarts suggests that regardless of their background, they aspired to middle-class status. In some cases they attained it, not only by making money but by gaining legal and academic approval for their publications.

Publishers and booksellers who risked arrest for distributing "obscene" and "indecent" materials performed a valuable service for public health, science, and literature. This may be measured by listing some of the exceptional writers they distributed in unexpurgated editions: the iconoclastic poets and novelists Rabelais, Pierre Louÿs, Arthur Schnitzler, and D. H. Lawrence; the pioneer birth-control advocates Marie Stopes, Margaret Sanger, and William J. Robinson; and the proponents of same-sex relationships Oscar Wilde, Radclyffe Hall, and Magnus Hirschfeld. Most of the sexually explicit books of the interwar period, however, would be judged today as simply ephemeral entertainments; some, from a current perspective, convey false information or rest on faulty assumptions. Though the same could be said of any publisher's list, prurience remained a selling point even for books by important writers.

Erotica dealers traded on the fact that sex, as a taboo subject, was associated with secrecy, mystery, special occasion, and privilege. Readers would buy books on the ways religious ceremony (*Magica Sexualis*) and social mores (*Sex Life in England, Chastity Belts*) channel sexual instinct if they could be brought to focus on the arcane and magical nature of the material, and to subscribe to the idea that its circulation must be confined to those whose curiosity was part of a scientific, dispassionate sensibility. The request to sign a coupon assuring the publisher of one's qualifications further incited curiosity and the sense of belonging to a special club. There was also the implication that information about sex, if not success and expertise in sexual relations, was to be identified with affluence and professional and community status. The descriptions of the lavish bindings and their gold stamped lettering, the watermarked paper, the elaborate decorations, frontispieces, and vignettes of certain varieties of erotica had an obvious appeal to those who wished to think their tastes were "exclusive." Such readers might have identified success in finding sex partners with a cool, affectless sensuality. The aloof, uncommitted sybarite, whom experience taught to consume sexual favors dispassionately, was an exemplar for some (Figure 1). Whether as author of, or character in, erotic stories, he or she was paraded before prospective customers, and was a steady seller.

Advertisements for erotica sometimes traded on the attraction of the "body beautiful," but they often emphasized instead the bizarre, morbid, or pathological (Figure 2). One brochure touted large numbers of "racial-erotic photographs" delineating "curious pregnancies," sexual organs deformed by disease or by "passing curious sex and erotic devices," tattooing, and other "savage arts" involving the human body.[3] Aboriginal peoples were the major source for examples of sexual abnormalities and diseases. Treatments of homosexuality and lesbianism were included in works of this type, and when mentioned in advertisements, "inversion" was heavily laden with a sense of both freakishness and degeneracy. It was "whispered about," a "riddle," an "abnormality" of a "shadow world."[4] Sadism was yet another selling point (Figure 3). Circulars for erotica focused extensively on the freakish extremes to which lust and desire could drive people. Books on chastity belts and male and female infibulation attempted "an astonishing history of genital curiosities," such as "methods of sewing up the sexes of

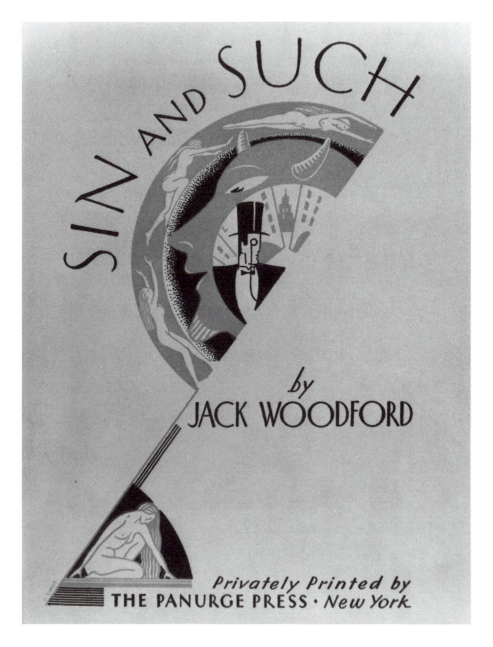

Figure 1. Title page of Jack Woodford, *Sin and Such*, published in an edition of fifteen hundred copies by the Panurge Press in 1930. Booksellers remember the volume for its binding, the patterned cloth of which they accurately describe as "lipstick red."

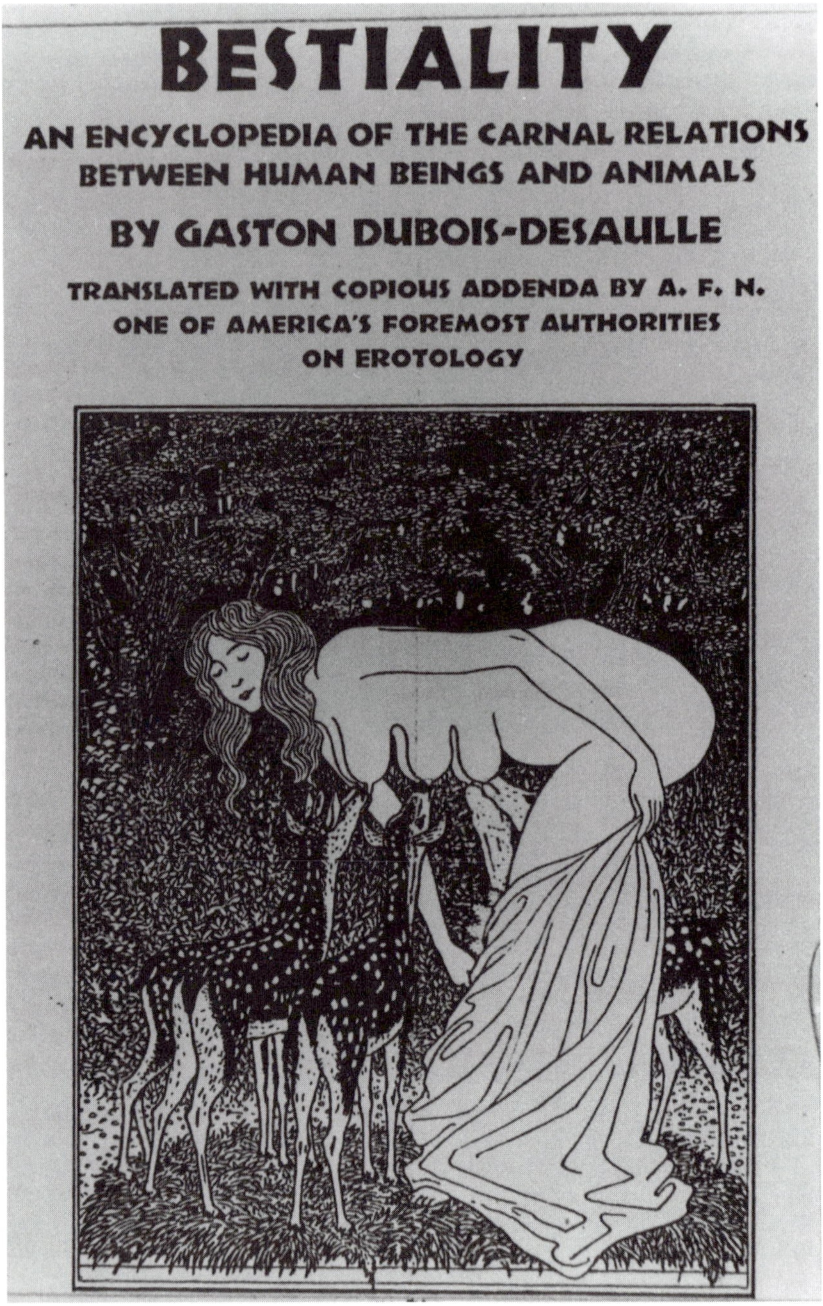

Figure 2. Brochure for Gaston Dubois-Desaulle, *Bestiality: An Historical, Medical, Legal, and Literary Study, with Addenda*, issued by the Panurge Press, 1934. Reproduced by permission of the Kinsey Institute, University of Indiana (KI Files).

WOMAN
AS A SEXUAL CRIMINAL

By ERICH WULFFEN, M.D.

Director of Penal Institutes and the
Minister of Probation in Saxony. Author
of: *Criminal Psychology: The Sexual
Criminal: The Sexual Mirror of Art and
Crime, etc.*

ONLY ENGLISH TRANSLATION

Masochist *tortured* in a "Massage Salon"
from the Criminal Archives of the Hamburg Police

Complete and Unexpurgated

●

Over 500 Pages

●

**FULLY ILLUSTRATED
WITH
UNIQUE PHOTOGRAPHS
FROM THE
SECRET ARCHIVES
OF THE
GERMAN POLICE**

●

Hundreds of Cases

●

**SOLD only by SUBSCRIPTION
To DOCTORS and LAWYERS**

Figure 3. First page of brochure issued by the American Ethnological Press for its edition of Erich Wulffen, *Psycho-Biological, Medico-Legal and Criminological Studies in Woman as a Sexual Criminal* (1935). Reproduced by permission of Dr. C. J. Scheiner.

women," "outrageous customs such as point-tying" (magical spells producing impotence), "eunuch factories," and "anaphrodisiacs."

Many of the fiction and nonfiction titles about Africa, the Middle East, or the Orient sold by mail or shelved in the curiosa or erotica sections of bookstores were actually serious anthropological studies or perceptive depictions of foreign peoples. But even this material was often advertised as an easy and direct way to comprehend the sexual prowess and feral proclivities of the black race. Phrases such as "the barbaric and raging sex-life of the African," their "darkest erotic practices,"[5] "the ruthless savagery of the dark continent," or "the jungle morality of the African races, their extreme sensuality,"[6] suggested that the "natives" were not only remote but voices from a barbaric past. Not just Africans but also Arabs and Asians in general were stigmatized as "incontinent," "adulterous and cruel."[7] It is not surprising to find racial scapegoating embedded in ambivalence about sexual urges. Since sexual desire was associated with secrecy, amoral decadence, violent excess, and disease, and yet was an irrepressible force, those who epitomized its carnality and the emotional confusion it caused must be barely human, threatening strangers. A major selling point in advertisements of this type was the white woman's attraction to the black man, often characterized as emerging after the man forced himself on a woman he had captured and brutalized.[8]

Sometimes, the white woman tempted the black man. A 1935 edition of a virulently racist turn-of-the-century novel declared this kind of behavior to be simply an "instinct of [the female] race, handed down from the slightly-clad lady who dallied with the serpent."[9] Distrust of "the weaker sex" was as endemic and mundane as that of the black. The perceived aberrancy and outlandishness of both women and blacks were used to incite prurience by identifying lust with frustration, misery, and degeneracy. Advertisements for many kinds of erotic books (Figures 2 and 3) worked in this way. Women could defeat "the most diabolical ingenuity of jealous husbands,"[10] become "teaser types" who "permit all embraces but the final embrace,"[11] or cleverly hide nymphomania by simulating modesty and virginity.[12]

All of the avatars of prurience just described have a common theme: the self-destructiveness of sexual desire. Looking objectively at the way erotica merchants sold sex in the 1920s and 1930s, one recognizes — and possibly notes ruefully how things have not changed much — that it was associated variously with loss of innocence, loveless exploitation and manipulation, indelicacy, irrationality, the infliction of pain, and the equation of sensuality or orgasm with suffering. It was assumed that people who could afford to indulge their sexual instincts did so with the aggressive use of physical, political, or economic power. Sex was a tool, often used tyrannically by sybaritic, subversive, or foreign individuals, with which to destroy the moral or social order. It was associated with the profane, with idleness, and with the coarse dissipation of both money and personal vitality. Erotica distributors insisted on the value of sex education and satisfaction of basic instincts, but the demands of the marketplace led them to present a picture of human sexuality saturated just as strongly with shame and fear as that embraced by those whom H. L. Mencken called the "Comstocks": the officers of the Watch and Ward Society and the New York Society for the Suppression of Vice (NYSSV).

A unique confluence of social factors during the 1920s and 1930s produced an unprecedented amount of erotica in America, which took many new forms. The revolution in printing technology was one factor. Another was the accelerated pace of social change, which made available more choices involving sex and provided a setting in which legal definitions of obscenity became liberalized. America's population in the 1920s was still more rural than urban, but the urbanization that had progressed for half a century meant that after World War I there was increased social mobility, especially for women, and greater opportunities for personal and professional triumphs and tragedies. New places of entertainment catered to human needs for escape from new tensions that had not existed in the settled routines of rural life, increasing the chances for sensual adventures. New trends in women's clothing, haberdashery, and perfumes, and the changing contents of books, magazines, and films reflected the need for vicarious escapes from the mundane too. All such outlets showed how deeply the moral codes more fitting for a rural family setting had eroded, as worried native-born elites were quick to perceive.

The antivice "preventive societies" of the Progressive Era emerged in reaction against this new social scene. These organizations tried to combat the "moral degradation" in the immigrant slums, which they saw as root causes of gambling, prostitution, and alcoholism, as well as pornography. They also sought to convince middle-class communities of the urgency of rectitude. Organizations such as Boston's Watch and Ward and New York's Society for the Suppression of Vice, laboring for a return to family-oriented values, championed reticence in sexual matters and hoped to restrict sexual expression to the marriage bed. They believed that bodily activities naturally evoked shame among virtuous people, who followed God's ruling that they should be kept private. Books should be morally uplifting; since the life of the human body stood as far from morality as self-centered sensual satisfaction stood from disinterested reason, all texts that focused on sex, whether marriage manuals, birth-control tracts, or steamy novels, spoke aloud what for the sake of spiritual health had to be kept hidden. These preventive societies operated through legal proscriptions such as the Comstock Law against obscene and indecent expression, through vigilant prosecution of offenders, and through forceful lectures and pamphlets about what decent behavior was.

But antivice crusaders, however well endowed with financial support and backed by traditional codes of personal integrity, could not stem the tide of revolution in manners and morals. Since sex was increasingly considered to be a significant element in a fulfilling life instead of merely a procreative necessity, the demand for information about it skyrocketed. By the early 1920s, a group of young New York publishers was providing Americans with literature from European writers whom the older publishers considered too subversive to touch. Beginning in 1922, a series of court rulings made it more difficult to suppress sexually explicit material that could not be termed flagitious by any general consensus. These rulings were the result of obscenity prosecutions for which determined publishers hired expert lawyers, who successfully refuted the charges. The possible demoralizing effect of a work on the most susceptible member of the community was no longer the criterion for obscenity. Instead, judgments were made on the basis of the tolerances of the average adult, his or her distinctions between obscene and realistic depictions of life and manners, and the literary or scientific value of a work, to which experts were allowed to testify. The entire book, not isolated passages, had to be evaluated.

In this context, frankly descriptive fiction became popular, but so did "anthropological" accounts of sexual customs and "sexological" analyses of behavior. Erotica distributors quickly assessed which readers would pay what for their wares. Sexually oriented books became accessible not only to the well-to-do, but also, via low-priced reprints distributed in stores and through the mails, and by lending libraries, to people with only a dollar to spare, and to adolescents. There were renewed demands for interdiction, calls for government action and for self-regulation by publishers and bookstore owners. But meanwhile, underground distributors, taking advantage of small cylinder rotary presses, papier-mâché printing plates, and photolithography, churned out large quantities of flagrantly obscene works, and reprinted domestically the banned modern and Victorian European classics.

Not only was more erotica printed and distributed in America during the interwar period than previously; more was written as well, especially during the Depression years. At that time, writers and publishers needed money as badly as almost everyone else. New audiences among the hoi polloi were created for cheap borderline materials, and the prurient itches of wealthy collectors were exploited as well. For the later, "combines" of young, needy writers turned out unpublishable material in typescripts sold in ribbon and duplicated copies.

After World War II, the conflict between erotica distributors and the authorities who attempted to suppress their products assumed a different character. The preventive societies were no longer a factor, although the Post Office certainly was. Mail-order booksellers, hindered in the late 1930s by Justice Department prosecutions, profited by taking advantage of new and more varied kinds of borderline books. As demographic patterns changed, with middle-class families relocating to the burgeoning suburbs, many downtown cigar- and bookstores of the big cities began to carry "sleaze," that is, more aggressively salacious hardbacks than those found in lending libraries and on dollar-book counters before the war. With the paperback revolution came suggestive cover art that made even the most innocuous literature seem racy and was visible to all, on newsstands and in drugstores. Moralists' concerns were redirected toward juvenile delinquency. By 1950 a very different kind of book from those of the 1930s was being labeled "vulgar," "sadistic," "incitive of drug use," "violent," "perverted," and "lustful." Bolder methods of advertisement and distribution had sparked a new round of moral indignation, perpetuating the symbiotic cycle as new kinds of "dangerous" books became a forbidden thrill. Not until the new sexual revolution in the early 1960s were erotic classics allowed to circulate freely and made cheaply available.

Erotica merchants, along with many other "middlemen," worked in morally ambiguous areas. Their critics viewed them as grabbing dirty dollars by profaning an aspect of human experience meant to be regulated by sacred authority and not amenable to public discussion. Conservative moralists stigmatized erotica dealers as lumpen parvenus and indecent subversive strangers. They were regarded as interlopers, bonding together with fellow ethnics to monopolize a marginal area of trade. The seeming low shrewdness and boundless venality were explained as the visible effects of these outsiders' inability to discipline themselves to accept American religious and ethical values. Erotica merchants were accused of controlling prices through an underground delivery system, of dealing unfairly with customers, and of being manipulative while contributing nothing to the larger community whose morals and mores they were thought both to disdain and to prey upon. Authorities crusading for decency took care to deny the ethnic middleman any official sanction, political power, or due process if they could. Erotica dealers learned to persevere, developing the necessary moxie to confront enemies, satisfy customers, and negotiate with competitors. Their character traits and professional abilities were typical of successful middlemen — and at times easy to confuse with those of successful criminals.

Bookleggers and Smuthounds begins with a discussion of the interwar erotica distributors as "pariah capitalists"; it deals with the skills of eastern European Jewish immigrants and their offspring that made them successful in the field. Also discussed are the kinds of erotica prevalent in the 1920s and 1930s, and the locations at which it was printed, rented, and sold. John Saxton Sumner, a chief moral crusader against printed material deemed obscene and Anthony Comstock's successor as secretary of the NYSSV, was a key player throughout this period. Sumner's organization aimed to eradicate a slew of physical and intellectual dysfunctions it attributed to the availability of obscene books, magazines, and pictures, including sins against God and barriers isolating citizens from achieving the American Dream. Sumner thought it necessary to defend a "one-hundred-percent American" moral consensus — an amalgam of sexual reticence, patriotism, and Christian piety — against the immigrant, the Bolshevik, the money-grubbing urbanite, the worldly sophisticate, and the effete intellectual.

The response of the New York book trade to these ideological pressures is another important part of the story. Out of the desire for a respectable public image emerged a false dichotomy between responsible bookmen and "smutmongering" pariahs, driven by the policies of publishers' and booksellers' professional organizations seeking to protect the public image of their profession. Also dealt with is the significance of developments in the late 1920s and 1930s when court decisions liberalized the criteria under which erotic books were deemed nonobscene. To some extent, the power of Sumner and other "moral entrepreneurs" of the antivice societies weakened, although that of the Catholic Church and the Post Office did not.

There were also in place extensive and lucrative mail-order erotica schemes, and the federal response to them shows how persistently the government pursued these booksellers. Even before Comstock, the Post Office took as its congressional mandate purging the mails of the "twin pollutants" of fraud and obscenity. Its work during the interwar period reflects the full range of its procedures and the machine-like, extraconstitutional rigidity with which they were applied. Determining what was unmailable through unilateral decisions of its own team of inspectors and counsels, postal authorities meshed with other components of the social order — clergy, politicians, spokespeople for the preventive societies — to create layers or "nests" of authority that humbled publishers and distributors of erotica.

The final chapter of *Bookleggers and Smuthounds* describes the career of Samuel Roth. No one knew better how to appeal to prurience to sell books — and no one was more scarred by the traumas of between-the-wars erotica distribution. By concentrating on the way Roth advertised his books, defined himself, and defied authority, I expose the conflicted motives and psychic pressures of dealing in erotica in the early to mid-twentieth century. Roth made his living by publishing some very good literature, but peddled classics and pulps in a uniformly titillating manner, for which the authorities punished him severely. Unable to cope with insecurity and alienation, Roth responded by portraying himself as a martyr to free speech, a subversive, which at best he was only imperfectly. His challenge of authority was never free from the economic reality of catering to the prurience that his prosecutors themselves helped perpetuate.

In bare but essential outline, the rules Roth was forced to play by are still in effect. Sexually explicit video- and audiotapes, telephone communications, and cyberspace web sites, usually not print media, now occasion fear that American youth are being debauched, but insistent calls for government censorship or self-imposed rating systems are part of the same strange symbiosis of condemnation and popularity. Artists and merchants who are subject to attack as sleazy or indecent today may easily identify with their predecessors, and profit from considering what was won and lost as they went about their business.

Traders in Prurience
Pariah Capitalists and Moral Entrepreneurs

In the 1920s and 1930s, when sexually explicit books and magazines and their illustrations, not the Internet and video cassettes, were considered a chief corrupting influence in American homes, censorious authorities pointed suspiciously at booksellers of widely varying types. Everyone in the trade knew about the "bookleggers," "Fourth Avenue pirates," and underground printers and publishers. Many carried their wares — sexological or anthropological tracts, titillating novels, histories of curious usages to which the human body had been subject, or under-the-counter banned titles sold to trusted customers. The owners of one well-established New York bookstore, Biblo and Tannen (later a reprint publishing house), made ends meet on Fourth Avenue during the Depression by selling pornographic pamphlets or "readers," staying open Saturday night until 1 A.M. to do so. The owners kept a sharp eye out for agents for the New York Society for the Suppression of Vice (NYSSV), hoping they did not work during the midnight hours, when the demand rose steadily.[1] All sorts of books about sex moved well, but there was a high risk that the existence of both borderline and flagrant types would electrify activists worried about declining moral standards in their cities. Consequently, police or their deputized agents might visit the often unsuspecting wholesalers or retailers.

The late Louis Cohen of the Argosy Book Store in midtown Manhattan recalled that he scrupulously kept his distance from erotica, even instructing his clerks never to refer a customer to stores whose owners felt that they would have had to close their doors without dealing in it. However, in 1935, Cohen received a subpoena from John Saxton Sumner, secretary of the NYSSV. One of Sumner's undercover agents had purchased a recently shelved book on flagellation from the Argosy's restricted-access curiosa section. At the hearing, the nervous bookseller armed himself with evidence of catalogs and customer endorsement, and the judge quickly dismissed the case.[2] But Cohen knew the fate of some of his colleagues; visions of padlocks and bankruptcy justifiably troubled his sleep. With Sumner on the loose, these could be any bookseller's fate.

The Town Censor and Broadway Sam

On 4 October 1929, Sumner and several of his agents searched the offices of the Golden Hind Press, at 122 Fifth Avenue, and impounded books of both dubious and notorious reputation.[3] The borderline items included *Oscar Wilde Three Times Tried*, Petronius's *Satyricon*, which portrayed three men's bisexual escapades, and *Hands Around*, a translation of Arthur Schnitzler's *Reigen* (*La Ronde*), a drama of linked episodes, each culminating in a sexual encounter. The owner, Samuel Roth, watched Sumner's men carry away cartloads of the *Kama Sutra* and a lucrative piece of hackwork, *Observations of an Old Man in Love*, which was a spin-off from Frank Harris's lubricious four-volume autobiography, *My Life and Loves*. The next day, at a storeroom also rented by the Golden Hind, the vice-eradicators found 2,290 volumes, a treasure trove consisting of many banned books, including unexpurgated copies of *Fanny Hill*, *Lady Chatterley's Lover*, and *Ulysses*, as well as "pictures, very filthy." Sumner also grabbed assorted correspondence from Roth's desk. Order forms for *Forbidden Books*, a catalog with erotic excerpts from works published by the notorious European pornographer Charles Carrington, and for *Fanny Hill* and *Lady Chatterley* were discovered.[4] These were from booksellers, including James A. Delacey of Dunster House, whose sale of these books would make him a defendant in one of Boston's most celebrated obscenity trials. Roth, his wife, Pauline, who was registered as proprietor of the Golden Hind, and his brother Max ("Moe") were all arrested.

Under the alias Harry Burke, Max Roth had personally contacted people he thought would be interested in purchasing back-room or under-the-counter books. As Samuel Roth's daughter later recalled, one was a lawyer named Marcus who, as bad fortune would have it, was a member of the NYSSV.[5] Marcus had received a Golden Hind circular for a book entitled *Bundling* and had thereupon contacted Sumner, who requested that he respond. He did, indicating that he already knew about bundling, a venerable puritan exercise in sexual restraint. Could the Golden Hind locate, as Sumner put it in his testimony at the trial, "any other spicy books" for Marcus?[6] Harry Burke called the lawyer and made an appointment with him. Burke brought to the man's office copies of *Lady Chatterley's Lover*, *A Night in a*

Moorish Harem, *The Amatory Experiences of a Surgeon*, and "probably ten other books of that type," as Sumner later testified. Max did not recognize that among three other gentlemen present, one was Sumner himself. He unwittingly sold three books to an undercover policeman, as well as a copy of *Chatterley* to Marcus. Max Roth was soon on his way to prison for possession and sale of obscene books.

So was Sam Roth, for violation of parole. In June of 1928, Sumner and his agents, "an evil, foul-smelling lot" in Roth's opinion, had prepared a net of deception in which to snare him and his wife at their Book Auction (Figure 4).[7] According to Roth, Sumner had forced a bookseller, who had been arrested just nine days before, to leave some illicit photos and drawings at the Book Auction the day before Sumner raided the premises.[8] They were not discarded, Roth asserted, only because he and his wife knew the man who had brought them in, Henry Klein, and knew that Klein was in trouble because Sumner had recently raided his store. They looked out for their colleague, assuming he would return for the material the next day. This may have been preposterous self-justification, or the claim may well have been true; what is almost certain is that the materials in question were not the only erotic ones on the premises. Roth, who had been arrested previously, swore to his probation officer that Sumner was "trying to frame him up."[9] The vice society's annual ledgers record Klein's arrest and his suspended sentence in 1928, even though he was a wholesaler.[10] They also record his workhouse sentence for possessing Harris's *My Life* in 1925, and his penitentiary sentence four years later. That Klein managed to avoid a jail sentence in 1928 might well indicate that he acted as Sumner instructed him.

While serving four months for his Golden Hind activities, Roth wrote *Stone Walls Do Not: The Chronicle of a Captivity*, in which Sumner had a place. In a long poem titled "The Censor," "S . . . ner"

> takes the precious volume
> From its own appointed shelf,
> And his eyes as he scans its pages
> Shame it even to itself; . . . .[11]

From his slightly shabby office in what used to be the dining room of an old Manhattan brownstone at 215 West 22nd Street, Sumner, the "town censor," directed a crusade against "immoral" plays and movies, burlesque houses, pub-

Figure 4. This small secondhand bookstore was owned by the Fourth International Socialist Workers Party in the 1930s, but in 1928 this (28 East 12th Street) was the location of Samuel Roth's Book Auction. John Sumner arrested Roth and his wife for having on the premises certain erotic photos and drawings, which Roth swore Sumner had had planted. © Collection of the New-York Historical Society.

lishers, and bookstores of every size and description. He was a recognizable figure to New Yorkers of all five boroughs (Figure 5), the equal in the public mind of fellow mugwumps such as Reverend Charles Parkhurst (witness to, and decrier of, East Side debauchery), Republican counsel Frank Moss (author of *American Metropolis*), and Judge Samuel Seabury (whose investigations into the magistrates' courts brought down Mayor Jimmy Walker).

Sumner was the hand-picked successor to the NYSSV founder, Anthony Comstock, the lifelong fervent crusader for moral purity, who, although a private citizen, was the author of the federal antiobscenity postal statutes that bear his name.[12] The law resulting from Comstock's efforts in Congress prohibited "every obscene, lewd, lascivious, indecent, filthy, or vile article, matter, thing, device, or substance; and . . . [e]very article . . . which is advertised or described in a manner calculated to lead another to use or apply it for preventing conception or producing abortion, or for any indecent or immoral use."[13]

The appeal of the Comstock Law was its assumption that in an era of social change and urban growth America was engaged in a life-and-death fight waged on behalf of "decent" people. At stake was the nature of the community itself. The enemies were two very different but equally pernicious types, either immoral sensualists or quick-buck opportunists. The former were the intellectual decadents advocating free love and birth control, thus challenging family structure. The latter were venal merchants peddling pornography. If left unchecked, both would destroy the moral consensus necessary for a Christian social conscience to prevail in America. John Sumner battled tirelessly against both kinds of offenders.

Sumner was a soft-spoken man, not a charismatic, fire-and-brimstone evangelist of the Billy Sunday type. He did not make a point of publicly labeling offenders as being of the wrong class, nationality, or faith — although he carefully observed these qualities in those he investigated. He was no vulgar demonizer of agnostic scholars, liberal clerics, and sex-obsessed writers for the delectation of scapegoat-hungry yahoos. He had, however, what historian Richard Hofstadter has described as the "one-hundred per cent mentality,"[14] that is, one who knew that the new-fangled "sophisticated" literature and drama that emerged after the Great War needed careful watching. He saw a strong relationship between religious orthodoxy, patriotism, and repression of the "animal passions." As leaders of the "preventive" or "purity" societies such as the NYSSV saw it, the interwar decades of the twentieth century presented an unprecedented set of enticements to immorality

Why the Art Exhibit "for Men Only" Upset the Vice Crusader

And the Old Battle Over What's Art and What Isn't Rages on Half-a-Dozen Fronts From Broadway to Boston and New Jersey to Detroit

A Copy of Giorgione's Famous "Sleeping Venus" Was Barred from a Broadway Exhibit "For Men Only."

John S. Sumner, Anti-Vice Leader, Sought to Suppress Seven Nudes and Was Sued.

SUPPOSE you were riding up Fifth Avenue on a bus and saw a banner draped across the classic facade of the Metropolitan Museum of Art with the words—"FOR MEN ONLY." Would that label transform some of the celebrated paintings upon the museum walls from works of art into a low form of exhibition? And would John S. Sumner of the Society for the Suppression of Vice be justified in taking action?

Recent developments in the eternal controversy as to what is artistic and what is improper, and whether the artistic can become the improper, make this a pertinent question. For it appears that, whereas in a Broadway storeroom is one thing to a vice crusader, and something else to someone else. Also that a ballyhoo copy of a masterpiece is to be regarded askance. Also that a work of art has its morality jeopardized by passing through the customs.

It sometimes boils down to the question of how a painting is presented. Even the courts are beginning to accept the viewpoint of the art world, that what determines the status of a painting, a book or a piece of sculpture is its appropriate presentation from the angle of taste.

This distinction was emphasized in a raid by Mr. Sumner on a Broadway display of nudes, the arrest of one Timothy Murphy who lectured on the exhibit, and now by the suit of Mr. Murphy, asking $100,000 for false arrest and malicious prosecution.

The Broadway show opened with a flourish and with these signs in the window: Admission 25 cents—Men Only—Men Over 18 only—FAMOUS PAINTINGS.

Jack Rothschild promoted the exhibit and engaged Murphy to enlighten the customers by explaining what the pictures of nudes and semi-nudes were about.

Mr. Sumner and three policeman swooped down on the scene, listened to a few words of the lecture, and promptly bundled Murphy and his nudes into a patrol wagon.

Lacking bail, the lecturer spent the night in jail. When the case was heard before Magistrate George W. Simpson, the prosecution argued that Murphy had violated the penal code prohibiting the exhibition of lewd pictures.

Former Judge Mancuso, for the defense, succeeded in identifying all seven of the paintings as copies of recognized old masters, one of them being Giorgione's "Sleeping Venus." Sumner insisted that though the works might represent similar paintings by masters, the copies were deliberately franker than the originals.

TIMOTHY MURPHY, a gray-haired Irishman of about 40, told the court he was an itinerant lecturer whose repertoire included Sex, Capital punishment, Art, Eugenics, Science and the Bible. When asked for his qualifications, he replied that he had been in the army.

The magistrate discharged Murphy, holding that the reproductions were artistically done, and that they could not be designated as indecent simply because they were exhibited on Broadway

"Portrait of a Young Lady" (Above) Done in Polished Bronze by the Rumanian Artist Brancusi.

or because women were barred.

So Murphy has assumed the role of aggressor in this battle of the nudes, and brought suit for $100,000 against the the secretary of the vice suppression society. His attorney, David Garrison Berger, plans to make this a test case to define the province of moral censors in the domain of "art" exhibition.

The Sumner attitude toward the question involved is mirrored in his answer to a query during the Murphy hearing.

"There is a great distinction," he said, "between showing pictures in an art gallery and showing some pictures on Broadway for men only under an air of mystery."

That the vice crusader is not always in the puritanic ranks on disputed matters of art is shown by his attitude toward a piece of sculpture by Edward Field Sanford, Jr., of New York, which was shown at the National Academy of Design.

Two members of the Harvard Law Club lodged a complaint against the figure as "immoral and indecent." Sumner investigated and said: "It's art."

Plainfield Art Students (Above) Walking Off With Their Exiled Nudes. At Left, the Mexican Artist, Diego Rivera, Whose Murals Started Rows.

Boston, long one of the citadels of conservatism in its slant or art, recently aroused the ire of Henri Burkhard, when his "Mater Doloroso" was removed from the Boston Museum of Arts as "irreligious." It is a Madonna and Child study.

This action he branded as "public exposure of narrow-mindedness" on the part of "old ladies." He indicated that he thought these "old ladies" were of both sexes.

NO question of impropriety entered into this difference of opinion, nor is it involved in the altercation between the eminent Mexican mural painter, Diego Rivera, and two of his patrons—Rockefeller Center in New York and the Institute of Arts in Detroit.

The Rockefellers halted Rivera's work on murals for the 72-story RCA building when he put Lenin in one of his brilliant plaster panels. The Mexican artist refused to erase the Russian leader, so the ultra conservative Rockefellers paid him off and put a screen in front of his mural.

Detroit art lovers, some of them, pounced upon one of Rivera's 27 panels for the Detroit Museum as "commun-

istic" and "irreligious." But his spon didn't back down in this controver

The 27 panels represent almost a of the artist's creative work. His o nal sketches were approved by the commission of Detroit, as well as by W. R. Valentiner, director, and E Ford, who gave them to the city.

The paintings are symbolic, and one which seems have aroused particular objection is titled "Vaccination." In treatment arrangement, adverse critics find in resemblance to the traditional group of the Holy Family, but the Mexican nies any intention of caricaturing theme.

Nudes upset the serenity of an art hibition in North Plainfield, N. J., long ago. Students of the Van Embu art school assembled 400 of their wo for a show in the Plainfield Pu Library. The as ment included nudes.

Sedate mem of the commu protested to the brarian, and the hibition was clo Most of the nu were charac sketches, but gardless of charcoaled—m sketchy, they sh ed the sensibili of some New seyites.

The showing continued in the lery of the school.

Everyone will call the recent barrassment of customs officials w the entry of certain Michael Angelo productions was barred. The original these challenged prints are to be fo in the Sistine Chapel at the Vati and when a minor official lifted a m

Timothy Murphy Gave Lectures on Art—and Sued the Anti-Vice Crusader.

(Continued on Page 16.)

and sensual gratification. Popular entertainments, especially in the burgeoning urban areas, titillated large numbers of people with allusions to taboo language and behavior. Amusement parks, dance halls, restaurants, saloons, nickelodeons, with their ragtime, hands-on dancing, dizzying ups-and-downs, raunchy clowns, musicians, and song lyrics, invited paying customers to enjoy themselves recklessly and for as long as possible, thus eroticizing leisure time (see Chapter 2).

Conservative moralists recognized that these pastimes were encouraged by a new and suspect group of businesspeople. These entrepreneurs realized the American Dream by pioneering new businesses in which restrictions based on class, sex, or ethnic background were absent. Any capable individual could rise to the top. Immigrants and their offspring were establishing themselves as prosperous restaurant and theater owners, actors, and publishers, all proud and grateful to call themselves Americans. They were not necessarily attuned to the moral and social proprieties that established bankers, property owners, and manufacturers, as well as veteran publishers, found easy to profess, and Sumner's crusade targeted those who used popular entertainment to make a wider public comfortable with sexual explicitness. Print media were not his only concerns, but became an area in which the vice squad, busied with prostitution, bootlegging, and gambling, needed help.

The NYSSV was one of the last of a breed of moral-reform organizations that had included the Committee of Fourteen (founded to fight "disorderly resorts") and the Anti-Saloon League. As Sumner put it, "Where there are so many subdivisions of commercialized vice, it is apparent that a city official having jurisdiction over the whole field cannot specialize in any one feature." [15] At his society's head stood Sumner, prominent among his fellow crusaders as a "moral entrepreneur," an enterprising crusader with social position, professional standing, expertise in the use of political influence, and — until the Depression — solid financial backing. [16] He had the respectful endorsement of a large segment of the general public and its political and religious spokespeople. Occasionally, when the general public could be moved to outrage at a particular moral transgression, the support was fervent.

Figure 5. A force to be reckoned with, if not respected: Sunday rotogravure article on John Sumner's distinctions between art (in the Metropolitan Museum) and obscenity (a Broadway art lecture "for men only"). From *New York Mirror*, 20 May 1933. Reproduced by permission of the Harry Ransom Humanities Research Center, University of Texas at Austin (JA Files).

Often, however, it was shallow and cosmetic. Real estate moguls, after all, benefited from the success of brothel owners, and bankers from that of the distillery business.[17] But if support among the urban social elite and professional classes was often not enthusiastic, that fact only hardened the moral entrepreneur's resolve. The pursuit of obscenity remained intense, and apparently uncompromising. Sumner, for example, showed no leniency for the heathens who peddled copies of *Fanny Hill* or who advocated Margaret Sanger's birth-control programs. To him, all were outsiders who professed to make the world better by their efforts but who really sought only to improve their financial status; all used moral standards repugnant to Sumner and his constituents in attempting to determine which books and ideas to distribute and how. It was this sort of impertinence that led Sumner to make special targets of merchants as diverse as Samuel Roth, Frances Steloff of the prestigious Gotham Book Mart, the irascible bookseller and translator Bernard G. Guerney, and the publishers Thomas Seltzer and Horace Liveright. If Guerney, Seltzer, and Liveright were literati, so much the better. Many citizens wanted to believe their own convictions would eventually prevail. Sumner could assure these supporters that the contumely of the highbrows would reinforce his society's standing among all "right-minded" people. Moral entrepreneurs, above all, needed the public eye. Most of Sumner's constituency were not literati, and knew purveyors of "dirt" when they saw them.

Samuel Roth was one of Sumner's most daring adversaries. "Broadway Sam" described himself as a pioneer publisher of modernist texts, and for thirty years pointed to his edition of Joyce's *Ulysses* as only one of his contributions to freedom of expression. But the edition was unauthorized, as were, most likely, excerpts Roth printed in one of his magazines. Not only Sumner but also Joyce and a large part of the outraged literary community did everything they could to stop him. In 1927 friends of Joyce put together an international protest against Roth's handling of the book.[18] His piracies of *Lady Chatterley's Lover*, both in expurgated and complete editions, provoked similar protests from the estate of D. H. Lawrence. In and out of trouble for decades, Roth in 1936 received the most severe prison sentence possible under the law for brazenly using the Postal Service to distribute flagrantly obscene books. For years, Roth deposited banned books in the mails, stored them in subway lockers, and then had them delivered in person to offices and homes. He teased postal inspectors so often with borderline items that they took to prosecuting him for fraudulently selling books that although touted as sexy, were in fact insignificantly so. Roth was the most often incarcerated, the most feckless, and quite likely the most resourceful booklegger of his time, challenging moral and legal authorities with a quixotic bravado. As fervently as Sumner pursued him, so fervently was he shunned by many of his colleagues in the book trade. And just as fervently, he defended himself against charges of purveying pornography and sullying the reputation of booksellers in general. He was preposterous, resourceful, and relentless. A writer himself, he was also capable of expressing on paper, and exemplifying in his own conduct, the emotional strains of venally exploiting prurient curiosity and of being censored (see Figure 46).

The Smutmonger

Roth and Sumner, their contemporaries must have thought, deserved each other. By their very presence and the nature of their operations, the erotica dealers provided the vice societies, police, postal authorities, politicians, and clergy with a clear and present enemy. Bearing the stigma of a moral degeneration spreading through their communities, Roth and his cohorts took their place alongside bootleggers, tenement and sweatshop managers, opium smugglers and traders, pawnbrokers, bookies, and numbers runners. They were pariah capitalists who did dirty jobs, and who could not have operated without the tacit sanction of established society.[19]

If the tenement managers were in a symbiotic embrace with wealthy owners of real estate, the bootleggers with distillers, the bookies with racetrack owners, the symbiotic relationship in which the publishers of sexually explicit literature found themselves was more subtle. The erotica dealers and the moralists and prosecutors whose reason for being they provided needed one another no less than the sweatshop owners required the legitimate "needle trade" outlets. In addition, only through the operations of the smutmongers could the authorities who indicted them on the charge of sex for its own sake augment their ideological, if not material, capital. So-called pornographers necessarily appealed to prurient fascination, and thus sexuality remained associated with the furtive and the shameful. It may seem as if the large number of erotic books made available subverted the moral consensus. In reality, they were themselves a form of repression — and a safety valve providing fantasies whose satisfaction allowed people to tolerate, not rebel against, conventional ideals of decency.[20] Many readers of erotica not only quietly and guiltily siphoned off the frustrations caused by their culture's restrictions on sexual impulse, but did so harmlessly — that is, without criticizing the ideology itself. Thus, ironically, conservative American institutions and their spokespeople were able to have their distrust of carnal instincts reconfirmed by the same erotica publishers and distributors who said (or who hired lawyers to say) that because their books had educational or artistic value, and because the average intelligent reader would not be debauched, they were fighting against puritanism in the name of freedom of expression.

The success of these selling tactics does not mean that people always and everywhere identified sex with prurience. The more we learn about how individuals really behaved, even at the height of the supposedly inhibited Victorian and Gilded Ages, the more we realize that people could think creatively about sex, and express their desires in a satisfying or imaginative manner. If and when they did so, they often took advantage of what distributors of erotic books made available to them, ignoring the language and illustrations of the advertisements, as they did the warnings of the dour moralists. This important qualification aside, given what Americans had been told about their sensual desires in the home, school, and church, and how their urges affected their psyches, their prurience was internalized. Distrust of sexual instinct and of people who wrote about it were, to borrow the beautiful phrase the poet John Sanford used to describe the ideological ambience of his time and place, "the color of the air."

In the crucibles of moral ambiguity and social change that America's cities had become, most booksellers would struggle mightily to avoid being thought of as cut from the same cloth as Sam Roth. But many different kinds of bookmen could be, and were, accused of obscenity and indecency. Roth evinces the single-minded determination associated with the exploitation of prurience, but he was a writer himself and a lover of literature. In that respect, he had much in common with other members of the book trade. It would be a mistake to think of the story of erotica merchants as merely a chapter in the history of twentieth-century obscenity legislation, for it is integral to the social history of American literature, and to modernism.

To be sure, some of those fined or imprisoned for dealing in obscenity were dispassionate predators. There were circumstances under which reputable publishers had every right to distance themselves from the "dirty underside" of their profession. In New York, if a publisher planned to bring out a book with an erotic flavor, he was forced to look over his shoulder at the Fourth Avenue pirates who might get wind of his edition. In 1932, Bennett Cerf wisely set the price of the Random House *Ulysses* at a reasonable two dollars and fifty cents, because he knew how easily it could be photolithographed and a cheap impression produced "with no plate costs." His inquiries with those in the know produced a likely booklegger. Cerf asked his attorney, Morris Ernst, to threaten the man with an injunction and confiscation of any pirated copies.[21]

However, evidence shows that a large number of erotica dealers had some claim to be considered men of letters or social reformers. Samuel Roth supported and published writers such as George Sylvester Viereck, poet, political controversialist, and self-styled "stormy petrel"; Clement Wood, prolific journalist, etymologist, novelist, and poet; Gershon Legman, erotic folklorist and analyst of sexual mores and the motives for censorship; and Milton Hindus, whose groundbreaking study of Céline was based on personal interviews. Samuel Curl, publisher through the Phoenix Press of lending-library sex-pulp novels, issued the first English edition of impressionist poet Walter Mehring's *No Road Back*, with illustrations by George Grosz, in 1944. Jacob ("Jack" or "Jake") Brussel, an erudite and energetic antiquarian book dealer, was one of the most resourceful of those who published and sold erotica, including legally banned works, first at his Ortelius Book Shop and then at other Fourth Avenue locations in New York City, as well as by mail order. In 1940, among the erotica traced to him was the underground "Medvsa" edition of Henry Miller's *Tropic of Cancer*, resulting in his conviction and incarceration.[22]

Joseph Lewis, founder of the Truth Publishing Company, professed atheist, birth-control activist, and advocate for separation of church and state, championed Margaret Sanger and Arthur Garfield Hayes. He was prosecuted by John Sumner in 1927 for publishing and selling William J. Robinson's *Sexual Truths*,[23] perhaps because the work reprinted Benjamin Franklin's famous "Advice to a Young Man on Choosing a Mistress." Beginning in 1921, the iconoclastic Lewis's edition of Robinson's *Sexual Problems of Today* included the following statement by the intrepid physician: "I know that the dissemination of any information regarding the prevention of conception carries with it the extremely severe penalty of a $5,000 fine or five years at hard labor, or both."[24] Robinson proceeded to describe, in a chapter so titled, "Four Absolutely Infallible Methods for the Prevention of Conception." He was obviously being sarcastic in listing only the ones he could suggest without landing in "Joliet or Leavenworth": abstinence for life; marriage to a woman no longer capable of conceiving; castration; or removal of the wife's womb. He ended the chapter by stating, "Oh, what a stupid world we live in." Postal authorities refused to see the irony, and threatened to have Truth Publishing prosecuted for fraudulent advertising, since it had included the chapter title in its circulars. At a hearing, one of the counsels stated that a federal indictment was being prepared against Truth, because it was suspected of sending not only information regarding contraception to certain customers but also prophylactics themselves.[25]

Two chief mail-order erotica dealers were Esar Levine and Benjamin Rebhuhn (Figure 6). Levine, as the introductions and notes for several of his Panurge Press titles attest, was a scholar; after the imprint's demise, he focused his efforts on analyses and compilations of wit and humor.[26] Rebhuhn was Levine's close friend and an aspiring novelist who, in the course of his life, developed close personal relationships not only with Frank Harris but also with two other renowned public figures: the free-speech crusader Theodore Schroeder and the architect Frank Lloyd Wright. Rebhuhn's commitment to free dissemination of information about birth control, and his opposition to the Catholic Church's policies regarding boycotts and licensing, led him to give away, possibly as premiums, many copies of a sixteenth-century account of Jan Hus's execution for heresy.[27] Levine and Rebhuhn specialized in mail-order sexology in the 1930s, and the Justice Department prosecuted them vigorously. These two men shared similar responses to inequities in government, methods of social reform, aesthetic standards in art and literature, and repressive conventions regarding social and sexual mores. Aspiring writers, they had met while students at the City College of New York. Together, they had attended Frank Harris's lectures during his visits to New York. In 1920, the young men purchased steerage tickets and sailed to Mexico, interested in the socialist reforms being fervently advocated in the country at the time, and in the possibility of its evolving a radically different regimen of individual conduct from that of the anxiety- and cash-driven United States. Probably they were inspired by the Mexican Constitution of 1917. As a way of becoming part of this new social order, they planned to open a vegetarian restaurant in Mexico City. For a time, Rebhuhn, who had tutored in English in New York and taught writing at City College, was employed by the University of Mexico, until he was released because of his radical political views. Revolutionary fervor and the country's uncertain economy forced Levine and Rebhuhn to leave Mexico in 1924. While there, they clandestinely distributed copies of volume one of the four-volume *My Life and Loves*, in which

Figure 6. Benjamin Rebhuhn (left), and Esar Levine, right, c. 1923. Reproduced by permission of Dr. Ronald Rebhuhn, Westbury, N.Y.

the iconoclastic Frank Harris cast himself as an Edwardian Casanova. They continued this enterprise, to their regret, in New York.[28]

The Ethnic Middleman

The hostility of the community toward those identified as erotica dealers, and the calling to account that accompanied it, was grounded on the way erotica seemed to subvert the moral consensus. There were other factors at play in the hostility, however, having as much to do with who the dealers were as with what they did. As was (and is) the case with other "middlemen minorities,"[29] erotica dealers formed a tight-knit, and therefore persistent, resourceful, and resiliently successful entity. They were easy to stigmatize as a group set apart from the majority, even if they had the same goals and methods of doing business as general book dealers.

In New York at least, during the period from 1880 to 1940, many were members of Jewish immigrant families. Jewish erotica dealers seem to have become prominent in the field soon after the eastern European immigrants began arriving in record numbers in 1880. The best evidence of this, apart from the names of offenders as reported in newspapers, are the listings in the yearly ledgers of the NYSSV, as compiled by Comstock and then Sumner (Tables 1 and 2).[30] These ledger entries for "Nationality" and "Religion" of people arrested may have been derived from police blotters and may not have been inclusive, although entries do seem to have been made in careful chronological order, with details regarding circumstances of offense and disposition of case. They include the various activities the society deemed violations of the Comstock Law: printing, publishing, selling, or lending offensive books, magazines, photographs, pamphlets, and artwork. The material was sold from cigar-, book-, or drugstores or newsstands, or peddled at hotels or burlesque houses. The figures may be skewed regarding Jewish

Table 1. Obscenity Arrests, "Religion" Column Ledgers of NYSSV, 1882–1919

	1882	1887	1897	1905	1915	1919
Jewish	3	9	18	54	61	22
Catholic	3	5	5	12	26	9
Protestant	7	5	11	19	25	10
religion not recorded	5	10	6	5	9	1

Table 2. Obscenity Arrests, "Religion" Column Ledgers of NYSSV, 1920–1939

	1920	1922	1923	1927	1930	1933	1937	1939
Jewish	13	8	13	13	9	29	10	28
Catholic	3	3	2	7	1	2	0	2
Protestant	11	5	6	4	5	1	2	0
religion not recorded	10	16	4	7	12	3	5	2

involvement given the important fact that the "Religion" column was left blank fairly often.

At first, the vice-society ledgers note, many Jews of German origin were cited (German immigrants were skilled printers, lithographers, and typesetters),[31] then many eastern European Jews, as well as some Austrians, English, and Germans. In New York, Jews do not seem to have replaced any other specific ethnic group in this industry. The ledgers list other religions (including "heathen" and "free lover or luster") much less often than Jews; non-Jewish nationalities are variously Italian, Spanish, German, and Irish. There is, therefore, no phenomenon similar to those documented in other contemporary immigrant workforces managed by innovative middlemen such as the construction trades, where lower-salaried Italian immigrants, well-organized by padrones, ousted Irish,[32] or the needle trades, where the success of Jewish middlemen-contractors, the "sweaters," in organizing a low-paid, largely female workforce drove independent German tailors out of business.[33] The absence of any single ethnic group of erotica dealers in New York City prior to the Jewish presence can be accounted for by the fact that, as compared to tailoring, construction, shopkeeping, domestic or municipal service, or clerical work, the erotica business supported a relatively small number of workers. The work itself did not have different organizational principles, or less need of innovative middlemen, than other emotionally taxing low-status occupations despised by more secure native citizens.

The Erotica Dealer's Modus Operandi

A close-knit group of colleagues who shared similar financial and social status and similar personal and career goals was as valuable in erotica dealing as in other immigrant-dominated professions, especially those entrepreneurial activities in which the Jewish settler felt most comfortable: peddling, shopkeeping, real estate. Such conditions helped limit the vertical structure of the business to people with the same financial expectations and the same capacity, at this early stage of residence in "the Golden Land," for coupling "ruthless underconsumption"[34] with hard work and hard-nosed risk taking. Coworkers also shared similar tastes in, and knowledge of, the classics, the steady sellers, the categories of "perversities," and the contemporary fashions in erotica. This kind of middleman activity, like others, had the advantage, whatever the risks, of being open to newcomers. Well-inured to hostility from native populations, Jews, when they found themselves excluded from a field of endeavor, turned to a profession in which they sensed they could eventually thrive by cooperating with colleagues in a community of effort. In New York this choice was very often the retailing business.[35]

In several cases, the erotica dealer's relatives were business partners. One could trust uncles and brothers, and possibly no one else. When Samuel Roth was sentenced to three years in prison in 1936 for interstate distribution of obscene literature, the judge deplored the fact that he had assigned his wife, son, and daughter administrative or clerical tasks in his operations.[36] Seven years earlier, his brother had helped with his clandestine distribution of piracies of *Lady Chatterley's Lover* and *Ulysses*.[37] The underground printing of many banned erotic classics, possibly including the above-mentioned titles, was the work of two brothers, Adolph and Rudolph Loewinger;[38] another pair, David and Jacob Brotman, was responsible for a large part of the lubricious under-the-counter pamphlets and paperbound books Boston's Watch and Ward decried as flagitious.[39] Jack Brussel, Sam Roth's partner at the start of the latter's career, enlisted the aid of his first wife, whose name appears on various Library of Congress copyright records. Benjamin Rebhuhn's office manager was his nephew, and his wife was listed as director of the Falstaff Press Inc.[40] Esar Levine and his brother Benjamin, close friends of the Rebhuhns, were editor and business manager, respectively, of the Panurge Press.[41]

Erotica distributors knew each other, on occasion remaindered each other's books, and consulted both on reasonable retail prices and on fees for the printers who would risk dealing with them. Brochures as well as books and mailing lists were transferred from one distributor to another.[42] Their stock was thus easy to liquidate, or at least readily transferable. One example is the Rarity Press editions of erotic classics, rights to which were transferred to William Godwin Inc. around 1932. Many Panurge titles were transferred to Falstaff in 1936 (and reprinted as new editions), and later became property of Metro Books, distributed by Benjamin Levine.[43] When Samuel Roth faced bankruptcy in 1933, he (mistakenly) thought he could arrange with colleagues to lend or sell them his books and copyrights in exchange for liquidation of debts.

A 1930 letter from the law firm of Greenbaum, Wolff, and Ernst to Ellis Meyers, secretary of the American Booksellers Association, affords an interesting example of the protocols among erotica dealers of the period. Meyers had written to John Sumner about the salutary changes promised by the proposed (later defeated) Post Bill of 1929–30 making publishers support their booksellers by standing side by side with them when their books were cited as obscene. Meyers sent a copy of Sumner's reply to the firm. Sumner thought booksellers needed more, not less, liability to prosecution. He listed the following offenders who balked at revealing their anonymous publisher-distributors: Earl Marks, Ben and David Rebhuhn, Solomon Malkin, Samuel and Max Roth, Alex Field, Henry Klein, Raymond Thomson, Al Picker, Joseph Seiffer, Max Gottschalk, and David Moss.[44] Morris Ernst objected to the vice-society secretary's listing David Moss of the Gotham Book Mart because Ernst's firm had defended Moss, in 1928, when a Sumner raid yielded some seventy-five titles. The lawyer stated that twenty-five of these had established imprints, but Sumner had prosecuted the more vulnerable bookseller, not the established publishers, who could better afford the legal expertise to convince the court that the items seized were of literary value.[45]

Insofar as Moss could be defended as a seller of such books, he should not have been grouped with the other individuals. But Moss needed to satisfy good customers who did not want to risk their reputations by dealing with people they could not trust. Like many other general book dealers specializing in modern literature, he had methods in common with specialists in the selling of underground books. What, for instance, of the interdicted titles — whether of literary value or not — confiscated by Sumner? Moss, or his friend and fellow bookman Martin Kamin, must have had sources among erotica distributors for the copies of *Maria Monk*, *The Merry Order of St. Bridget*, *My Life*, *Ulysses*, and Fuchs's *Geschichte der Erotischen Kunst* (illustrated with reproductions of erotic paintings and caricatures) found in Moss's storeroom.[46] Fuchs's work and *Ulysses* may have been smuggled through Customs, or sent from Europe to nondescript residential addresses; once delivered, certain middlemen brought them to the booksellers who had placed orders. It may safely be assumed that Moss or Kamin, middlemen themselves, would have been no more likely to reveal the identity of such bookleggers than would booksellers notorious for their under-the-counter items. "In the vast majority of cases," Sumner explained to Meyers, "the source of the books on which prosecutions are based are secret sources, so situated, that a quick getaway is easily accomplished." Whether or not the underground distributors a frightened bookseller might finger were successfully collared, he himself would be forever cut off from his sources of supply, for he would never be trusted again. He had no choice if he wished to remain in the business. Nor did Moss, if he wanted to continue to offer such materials to trusted customers.

Erotica merchants did more for each other than protect sources of supply and watch out for whatever heat Sumner or the police could bring to bear. They also shared information about remaindering deals, imprint changes, what legal or financial troubles had caused them, and which parties had cooperated in the deal. Any underground bookseller or distributor, and even a printer, could decide to take a chance on publishing a spicy title. If successful, he tried again, especially if encouraged by his customers. Once someone established a particular specialty, it was imprudent to compete with him, although this did happen with especially hot properties. Legally interdicted books could of course be expensive, and one quickly discovered what the market would bear. Therefore, prices do not seem to have varied very much, whether for purchase, rental, or mail-order materials. Erotica dealers also shared information about reliable and possibly unreliable customers for the underground material most in demand, about new authors and popular titles ancient and modern, about the safest procedures for having books smuggled into the country from abroad, and about which printers were available when and where.

This is not to suggest that erotica dealers formed a brotherhood pledged to open dealing. Competition, especially when the property was hot, notorious, and lucrative, could be cutthroat. Sam Roth's 1928 imprisonment may have been occasioned by Henry Klein's accepting Sumner's offer of a plea bargain. The experience of Esar Levine and Benjamin Rebhuhn, who in 1926 found themselves as hapless fledgling erotica dealers in the United States, despite their experience a few years earlier with smuggling copies of Frank Harris's *My Life and Loves* in from Mexico, epitomizes the pariah bookseller's vulnerability to exploitation. Struggling for capital, technological resources, and influence, both inside and outside the erotica dealers' vertical structure, they were robbed and abandoned by their contacts.

Levine was arrested in June 1925 while arranging at a printing plant the typesetting of volume 2 of the autobiography.[47] He and Rebhuhn solicited the help of a Tammany politician, a fixer with ties to the corrupt magistrates' courts. For a week in late January 1931, at the time of the press-stopping Seabury investigations into these courts, the front pages were full of the affairs of one Ben Miller, characterized by the *New York Journal* as having "more aliases than a dog has fleas."[48] The dailies headlined his involvement with "Frank Harris' Love Diary," about which the fixer refused to speak until threatened with contempt of court.[49] Investigators ascertained that Miller first asked Rebhuhn and Levine for $250, to be given to him within twenty-four hours, with which he could begin to arrange to have Levine's case dropped and the plates returned to them from the printer.[50] Perhaps the need to bribe several officials was part of the reason — separate from the printer's demands — that Miller required another $750 to complete the deal.[51] Some six hundred books, and apparently the plates, were returned.[52] Miller said that because of his "protection," Rebhuhn and Levine could begin selling volume 2 to local booksellers. He also assumed, because of the "protection" he had arranged, "a sort of partnership in the business,"[53] which meant that he decided when and where more copies of volume 2 should be printed and released to the trade. Miller further enmeshed Harris's two friends by lending them money with which to arrange for the printing, binding, advertisement — to a carefully selected set of mail-order customers — and distribution of the expurgated volume 1, which would be released only when he could arrange for the right judge to "declare it legitimate."[54]

Miller was either unable or, more likely, unwilling to get Levine a light sentence. The 1926 ledgers of the NYSSV state that on 26 February Levine was sentenced to three months in the "workhouse."[55] This was a stiff sentence for publishing and selling obscene material under the state Comstock Law (conviction on the federal offense of sending it through the mail carried a much harsher penalty).[56] The reason for Levine's sentence might have been a second, Sumner-engineered raid the previous August.[57] Rebhuhn's account was that the printer had, "against our orders," gone to the bindery to pick up some eleven hundred copies of *My Life and Loves*. "This means more advertisement [circulars needed] for the book and more money going to get the printers out. Another Miller job."[58] Levine's case was docketed separately from that of the two printers. The reasoning may have been that at the time of his arrest, he had revealed his role as publisher.[59] On

11 October, Frank Harris wrote that he could "not understand why Esar's case was not tried with the others."[60] John Sumner could, and perhaps for different reasons, Miller could also. He may have suggested it to the magistrates, most of whom owed their positions to Tammany. With Esar Levine out of commission, he could continue to have his way with Frank Harris's love autobiography. Eventually, Rebhuhn learned that mail enclosing requests for volume 2 had been "robbed."[61] That is, Miller, "in his aggressive and rude way," had been opening the mail, taking the money, and discarding the orders. He may also have been selling volume 2 without informing his partners, transporting the plates stored in his cellar to a printer for the production of various impressions. Someone would have had to clue him in as to which booksellers would sell or rent the item, or as to a middleman who would approach them. He could have made it worthwhile for the printer, or friends in the police department, to do that.

It took the intervention of Harris's New York lawyer to extricate the writer's friends from Miller.[62] The fixer, however, was hardly their only problem. In the fall of 1926, it became clear that someone was underselling them, at seven or eight dollars a copy as opposed to ten. This was true not only in New York, but in Chicago, as Levine found on a trip there in September.[63] Miller was not suspected; rather, the police themselves were. Obscenity dealers were easy targets for this sort of drain on their profits, and Rebhuhn speculated that of the more than nine hundred volumes confiscated (including two hundred unbound copies taken in the second raid), more than half found their way to distributors "from the police commissioner's office."[64] It occurred to him that the binder, who had several hundred copies,[65] had also sold books. This was less likely, because if distributors found that had happened, they would not take any more business to him. Rebhuhn and Levine had by this time joined with a third party to form the Frank Harris Publishing Company, and were entrusted by Harris clandestinely to print and distribute volumes 3 and 4 of his autobiography in the United States. Truly disciples of the writer, this "Trinity" (Harris's appellation) attempted to adhere to their "master's" unwieldy and naive plans for two volumes in which the "naughty" chapters were present in some copies and excised in others. The former were much more expensive, and to be placed in the hands of a trusted clientele. Stealthily, the Trinity took the papier-mâché plates that friends of Harris smuggled past Customs to a printing concern they had located.[66] They waited patiently for the printers to work out a way to get the sheets of both the pornographic and "conventional" chapters completed and bound. A few copies were ready in May 1927 (Figure 7), the only books to come into their hands. After the first small delivery, the printers refused to deal any more with the Trinity and simply pirated the text of volumes 3 and 4, publishing a new one-volume edition, without bothering to make any explicit passages detachable.[67] That was probably the original reason they decided to risk doing business with the Harris men.

The nonplussed Frank Harris considered his young American friends fools. But it is easy to understand how any effort to publish a notorious and widely proscribed book in the late 1920s might have foundered. Erotica distributors were not sadistic thugs, nor were they power brokers. Therefore, they sometimes needed to contact the latter. They worked without the ability to control — with financial, physical, or political strength — the colleagues who actually produced the goods necessary for success, and whose self-interest was not restrained by the codes of professional ethics that legitimate enterprises feature. Those who pirated volumes 3 and 4 from Harris's Trinity had many equally resourceful bookleggers to contend with, Samuel Roth among them.[68] His *Observations of an Old Man in Love* — subtitled *An Interlude in the Life and Loves of F. H.* — which Sumner found at the Golden Hind Press, huddled together thirty-two brief excerpts from *My Life*. For further delectation, Roth appended "the quimbolexicon," a list of words and their definitions related to the female "quimbo."

Other "pirates" — the term is equivocal because "pornography" like Harris's could not be copyrighted — were about to cash in on the excitement. In 1931, a one-volume compilation of all the erotic episodes in *My Life and Loves* appeared. Titled *My Love Life: A Love Autobiography*, it contained a foreword, pirated of course, and bore an imprint similar to the other *My Life* volumes.[69] The typography, endpapers, and binding design resemble some of Sam Roth's productions. But neither he nor Ben Miller was behind it, or at least not exclusively. It appears that Solomon (he favored "Sol") Malkin, a bright young college student who had clerked in Jake Brussel's Ortelius Book Shop and later studied at the Institute for Sexual Science in Berlin, was one of those who arranged it.[70]

Erotica dealers with experience had to be tough, although not necessarily predatory, and the business was not for the timid or scrupulous. But the criminality of erotica dealers did not extend beyond bookselling into organized racketeering; Al Capone and Meyer Lansky were not role models. A figure like A. G. Geiger, the dirty-books racketeer in Raymond Chandler's *Big Sleep* (1939) who supplements

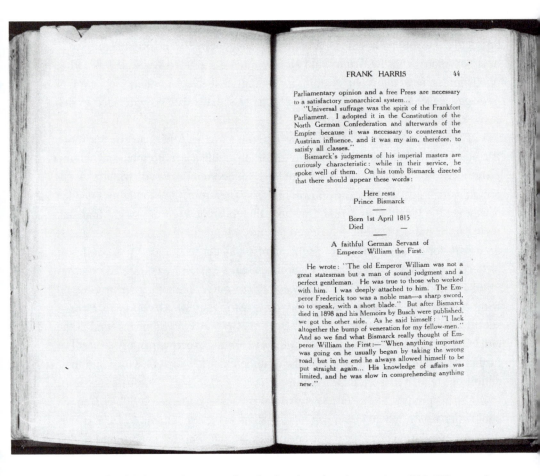

Figure 7. Harris's instructions regarding the first American impression of *My Life* were that the "naughty" chapters of volumes 3 and 4 be detachable from the rest of the book. This two-page spread from volume 3 shows a blank page. On the reverse side is the first page in "conventional" chapter 4. Opposite the blank is the second page. The start of chapter 4 and this blank are on the eighth and final leaf in the gathering, most of which is "naughty" chapter 3a. Chapter 3a is detachable, but if it were removed, some of the conventional text would go with it. These irregularities are representative of those caused by Harris's instructions, and show that censorship definitely affected the look and structure of a banned book. Reproduced by permission of Dr. Ronald Rebhuhn, Westbury, N.Y.

his business activities as owner of a pornographic lending library in Hollywood by arranging sex orgies and blackmailing rich customers, is a fascinating but lurid exaggeration. However susceptible film personalities were to blackmail, it was not the métier of book dealers. Equally misleading was a 1929 article in the *New York World* that purported to expose that city's "smut racketeers." Its author reported the existence of two warring "gangs" of distributors of "forbidden translations, prohibited works of genuine literary quality, and out-and-out pornography." Each gang strongarmed the retail outlets with customers for erotica — "some large and well-established bookstores, some little hole-in-the-wall shops, some little more than cigar stores with a curtained shelf" — into taking their wares, informing John Sumner if an owner refused.[71] The article is undocumented, and fanciful. If such gangs of middlemen existed, they would have supplanted the côterie of close-knit colleagues who comprised the "vertical structure" of the business. The *World*'s reporter had a much more lucrative, and therefore centralized, enterprise in mind: bootlegging.

Individuals, not gangs, organized the erotica trade of the period. The Roths, Fields, Brussels, and Brotmans contracted to have volumes of classical or modern sexually explicit literature, pamphlets, playing cards, and scatological "dirty comics" printed in quantities of a few thousand, and sold them to individual peddlers or store owners willing to retail them. Various printers produced the different kinds of erotica, for discrete distributors who specialized in getting these into the hands of diverse retailers. The number of workers in this field was limited, and one needed to be part of the network and know its modus operandi to flourish.

Erotica Dealers' Shrewdness, Objectivity, and Chutzpah

What personal characteristics and abilities allowed these men and women to be successful at their trade? Successful publishers were first willing to work the long hours required to arrange details with printers and distributors, transport heavy boxes, make occasionally surreptitious contacts with customers, place advertisements, write advertising copy, handle finances, and deal with legal problems. They were able to exchange immediate gratifications for hard-earned success, postponing the former until a future, secure situation developed. For the same reason, erotica dealers stoically underwent short-term deprivations such as confiscation of their stock, visits from undercover agents, decoy letters from postal inspectors, fines, and imprisonment.[72]

Second, the erotica distributor had an objectivity that allowed shrewd observation of the needs of his customers.[73] The successful marketing of novels that titillated the imagination of lending-library and drugstore patrons are evidence of this shrewdness. Another prime example was the mail-order distributors' sensitivity to how important knowledge of the varied pleasures of "the marriage bed," sexual aberrations and diseases, and the alternative sexual roles and choices that sociologists and anthropologists had uncovered was to the American people. This focus on sexology fueled the considerable success of the mail-order operations of the 1930s.

A third characteristic of the pariah-capitalist erotica distributor was, eminently and vitally, his or her willingness to trade in taboo material. This required an extra measure of daring and emotional stamina. It meant disciplining oneself in equanimity when the pressures of public disdain led to the warrantless confiscation and court-ordered destruction of one's stock. It meant unavoidably inciting, and then accepting with resignation, the carefully timed moral indignation flowing from political platforms and church pulpits. It meant knowing when to persevere in the face of police action, character assassination from crusading moralists, and threats from Sumner and his undercover agents. That is to say, the distributor had to have chutzpah, or moxie. The former connotes boorish self-confidence, but also, since the nineteenth century, daring, hard-edged practicality, an ability to persevere (for either idealistic or practical ends) despite public opinion and police suspicion, and an underdog's unlikely triumph over powerful obstacles and entrenched authority. The latter word, in American slang, suggests initiative, shrewdness, nerve, and, in underground usage, arrogant assurance.[74]

The adventures of the friends of Frank Harris provide a remarkable example of chutzpah. Ben Miller arranged for a New York magistrate to declare an expurgated edition of volume one of *My Life and Loves* fit for public distribution. Thus he turned, through the action of gold crossing palms, a "flagitious" work into a borderline (other terms were "gallant" or "polite") one. Judge George W. Simpson, considering the revised book in accordance with "the mores of the day," dismissed the case.[75] Miller may have been able to time the arrest occasioning the decision so that Magistrate Simpson presided in the Tombs court, and with good reason. This magistrate had taken $2,000 from Miller to rule that the expurgated volume one would not debauch modern-day New Yorkers.[76] (In 1931, the Seabury Investigations into corruption in the magistrates' courts cost Simpson his position on the bench.)

Miller plotted a charade involving a crony, who acted as salesman, and an arresting officer, to whom he promised a promotion for his part.[77] The affair had been arranged to milk maximum publicity and pump up interest in sales. In its account, the *World* did not mention that the book was the expurgated version, and noted that two "salesmen" were sentenced to jail the previous December for selling *My Life and Loves*.[78] The paper printed a clarification the next day, stating that the distinction had been called to its attention by the lawyer for the salesman who had been arrested.[79] The lawyer had "asked that a correction be made in fairness to Magistrate Simpson and his client." Possibly, Miller "arranged" for the April 2 article to read as it does. With its headline at the top of the right-hand column on page 3, and its stress on the recent arrests for selling the book, it seems calculated to make it possible for readers to ask their booksellers about the title's availability, even if they assumed, as the *World*'s reporter apparently did not, that to make Harris's book available without expurgating it was impossible. Whether the April 2 article was serendipitous or the fruit of bribery, the Friends of Harris seized the day with dispatch, incorporating it in an advertisement and "soliciting orders on the basis of this dismissal of the case."[80] As planned, the advertisement referred to the boldness and frankness of the work. For documentation, they could point to a passage which Simpson had ordered excised, but which was not. It concerned the syphilis contracted by a none-too-wise cowboy named Charlie, with whom Harris rode the range during his salad days. The inclusion of "the Charlie incident" stands as redundant proof of Miller's shrewdness, and that of Esar Levine, who prepared the expurgation in consultation with Miller.[81]

Benjamin Rebhuhn spent months in federal prison in the late 1920s after being caught selling interdicted erotica, including Frank Harris's autobiography.[82] After his release, with a lot of experience under his belt, he founded his Falstaff Press, and for several years promoted the firm by suggestive ads and circulars, on which Falstaff's leer was ever present (Figure 8). He persisted even after repeated warnings by postal authorities and the district attorney to desist, and a subsequent indictment. The business was lucrative. At his 1939 trial for interstate distribution of books and circulars, Rebhuhn refused to plead guilty. He had not been intimidated by the twelve hundred complaints from those receiving circulars from

Falstaff.[83] As befitted a friend of the crusading First Amendment advocate Theodore Schroeder, he wished to defend his Falstaff Press's "vital [sex-educational] function." His former partner Esar Levine himself had entered a guilty plea to avoid jail for his Panurge Press mailings. He disappointed Rebhuhn utterly.[84] For the latter, if jail beckoned, so be it. At least, he felt, he had his principles.

This irrepressible insistence, seen as characteristic of Jewish merchants in particular, and of ethnic middlemen minorities in general,[85] helped confer pariah status on the erotic book dealers. Here, the one-hundred-percent moralist warned, was a tightly knit group of workers single-mindedly driven to material success, an apparently autonomous minority that had chosen to pursue its own "godless, un-American" goals with a strange and foreign intensity. When added to the disreputable nature of the business, as attested to by the denunciations of various authority figures, and by police action against the "promoters," as postal inspectors termed them, the identity of the erotica distributor as clannish — employing "their own kind" — and aloof — with their own, ethnic, allegiances — became fixed. Here was a kind of "parasite" with whom one would, on occasion, itch to deal, but would remain chary of trusting, especially because the dealer was so good at what he did.

What respect had a publisher of smut for American moral values, American standards of fair and lawful business dealings, and American freedoms? In spite of Sumner, Post Office inspectors, and organizations dedicated to maintaining decency, those involved in distributing erotica had a great deal of confidence in American democracy, and not because they could manipulate the legal system to continue to do business. Only in America, albeit in sweltering and freezing tenements lining streets overrun with ganefs, could they have begun freely to compete, as pushcart peddlers, dusty printers in ink-sodden lofts, or clerks in shadowy secondhand bookshops, for consumers' dollars. They often protested that they had studied the nation's laws and acted within them, exercising those protections given by the First Amendment. Certainly they sensed that the business in which they were enmeshed could get beyond their control — not only because of changing markets and clever competitors but also because of police action against "obscen-

Figure 8. A pulp magazine advertisement for the books of the Falstaff Press, one of the most successful mail-order erotica businesses of the 1930s. From *Film Fun*, Feb. 1934, inside back cover.

ity," which was not accorded constitutional protection. They were after all piloting uncertain craft in murky waters inevitably to become stormy.

The erotica dealer sometimes had to rely on his lawyer's closing arguments to judge and jury to rescue him or her from fines and jail terms, as well as the twin stigmas of con person and smut merchant. During such courtroom hours, these businessmen and -women must have struggled to find the patience and self-control that might have been needed in anticipation of a harsh judgment by their fellow citizens. In the agonizing moments before a verdict, they would be found contemplating the ultimate harbor toward which they had willed their secular career to steer — the Yiddish word is *takhlis*. It can mean "brass tacks," in a narrowly practical sense, but also worldly goal: a fate that God controls, ultimately for the best, for He sees the orderly design beyond the confusions and paradoxes that stymie mortals. Moses Kligsberg asserts that the eastern European Jewish people's sense of how and where to fulfill *takhlis* was a chief motive for the immigration to America, and so explains the perseverance, enthusiasm, respect for education, community and family solidarity, and malleability that other sociological analysts attribute to traits of middleman minorities.[86] The prosecuted erotica dealers could only submit to fate and promise themselves that, even if they went to jail, their sons and daughters would recognize that they had been fighting puritanical taboos, not selling smut, and were accepting the setbacks that presented themselves as they endeavored to accomplish legitimate goals.

Political Vulnerability

Political dependence on authorities, according to sociologists, is part of the dynamics of pariah capitalism: the minority status of the group that is allowed control of a particular trading activity makes it easier for the political elite to control it. Although the minority group has money, theirs is "weak" capital — that is, subject to the vicissitudes of legal actions, or to public indignation against the group and resultant loss of patronage or attacks on property.[87] Because of the distrust of the majority, the middleman minority is subject to scapegoating. Patrons have to deal with the minority to attain a particular disreputable but coveted commodity, and they find the group to be both clannish and audacious in their pursuit of success. In addition, its members are highly visible, and, due to their "weak money," vulnerable to censure.[88]

The hostility endured by the erotica dealer often revealed its virulence strikingly in the form of political vulnerability. Enmity was expressed on behalf of the community and its belief system by authorities who may have shared ethnic affiliation with the suspected middleman. Rabbi Stephen Wise was just as indignant about obscene books as John Sumner; Alfred Knopf was as wary of being connected with them as was Doubleday or Houghton. Samuel Roth hated both Knopf and Wise, whom he dubbed "a priest disguised as a rabbi."[89]

After Esar Levine was arrested while supervising the printing of *My Life and Loves*, his lawyers argued that the police had possessed no warrant to raid the printer. It was Judge Aaron Levy who ordered the lifting of a temporary injunction the lawyers had obtained; if the books were obscene, the police had acted properly.[90] There was a successful appeal, but that only gave Levy an opportunity to reaffirm his earlier decision. Declaring Harris's book "neither literature nor art," he feared that if the evidence were suppressed, the publishers would "dispose of their vile and vicious wares and scatter corruption and perversity."[91] Here, various levels of authority — police, judges, the NYSSV — worked together, using the law and public opinion as stringently as possible to protect "decent" people from moral pariahs. The lawyer for Levine and the printers had argued, soon after the arrest, that protecting homes and offices from "unlawful entry by police officers" was a greater threat to democracy than one thousand copies of a privately printed book of limited interest.[92] This claim was ignored. Perhaps the judge's language reflects not only his view of the effect of sexually explicit books on the average person but, especially considering the timing of his decision, his indignation at Harris's disciples' chutzpah — for by then their continued attempts to get *My Life* clandestinely printed had come to light. Even if Levy's decision might have been made at Ben Miller's behest, in order to clear the way for his own schemes, it is an example of political vulnerability, just as was Levine and Rebhuhn's need to rely on political fixers and underground printers in the first place. Many retailers of erotica were so constrained.

Both the left and the right sided against the pariah erotica dealer. In order to build on its ideological and political stature, hard won since the mid-1920s, the National Council for Freedom from Censorship (NCFC) felt it had better adopt a "hands-off" policy toward what might be regarded as sex for its own sake, distributed by those operating in bad faith. It was in this spirit that Alexander Lindey, a lawyer for the NCFC, "doubt[ed] whether the Council would want to defend Frank

Harris' [*My*] *Life* [*and Loves*], and *Immortalia*, [which] may turn out to be rank erotica."[93] That was sound politics, as practiced by an organization which needed to establish credibility and respect with customs and Post Office inspectors, newspaper and magazine editors, bar associations, publishers, and elected officials. The council required the ideological and financial support of liberal-minded citizens. To this end, it could not afford to be seen as helping smut merchants evade the law.

The NCFC, along with the liberal Vanguard Press, supported the Post Bill of 1929–30. Had it become law, those publishers with the status and money to afford lawyers would have been protected, as would their retail outlets; those who could not — and who could not, in fact, even be identified because they printed "privately" and flew by night — would have continued to hide while their "indecent" distributors faced spokespeople for the outraged community. The bill would "stimulate respect for the integrity of all business houses who will stand behind their product."[94] The celebrated First Amendment–advocate Morris Ernst and Lindey tried to revive it in the mid-1930s.[95] Had they been successful, it would have further hindered Sumner's efforts to interdict sexually explicit modern literature meriting the approbation of the literary community. Notably, it would also have further dichotomized the trade into "respectable" and "pariah" camps, or, as the vice-society leader himself put it, "those acting in good faith" and "those acting in bad faith."

The NCFC advocated protection of the basic constitutional rights of even bad-faith entrepreneurs. Sumner sometimes behaved as if he did not follow this caveat. This was especially evident when he equated moral and political subversion on one hand and sexually explicit materials on the other as twin evils. Erotica dealers were thought to be responsible not only for repulsive expressions of degenerate behavior but also for scurrilous, "indecent" attacks on established ethical and religious doctrine — and sometimes on righteous public officials. In June 1927, Sumner raided the printers as they were setting up *The President's Daughter*, an autobiography by a woman who claimed to be the secret paramour of sitting president Warren G. Harding. According to a special statement the publishers printed as front matter, "six burly men, and Mr. Sumner," broke into their printer's shop, took plates and printed sheets, and tried to prosecute. Sumner's motive is unclear, but political partisanship cannot be ruled out. The magistrate rejected his claim that the book was "obscene, lewd, lascivious, and indecent," but quite possibly because of the publicity he generated, newspapers at first eschewed reviewing it, and many stores refused to carry it.[96] The author and her business manager had tried to keep the book a secret until publication, so that no accusations of "indecent" sensation mongering could be used to hamper its appearance. After the raid, as the author herself recounted, the Post Office investigated the publisher on suspicion of fraud. An Arkansas senator denounced the book as "lewd," "brazen," and the "grossest attack ever launched." Due to this kind of pressure (which may have come from the Republican Party, Harding's survivors, or both sources), several outlets, including Macy's, would not carry *The President's Daughter*; Baker and Taylor would not distribute it; *Publishers Weekly* did not announce it.[97] Despite all its problems, the book sold brilliantly.

The Pariah Capitalist as Subversive and Parvenu

Although avoiding ethnic scapegoating, John Sumner sometimes specifically described the purveyor of "obscenity" as a Jew (or Italian or German). Rooted in his opposition to erotic literature was a fear of contamination by the unclean outsider. Society as a whole, as well as the immigrant neighborhoods, was in danger of contagion. Sumner's annual reports stigmatize individuals arrested (whether convicted or not) as "foreign looking," "mentally defective," "exhibitionists," "fly-by-night." "Most of these defendants," he wrote in his 1928 report, "were of the young, radical, irreligious and over-educated type. Their personal writings wherever found, indicated an utter disregard for the law, public decency or any of the proprieties of organized society. They are literally anarchists."[98]

The erotica dealer took care of his own, like the Jewish "sweaters" and the Italian padrones, who recruited cheap immigrant labor so that they could fulfill contracts with clothing and construction magnates, and the Irish saloonkeepers or ward heelers, who bought votes with political favors.[99] The vice societies were appalled. According to Sumner and other patrician observers — in whose hearts superiority and "civility" were closely interwoven — such narrow, self-involved, venal conduct of life was typical of immigrants, and revealed their intrinsic inferiority to the civic-minded gentlemen who offered disinterested services for the impartial improvement of the public. If immigrants were not brought to conform, at whatever cost to themselves or the government, the country was in danger. Were the unassimilated immigrants' loyalties not to their own people, rather than to their new country and its values; and did they not isolate themselves in their own enclaves, disdaining intimate contact, and certainly intermarriage, with their hosts, as if they were a "chosen" people?[100] Further, would they not exploit with cynical expediency court decisions such as that granting *Ulysses* literary value, thus flooding shops and newsstands with prurient potboilers?

Fear of the indecent subversive lead easily to contempt for the vulgar parvenu. Both attitudes marginalized German and eastern European Jews generally. Driven toward, and attaining, considerable success, they were seen as cunning social climbers pushing themselves toward legitimacy through dressing ostentatiously, vacationing at fashionable resorts (or, when excluded, opening their own opulent hotels), matriculating at prestigious colleges and professional schools, and conspicuously appropriating cultural icons and technological conveniences.[101] There is a striking example of sensitivity to parvenu status in the letters of the wife of one of Sumner's targets, the idealistic young publisher Thomas Seltzer. In 1922 Seltzer was prosecuted, unsuccessfully, for issuing three "obscene" titles, including *Women in Love*. Adele Seltzer wrote of her situation with a pride born of *takhlis*, but tainted by accusations she needed to fight off: "I go about with an ever-present sense of wonder that we, Thomas & I, little, little Jews, should be the publishers of the great English giant of this age . . . not because with Jewish shrewdness we outwitted some other publisher & got Lawrence first, but because Lawrence's 'Women In Love' went begging for a publisher, and we were the only people who understood its greatness."[102]

Craving legitimacy and respect, publishers and booksellers (or their lawyers) asserted that their efforts had discredited the older Hicklin test criteria used to interdict works which might corrupt immature readers "into whose hands" they might fall. The Hicklin test was being replaced by progressive ones by which literary value was distinguished from smut. As a result, the average adult's freedom to read and think was liberally extended. However, what was evident to many respectable citizens, law-enforcement authorities, and moral entrepreneurs — sometimes in protest against a Lawrence novel or a Schnitzler play, but especially when they looked at full-page magazine advertisements such as the one reproduced in Figure 8 — was a pandering to prurient curiosity. Obviously, marketing of this nature, and to a lesser extent advertisements noting the attempts to censor Lawrence or Schnitzler, increased sales. These appeals could just as easily lead moralists to portray the works as either unworthy of serious notice or downright degenerate. Whether erotica dealers' activities resulted in social ostracism or legal interdictions, their accusers felt those they indicted had brought the opprobrium upon themselves.

There is an undeniable half truth in this. The minority middlemen knew what to do to attain material success. With personal resources, and perseverance nourished by chutzpah and *takhlis*, they recognized the values and espoused the tactics of fellow citizens, explored the erotic fascinations of the latter, and manipulated and accepted the manipulation of those with whom they dealt. Middlemen were part of the action, and accepted the rules of the game. What erotica dealers wanted was not bald power to impose their wills but fulfillment of the American Dream: protection from material wants, the deference that financial security yields, and a secure identity as a citizen enjoying the privileges of a democratic society. Erotica dealers may have been coffeehouse socialists; they may have supported the loyalist cause in Spain, or the Zionists in Palestine; they may have admired Mexico's attempts to resist American corporate manipulation; they may have admired D. H. Lawrence, Isadora Duncan, Marie Stopes, or Leon Trotsky. But whatever their self-images may have been, in their actions they were not subversives — political, moral, or sexual. Those who were Jewish immigrants or the sons and daughters of immigrants were especially interested in assimilating into American culture. In their own way, they wanted this as much as Hollywood's movie moguls or the "Jewish humanists" who edited and wrote for the *Menorah Journal*, Louis Untermeyer, Walter Lippmann, or Bernard Baruch.[103]

Hannah Arendt defines the Jewish parvenu as someone who has accepted whatever set of economic and moral imperatives is necessary to become part of the bourgeois community.[104] The minority middlemen gave people what they wanted, publishing sexually explicit books, magazines, and photographs. Sometimes, they justified their businesses as a contribution to society, enlightening people about, or entertaining them with, varieties of sexual experience. Not surprisingly, those most active as pariah middlemen made this claim most often. Three important distributors with which this book deals — Rebhuhn, Levine, and Roth — were most strident about it. Sifting carefully through their claims, one acknowledges that their publications — fiction, manuals on contraception and sexual stimulation, birth-control tracts, and anthropological studies of alternate sexualities — brought before the public eye what authorities had tried to keep hidden. To some, such information was a blessing, increasing health and lighting a path to self-exploration. To others, it was "snappy" entertainment, paralleling what movies and stage shows offered.

However, there was a deeper contribution. Erotica dealers were as vital a part of a dynamic process as the moralists who pursued them: they dealt in, and transmitted the experience of, prurient fascination in a way that was essential to keep sexuality identified with the furtive and with guilt. Only people sophisticated in commercial enterprise and at the same time endowed with pariah status could do that.

2

"Sex O'Clock in America"
Who Bought What, Where, How, and Why

In a work translated into English in 1932, the sociologist Leopold von Weise observed that modern men and women, cloistered all day in offices and factories, were denied communal outlets through which aboriginal societies released natural impulses. In their public lives, they were restricted to a decorum of behavior, language, and gesture based on their proper place in an impersonal pecking order. When released from their places of employment, city workers needed "surrogate activities" safely to work off their frustrations and gratify their fantasies, a need that made the amusement business a fast-growing one. One popular category of "surrogation," von Weise stated, "is bound up with the sex urge; instances are found in: 'T[ired] B[usiness] M[an]' musical comedies and burlesque; 'taxi dancing'; the libidinous French postcard, novel, short story, 'unexpurgated edition,' 'confession' magazine, 'Captain Billy's Whiz-Bang,' 'Art Lover's Magazine,' and all the *erotica* that the little 'arty' bookshops disseminate; masturbation, some kinds of homosexuality, prostitution; and so on."[1] Those who sold or rented erotica in the 1920s and 1930s shared a sure instinct about the kind of surrogation the public wanted, and a rough-hewn opportunism regarding the people's need for sexual frankness. As one bookstore owner remembered:

Many of our customers [in the early 1930s] were unable to pay their bills. . . . We began to examine what other possibilities there existed to bring in additional revenue and fell upon the idea of adding pornography to our rental library. Pornography in those days was something clandestine and furtive, like bootlegging. . . . The finest people drank illegal booze and some of the best customers of the speakeasies were among them; but only perverts and degenerates were supposed to read pornography. Of course we were cautious and loaned books only to people we knew. It was revealing to discover that some of our leading citizens were among our best customers.[2]

During the interwar period, selling erotica was increasingly profitable; with the Depression economy, it became even more attractive. By the early 1920s, if not before, it was "sex o'clock in American literature."[3] Increased interest in analyses of, and stories about, sexual desire and behavior was inevitable after large numbers of people came to live in urban areas, where new and freer ways of conducting oneself in public and in private were desirable for social viability and personal satisfaction. City dwellers felt the pressure of imitating, and dreamed of attaining, these patterns of behavior, and enjoyed seeing them satisfied, if only vicariously, through the popular entertainments the city offered. The "commercialization of sex"[4] was a phenomenon of urban life that satisfied people's needs and created new ones. Clothing manufacture, hairstyling, nightclubs, stage performances, films, magazines, and books grew more sophisticated as these businesses, in the hands of increasingly clever and observant entrepreneurs, attracted more and more customers.

The Eroticization of Leisure Time

The popularity of the surrogate entertainments von Weise listed indicates that the ideal of sexual reticence, which had been a workable guide to conduct before the turn of the century, had now eroded. Previously, sex-for-hire had been available only in working-class, especially black and immigrant, red-light districts, and few middle-class men dared join the decadent aristocrats who ventured into what seemed like exotic dens of vice. These were the well-marked places of the Devil. The home and workplace had been sacred precincts of modesty, thrift, self-sacrifice, and pious contempt for sensuality; the paterfamilias ruled the pulpit and political platform, as well as the hearth. But by the early 1900s, what Rochelle Gurstein has called "the repeal of reticence" was well underway, with attacks on traditional marriage, advocacy of free love and of sex as an important part of people's lives, and the popularization of Freudian ideas, which before the war were confined to academic settings.[5] World War I provided a breathing space for advocates of conserving reticence, as the publishing industry, paying homage to the image of the American soldier as pure-hearted crusader, effectively regulated itself. After the war came the Justice Department actions against suspected subversives, during which writing deemed indecent, as well as anarchistic, was seized. As often happens after a period of war and austerity, people became suspicious of such allegiances to purity,[6] as they did of the motives of the authorities in general.

With urban populations freer to spend their money where they wished, the ethos of downtown gratification struggled fiercely with the traditional code. The places of temptation were expanding: in a location such as Manhattan's Times Square, one could find

glorified dancing girls and millionaire playboys, and, on a different plane, dime-a-dance hostesses and pleasure-seeking clerks . . . gangsters and racketeers, panhandlers and derelicts, youthful stage stars and aging burlesque comedians. . . . An outer shell of bars and restaurants, electric signs, movie palaces, taxi dance halls, cabarets, chop suey palaces, and side shows of every description . . . fruit juice stands garlanded with artificial palm leaves, theater ticket offices, cheap lunch counters, cut-rate haberdasheries, burlesque houses, and novelty concessions.[7]

With the spread of print and broadcast media, erotica was moving right into the home. Moral order was under siege, as a sermon preached at St. Patrick's Cathedral in 1937 made clear: "In this age of sophistication and deified liberty the home has been demoralized because authority has been defied and denied . . . I think the desire of husbands and wives to indulge all their premarital social activities even after the marriage is one reason for the breakdown. . . . The night clubs have supplanted the nursery; the tooting saxophone has taken the place of the lullaby; Kleig lights have replaced the fireside."[8]

The newsstands, cut-rate bookshops, cigar and drugstore lending libraries, and burlesque houses that John Sumner and his colleagues decried were easily found along the edges of the neon pleasure zones. The New York police chaplain found them in 1933 and called for the licensing of all bookstores.[9] One year later, he inveighed against the Times Square area, "the filth center of the world," with its bookstores that "pander to the lowest forms of vice," and its newsstands, whose magazines were calculated to make "a respectable savage blush."[10] For those who would not actually consort with gangsters, prostitutes, con men, and gigolos, a vicarious participation was provided through the printed word, the retouched photo, and the off-color novelty item. "Indecent" books and movies, available to so many at so low a cost, seemed to present a special temptation to fantasize about prioritizing sensual indulgence over hard work, modesty, and family responsibilities. Films and books allowed customers to identify safely with the heroes and heroines of stories about seduction, kept women, nudity, crimes of passion, white slavery, adultery, and divorce.

The thrills movies delivered were more spontaneously attractive than those to be found in books, and the audience for films was more extensive. As movie czar Will Hayes, who, as president of the Motion Picture Producers and Distributors of America, was in charge of restraining Hollywood's excesses of "indecency," put it, moviegoers constituted "the vast majority of Americans, who do not fling defiance at customs and conventions, but who cling with fine faith and devotion to the things that are wholesome and healthy."[11] He must have felt that this majority might be tempted, because he joined with the Catholic authorities who, backed by a monolithic constituency, successfully pressured film executives to oversee what the industry produced. Thereafter, the film industry's "merchants of leisure" were most vigorously subjected to regulatory codes.[12] No such agreements had been hammered out with publishers, and no such enforcer existed, although the printed media on newsstands, in burlesque houses, in drugstores, cigar stores, bookstores, and lending libraries offered similarly questionable entertainments. Producers and publishers, theater and bookstore owners, were in the same kind of business (Figure 9). Segments of the print media needed to market sex. Their enterprises would grow most strongly if moral reproaches and legal entanglements could be minimized. Could they be trusted to act responsibly without coercion?

The founding of the National Organization for Decent Literature (NODL), which sought, with limited success, to impose strict codes of acceptability on printed materials, followed the advent of the Legion of Decency (1934) by only a few years. The legion was dedicated to policing popular films for emphasis on "sex," "vulgarity," "crime," sybaritic recreations ("dances," "costume"), and irreverent treatment of family, patriotic, or religious values.[13] The NODL campaigned against newsstand and bookstore materials "glorifying" crime, drugs, and licentiousness, starting in 1938.[14] Both organizations represented Catholic-supported attempts to persuade filmmakers and publishers to restrict their production of salacious material. Although their strategy involved legal censorship rather than self-regulation, the Progressive reformers of the purity societies had long been preparing the public for such organizations. The attempts of motion-picture producers and distributors to meet their objections, as well as those of fundamentalist Protestants and Catholic authorities, date from 1922. The New York Society for the Suppression of Vice (NYSSV) had been warning the public about dangerous books and plays for at least a generation; films and other new forms of entertainment alarmed them equally. Increasingly throughout the 1920s, both books and films took their place alongside cosmetics, clothing, jewelry, mouthwash, and soap as com-

Figure 9. The corner of Lexington Avenue and East 42nd Street, Manhattan, in 1928. A cigar store occupied the ground floor of the corner property. Next to it on the 42nd Street side were a men's shop and a movie theater. These were sites in which men could experience the "eroticization of leisure time" (both borderline and "flagitious" lending-library erotica, formfitting clothing, and daring movies) about which the antivice societies were concerned. Perhaps in a hotel room above the cigar store one could locate a peddler who traded in pornographic readers, or copies of *My Life and Loves* or *Lady Chatterley's Lover*. © Ewing Galloway, Inc. All rights reserved. Reproduced by permission of Ewing Galloway and the New York Public Library, Astor, Lenox and Tilden Foundations, United States History, Local History and Genealogy Division (Collection: Photographic Views of New York City).

modities gratifying sensual needs. But to the idealists of the reform societies, their effects on the consumer seemed especially corrosive.

The commodification of leisure, of which the commercialization of sex is but one facet, was not the only factor contributing to the new morality of the 1920s. Prohibition brought a general disrespect for laws against activities for which there seemed to be no victims among the adult population, including selling erotica and gambling. There was also greater social mobility, especially for urban women. But movies and books as well as nightclubs and speakeasies facilitated the new morality's assimilation into mundane experience, making extramarital sexual experience much more possible than before World War I, and providing a stronger sense that in general one owed it to oneself to fulfill urges for gratifications of all sorts, including sexual ones.[15]

Also loosening old restraints were the increased mobility that the automobile provided, the excitement of defying Prohibition, the emergence of the newly autonomous collegiate "flaming youth," and the romance attached by advertisers, popular novels, and films to freedom and love of experimentation. At first largely confined to the youthful, affluent, and urban participants in the Jazz Age, the revolution in manners and morals became even more a part of the fabric of ordinary American life, thanks to the resourcefulness of the commodifiers of sex, after the Crash of 1929. By then, many "modern" Americans of all ages had an increasing fund of information about how the body functioned and what the consequences of sexual behavior were. As John D'Emilio and Estelle Freedman's history of sexuality in America shows, birth control and family planning, although still considered radical in 1920, had been made increasingly visible by Margaret Sanger and her clinics. The percentage of women who had premarital intercourse rose sharply during the 1920s, as did motivation to marry for emotional fulfillment — companionate marriage — rather than as a duty. With the ability to separate themselves from their parents by having their own places to meet, by using automobiles to get there, and by reading about the gaiety of college life, middle-class youth were able to develop their own subculture. It was obvious to practical-minded parents that their adolescent offspring ought to educate themselves about how to experiment with sex in a responsible and healthy way.[16] It was not simply the hope of appearing modish and the search for titillation that made people seek access to sexually oriented fiction and nonfiction but the need to participate in a new freedom. The way one did so could either increase one's chances for happiness or cause emotional or physical disability. No wonder moralists had little trouble getting parents to listen when they warned about the kinds of films and books about sex now on the market.

Since sex was so controversial and marketable, neither distributor nor reader could easily separate teaching about it from entertainment involving it. People could learn about the sex instinct from sober treatises or from teasingly salacious novels. Both kinds of books, advertised in various media, were increasingly available to readers of all ages and levels of sophistication. Therefore, it would be a mistake to assume that age and social class determined the quality of what was read. For example, Emanuel Haldeman-Julius's educational Little Blue Books — at five cents apiece, a kind of poor man's university — included many about courtship, marriage, venereal diseases, birth control, prostitution, and Freudian psychology. They sold equally well among readers of the *New York Times*, the sensation-mongering tabloid the *Daily Graphic*, and *Liberty*, a low-priced general-interest magazine for middle- and working-class readers.[17]

Dollar Novels to Deluxe Editions

Not all erotic books were within the price range of those who wanted them. In the 1920s, prices were high, not for the items openly published by reputable firms and promptly decried as indecently frank, but for the various genres of sexology, explicit fiction, and underground pornography. Many publishers, notably Covici-Friede, Brentano, and Liveright, issued expensive editions of eyebrow-raising books by well-respected writers without fear of censorship. The authorities did not in these cases press the "into whose hands" issue, because the books were limited to print runs of between one thousand and fifteen hundred copies that had been sold by subscription before publication, at prices of between five and ten dollars, ostensibly to people with credentials as scholars, rare-book collectors, physicians, or writers.[18] High prices meant limited circulation, which was reassuring to those concerned that large numbers of people would find their moral convictions weakened if given the opportunity to read the "wrong" sort of books. The catalogs of Harry F. Marks, a carriage-trade New York antiquarian bookseller, for "belles-lettres, classical literature, and anthropological works" feature a quotation from Macaulay on the back cover that reads in part: "No Book which is Valuable . . . should be withheld from the Student." The student had to prove that he or she had proper credentials. The bottom of the front cover states: "Subscriptions taken only from Doctors, Lawyers, Educators, Students and Members of the Learned Professions."

Writers and sellers of the sorts of erotica that most directly flaunted obscenity laws wanted to reach as many readers as possible, but most often their first concern was safe distribution. Frank Harris made varying suggestions to his American disciples about pricing the version of his autobiography with the "naughty" chapters present, but the figure most often stated was ten dollars per volume (this was the wholesale price, which meant it retailed for much more at bookstores). The print run of the expurgated volume 1 sold out at fifteen dollars per retailed copy.[19] According to D. H. Lawrence, piracies of *Lady Chatterley's Lover* fetched from ten dollars to fifty dollars;[20] by the mid-1930s, there were two attractive deluxe editions of the novel, published in Chicago and California. Harry F. Marks listed finely printed and bound "anthropological works" at forty-five dollars or sixty-five dollars, and other "belles-lettres" at three dollars and fifty cents to twenty-five dollars.[21] Those printed by the chief European erotica publisher at the turn of the century, Charles Carrington, were particularly valuable. Marks's titles included the unexpurgated *Arabian Nights*, *The Merry Order of St. Bridget*, *Opus Sadicum*, the famous Hindu manual of love-making *Ananga Ranga*, Wilhelm Stekel's psychoanalytical books on homosexuality, Earl Lind's *Autobiography of an Androgyne*, and Pierre Louÿs's novel *Aphrodite*. These are all titles John Sumner interdicted — not proceeding against Marks, but when he found them circulated in cheaper under-the-counter editions.

During the Depression, well-produced books of this nature, printed on quality paper, with attractive binding and endpapers, gilt edges, and well-designed typography, did not drop much in price. There was still a small but active market for the expensive books, both for borderline mail-order offerings at five dollars and for classical and newly issued works deemed flagrantly obscene at three times that. Literary publishers of erotica may have taken heart from the experience of George Macy. Founded just as the stock market crashed, his Limited Editions Club offered classical (not erotic) titles at ten dollars each and was well supported throughout the early 1930s.[22] During the Depression, as in the previous decade, national distribution of income was extremely uneven. Thirteen percent of Americans made more than five thousand dollars per year in 1929; 11 percent remained in that grouping in 1936.[23] Most of the rich stayed rich, and those who were comfortable before 1929 continued to afford some luxuries in the 1930s. An erotically illustrated edition of Clement Wood's short-story collection, *Flesh*, sold for twelve dollars and fifty cents (a typical price) in 1930. Catalogs of the Argus Book Shop in Chicago[24] and the Anthropological Library in New York[25] list offerings ranging from three dollars to one hundred twenty-five dollars. London and Paris editions were the most expensive, with strictly sub-rosa items, such as individual volumes of the Victorian magazine *The Pearl*, offered at twenty dollars each. The two-volume Carrington edition of *Untrodden Fields of Anthropology* cost fifty dollars at the height of the Depression; a 23rd Street bookseller entrapped into selling *White Stains* in 1934 was asking seventeen dollars.[26]

Exactly who could afford these rates? Esar Levine, who in the early 1930s owned the Panurge Press, was one of a number of astute mail-order specialists and bookstore owners with well-cultivated mailing lists. Panurge classified its clients into groups. There were twenty-five "prominent individuals," including the department store owner Rodman Wanamaker, the actor Eric von Stroheim, and the rubber magnate C. W. Seiberling; ten "professors"; fifty "army officers"; twenty "reverends"; two hundred eighty "lawyers," and fourteen hundred "doctors," including more dentists than physicians — thirty-five fully typed pages were needed to list them.[27] Panurge was a mail-order house, which priced its newly published books, whether sexology or fiction, at five or six dollars.

However, Panurge and its competitors needed to reach a general audience of middle-class men and women as well. Therefore, as advertising matter indicates, after the market among the affluent had been exhausted, one could buy at $3.90, $2.50, $1.98, or $1.50.[28] Even that was steep for some people. The book trade, although initially optimistic after the Crash, saw the need to reduce prices by 1932.[29] A two-dollar book would have been 5 percent of the weekly wage of someone making $2,000 per year in 1929, or about $40 per week. Even cheaper books were a luxury for the 26 percent of the population at this income level. By 1936, that percentage had risen to 29 percent. The number making between $2,000 and $3,000 in 1936 comprised another 21 percent of the population; it had been 29 percent in 1929. Calculations using the Consumer Price Index suggest that a book that cost $12.50 in 1927 would be the equivalent of $117 in mid-1998 currency. By 1935, such a book would cost the equivalent of $149, and a six-dollar 1935 first edition of a Panurge or Falstaff Press text would cost the equivalent of $71. To pay even one dollar for a novel in 1935 would be comparable to paying $12 in the late 1990s. It is not difficult to imagine, therefore, how unlikely it would be for more than half of all adult Americans to afford a book of three, five, or ten dollars in the mid-1930s. People with weekly salaries of thirty-five or forty dollars per week were applying for relief. No wonder that pulp magazines and lending libraries were popular then, and that some of the latter specialized in providing both over- and under-the-counter erotica. Dollar novels were published in increasing numbers, and often formed the core of a lending-library's offerings. After 1930, printers worked more cheaply, and publishers, distributors, and bookstore and lending-library proprietors found new ways to interest people of diverse income levels as evidenced by the alarm raised by antivice societies, politicians, and clergy against lending-library and newsstand materials. Young men, and especially young women, spending time in specialty shops and bookstores were being exposed in growing numbers to texts that treated birth control, companionate marriage, and sexual experimentation.

Nineteen thirty-three was a crisis year for the book trade: the number of new titles declined, as did prices, and raw materials became harder to purchase. Remainders were so plentiful that a purchaser could expect a new title at two dollars to soon be on sale for one dollar and twenty-five cents.[30] New and inexpensive editions were to be had on "dollar book" counters or through notices placed in pulp magazines. The Franklin Publishing Company of Chicago ran many full-page advertisements in *College Life* from 1928 to 1931 offering individual titles only recently released from the bonds of prudish convention, such as the *Decameron* ("at last Censorship no longer denies you this thrill of thrills"). The availability and popularity of reprints had long been a cause for concern for the publisher of new fiction.[31] Now erotica dealers, recognizing that the reader's interest was growing while his or her budget was shrinking, discovered the inexpensive mass-produced reprint, and the value of titillating advertisement. In 1932, William Godwin Inc. used the imprint Rarity Press, and the text and illustrations of books originally published by the Fortune Press and John Lane, both of London, to bring out impressions of erotic classics that enjoyed "tremendous sales at Macy's and Hearn's at a dollar a piece."[32] Such books eliminated the chances for a general sale of more expensive, and more lavishly produced, editions of the same works. The latter, now mere shelf fillers, could be had for loose change on remainder counters. And yet by 1933, the Godwin editions seem to have met with a similar fate, according to *Publishers Weekly*.[33] Because the works of Boccaccio, Martial, Margaret of Navarre, and other writers once decried as prurient were now made widely available, and also had been cleared by the courts, or ignored by Customs officials and vice-society investigators, it became fruitless to try to tempt people with them. Meanwhile, cheap books on erotology, birth control, eugenics, "inversion" and other "sexual abnormalities," and the restoration of "lost potency" were commonly listed in the classified sections of pulp, romance, movie star, adventure, and humor magazines. They continued to draw fire from postal inspectors and outraged parents, but were increasingly attainable. What had taken place was "a sudden cheapening and popularizing of erotica, by publishers who saw no other way of making money. . . . At last, the great body of readers know what erotica is; they purchase erotic books in cheap editions, and what they buy, they buy sanely and in moderation."[34]

Greater familiarity extended to the most blatantly obscene pamphlets and paperbound books. It is possible that people ordering erotic classics by mail would have been sent advertisements for interdicted volumes that could not be offered in a newspaper notice: in 1938, the Arden Book Company did so, with Sam Roth's edition of the *Ananga Ranga* (which he entitled *The Secret Places of the Human Body*), and with two books entitled *Strip Tease* and *Something to Do in Bed*.[35] The same year, the National Library offered the same books, in a "Book Bargain" circular sent to college students who had responded to advertisements for a civil service handbook.[36] As John Sumner stated in the NYSSV annual report for 1933, the Depression drove down prices for "books which are so flagrantly offensive that they are printed secretly and distributed with stealth and cunning . . . [thus] making these publications potentially more harmful due to the possibility of greater circulation."[37]

The Scale of Lubricity: From Borderline Distasteful to Obscene and Unlawful

Few American establishments would have stocked the full variety of erotic books and magazines available. Bob Brown, freelance pulp writer and symbolist poet, offers a vivid contemporary description of a Paris bookstore in which American tourists would have felt at home because its contents were similar to those in an American shop. There were

a handful of second-hand breath-taking American romances in smart crimson and green jackets in the show windows as a blind. In a surreptitious case inside . . . prying pornographers unfailingly find the goods; . . . ferocious Masochs, boarding school true stories . . . the *Museo Secreto* all about Herculaneo and Pompeii, Frank Harris' "My Life and Loves," preposterous phallic boastings with duly magnified illustrations . . . suppressed first editions, "Sadie Blackeyes" [a French fetish novel], doctor's books and the East Indian standby painfully depicting the 69 approved pleasurable positions.[38]

Pierre Louÿs

THE

SONGS OF BILITIS

TRANSLATED FROM THE GREEK

This volume, issued by The Pierre Louÿs Society, is one of the most beautiful ever printed, produced in the most luxurious manner, regardless of expense.

The translation was specially done by M. S. Buck, the eminent scholar and bibliophile, and the work is divided into three parts: the first, a series of delightful pastorals; the second, narrating incidents in Bilitis' life on the Isle of Lesbos; and the third, her experiences while living as a courtesan on the Isle of Kypros.

The volume is superbly illustrated in the most resplendent manner with reproductions in full color of twenty-four full-page designs of Franz Felix.

This re-issue of this delightful book is limited to 1250 copies; bound in green boards, with printed paper labels; and, like all previous limited editions of The Pierre Louÿs Society, will undoubtedly be quickly over-subscribed, and copies will command a premium in the very near future; it is therefore peremptorily necessary that your order should be given immediately.

THE PRICE IS $15.00

If such a store were in the United States, browsers would also have found, scattered throughout and inserted in erotic volumes, enticing circulars for books to be purchased either by mail order or sometimes by special order in the bookstore itself (Figure 10).

The upscale store catering to the mid-Manhattan carriage trade, the Fourth Avenue secondhand shop, and the backdate magazine place each had its proper ambience, and its own preferred items. It was only a matter of where a customer chose to go. If there was little mystery about who could get what, this was owing to word of mouth, which was of supreme importance in finding out where to locate legally proscribed erotica. Bern Porter, chronicler of Henry Miller and habitué of the erotica scene, states that not only secondhand booksellers on Fourth Avenue and elsewhere but also the great "art erotica" suppliers such as Jake Zeitlin, Harry F. Marks, Ben Abramson, and David Moss "operated by word of mouth advertising as opposed to printed public advertising, . . . with sellers purposely going to bars in their neighborhood saying to all 'we have it at our address.' " Jack Biblo of Biblo and Tannen confirms that through word of mouth, sellers and buyers alike could learn whom to trust, something that could not have been accomplished by the impersonal sales pitch of a circular or classified advertisement.[39]

Items of trade fell into five broad categories: gallantiana, sex pulps, erotology and sexology, "bibles" and "readers," and classical and modern books judged to be rankly indecent. These terms are not those used by the censors. Although they sometimes used similar labels, those they favored were consistently pejorative, even in the case of the "milder" categories. For the moral entrepreneur, all categories of erotica were deplorable. In the 1930s, an example of the contempt accorded both merely titillating and "flagitious" literature is the way those terms parallel the distinction between a "parlor show" and a "whore show" in burlesque. To a judge considering the appeal of a burlesque theater for renewal of license in 1941, both

Figure 10. First page of a folio-size flyer, printed in red and black, for the Pierre Louÿs Society's edition of *The Songs of Bilitis*, with illustrations by Franz Felix. The price (fifteen dollars) is given, but there is no order form. The summary of Bilitis' life on Lesbos states that, with husbands occupied with drinking and "dancing-girls," the women united and "softened to those delicate loves to which antiquity has given their name and which have, whatever men may think, more of true passion than of studied viciousness." In possession of the author.

forms of entertainment were worthy of disdain, although he termed the former "respectable," and the latter only for those "degenerately affixed on sex." (The appeal of the theater in question was rejected, probably because it offered strip tease.) New York's commissioner of licenses at the time sided with John Sumner on such matters as burlesque and spicy magazines, and the judge seemed to echo the beliefs of both men. Regulatory power, he said, may be at odds with freedom of speech but the alternative is "social anarchy and oppressive license."[40] The preventive societies would have agreed.

Gallantiana

The term "gallantiana" (synonyms are "curiosa" or "facetiae") is that of Gershon Legman, an articulate and passionate participant in, and observer of, the erotica scene, and an extraordinary historian of the same, prose stylist, and bibliographer. He learned about the business in the 1930s by working with New York erotica publishers and booksellers. He knew such mainstays as Samuel Roth, Jake Brussel, Benjamin Rebhuhn, and Esar Levine, and had his own troubles with the postal suppression of his highly original study of American sexual taboos, *Love & Death: A Study in Censorship* (1949), because it contained some four-letter words. For Legman, "gallantiana" denotes "those marginal elements of unexpurgated literature such as jest-books and balladry, works on (and against) women and love, facetious treatises in prose and in verse, and the hinterland of scatologica."[41] "Gallant" literature also includes many novels and literary classics that had, or were perceived as having, erotic themes.

Charles H. Bodwell, the secretary of Boston's Watch and Ward Society, supervised a board whose members read many borderline titles each month in order to pass their judgments on to the Boston booksellers. Bodwell distinguished "polite literature" — "contemporary novels" that he thought focused too strongly on the erotic — from "pornography."[42] Judging from examples of titles contested in Boston, *Elmer Gantry* and *The Sun Also Rises* would have been examples of such literature. Reverend Henry N. Pringle, law-enforcement director of the International Reform Federation, drew up a sixteen-page list of "protested books," to which Bodwell and Sumner were asked to contribute titles, whether of polite or blatantly obscene works.[43] Pringle included "remarks" specifying the offensiveness of curiosa such as *Casanova's Homecoming* ("rake's conquests"), Balzac's

Droll Stories ("French filth for America"), *Flaming Youth* by Samuel Hopkins Adams, writing as Warner Fabian ("reeking with indecency"), the *Decameron* ("amours ad nauseam"), *The Perfumed Garden* ("coitional particulars"), Claudia de Lys's *How the World Weds* ("full of pruriency"), and Louÿs's *Woman and Puppet* ("Seville at carnival time").

What was the source of Pringle's distress regarding these books' infringements of propriety? *How the World Weds* is about marriage customs; its third part, the flap of the dust jacket states, "deals comprehensively with aberrations and irregularities in marriage." Handsomely quarter-bound in cloth with decorated paperboards and red endpapers, it is illustrated with three black-and-white drawings of near-naked men and women, surrounded by demons and snakes, and framed with poles and sashes; perhaps these were thought to encourage a priapic cast of mind. One of *Flaming Youth*'s feature scenes shows young people swimming in the nude with a poolside spotlight trained on one naked body or another. The ribaldries of *Droll Stories* and the *Decameron* are many and focus not so much on the marriage as on the adulterous bed, into which women and men climb joyfully. Each of these stories, however intelligently and gracefully written, speaks openly about sexual desire, and Pringle, Sumner, and Bodwell were not inclined to distinguish that from obscenity. In addition, these books were by "foreign" writers, and so for the chauvinistic American moralist the exoticism was easier to identify as degenerate. The purity societies never stopped trying to interdict gallantiana.⁴⁴ In the 1920s, several of these titles were banned by various municipalities, U.S. Customs, and the Post Office, which continued to rule many of them unmailable throughout the interwar period.⁴⁵ Nonfiction curiosa, and contemporary novels, including those by Ernest Hemingway, William Faulkner, Erskine Caldwell, Ben Hecht, and Aleksandr Kuprin, were boycotted by the Catholic Church.

One could easily find abridged, expurgated editions of Roman, Renaissance, eighteenth-century, or contemporary literature with text or illustrations just sexually explicit enough to appeal to prurient interest and to awaken Pringle-esque censoriousness (Figure 11). Their unexpurgated counterparts could also be found in bookstores, which did not necessarily mean that those stores were in danger of prosecution. However, no one could completely predict at which books the police and the antivice societies might take offense. Often it was the illustrations that triggered attempts at censorship. A large number of prosecutions involved unexpurgated editions of modern memoirs, novels, and plays that a particular police-

THE FORTUNES *and* MISFORTUNES ⸏

OF THE FAMOUS

MOLL FLANDERS

by DANIEL DEFOE

∽ *with illuftrations by* ∽
JOHN ALAN MAXWELL

THE · BIBLIOPHILIST · SOCIETY

Figure 11. This 1931 edition of *Moll Flanders* (n.d.: The Bibliophilist Society), "profusely illustrated" with drawings of a bare-breasted heroine, may not have been prosecuted because it was a literary classic, but it would have raised eyebrows and moralists' hackles.

man, a vice-society investigator, or even a private citizen brought to the attention of a magistrate or postal authority. Sometimes such books, when sponsored by established publishers who could afford lawyers' fees, were permitted circulation, at least temporarily and locally, and of course grudgingly. Reasons included the vice-societies' reluctance to be the subject of disapproving newspaper editorials, to lose a case in court, or to have their own members wonder at their choice of targets.

Literary classics with boldly uninhibited erotic passages had been sought out by prurient readers since the eighteenth century. As cultural historian Peter Gay has documented, in Victorian times young men either enthusiastically or furtively (depending on temperament) filled their libraries with eighteenth- and nineteenth-century complete editions of classical novels, poems, plays, and memoirs, such as the works of Martial, Suetonius, Aristophanes, Ovid, Aretino, Boccaccio, Rabelais, and Casanova.[46] No less desirable were Margaret of Navarre's amatory stories modeled on Boccaccio's, the licentious novels of Mirabeau and Crébillon fils, Brantôme's accounts of the "fair and gallant ladies" of the sixteenth century, Burton's unexpurgated volumes of the *Arabian Nights*, and the *One Hundred Merrie and Delightsome Tales*, a Renaissance compilation of amorous stories. Among the titles John Sumner thought the Gotham Book Mart had no business distributing in 1930 were Louÿs's *Songs of Bilitis*, Gautier's *Mademoiselle de Maupin*, Cabell's *Jurgen*, Lawrence's *Women in Love*, and *From a Turkish Harem*, an anthology put together by Martin Hartman and translated into English from German. The library of Clara Tice, an artist well-known in New York bohemian circles and herself a prolific and daringly explicit illustrator of gallant books, especially for the Pierre Louÿs Society, displayed other examples: Apuleius's *Golden Ass*, Longus's *Daphnis and Chloe*, Balzac's *Droll Stories*, Beardsley's *Under the Hill*, Flaubert's *The Temptation of St. Anthony*, Laclos's *Les Liaisons Dangereuses*, Smith's *Poetica Erotica*.[47] The law firm of Greenbaum, Wolff, and Ernst added the entire set of the Rarity Press reprints of such classics to its reference collection.[48] The firm had itself helped to have some of them declared not obscene and in the early 1930s assumed it would need to continue with its efforts, therefore putting the set to good use.

Such classics by the 1930s became widely and cheaply available. Moralists, however, continued throughout the decade to deplore them unless their eroticism was bowdlerized. Complete editions often were issued as "privately printed." A publisher who placed the firm's name on the title page as well as this rubric was simply increasing curiosity; thus the Godwin reprints were dubbed "Privately

Printed for William Godwin Inc." Frankly obscene erotica was issued privately because anonymity was essential to avoid arrest. In prosecuting Thomas Seltzer's editions of *Women in Love* and *Casanova's Homecoming* in 1922, John Sumner stressed as evidence of their grossness their having been issued in limited, privately printed editions, at fifteen dollars and ten dollars a copy, respectively.[49] Seltzer's name was not in either book. Private printing, opined critic Henry S. Canby, was "a sign usually of weakness in the book, distrust of the reader, or fear of the hand of authority."[50] The enticing flavor of the disreputable helped sales, and so the designation continued to be found on title pages of books no longer proscribed — a signal, like the wink of an eye, of the sexual frankness of the text. Consider the advice Esar Levine gave the wife of the aging and impecunious Frank Harris in 1930:

Have a French printer set up the "Yellow Ticket" volume of short stories. Have it "privately printed" by the author. There are half a dozen short stories in that volume which an indiscriminating public will consider off-color. . . . If you do this, the public will buy hundreds of copies — provided this book contains only such stories as I suggest, the snappy ones. Such a volume would sell ever so much faster than Frank's later volume of short stories which are on a far higher level. Briffault Brothers or Groves and Michaux could sell hundreds of copies at $5.00 a throw. You have no idea, Nellie, what a magic effect "privately printed" on the title page of a book of snappy stories would have![51]

Another of the authorities' concerns regarded "abridgments" that left intact what they considered the eroticism. The 1930 annual report of the NYSSV expressed alarm at this as a trend. Therefore, publishers were also concerned, and sought advice before committing to either complete or abridged editions. If they were sexy, who knew? In 1930, Art Studio Books ("Publications of Unexpurgated Translations in Limited Editions") requested that Greenbaum, Wolff, and Ernst determine whether its "beautiful edition of Ovid, unexpurgated and translated by Alexander King," could safely be advertised and sold. This law firm and others were often approached by publishers concerned about prosecution.[52] Art Studio distributed to bookstores and may also have done mail-order retailing. Its staff might have included editor Thomas R. Smith, compiler of the privately printed *Immortalia* (an important, and banned, 1929 anthology of erotic folklore) and, for Boni and Liveright in 1921, *Poetica Erotica*. The latter could qualify as gallantiana; the former was stronger stuff. By 1934, in the depths of the Depression, Art

Studio was taking a risk — unsuccessful, as it turned out — by publishing underground erotic classics for which anyone could be successfully prosecuted.[53]

When packaged with respectable discretion, erotica could be consumed conspicuously. "Gallant" suggests courtesy, graceful (if amateurish) erudition, and "class." It generally implies that the reader has legitimate reasons for examining the work of Ovid, Boccaccio, Schnitzler, or Louÿs, which in the hands of the vulgar, unlettered masses would become "demoralizing." Grete Meisel-Hess's *The Sexual Crisis* (1917; reprinted in translation throughout the interwar period) respectfully described "gallant love" as a very different experience from mere bodily arousal; it was instead a set of intellectual contretemps that forced sophisticated lovers to explore each other's sensibility. The intimacy resulting from "feelings of sympathy, friendship, and tenderness . . . suffice to justify a woman's self-surrender to a man. . . . Only in highly cultivated hands is gallant love able to maintain its value."[54] Those responsible for the production of gallantiana in the 1920s, whether unbarbered or "abridged," often sold the aristocratic refinement the gallant experience embodied by attempting fine printing: black gold-stamped boards, linen spines, decorated endpapers, top-edge gilt, and untrimmed edges. All held a certain kind of prurient appeal — a very enticing kind. "Furtive tomes in tasty bindings," Bob Brown called them. "Pale pallid twitchings on the titillating tender edges of things."[55]

Sex Pulps

Upon entering a general-interest bookstore whose owner was not overly concerned with scrutiny by the preventive societies, a browser might encounter a wide selection of gallantiana just described, collections of bawdy jokes, books about the "strange careers" or "secret lives" of political or showbiz celebrities, and "racy" romantic or mystery novels devoid of four-letter words or explicit descriptions of intercourse. If the store featured backdate magazines, one could also scan display racks of gossip, pinup, art, and nudist magazines (with airbrushed models). Certain periodicals featured quite a few pictures of female nudes for their mainly male readers: *Broadway Brevities, Smokehouse Monthly, Police Gazette, Captain Billy's Whiz-Bang, Artists and Models, Wow, Spicy Romances, Jazza-Ka-Jazza, Pan, Paris Nights,* and *Hot Dog* were popular throughout the 1920s. Their counterparts for women were the conventionally romantic "confession" magazines, pioneered by Bernarr Macfadden's *True Story*. The racy books, in contrast, were written and packaged with both sexes in mind. However, they targeted specialized audiences as carefully and astutely as did the magazines. Their paper was not wood pulp. But their formulaic story lines, inexpensive format, and "spicy" dust-jacket illustrations represented a marketing strategy similar to that of the pulp magazines, and thus I characterize these books as "sex pulps."

Sex pulps featured brightly colored jackets, plain cloth bindings, inexpensive paper, and were small enough to be held in one hand as part of a cigar or drugstore shopper's purchases. A result of the post-Crash need for cheap escapist fare, they were a new kind of book: aggressively rather than discreetly titillating, parvenu rather than genteel in sensibility, garish rather than sophisticated in their packaging, and issued in large print runs rather than limited editions. Imprints included William Faro (Sam Roth), William Godwin (for whom Jack Woodford and Peggy Gaddis were starting long careers as writers of mildly sexy potboilers), Arcadia House, Phoenix, Blue Ribbon, Macaulay, and Grosset and Dunlap. Grosset and Dunlap included Tiffany Thayer — whose *Thirteen Men* (1930) demonstrated his ability to create diverse characters with shadowy pasts and dubious sexual tastes — in its large genre list, and reprinted the Knopf expurgated edition of *Lady Chatterley's Lover*. Covici-Friede, now publishing lower-priced books than it had before the Crash, aggressively marketed a number of titillating stories, leading off with *Speakeasy Girl*, which the firm advertised by placing a design from the dust jacket on cocktail shakers that were sent to bookstore personnel; various movie producers received free advance copies.[56] Clearly, these firms did more than publish borderline erotica; even the jointly owned Godwin and Phoenix, which pursued the audience most aggressively, had many other publishing aims. Godwin specialized in social science, and was responsible for the tony magazine *Modern Quarterly*.[57]

Women who visited the various stores that displayed novels and magazines were important target audiences for sex pulps: receptionists, salesclerks, teachers, office-pool typists, and neighbor-conscious housewives all bought them. Women may also have served as lending librarians in drugstores and department stores. One clever innovation of the late 1920s or early 1930s was the "office library," or "bag" system, whereby a representative of a lending-library distributor made weekly visits to office buildings for the convenience of the workers, who would borrow one or more titles for between fifteen and twenty-five cents per week.[58] Gershon Legman claimed in 1945 that after the success in the 1920s of "wish-fulfillment novels like *The Sheik*, full of rape and roughness and other touches aimed at the woman public," these readers began to "[insist] on sex in the novels they borrow from the very influential lending-library chains."[59] However, sex-pulp writers and publishers apparently did not share Legman's opinion of what women wish for; their story lines did not attempt the exotic romance, let alone the sultry aggression, that E. M. Hull managed to infuse into her 1921 novel. The lending-library potboilers did strive to fulfill working women's fantasies of romantic encounters that led to handsome men and comely young women sleeping together. But this result was only lightly suggested.

The story lines invariably featured a strong silent hero, an ingenue heroine, her desire for romantic adventures and fulfillment, the futile resistance of family and peers, glamorous supporting characters and locales, melodramatic plots and counterplots involving crooks, femmes fatales, or filthy lucre, and at the end, marriage, self-realization, worldly success (Figure 12). But by no means did the stories simply ring tired changes on such clichés. During the Depression, new recreational reading patterns and markets were discerned, and older ones were more aggressively exploited. Since the end of World War I, young women both single and married had come to, and sought work in, large cities,[60] and Macfadden's magazines had tapped this market. By the early 1930s, it had probably increased, since more women had to leave the shelter of the home and expand their horizons in the workplace, especially with low-paying office employment. Publishers of sex pulps now fully recognized this market's potential. Like Hollywood, they began to put more creative effort into advertising their wares to a mass audience. They sought purchasers, and borrowers, of all ages, occupations, and tastes, anyone who was curious about success, sports, romance, crime, popular psychology — and sex. They favored stories that featured "modern" protagonists whose aspirations and problems were familiar to their readers and with whom they therefore could identify. Heroines were secretaries, or even business executives; the men were typical of the bachelors whom young women, in urban or rural areas, might date; the married couples' problems were both physiological and emotional, involving when to have children, and how to maintain sexual ardor; settings were recognizable as American, although similar to locales depicted in sensationalist tabloids or the movies. The more a story hinted at creative foreplay, contraceptive

Novels that throb with warm life and passion

BROADWAY VIRGIN
by Lois Bull

The kissable but unkept Nina, a bright feature in the hot spots of night life, is innocently entangled in a bloody gang war. How she is rescued by a brown-eyed stranger, to become the sweetheart of Paris and all Broadway.

LOVE GIRL
by May Edginton
author of MONEY! MONEY! MONEY!

Louie, the Love Girl, has just discovered the thrill of being a beautiful woman in a world of susceptible men. But her money-mad father dangles her in front of wealthy directors and Louie's romances get in a jam when several other men are entranced.

PAVEMENT LADY
by Marguerite Brener

The downfall and degradation of a girl in whom the fine possibilities of love were cheated, told with convincing realism. How a bad start betrayed her into the hands of men who were cowards without honor.

GROUNDS for INDECENCY
by Milton Herbert Gropper and Edna Sherry

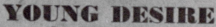

To save her father from ruin and suicide, Nita offers the treasure of her beauty to the creditor who would save him. A young copper magnate comes to the rescue and tries to resist Nita's firm intention to sacrifice herself.

YOUNG DESIRE
by Clem Yore
author of RANGER BILL; HARD RIDING SLIM MAGEE

A novel of stormy passion. A California girl's love madness is awakened by a vagabond artist. It dominates her life in spite of all the forces that strive to crush it, and it leads her to renounce a great career.

THE NUPTIAL NIGHT
by Dolf Wyllarde
author of THE LAVENDER LAD

A series of tragic, scandalous, yet curiously agreeable surprises overtook a girl on her nuptial night when she discovered she did not love her bridegroom.

MACAULAY   •   **Publishers**   •   **NEW YORK**

techniques, responses of the body to sexual instinct, the better — without, of course, explicit sex scenes or scatology.

To witness these strategies in operation, one need only cast an eye at some of the advertising blurbs:

The kissable but unkempt Nina, a bright feature in the hot spots of night life, is innocently entangled in a bloody gang war. How she is rescued by a brown-eyed stranger, to become the sweetheart of Paris and all Broadway. (*Broadway Virgin* [Macaulay Co.])

Lilly Miller, a typical American girl born to the calico, aspires to ermine. "You've got *star lust,*" Perry Hatch told her. . . . "You'll see . . . your ethics and principles yield just as freely as your more or less innocent body" (*Star Lust* [Wm. Godwin Inc.])

"Strangers in Love" is a novel dealing with the ever present problems of frustration in marriage. . . . The experiences . . . are so true to life that the story — shocking and honestly frank — might have been the story of your next door neighbor — or yourself. (*Strangers in Love* [Wm. Godwin Inc.])

Everyone is familiar with the dentist's office and the girl in the white uniform, the combined receptionist, assistant, laboratory helper and bill collector. Sometimes the girl's eyes show she does more also, and suggest so much of hard acquaintance with life. (*Receptionist* [Phoenix Press])

When Dora Drummond came to him with the suggestion that he provide her with a mate for a eugenic baby, even the resourceful practitioner was baffled. (*Doctor's Office* [Phoenix Press])

Lovely Judith Brian, independent young business woman of today, plays a daring game of love — but plays it by a staunch and loyal code. (*Playgirls in Love* [Grosset and Dunlap])

Of course such plots did not go unchallenged by moralists. Protests against sex pulps, at least in the big cities, often originated in the Catholic pulpit.

The publishers developed a wary approach to sexually explicit material. Arcadia House was founded in 1934 as a division of William Godwin and Phoenix by the joint owners of these firms, Alex Hillman, Sam Curl, and the Wartels brothers. Godwin and Phoenix had and continued to have censorship problems because

---

Figure 12. The back panel of this dust jacket of Maurice Dekobra's *Venus on Wheels* (New York: The Macaulay Co., 1931) lists the kind of sex-pulp romances popular in bookstores and lending libraries during the 1930s.

some of their sex pulps focused strongly on extramarital affairs. Arcadia gave them a chaste line under which they could shelter, while continuing to market a slightly "spicy" line for mainstream consumption by commonsensically unprudish readers, and more frank, explicit offerings, the sales of which would be nicely increased by official censure. Arcadia titles were "Light, Clean, Wholesome Romances particularly suitable for all public and privately operated libraries. . . . Entertaining to all and offensive to none."[61] This bland, sinless, wholesome fare supposedly "reflect[ed] the idealism and optimism of American youth." The strategy of balancing sex pulps with treacly romances was in imitation of the spicy-story and confession magazines of the mid-1920s. The periodical editors, led by Bernarr Macfadden, had a double-edged commitment to stories of unconventional sexual experimentation and happy endings saturated with moral regeneration and selfless dedication to One Who Cares. In some novels, both plot elements were present. Writers in periodicals as varied as the *New Republic* and *Commonweal* gagged over the smug hypocrisy of this formula at the time.[62] The newly formed National Organization for Decent Literature (NODL) was still hacking away at it in the late 1930s: "sin, suffer, repent and sin again."[63]

Shrewd publishers sensed a storm of conservative moral protest gathering above the drugstore book. The merchants most likely to survive it would have established the kind of diversity of Godwin and Phoenix, which in 1935, 1936, and 1937 issued eighty-nine, ninety, and thirty-four, and twenty-nine, fifty-eight, and seventy-three titles respectively (Arcadia House published twenty-six in 1937).[64] On 24 March 1934, Godwin placed trade notices for *Second Sight* ("the confusions of a generation") and *Blondes Play Too Rough* ("the jam a man gets into when he thinks he's having a good time taking pretty little blondes here and there"). Recognizing the spicy nature of these books, the firm noted that "both of these books will be extensively advertised. You take no chances [of legal expense] under our policy of complete protection."[65] This meant that they would provide assistance if a bookseller faced police action because of one of their titles.

George Orwell gives a vivid contemporary description of the sex pulps sold in stores or placed in lending libraries in the early 1930s in his novel *Keep the Aspidistra Flying*. Gordon Comstock clerks in two London bookstores in neighborhoods of varying degrees of seediness; the wares and the clientele seem identical to what would have been found on this side of the Atlantic. The books, published by "special low-class firms," are categorized as "Sex," "Crime,"

"Romance."[66] One typical customer, a shop girl, requests "a good hot-stuff love-story . . . modern. Sex-problems and divorce and all that."[67] Two boys and a girl, she with "a fit of the giggles," look through the stock for "something with a kick in it": "There were hundreds of ['sex' books] in the library. They had titles like *Secrets of Paris* and *The Man She Trusted*; on their tattered yellow jackets were pictures of half-naked girls lying on divans with men in dinner-jackets standing over them. The stories inside, however, were painfully harmless."[68]

Erotology and Sexology

The kinds of sexually explicit literature most helpful to people who wanted to know more about themselves and their sensual instincts were erotology and sex-ology. The former concerns the techniques of sexual stimulation; the latter is the serious sociological or anthropological study of sexual behavior and sexual hygiene. Both kinds had obvious prurient appeal, as distributors, who sometimes substituted new and suggestive titles for the originals, knew. These genres were carefully monitored by various authorities. The International Reform Federation's Reverend Pringle's annotations to the sexological books in his list of protested books are exemplary: *Curious Perversions* ("tribadism [lesbian erotology] and sapphism"), *Physiology of Vice* ("all vices, perversions"), *Sex and Sex Worship* ("filth from classic quarries"), *The Sexual Question* ("distorted passions").

Charles Carrington was seen variously as the most notorious, the most heroic, and the most tragic figure in late nineteenth- and early twentieth-century erotica publishing, depending on the moral and aesthetic sensibility of the spectator. He was certainly the most influential. Born Paul Fernando in England to a Portuguese emigrant, he left there for France as a young adult after learning the book trade and participating in the bohemian life of the 1890s. In Paris, he dealt in erotological and sexological books for English and American readers. His openly sold editions, some of which he extensively annotated, include books on flagellation as a form of discipline, anthropological studies, and literary classics; these were much pirated and otherwise reprinted and smuggled through Customs around the world. The typography and page layout, and the author's persistence in the face of prosecution, were envied and imitated.[69] Samuel Roth and Esar Levine had extensive collec-tions of his editions.

Attractively produced erotology and sexology from the later nineteenth century through the 1920s could be classified within Legman's category of gallantiana, under the subheading of "works on (and against) women and love." But by the 1930s, sexology was a specialty of mail-order houses appealing to whomever could afford three to five dollars. The most resourceful houses took care with the look of the book, but in a different way than had previous publishers, whose clients expected well-printed works, which they might have specially rebound for their personal libraries. These clients, well educated and often with professional credentials, made their purchases in bookshops, or possibly directly from the publishers' catalogs. Mail-order houses of the 1930s reached a wider, sometimes naively curious, middle-class audience that returned coupons found in a wide variety of magazines, newspapers, and almanacs. Public officials, especially spokespeople for the Postal Service, complained about the prurience of the advertisements for erotica. No longer did one need to rely on word of mouth to be in the know, at least about borderline materials. Once a mail-order house received the coupon, the prospective purchaser received circulars allowing him or her to reassure the distributor that he or she was twenty-one years old and seriously interested in scientific subjects. The wisest distributor-publishers of mail-order books knew their clients would be tempted by an aggressively marketed version of what passed for gentlemanly sophistication in book design. Depending on the publisher, that version could be an accurate representation of late nineteenth-century typography using contemporary materials, or an ostentatious show of display type, colored paper, and quasi-leather paper-covered boards. Whatever the case, something new had been developed from long popular materials, this time to the advantage of the mail-order houses.

Sexology included encyclopedias of sexual topics (Niemoeller's *American Encyclopedia of Sex*), historical and anthropological accounts of sex customs in various parts of the world (Dr. Jacobus X's *Untrodden Fields of Anthropology*), treatments of "inversion" and its causes (Hesnard's *Strange Lust: The Psychology of Homosexuality*), and analyses of sexual pathology (Féré's *Scientific and Esoteric Studies in Sexual Degeneration in Mankind and in Animals*). A popular treatment of classical Greek and Roman sexual relations that described various intercourse positions, and was strictly under-the-counter, was Forberg's *Manual of Classical Erotology*.[70] Manuals of birth-control information by such writers as Marie Stopes, T. Van de Velde, and H. W. Long had theoretically found legal acceptance by 1930, but in practice they were still suspect, especially in communities with substantial

Catholic populations, and especially after Pope Pius XI's 1930 proclamation against contraception.[71] If it was not clear that such books were soberly produced and marketed for "experts," or for the improvement of health or marital compatibility among responsible adults, they could be, and were, proscribed.[72] Their appearance in all but the most reputable bookstores could be interpreted as an "enticement" to prurience. Lending-library copies, like treatments of birth control by magazines sold from newsstands, often resulted in the proprietor's being threatened with a boycott.

By 1930, books and magazines on nudism could be openly sold if published under established imprints. Many of them, by eschewing prurient stories or pictures, made strong claims to legitimacy. In 1934, the International Nudist Conference labored to convince the antivice societies that nudism was a serious, not salacious, subject.[73] When Ilsley Boone, editor of *Nudist* magazine, wrote to Charles Bodwell of the Watch and Ward to assure him that the February issue was not obscene, Bodwell asked Sumner's opinion.[74] He was informed that "all of these nudist publications with their illustrations are highly objectionable for public display and circulation."[75] Pringle must have believed this also; for him, "challenged" and "offensive" were coterminous. His comments regarding nudist books note "89 photos of mixed [men and women together] nudists" and "principles of nude culture." Although Sumner acknowledged that the police and the courts did not feel the need to censor such materials, he prosecuted them in any circumstances that suggested prurient enticements: for example, if booksellers displayed them in their windows.[76] Calling nudist magazines "art studies," because many of them used the word to legitimatize the genre, Sumner wrote to his constituents of the large number he confiscated in the late 1930s.[77] When an enterprising second-story bookseller rented the ground-floor display windows of a Long Island drugstore to show seven copies of Royer's *Let's Go Naked*, each copy open to a different illustration, Sumner dispatched an investigative agent to the spot. He found a group of truck drivers and schoolchildren ogling the "hot stuff," the naughty parts of which had been tantalizingly obscured by strips of black paper by the time he intervened. The vice society, unmollified, prosecuted the bookseller.[78]

One would expect that books on flagellation would be summarily condemned. Until the mid-1930s, however, they seem to have been considered either borderline erotica or medical curiosa, and so could be openly sold.[79] Examples are *Experiences of Flagellation* ("A Series of Remarkable Instances of Whipping Inflicted on Members of Both Sexes") and *Nell in Bridewell* ("The System of Corporal Punishment in the Female Prisons of South Germany Up to the Year 1848, A Contribution to the History of Manners"). Good evidence for their legitimate or, at worst, borderline status are the mail-order catalogs, printed and mimeographed, of the Anthropological Library of Jersey City, New Jersey, and New York City.[80] Some of these have lengthy sections titled "Flagellation." Gargoyle Press, a mail-order firm, specialized in flagellation.[81] Gershon Legman mentions two mid-1930s publishers of "openly-distributed (and very nasty) flagellantiana."[82] These books must have been no more susceptible to prosecution than the *Arabian Nights*, *Married Love*, or *Crossways of Sex*. There was a large and time-honored body of work on the subject considered as an ascetic religious discipline and as a tool of criminal correction.[83] Not until the mid-1930s did campaigns against the increasing production of cheap under-the-counter erotica regularly take note of the literature of flagellation.

Perhaps it was then that authorities realized flagellation was not just a subject from which a few "deviants" received sexual stimulation, but rather a widespread sexual variation of interest to many. At that point, it could be made the subject of moral indignation as a dangerous perversion. According to a contemporary journalist with access to law-enforcement files, "there are numerous known flagellants or 'spankers' in practically every city, practically immune from supervision, due to lax laws."[84] Havelock Ellis, remarking on the frequency of flagellation in America, mentioned Chicago newspaper advertisements offering it.[85] The first multiple listings of arrests for books on flagellation in John Sumner's ledgers occur in 1937. Sumner's annual report to constituents that year suggests that perhaps this was a new strain of offensiveness: "Other books which occupied our attention during the year included a low grade of paper covered volumes on the subject of flagellation. The illustrations and text tended and were intended solely to appeal to a perverted sex sense. Books of this type might very well arouse sex excitement in a person of unbalanced mind, leading to vicious anti-social acts."[86] It should be noted, however, that Henry N. Pringle's 1931 and 1934 lists of protested books include several works devoted to what Pringle describes as "the erotic cult of flagellation." As early as 1932, he was prosecuting mail-order dealers in the "perversion."[87]

If construed as at all prurient, the advertising circulars for flagellantia, and for sexological tracts in general, could get the publishers cited for pandering, whether the circulars were found in the mails or in bookstores. A mail-order publisher collared by Sumner in 1935 had distributed an edition of Pierre Guenoles's historical survey of whipping, including its psychosexual uses, under the title *Tender Bottoms* (see Figure 33).[88] Usually, the circulars and the prefaces to the books themselves carefully described them as directed only at "adult collectors of literary curiosities," or at physicians, lawyers, and sexual researchers. Sexology was indeed a serious study by the 1930s, but the impression readers got from perusing a circular's text or illustrations was that they would be purchasing a book with a level of sexual explicitness that would shock and titillate.

All the materials listed so far could well have been found on the open shelves of a bookstore whose owner accepted the fact that any sexually oriented materials might, at a given moment, lead to public disapprobation or police attention. The next two categories involve clearly unlawful material, kept under the counter, or, far more likely, in some other location, inaccessible to all but the fully trusted regular customer. On the trail of something "hot," the customer, making his (most likely not her) way beyond the store's display areas with the proprietor, might find himself in a small back room, where he would very quickly be told the price of what the owner had on hand (a price that might vary based on the owner's assessment of the customer's financial status). The customer would pay in cash, and perhaps be asked to leave by the back door.[89]

"Bibles" and "Readers"

The truly "hot stuff" might have been kept in secret drawers or boxes. A customer might have wished to buy a "reader": a paper-covered, side-stapled pamphlet with a title such as *Venus in Love*, *The Cracked Virgin*, or *Delightful Pastime*, that had appeared under such imprints as "M. Seuffrin . . . Nice, France," "Phedrin Publishing, Havana, Cuba," "Paris: Bibliothèque St. Germaine," "All Sports Fornication Press," and "Camel Publishing Company, Humpville, Illinois." Generally these were thirty-two or sixty-four pages long, and featured between two and seven grainy photos or line drawings of uncommon copulation positions, naked grinning women, or naked men and women fondling each other. The text was comprised of scatological stories of approximately ten thousand to twelve thousand words, centering exclusively on sexual conquest and gymnastics, often of a prodigious nature

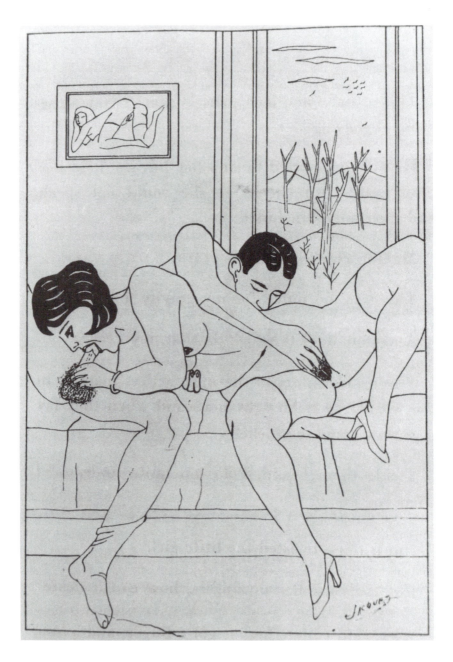

Figure 13. A reader. Illustration for *Between Her Legs Lay Paradise*. "Published for Private Circulation Only, Paris, France."

(Figure 13).[90] Readers often measured 8¾ by 5¾ inches, but could be pocket-size, which may mean they were published later than the 1910s or 1920s. I have been unable to determine when readers first appeared. The illustrations offer few clues, although hairstyling of the men and women posing in some cases seems Edwardian, and typography, headpieces, and vignettes occasionally suggest turn-of-the-century European styles. A few readers contain poems or anecdotes instead of stories. Some narratives could have been excerpted from full-length works that, like the illustrations, had first appeared a generation before the reader itself. As long as the sex scenes climaxed in a way that left all parties — participants and readers — satisfied, the latter would hardly notice, or care about, when or how the booklet had been put together. The writers were anonymous or pseudonymous ("Ramrod," "Senorita Delores De Haita"), but some became successful professionals, such as Gene Fowler, biographer of John Barrymore and chronicler of Hollywood high life.[91]

If he did not choose a reader, a customer might have walked away with the kind of comic book sometimes referred to as "Tijuana bibles," "eight-pagers," "blue cartoons," or "little dirty books." They were pocket-size, and consisted of one gathering of four leaves with one panel per page. They starred newspaper comic-strip characters (Orphan Annie, Andy Gump), famous name-altered stage and screen stars ("Mae Breast," "Douglas Farybanks") or gangsters (John Dillinger, "Baby Face" Nelson) in adolescent masturbatory fantasies, full of sexual and racial stereotypes, and wildly contemptuous of all authority.[92] In the 1920s, these comics were peddled around speakeasies, the plates having been manufactured and the comic books printed at the same underground locations that provided bootleggers with fake whiskey labels.[93] Those may have been early examples; recent commentary on bibles places their origins at about 1930.[94] By the late 1930s, Sumner's ledgers record huge caches of them: "7,000 cartoons," "280 large readers," "2,700 small cartoons," "approx. 2 tons (300,000 items)." They could be found in every kind of specialty store that handled under-the-counter items; the 1939 World's Fair in New York provided distributors with an irresistible market (Figure 14). There is a brilliant delineation of their contents by novelist Bernard Wolfe, who once applied for a job as a writer of the words (many four-lettered) that appeared in the "balloons" and captions: "These carefree cutups didn't have any problem relating to others, they were relating in every way the epidermis allows, variously coupling, tripling, communing, nosing, mouthing, fingering, backbend-

Figure 14. A Tijuana bible. Produced for the 1939 World's Fair in New York, this is the first interior panel. The cover title reads "Monkey Business at the World's Fair." These eight-pagers may have been sold at the Amusement Zone, where there was a lot of topless dancing and other "spicy" entertainment in the second year of the fair. Of course, they could also have been sold throughout the city.

ing, splitting, three-decker-sandwiching. Moon Mullins was ringmaster to a tightly interwoven daisy chain that Dagwood was working hard to unravel."[95]

Classical and Modern "Flagitious" Books

"Flagitious" is the term employed by Henry Pringle of the International Reform Federation to specify what today is termed "hard-core" pornography.[96] Bodwell of the Watch and Ward preferred the epithet "flagrantly obscene," distinguishing such works from those with "polite" indecencies. Those leading the fight against erotica distribution compiled lists of flagitious books, but tried to keep their lists confidential, for the use, in Pringle's words, of "mature persons, trying to restrict or abolish erotic and crime literature at the source of publication, distribution and sale."[97] The U.S. Customs Office circulated — strictly for the use of its agents — lists of books "which have from time to time been detained and proceeded against."[98] When Senator Bronson Cutting requested a copy to prepare his proposals for liberalizing federal censorship, Customs refused.[99] Secrecy was essential in order to discourage prurient curiosity, but there was also a political motive: only those who shared the censor's ideology could be trusted.

For the bookseller, secrecy was important, too, to fend off arrest. Most secondhand booksellers had a back room or other location, off limits to most clients, where expensive volumes were stored to safeguard them from shoplifting.[100] The back room's most lucrative purpose, however, was as a hiding place for the real "porno" (one bookseller recalls this term, not "porn," as being the preferred argot in the interwar period).[101] These books were not simply "protested," or read over carefully by purity societies for suspected indecencies. They had been officially proscribed and were being actively sought by the U.S. Postal Service, Customs, and the local police (Figure 15). "List thirteen outstanding works of pornography without which no library is complete," reads Question 11 from the 1934 second series of *Anecdota Americana*. The answer provides a beginner's catalog of flagitious pornography: "Fanny Hill, Perfumed Garden, My Secret Life (Eleven Volumes), Marquis De Sade's, [*sic*] The Boudoir, Grushenka, Anecdota Americana I and II, Voluptuous Army, Susan Aked, Immortalia, Rosa Fielding, Randiana and Forberg's Manual of Classical Erotology."

Distributors of flagitious materials — whether Tijuana bibles, readers, or editions of works like the Victorian narrative *Randiana* or *Memoirs of a Hotel Man* — could do good business in the 1930s. When a reporter queried Sumner in 1935 about "the state of vice," the reply was that fifteen- to thirty-five-dollar deluxe editions were passé but that "the big trade in erotica now had to do with paperbound volumes of some 30,000 [*sic*; 3,000?] words which you could buy for a quarter in places wherever you were known as an old erotica addict."[102] Such readers would have cost more than a quarter; two dollars would have been more like it. Perhaps Sumner, or his interviewer, had in mind decks of playing cards or

photos.[103] Not only paperbound pamphlets, but "flagrantly obscene books, both paper covered and cloth," were printed and distributed.[104] These volumes would have been readers three times as long as the pamphlet type, or flagellation titles published by "Cranston Publications," or "the Clacker Press," or possibly classics such as *Fanny Hill* set in eight- or ten-point type. The importance of these operations is clear from the amount of money and equipment involved: fifty thousand dollars' worth of printing and binding presses;[105] two thousand books and plates;[106] six police wagon loads of books and equipment (after a 28 March 1937 raid at "718" [518?] East 11th Street);[107] fourteen thousand readers, type, and plates, in the second raid within the week at the end of June 1934;[108] eleven thousand "obscene pamphlets";[109] forty-six thousand books and four hundred electrotype plates, some titles being *Crimson Hairs*, *Anecdota Americana*, and even *My Secret Life* (the rarest of underground Victorian erotica; surely an incomplete version was involved).[110]

By 1935, publishers of this kind of erotica, and those distributors who contracted with its publishers, used a system of reaching consumers that was completely separate from the networks and methods employed by the distributors of gallantiana, sex pulps, or sexology. Perhaps this system was modeled on that used by bootleggers in the 1920s. Given their mobility, the distributors were possibly former rum runners in reduced circumstances due to the repeal of Prohibition, who could stash the goods in their automobiles as well as in steamer trunks.[111] The fact that their wares had been printed at the same locations as whiskey labels lends further credence to this theory. The offenders were persistent: the same names occur in records of arrests from the early 1930s to the end of the decade.[112] Sumner noted that his society, in doing its undercover work, had "benefitt[ed] by the squabbles among the racketeers"[113] — racketeers here meaning an organized group of tough-minded people engaged in illegal but not necessarily fraudulent activity. There is no evidence he knew of their involvement in liquor traffic. Sumner states

---

Figure 15. Title page of a paperbound, staple-stitched 132-page edition of *Fanny Hill*, the eighteenth-century classic, c. 1930 (no publisher, no date). This version may have been published by Jack Brussel. It includes the passage describing sodomy that has been one of the most objectionable parts of the novel since its first appearance. The illustration (probably reproduced without permission) is most likely by Clara Tice. Reproduced here by permission of Elizabeth Yoell.

that evidence against one of them was difficult to obtain because "people working for or with him refuse to give information involving him."[114] Distributors of bibles and readers would have been constrained by the same kind of middleman protocols that prevented booksellers in the 1920s from naming distributors and printers of their "privately printed" editions. Locations apparently supplied with one or more items included not only bookstores, cigar stores, and backdate magazine stores, but also lunchrooms, barbecue stands, dine and dance halls, barbershops, gas stations, hotels, fraternal organizations, fire brigades, auto supply houses, and grocery stores.[115] Sumner's agents, and also those of the New York vice-fighting Committee of Fourteen, occasionally found not just bibles, but also spicy magazines and pamphlets being hawked at burlesque shows.[116]

Widespread distribution of flagitious pornography through new networks was not the only innovation during the 1930s; a lot of new material was written, as well. Booksellers and literary agents would approach professional writers of fiction to provide stories for either wealthy individual customers or groups of readers.[117] The former would be produced in an original ribbon copy for the middleman to deliver to the client — with one or more carbon copies kept for distribution when the time was right. The latter might be "mimeographed or rotogravured or actually printed and bound, as your budget allowed." C. J. Scheiner states that an "organization" of writers, agents, booksellers, and customers came into existence. It is not clear when this erotica combine started to work, but one of its productions was a set of tales, circa 1938, known collectively as *The Oxford Professor*. According to Gershon Legman, Gene Fowler, one of several Hollywood members, wrote *The Demi-Wang* and *Nirvana* under the organization's auspices "in the early thirties."[118] Its most notorious efforts were those sent around 1940 to an Oklahoma millionaire who commissioned pornographic short stories, which he needed to keep in constant supply, because each one brought him to tumescence only upon first reading. There are several accounts of this enterprise; Gershon Legman states that Clara Tice illustrated some of the materials sent to Oklahoma, and that he introduced Anaïs Nin to the millionaire's agent, a New York bookseller, at the Gotham Book Mart, having been wised up about the enterprise by a book scout "on the recommendation" of Samuel Roth.[119] Other accounts of the collector and work commissioned for him are by Nin, in volume three of her *Diaries*, and by Bernard Wolfe, who was one of the organization's writers.[120] Scheiner lists others, whose fee was often a dollar a page, as Clement Wood, Jack Hanley, Tony Gud, and Robert Sewall.[121]

These individuals wrote for the collector, but they and others would have done similar work whenever contacted.

All this is evidence that erotica production and distribution is part of the larger story of American literature. Writers such as Legman, Miller, and Nin, distributors such as David Moss of the Gotham Book Mart in New York and Ben Abramson of the Argus in Chicago, conservative and liberal public officials (postmaster generals, senators, investigators employed by antivice organizations), judges and lawyers were all as integral to the story as underground publishers, clandestine writers and artists of Tijuana bibles, and booksellers with surreptitious back rooms and pornographic rental libraries. When Samuel Roth, known publicly as an incorrigible pornographer, described himself as a man of letters, he could offer as evidence that some of his productions were on sale at the Gotham and the Argus, that he had offered Joyce and Lawrence to the public when it took the chutzpah of a "jolly Roger" to do so, and that he had the taste and discretion to collect the editions of Charles Carrington and instruct his illustrators to follow the examples of Aubrey Beardsley and Salvador Dalí.

Printers and Bookleggers: Some Special Problems

In New York, printers of underground erotica were to be found in lower Manhattan, mostly in the Union Square and Canal Street areas. They would work at night or during off-peak hours, charging for a thousand copies at a time, and so that was often the number of copies printed. In the 1920s and 1930s, most interdicted and borderline erotica was printed domestically, thus bypassing any involvement with U.S. Customs. During the Depression, more printers were willing to risk doing this kind of work. Printing a book involved many separate steps: arranging for the paper, typesetting, preparing metal or photolithographic plates, completing presswork, electroplating (for letterpress illustrations, or text and illustration together), and cutting, folding, and binding the sheets. Since all this work took some time and involved cooperation among several individuals, there was always a chance that Sumner's undercover agents could learn about the impending printing of sub-rosa items. The printers themselves kept mum, for if they did not, they would not get more work. The problem lay with their helpers.

Publishers and middlemen were reassured when the printer or binder with whom they contracted hired a number of recently arrived immigrants: loose lips would be less likely to sink ships if the words they uttered were incomprehensible. The printing trades during the period were very largely manned by "native-born white" workers, but there were French, Italian, and "Hebrew" union members.[122] As the restrictions on immigration in the early 1920s eventually lowered the demand for foreign-language publications, pressmen and compositors who could no longer turn a profit producing them may have been especially susceptible to contracting with publishers of erotica. In New York, printers who spoke German, Italian, Spanish, and Yiddish, based in Brooklyn or along Canal Street, could be commissioned.[123]

By 1928, offset lithography radically simplified the printing process; with just two copies of a banned book, a pirated impression could be run off speedily, and much more cheaply, since no type needed to be set. After 1930, prices for typesetting, printing, binding, and storing dropped, as worsening economic conditions constricted the market for deluxe editions, erotic or otherwise. Some printers had other contracts, some were on the edge of bankruptcy, but all knew that they could be involving themselves in criminal proceedings, and that the publishers they were obliging were as a rule not on sound legal and financial footing. Therefore, unless a publisher had earned their trust and respect with prompt payment for many orders, printers worked on a strictly cash-and-carry basis.

More than one printer might have found himself occasionally forced to become an erotica publisher in order to dispose of unpaid-for sheets, for it was pointless to allow the risky material to gather dust in his storage area.[124] It behooved the publisher not only to have the cash on the barrelhead, but to pick up printed sheets quickly, so that smuthounds might not get wind of the edition and track it down. Sometimes, competitors would deliberately tip off the authorities to locations where materials were being printed and bound, or could be tricked into revealing this information. The 28 March 1936 raid on a lower Manhattan loft netted "an electric printing press, feeders, cutters, binders, type, electroplates — worth $50,000."[125] The printers would have used the electroplates to print letterpress text and illustrations together for the readers and Tijuana bibles. The Police Confidential Squad, which had worked with Sumner to arrange the raid, needed most of the day to remove six wagon loads of books, readers, bibles, photographs, and playing cards from the East 11th Street loft (Figure 16). These items were manufactured at plants such as those Sumner often raided in the 1930s, with the aid of undercover work by the police and other preventive-society workers.[126]

Special hazards presented themselves to bookleggers if it was impossible to manufacture a book domestically. Dealing with Customs regulations and agents gave rise to crafty schemes involving bribery and smuggling. We have mentioned Ben Miller's (apparent) efforts on behalf of Levine and Rebhuhn as well as the smuggling of papier-mâché plates through Customs by other friends of Frank Harris. On one occasion, Miller's "closeness" to Customs officials helped make the most of a terrible muddle, exploiting the cash-driven aspect of the symbiotic relationship between law-enforcement officials and erotica distributors. Harris had sent five cases of *My Life and Loves* and one of *Oscar Wilde: His Life and Confessions* to New York; one of the six cases was earmarked for inspection. However, another was opened instead. The preferred solution — additional bribery — was inoperative at this point because one of the Customs officers, a Catholic who had been warned of the "virulence" of *My Life*, would not take the money. Miller suggested that four cases of *Oscar Wilde* be sent from Nice. When they arrived, less religious and more mercenary agents allowed these cases to be substituted for the same number of cases of *My Life*, and the latter were smuggled out of the Customs hall.[127]

Finding the "Hot Stuff"

During the first two decades of the twentieth century, Anthony Comstock had arrested several pushcart peddlers. He found them selling postcards and pamphlets they had received from "jobbers,"[128] freelance middlemen whom Sumner, after the pushcart era ended, referred to as "peddlers." From whom they received what they sold, and how they transported it, is unknown. Sumner personally arrested several, sometimes in their hotel rooms, even at an American Legion Convention.[129]

People could also order banned books over the phone, but from whom is unclear. Word of mouth would have been essential. They needed a numbered list of those available from a "friendly booklegger" at the other end of the line, who might be a peddler or a bookseller; the volume would be delivered in person and paid for in cash.[130] One could also arrange a visit from a valise-toting salesman, a variation on the lending-library bag system. Both strategies were used in many cases when the book was one vice-society agents especially wanted to track down. Columnist Louis Sobol, reflecting on his bookish youth, admits to encouraging visits from a peddler of erotica:

I'm a fellow who had my schooling in all the forbidden "literature" — from Fannie [*sic*] Hill and Frank Harris' Confessions to that final chapter of "Ulysses," and I am going to stick out my chin boldly and confess that they did not prod me at the time into running to the sink and scrubbing my eyes with soap. . . . There was even a time when I collected pornographic rarities — illustrated. In fact, there used to be a mild-mannered chap who would drop into my office every so often and out of a tattered Gladstone bag, tug a few books, place them reverently before me and whisper. Sometimes I bought.[131]

Finally, a dealer or collector could simply advertise in newspapers or *Publishers Weekly*. At least for a period in the late 1920s, its classified book-exchange listings contained requests for *Lady Chatterley's Lover*, *Madeleine*, *Poetica Erotica*, *One Hundred Merry Tales* (i.e., *One Hundred Merrie and Delightsome Stories*), and other underground books and gallantiana. Just before Esar Levine began his Panurge Press, he placed a series of notices for "any books published in English by 1. Charles Carrington 2. Isadore Liseux, and other titles of similar interest." Often, erotica dealers disguised desired titles to get by the editor, Sumner and his agents, or the Post Office. "Secret Court Memoirs Dr. Cabanes" (the *Erotikon*) for example, or "Harris, Frank. 3 volume work" (*My Life and Loves*).[132] Some wise bookmen and -women fished there. Most resorted to shops.

Upscale Bookstores

The Gotham Book Mart was a special target for John Sumner's vigilance; clearly Frances Steloff's commitment to literary excellence included distributing works by some writers with erotic sensibilities. Not only boldly outspoken modernists, how-

---

Figure 16. On 28 March 1936, police raided an East Side printing plant and confiscated readers, books, photographs, and playing cards destined "for hundreds of peddlers from coast to coast." The equipment included an electric printing press and machinery for cutting, sewing, and binding the books and pamphlets. A cutter is beyond the table (center). A paper press stands in the right background, to the right of the man with his back to the viewer. In the foreground are machines for sewing. The press is not shown, but should be close to the cutter. On the table in front of the cutter are sheets, of either playing cards or comics, waiting to be cut. The detective on the left seems to be holding printed, but possibly not yet stapled or sewn, books. Source: Staff photograph, *New York Daily Mirror*, 28 Mar. 1936. The photo, with caption but no accompanying story, appeared on p. 15 of the *Mirror*'s "Extra 3-Star Edition." Reproduced by permission of the Harry Ransom Humanities Research Center, University of Texas at Austin (JA Files).

ever, made this bookseller one of Sumner's most closely watched suspects. Like other upscale bookstores, the Gotham stocked various kinds of literary and scientific erotica. Moralists also had reason to suspect Steloff's New York colleagues Harry F. Marks[133] and the Holliday Book Shop.[134] In other cities suspicion fell on Horace Townsend and Leary's bookstore in Philadelphia;[135] on Dunster House in Cambridge, Massachusetts;[136] on Covici McGee, Kroch and Brentano's, and Ben Abramson's Argus Book Shop in Chicago;[137] on Harry Schwartz and C. N. Caspar in Milwaukee;[138] on Jake Zeitlin,[139] the Satyr Book Shop,[140] and Stanley Rose in Los Angeles; and on Paul Elder in San Francisco.

These people and their shops, whether they specialized in antiquarian, classical, modern, or scholarly literature (and in many cases a combination of these categories was available), were important in American literary circles, and their clientele trusted and respected them. The risks they took were in the service of something they and their customers — whether writers, scholars, or general readers — considered worth the attendant suspicion and legal difficulties. "High-hat" or "Fifth Avenue" stores shared this motive for risk taking with small, less prestigious ones. The differences lay in the class and income level of the customers and the ability of the owners to defend themselves from charges of obscenity, with the attendant drain on their finances and community status (see Chapter 4). The vulnerability of high-hat shops to police action was also lower — the more secure the community status of a bookstore, the smaller the chance of what the antivice societies would call "fair" media coverage.

Clients in public life might be careful to purchase books at establishments with solid reputations. In case of police action they may have wished to count on the owners' discretion; sometimes they undertook to speak with confidence on behalf of those owners to authorities. Upscale store owners may have handled *Chatterley, Jurgen, Immortalia, The Sofa*, the *Decameron*, or sexological or anthropological studies of marriage and courtship, but it would have been gauche, and futile, to ask in their shops for readers, eight-pagers, action photos, or pornographic decks of cards.

Secondhand and General Bookstores

For a wider range of sexually oriented works, one could avail oneself of the bookstores specializing in secondhand or general stock (Figure 17). In New York,

Figure 17. A Fourth Avenue bookstore, July 1933: Schulte's, numbers 80–82, between 10th and 11th Streets in Manhattan, one of two dozen on "Book Row" at the time (counting the several in Bible House). A landmark, Schulte's had opened in 1917. Its customers included Franklin Delano Roosevelt, O. Henry, Marlene Dietrich, the musician Fritz Kreisler, and the actress Marion Davies. Next door to Schulte's is another secondhand store. Reproduced by permission of the New York Public Library; Astor, Lenox and Tilden Foundations, United States History, Local History and Genealogy Division (Collection: Photographic Views of New York City).

these concentrations of browser's delights, along Fourth Avenue and elsewhere, was dominated by a tightly knit group of bookmen (proprietors, clerks, kibitzers, illustrators, translators). They included Jacob Brussel, Thomas Schulte, Samuel Roth, Eugene Nussbaum, Christian Gerhardt, Henry Klein, Louis Shomer, Solomon Malkin, Gershon Legman, Mahlon Blaine, and Keene Wallis. Sumner's ledgers record many raids on general and secondhand bookstores. Those on West 15th and East 17th Streets in New York yielded copies of *My Life*; *Venus in India*, *Anecdota Americana*, *Pauline*, and *The Merry Muses* were taken from an establishment on West 84th Street; *A Young Girl's Diary*, *Replenishing Jessica*, and *Crimson Hairs* were found in a Water Street store.[141]

The owners of the secondhand stores had experience in locating volumes from private libraries and from far-flung colleagues. Individuals felt comfortable posing queries regarding their own copies of erotica in a comprehensively stocked, unpretentious store with a number of anonymous browsers, and where the owner expected to be asked by all sorts of people about all sorts of volumes. These stores were also more daring in stocking a broad spectrum of the most flagitious titles (i.e., not only banned classics, but also readers and bibles), along with expurgated editions (whether stated as such or not), sexology and flagellation titles, and suggestive potboilers that some high-hat shops would not carry, either because the publisher could not be trusted or because the writing was judged meretricious. When the Justice Department needed to supply the sentencing judge with copies of Samuel Roth's books after his 1936 conviction for interstate distribution of obscene literature, its agent purchased the borderline volumes from Schulte's on Fourth Avenue.[142] Possibly, the Gotham, Brentano's, or Harry F. Marks would have stocked Roth's editions of Norman Davey's or Rhys Davies's stories, despite the vignettes of bare-breasted females, but not his "version" of Havelock Ellis's *Kanga Creek*. The inimitable Roth had embellished the text, and that of three other stories in the volume, with pasted-in drawings of completely or nearly nude young women; a few vignettes of both men and women featured full frontal nudity. Had the agent gone to an upscale store, the clerk may have helped him by pointing out that the edition he sought might be a pirated, expurgated, inexpertly printed, or vulgarly spicy version. But such an establishment might not have carried the book at all.[143] The agent may have decided that access to many questionable titles was a safer bet on Fourth Avenue than uptown. In this case, it was not Schulte's but Roth who got in trouble.

Chain and Department Stores

Chain stores became increasingly important as booksellers in New York and elsewhere in the 1920s. Examples in New York included Brentano's, Doubleday's, Womrath's, the department-store bookstalls at Lord & Taylor, the Pennsylvania Terminal, and Liberty Tower. Doubleday's managed outlets in St. Louis, Cleveland, and Newark. Chain stores seem to have had only minor problems with objectionable books.[144] An exception to the immunity from prosecution came with the decision of both Doubleday's and Brentano's to make window displays of illustrated nudist books (*Let's Go Naked* and *On Going Naked*). Sumner scored them as "lewd, indecent, and immoral."[145] Such incidents were rare because chain and department stores, with their varied but largely female clientele, were careful to sell — or rent — materials reasonably but not, of course, automatically categorized as innocuous. They carried the mildly titillating sex pulp romances of Phoenix, William Godwin, Arcadia House, or Grosset and Dunlap. Godwin's retooled Rarity Press editions, dubbed "the Forbidden Classics," did well for a while at New York department stores. In 1932, Rarity boasted in full-page notices in *Publishers Weekly* that fourteen titles had been tested in forty-eight stores "from coast to coast"; the lowest number of sales in a three-week period was four hundred.[146] Similar cheap editions of classic literature, including gallantiana, were offered by the Illustrated Editions Company and the Three Sirens Press.[147] Department-store shoppers could also find copies of titles recently cleared by the courts, and of authorized abridged editions of Rabelais, the *Arabian Nights*, or *Lady Chatterley's Lover* — the Grosset or Knopf versions, bowdlerizations fashioned after Roth's. In 1930, Simon and Schuster were able to place their edition of *Casanova's Homecoming* — a book apparently cleared in 1922 but newly challenged by Sumner — in Macy's, Gimbel's, Wanamaker's, Bloomingdale's, and Abraham and Strauss.[148] D. H. Clark's *Female* was being sold at Macy's, Gimbel's, Womrath's, Dutton's, Scribner's, and Doubleday, Doran when Sumner, capitalizing on concern about lending-library and drugstore displays of borderline erotica, bypassed all the "reputable book stores and department stores"[149] stocking the book to prosecute the proprietor of a stationery store with a lending library.

Many chain stores had lending libraries, stocking the same semisalacious novels that were available in drugstores and cigar stores. Such books were more likely to arouse concern when spotted in the latter locations.

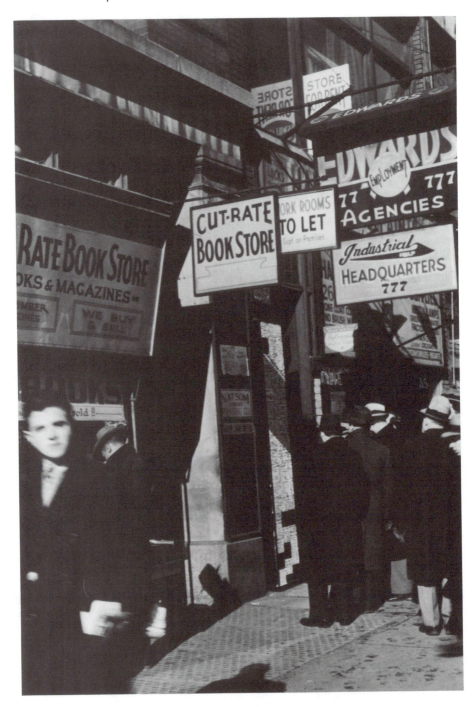

Figure 18. A backdate magazine and bookstore, West 26th Street, January 1939. Reproduced by permission of the New York Public Library, Astor, Lenox and Tilden Foundations, United States History, Local History and Genealogy Division (Collection: Photographic Views of New York City).

Backdate Magazine Stores

The proprietors of hybrid used-book and backdate magazine shops were generally enterprising, if threadbare, bookpeople in the know (Figure 18). Sumner harried these establishments as much as he did the peddlers and secondhand book dealers, especially in the late 1930s, when he found flagellation pamphlets being sold in them.[150] At such places the trusted customer could find magazines with pinup and nude photos, readers, blue cartoons, and unexpurgated erotica. However, unless the owner and his business were unusually prosperous, the more sought-after and notorious contraband, expensive to both retailer and customer, might not be stocked. If admitted to the store's cut-rate periodicals counter or back room, the customer might find magazines such as *Real Boudoir Tales*, *Real Forbidden Sweets*, *Real Temptation Tales*, *Real French Capers*;[151] Peter B. Everhard's blue cartoon version of "Moon Mullins"; a Tijuana bible such as *Sexperiences*; cheap editions of *A Night in a Moorish Harem* or *Crimson Hairs*; or a version of *The Memoirs of Casanova*. Most likely not available would be more expensive banned books such as Cabell's *Jurgen*, Wood's *Flesh*, an unexpurgated, smearily photolithographed piracy of the Orioli edition of *Lady Chatterley's Lover*, or Jack Brussel's American piracy of the Carrington printing of Forberg's *Classical Erotology*. For these, one had to find more eclectic outlets.

One of the most remarkable examples of Sumner's persistence can serve as evidence of the significance of the backdate magazine store in selling erotica. In October 1934, the secretary and the police tailed a boy with a wheelbarrow moving new, not used, magazines (the four "real" titles mentioned above) from a far West Side warehouse to a nearby bookshop, where they confiscated the whole shipment.[152] It seems that the distributors had the original notion of bypassing newsstands and moving directly to the secondhand outlets, probably owing to agitation on the part of churches and private citizens regarding smutty materials on display where children could see and purchase them.

Lending Libraries in Bookstores and in Other Outlets

Although critics of the "smut" in lending-library books directed their concern to those available in drugstores, cigar stores, and candy stores, they were even more incensed about the larger variety available through specialized circulating libraries.

Below are classified advertisements for two New York concerns as they appeared in the February 1935 Sunday book supplement of the *New York Herald Tribune*. Note such code words for "erotica" as "esoterika," "anthropological" (having to do with naked, libidinous natives and their curious customs), "privately printed," and "rare." Similar tip-offs would have been provided by use of the words "facetiae" and "curiosa."

READ RARE BOOKS. Members read without buying, rare, scarce, out-of-print books, limited, privately printed editions, unabridged translations. Write for information, giving age and occupation. ESOTERIKA BIBLION SOCIETY, Dept. 33, 15 E. 45th St.

ANTHROPOLOGICAL LIBRARY. 41 Union Sq. Limited and out of print editions, obtained on rental basis. Particulars furnished on request.

In 1935, many readers were happy to borrow what they were led to believe was erotically enticing. At that time there were many sumptuously illustrated and bound remaindered volumes for the operators of lending libraries to acquire cheaply. Both the Esoterika Biblion Society and the Anthropological Library had very extensive catalogs.[153] The former's reading charges were between fifty cents and five dollars per volume; the latter's, between fifty cents and one dollar. Books were divided into classes, the more expensive being the most explicitly erotic items; one assumes officially banned and thus uncatalogable titles, such as *Lady Chatterley's Lover*, *Tropic of Cancer*, or *My Life*, might have been made available to discreet borrowers. The Anthropological Library, despite the risks, lent largely through the mails. The usual disclaimer limited membership to physicians, teachers, clergymen, lawyers, and students of "psychological and social research." Two other New York erotica distributors that included lending books in their operations were the Gargoyle Press, which specialized in flagellantia, and Radio City Books.[154]

Several kinds of specialty stores could lend customers notorious underground books,[155] at a rate much higher than the two cents a day, or twenty cents a week, that other materials (including sexually oriented romances) would fetch. The ledgers of the NYSSV record that in drug-store lending libraries Sumner and his agents uncovered copies of *Venus and Tannhauser*, *Hands Around*, *My Life*, *Lady Chatterley's Lover*, *Woman and Puppet*, *Flossie: A Venus of Fifteen*, and *The Horn Book*. In reporting one of the Frank Harris seizures to his constituents, Sumner revealed concern that the offense had been committed at all, even if its effects in the community were slight: "the loaning was confined to an evil-minded element in the neighbor-hood. It was, however, a commercial exploitation of flagrant indecency."[156]

Any one drugstore or cigar store could distribute only a few underground "por-nographic" books at any one time, and those only to trusted "fellow-degenerates." In a city such as New York, however, it was felt they might proliferate at any moment, threatening to overwhelm the body politic with their cancerous degener-acy. Strong action needed to be taken. The liberalizing decisions of the New York Second Circuit Court and, after 1934, U.S. Customs, made it safe to circulate books with clear literary or social value. Examples were *The Well of Loneliness*, *The Sex Side of Life*, *Casanova's Homecoming*, and *Ulysses*. (For a discussion of how this came about, and of Morris Ernst's role in it, see Chapter 4.) In the eyes of the purity societies, such developments, combined with the effectiveness of the smutmongers in making their borderline wares available cheaply to a wide audience, made for a clear and present crisis. They feared a flood of bad books now that the borders of the taboo had been pushed back. Perhaps, they suggested to supporters, Frank Harris and *The Horn Book* would presently become as legally and morally acceptable as *Casanova's Homecoming* or the *Decameron*.

The new genres of smutty novels confirmed the fears of purity crusaders such as Sumner. This kind of erotica would probably not have flourished as strongly as it did without the growing importance and popularity of the lending libraries during the Depression. Economics, no less than changing moral codes, contributed to their spread. While many were run as independent businesses, and others, as mentioned above, were housed in department stores, all sorts of merchants now found it worthwhile to supplement their incomes by offering, in some corner of their stores (say between the trusses and the perfumes), a lending-library service.[157] As O. H. Cheyney reported in his then celebrated 1930 survey of the publishing industry, nonbookstore outlets, whether they lent or sold, were of only marginal interest to distributors. A druggist or candy store owner might deal in a small way with books him or herself, or allow an independent concern (the Union Library Association, Womrath's Agency, the American Library Association)[158] to do the lending.[159] Either way, the business was limited to selling or renting a small range of cheap (often "dollar") hardbacks. Unlike department stores, the cigar store or drugstore could not respond to customers' special needs or handle even a moderate range of genres,[160] unless it risked the rental of flagrant pornography, which may be one reason some proprietors did so. At the cigar store, the all-male ambience and the close acquaintance between steady customer and owner were factors indicating the profitability of selling or lending mild or spicy — and possibly, via the peddlers mentioned above, banned — erotica. Bookstore owners usually resisted renting stock because the profit margin was too low. But most readers could not afford to buy as they had before the Crash. This drove the bookseller — and the specialty-store owner — to lend books, despite the additional burden of record keeping, and the chance that the borrower and his friends would like the book so much they would abscond with it.[161]

Once resolved to lend, the bookstore faced strong competition, not only from the specialty stores whose small stock partly replicated their own, but from mail-order and delivery concerns, chain and department stores, and the aforementioned office library system. Lending libraries were possible in "gift shops, stationery stores, tea rooms, jewelry, radio, art, music, and other such luxury businesses [as well as] . . . clothing stores," and "hotels and clubs." "Every church, school, college, university and home is near rental libraries," complained the head of the American Civic League of New Orleans, writing directly to President Roosevelt in 1936. And then he got to the heart of the matter: they were circulating sex pulps for a few cents a day.[162]

Writing in 1933 in the Catholic weekly *America*, of which he was literary editor, Father Francis X. Talbot, S.J., discussed three categories of erotica that could be purchased at drugstores and cigar stores or obtained, even more cheaply, from their lending libraries.[163] The "scientific, reputedly, treatise on sex life and sex living" is larded with "medical jargon" and excuses itself from prosecution because it "profess[es] to be written for only the sadly married." The "quasi-humorous outlines of indecencies through the ages" also "siltheringly" seek legit-imacy on the basis of historical or literary value, as do unexpurgated editions of classical erotica.[164] "In many drug stores, [rental books] crowd out the legitimate drugs in the display windows." They, and the sex pulps, are "forced into the hands of the unwary and the innocent and the young." The last distressed him most. Quoting advertising blurbs, he cited "sex mad" stories of boys who contract vene-real disease, of "girls awakening into womanhood," of lustful contretemps in nightclubs, of white slavery, of the private and professional lives of physicians involved in "psychology, anatomy, physiology, and various aberrations." "As might be expected," he concluded, "the leprous record contains pages devoted to birth control, abortion, and astounding kinds of degeneracy." These fulminations came just a few years after the Church's interdiction of birth-control information, a response to the Anglican Church's toleration of it. The Catholic hierarchy's campaign against advocates of birth control was in full swing, and its call for citizen action paralleled Sumner's (Figure 19).

The censors were not alone in protesting. A facetious journalist of the day categorized the popular fiction genres attractive to borrowers as "crimers," "lovers," "westers," and "sexers."[165] He fretted that their sellers or renters had reduced the book to an ephemeral product meeting only the practical needs of workaday modern folk, of the same mundane significance as the truss, toilet water, vitamin pills, or laxatives.[166] He ended with a suggestion that the "warmer sex novels [should] be all ready wrapped in plain white paper so that diffident ladies can just whisper a word to the clerk and receive the book without undue blushes." This sneer was directed at dust jackets on which languid and smiling young women either gazed into the distance or blissfully relaxed in the arms of a handsome and well-tailored male. The women, in their low-cut ball gowns, not only got "diffident ladies" interested; they were also directed at the big-city or small-town man with a roving eye and prurient imagination.

Although there is little evidence, it seems that the garish dust jackets on cheap novels were retained on volumes in lending libraries.[167] In case they were not, the publisher repeated the jacket blurb on the first page. Jacket illustration and blurb worked to get the prospective reader "under cover." In the 1940s, cheap paperbacks — often reprints of these same 1930s clothbound sexers — would use lurid covers to accomplish the same purpose. The drugstore or five-and-ten book, for rent or purchase, had to compete, in the window displays[168] as well as on the shelves, with other nonessential commodities, such as those listed above, by appealing to escapist fantasies about self-improvement and widened horizons; advertisement copy, color design, and illustrations bear this out.

Once a client chose a book, the jacket itself may have been covered by the "house" jacket, sometimes color-coded, sometimes carrying blurbs for the library's holdings, often with advertisements for stationery supplies. Advertisements in trade journals suggest that these were common, although an added expense for the library proprietor. Thus, the borrower of a sexer from the house of Godwin, Phoenix, or Faro might avoid stares from her fellow shoppers at Whelan's or Walgreen's drugstores (as the journalist suggested), or jibes from his friends at the cigar store. An important caveat hidden among these tactics to rent or sell cheap

Figure 19. At the time of a clean-up campaign of Brooklyn lending libraries, Rita C. McGoldrick of the International Federation of Catholic Alumnae points out for District Attorney William F. X. Geoghan "obscene passages in a book rented for 2 cents from a circulating library." From "Geoghan Sees Evil," *New York American*, 1 Mar. 1933 ("N.Y. American Staff Photo"). Reproduced by permission of the Harry Ransom Humanities Research Center, University of Texas at Austin (JA Files).

books is that most consumers of sexually stimulating literature needed to maintain a modicum of self-confidence and respectability. They could be unresponsive to either overtly furtive or overtly genteel (thus patronizing) packaging. The clever publisher and rental-library proprietor took note.

Like the Catholic clergy, John Sumner regarded the drugstore book as disseminating the doctrine of self-indulgent obsession with sex among the working class, especially women, in an alarmingly broad fashion. The simultaneous appearance of films, magazines, and stage performances with similar selling points only deepened the urgency. Popular culture was presenting new challenges to parents' ability to protect their children from degenerate influences tossed in their paths by the merchants of vice. Birth control, companionate marriage, and extramarital affairs were all stations on the way to degeneracy. To the moral entrepreneur, interest in these subjects could only be wanton, and those responsible for exciting public interest in them could only be greedily exploiting the susceptibility of those members of the community most lacking in moral discrimination. In the mobilization of community outrage that followed, all sense of proportion went overboard and any book at all could be seized by police raiders. For example, in the swag of more than fifty volumes impounded at a Detroit lending library in December 1934 were Abbé Prevost's *Manon Lescaut*, Knut Hamsun's *The Road Leads On*, Hugh Walpole's *Captain Nicholas*, and even Professor Walter Pitkin's bestseller *Life Begins at Forty*.[169]

Erotica dealers were endlessly resourceful in interesting people in the widest possible variety of sexually oriented materials. Whether by means of bookshop or mail-order circulars, magazine advertisements, telephone or itinerant peddlers, personal browsing in, or gaining entrance to, back rooms of bookstores or various specialty shops, the average adult, whether he or she lived in a city or the country, was made aware and curious about at least some types of available material. That curiosity, aroused through prurience, shocked the moral entrepreneurs into vigorous responses. They knew how to use shame and guilt to solidify their own power.

3

"Hardworking American Daddy"
John Saxton Sumner and the New York Society for the Suppression of Vice

Samuel Roth's nemesis, John Saxton Sumner was New York City's preeminent smut fighter during the period between the two world wars, a formidable figure who became the metropolis's town censor not only through the strength of his moral convictions, but also by virtue of the efficiency with which he worked and the variety of reading matter he targeted. One irate bookseller characterized him as "John S. Smutrat: Vicesnoopia Filtheatia" (Figure 20).[1] He was hated not only by booksellers but also by publishers and authors, for his rigid moral standards as well as for his power to enforce his judgments and to stigmatize offenders. James Branch Cabell wrote that after Sumner tried to have his novel *Jurgen* proscribed in 1920, the author had become, in the eyes of literate collectors of erotica, a "connoisseur of copulation." Ever since, Cabell said in 1934, he had been doomed to receive a dozen letters a week requesting such favors as an opinion about the "most lively passage of an erotic nature" he had written, so that the correspondent could commission an artist to illustrate the scene for a bookplate.[2]

The journalist and political commentator Henry F. Pringle offered the following anecdote as a clue to the way Sumner carried out his duties. The vice crusader had gone to the offices of a lurid "art" magazine, presenting himself as an anonymous customer in order to purchase a copy for evidential purposes.

The editor happened to be in the outer office, and he knew the crusader very well. So he cupped his hands and called loudly to his staff, working inside. "Hey," he bellowed, "come out and take a look at Sumner!"
The staff crowded up as the editor, with heavy sarcasm, urged his visitor to stay for tea.
Mr. Sumner, handling himself very well, declined the invitation.
"I wanted to purchase a copy of *Art Lure*," he said.
"We're awfully sorry, but we can't sell you one," replied the editor.
"Ah!" said Mr. Sumner politely. "Some other day, then. You win this time."[3]

Figure 20. Caricature of Sumner, titled "John S. Smutrat: Vicesnoopia Filtheatia," appearing in a tabloid-style newspaper, *Jack Ketch the Hangman*, published by the 22nd Street bookseller Bernard Guibert Guerney, July 1932. Sumner raided Guerney's Blue Faun Book Shop and confiscated the print run of the publication, then filed a criminal libel suit. Most of the copies were burned with other "smut" in the police headquarters furnace.

Pringle's point was that Sumner was perhaps "a shade too refined for his job."[4] However, in his own view, Sumner had been prudently chosen by the New York Society for the Suppression of Vice (NYSSV) to carry Anthony Comstock's mantle. The founder "was somewhat of a religious fanatic who loved notoriety,"[5] but now the Society needed a younger, more quietly effective leader: a conservative, as he told Pringle, in contrast to the table-thumping ranter whose stern features, muttonchop whiskers, and pot belly invited derision, and whose occasional indignant manhandling of suspects and gloating pronouncements about their penal sentences provoked anger. Comstock's hands-on vigilance was bereft of dignity and restraint, requisite virtues prized by the gentlemen who volunteered time and money to maintain the society. Sumner, in contrast, had a reputation for expressing articulate, knowledgeable, and reasonable viewpoints to a general audience, even in forums and debates with ideological opponents. One could hardly imagine Comstock writing an article for *Smart Set* magazine advising parents to speak frankly to their flapper daughters about their bobbed hair, love of jazz, and visits to dance halls. But Sumner did, describing himself as a "plain, ordinary, everyday, hard-working American daddy." His words of wisdom: "it's hard to keep them from knowing things. . . . There wouldn't be half the harm in those sex plays and sex movies and sex books . . . if you parents did your job." This 1928 essay was most likely heavily edited for easy magazine reading, but in it Sumner spoke confidently and plainly as a typically responsible family man.[6]

One would not expect American booksellers in the 1920s and 1930s to view the NYSSV as a humanitarian group on the order of the Society for the Prevention of Cruelty to Children, the American Society for the Prevention of Cruelty to Animals, and the City Vigilance League. This is how its supporters saw it, however, and how they wanted the public to acknowledge their work. From its inception, the NYSSV had been backed by men of wealth and prestige such as J. P. Morgan, copper magnate William E. Dodge, Samuel Colgate (founder of the soap dynasty), and other well-respected bankers, lawyers, attorneys, and several long-established publishers. They were philanthropists who, however their high station had come about, declared it their duty to raise their communities' moral standards.[7] The antivice societies throughout the country shared especially close ties to other organizations, such as the Women's Christian Temperance Union and New York's Committee of Fourteen, dedicated to eliminating prostitution and sexually transmitted diseases, which had emerged in response to the burgeoning of dance halls, saloons, and "lobster palaces" in the years of industrial and urban expansion after the Civil War. The NYSSV won large-scale public support throughout the last twenty-five years of the nineteenth century, but opposition came from advocates of sex education, birth control, and free love, as well as from entrepreneurs of popular entertainment. The eroticization of leisure was a force no warning voice could stop. By the early twentieth century, it had become integral with mainstream culture. Although during the 1920s and 1930s many continued to identify sexual reticence with decency, nonprocreative sex was on view everywhere, in advertisements for items ranging from contraceptives to clothing.[8] However transparent the venality, not everyone thought sexual explicitness in popular culture was a problem.

Preventive societies, including the antivice groups, understood that part of the reason for crime and disease was overcrowding and poverty, and that reform would come through practical political initiative. However, a large part of their message was that degenerate social conditions were remediable by character development. People like Comstock proposed substituting moral discipline for weak-kneed licentiousness: that is, Yankee initiative must drive out ignorance, laziness, and fatalism. He doubted the average person's ability to develop moral resolve unaided. For him, smut peddlers, and what he called "free lusters," were a social cancer; they could not be permitted to corrupt the masses. Executives of the preventive societies were assured that their aims were disinterested, and that they were shared by the "best" people in American society, the Christian gentlemen. They spoke with an infectious conviction.[9] Comstock was a leading example. He almost single-handedly lobbied through Congress the federal antiobscenity postal statutes in 1873. His efforts, vivified by an extensive collection of sexually explicit materials, showed just how successful an idealistic private citizen could be when he or she gave elected officials a chance to share his or her own rectitude. Returning to New York, he founded the NYSSV, a more powerful version of its predecessor, the Young Men's Christian Association's Committee for the Suppression of Vice, which had subsidized his efforts in Washington.[10]

Dismayed by the failure of municipal statutes and police enforcement to eradicate vice, preventive societies assumed quasi-legal power to identify offenders. Comstock and his fellow crusaders led organizations that acted without respect for proper warrants, and conducted massive and violent raids on suspected premises.[11] Comstock's success in Washington earned him a commission as special agent of the Post Office;[12] he wrote letters under assumed names to trap offenders, and also summarily removed from offices and stores whatever he suspected might be evidence. On occasion the tactics of the preventive societies were vigilante-like. At times, they joined elected law-enforcement personnel in showing little concern for suspects' constitutional protections. Where Sumner differed from Comstock was in his serene demeanor and his seemingly dispassionate defense of these actions as necessary to cleanse the community of degeneracy, and to improve the chances of its most needy members to purge themselves from vice and become better citizens.

The antivice societies grew up in the enlightened, well-educated Protestant constituencies, not among groups who took the Bible literally, howled about the vices of the city and its immigrant population, and criticized the urban churches as vacillating and increasingly secular.[13] If fundamentalists thought dimly of a man like Sumner, however, they would have been surprised upon closer scrutiny. It is true that Comstock's successor was gentlemanly, secular, and patrician. But he was neither weakly committed to his ideals nor accommodating to liberal social thinkers or to the sexual suggestiveness of popular entertainments.

Sumner's Modus Operandi

Sumner, the son of a rear admiral, was called to the New York bar at the age of twenty-eight in 1904. He specialized in stockbrokerage law until his appointment as associate secretary of the NYSSV in 1913. Upon Comstock's death in 1915, he was appointed secretary of the society, in which position he diligently served until his retirement in 1950. He was a teetotaler, an Episcopalian, a Son of the American Revolution, a member of the Founders and Patriots of America, and, politically, an independent.[14] Proclaiming himself no "censor," he would reiterate to the press that his organization did not make laws but merely sent out agents to uphold moral stances sanctioned by codes of "decency." The NYSSV was deputized by the district attorney to investigate suspected violations, which were stipulated by section 1141 of the state penal code. The society's sanction to help enforce the obscenity statute, which came direct from the state legislature in its year of incorporation, was reflected in section 5 of its own charter.[15] Nor did Sumner's agents entrap, he claimed disingenuously; they merely investigated. The police, noting the contro-versies generated when booksellers and publishers were arrested for obscenity in the 1920s, were probably increasingly happy to have the NYSSV take some of the pressure off their shoulders, though this was not a reason the society acknowledged.

Sumner had learned procedures from his predecessor. He kept careful track of all books seized by Customs agents, interdicted in the courts, or declared unmail-able by the Post Office. He also found suspected titles in letters from private parties outraged by what they saw in bookstores or newspaper advertisements. Correspon-dence with other antivice society executives was another rich source of informa-tion.[16] Furthermore, a member of the board of directors of the society might suggest that a certain title be proceeded against, although Sumner did not always consult his board before proceeding.[17] When conducting raids on stores selling question-able books, he would take as many copies as he could find of books he suspected and scour the premises for other offending materials such as magazines, playing cards, and readers. The more books he carted off, the greater the chance of winning the case on the basis of the contents of one or more of them. But before taking any action, he had to visit a New York magistrate with copies of the materials he suspected. All he needed was a single judge who would look with raised eyebrows at one or more of the books he removed from his briefcase.[18] It was a special success to find a magistrate who, in banning a book, overruled a liberal colleague who had recently ruled a particular text nonobscene.

Sumner described his tactics in a letter to Charles Bodwell of the Watch and Ward as follows: First, it was necessary to obtain a copy of the book surreptitiously, mark its objectionable passages, then present "complaint, warrant, and [unsigned] search warrant" to a magistrate. If the latter thought the complaint valid, he signed it, and the society agent who made the purchase swore to it (this was the first of several court appearances for the agent). Then, the magistrate issued a summons and the search warrant, which were executed by a policeman. The latter was accompanied by Sumner or his designee, "to advise on the execution of the search warrant and the matters to be taken." Finally, the defendant was arraigned, the books being "retained by us for safe keeping and subject to the order of the District Attorney." If the magistrate found there was probable cause, the defendant was held for trial in special sessions court, "which tries misdemeanor cases and consists of three judges sitting together. In this court we again appear as complaining witness and give testimony."[19] "While we have been attacked as a sinister organization," Sumner cannily told a City College of New York interviewer, "our position before the law is simply that of a complaining witness"[20] (Figure 21).

Locating the particular bookshops in which one could find gallantiana, sex pulps, or recently cleared volumes that Sumner wished to present to a magistrate for a second opinion was easy. The agent, or possibly Sumner himself, purchased a copy from an unsuspecting (or at least indifferent) clerk. However, if the proprietor knew a book was interdicted, or likely to be, he or she kept it under the counter. In this case it was necessary to deceive the suspect into selling. Sumner would have an agent work undercover, putting him on the trail of prosecutable books and magazines, and also of the numerous advertising circulars to be found somewhere on the premises of suspected dealers in erotica (Figure 13). In using an undercover agent, Sumner was following the lead of Comstock and the Post Office, whose team of inspectors would write decoy letters to entrap perpetrators of fraud and obscenity schemes. Boston and Chicago vigilance groups did the same.

However, the most notorious NYSSV tactic was even closer to the line that separates investigation from enticement to commit crimes. This was the personal visit to the bookstore or publishing house, a specialty of Sumner's chief agent, Charles Bamberger. Efficiently trained under Comstock, Bamberger had such self-confidence, and such contempt for the intelligence of his enemies, that he at one point identified himself on calling cards and fake letterheads as a dealer in "books and novelties" named "Evic Rotacidare" — Vice Eradicator (almost) spelled backward.[21] Instead of simply writing for books, he would work his way into a bookseller's confidence, returning to the shop several times to talk and occasionally making innocuous purchases. After a while, he would softly confide that he was after some "hot stuff." After procuring and paying for the books he had solicited, he would signal the police lurking outside the shop.

Distrust of police competence and honesty was part of the credo of preventive organizations, so many of them relied on men of Bamberger's abilities to initiate arrests. The practice was not limited to conservative Christian groups. The affluent German Jewish community, for instance, organized its own "Kehillah," or "communal body," with a Bureau of Social Morals, and employed its own spy to document gambling, prostitution, thievery, and strong-arm racketeering in lower Manhattan; the information was duly passed on to the police, who, sadly but not unexpectedly, often did not use it, because of the Tammany Hall political machine's relationship with the underworld.[22] Smut hunters, however, used under-

Figure 21. John Saxton Sumner in court, 1937. Photo accompanying "Obscene Book Trial Yorkville Court," *New York Journal American*, 3 Feb. 1937. Reproduced by permission of the Harry Ransom Humanities Research Center, University of Texas at Austin (JA Files).

cover agents, and decoy letters, for a different purpose than other reformist and preventive groups. They had little reason to believe that policemen or magistrates had nefarious motives regarding the enforcement of obscenity laws. Smuthounds used undercover tactics simply as the most effective way of locating offenders — which, in the case of the NYSSV, they were deputized to do. Erotica distributors lacked the capital and political power of racketeers, so they were unlikely to engage in graft or bribery. Rebhuhn and Levine's ill-fated reliance on Ben Miller would have cautioned others in the business against such finagling unless one knew exactly how to harness political influence efficiently. There is little evidence, save for the Miller affair, that bribery of public officials ever stymied Sumner in his fight against erotica dealers. But H. L. Mencken tells how, in 1916, he and his fellow editors of a pulp magazine were advised to give five hundred dollars to one of the three judges of Special Sessions hearing the case. They did so, and the case was dismissed.[23] As his power waned in the 1930s, Sumner took relief from his frustrations by muttering about the timidity of magistrates, and by wondering about the honesty of "liberal" judges who, until the Seabury antigraft investigations in 1931 and Mayor Walker's resignation, were Tammany-controlled. Sumner never made any public charges of judicial corruption, although one 1934 acquittal prompted the comment in his ledgers "D. A. incompetent or — ." He lacked hard evidence, and realized that he needed to work with judges. He would not wish to be looked upon with suspicion as a lawyer hostile to magistrates.

Occasionally, Sumner himself attempted to purchase banned books under assumed names, or assigned this task to his financial agent, an employee who made the rounds of potential contributors (among whom were some booksellers).[24] His regular staff consisted of only Bamberger, a financial officer, and a stenographer, although he sometimes hired local characters — "stool pigeons," his enemies called them — who were paid to supply him with information about clandestine printing and wholesaling as well as retailing of books.[25]

There were some advantages in skirmishing against the bookleggers of New York with such a small cadre: shared purpose and reliability. Boston's Watch and Ward Society habitually used undercover agents whom it employed not only to trap booksellers but also to deal with gamblers, bootleggers, and pimps. They were themselves of dubious moral character and often embarrassed the society.[26] Sumner avoided this pitfall by relying on his stool pigeons sparingly. The condemnation directed against the Watch and Ward after it entrapped the proprietor of Dunster

House in Cambridge into selling copies of *Lady Chatterley's Lover* to professors was strengthened when journalists ascertained that several of its undercover men were ex-convicts.[27] The Illinois Vigilance Association also suffered irreversible loss of prestige when newspaper publicity spotlighted not only Superintendent Yarrow's belligerent zeal but his use of "informers."[28] Bamberger's deceptions were also revealed, and in 1918 Frank Harris, in high dudgeon, accused a Sumner agent of stealing and reselling "obscene photographs" from "an extensive store-room of the Society."[29] But the disapprobation directed at the NYSSV did not become as explosive or as damaging as in Boston or Chicago. Sumner's equanimity and common sense, and the tightly organized operation he presided over, prolonged his career despite the declining influence in the 1930s of the preventive societies, including his own.

If the use of undercover agents was of dubious legality, so were other strategies Sumner used to stop the spread of sexual explicitness. He would speak to the proprietors of bookstores whose windows featured displays that included books he considered undesirable. According to booksellers to whom this had happened, the books he pointed out had not been the subject of court action, but were ones that Sumner himself thought were indecent. Sumner did not explicitly state that the bookseller was in imminent danger of arrest, but simply indicated that he or she was not to display certain works. The unstated warning underlying these conversations was that if the books were not withdrawn from the window, the shop might come under scrutiny for other titles.[30]

Sumner also occasionally gave opinions on whether or not he might prosecute certain books if they were sold, or published.[31] Sometimes these opinions were solicited, and sometimes they were not. When, in 1922, Horace Liveright contemplated publishing an edition of Theodore Dreiser's *The Genius*, H. L. Mencken, at the request of his friend, Dreiser's lawyer, sought and received Sumner's advice on possible expurgations.[32] As a fledgling publisher, Richard Simon was enthusiastic about his friend Joseph March's narrative poem *The Wild Party*, a ribald and profane event attended by prostitutes, men on the make, hard-boiled types, lesbians, and male homosexuals, which is brought to closure when one "Queenie's" bed partner for the night shoots the man with whom she had been living. In 1926, Simon asked Sumner "what he would do to us if we published it." The answer, of course, was "he'd put us in jail." Pascal Covici published *The Wild Party* in a limited edition in 1928; it was one of the books Sumner confiscated during a raid on the Gotham Book Mart that year.[33] In 1930, upon hearing that Simon and Schuster were about to publish an edition of *Casanova's Homecoming*, for which Sumner prosecuted Thomas Seltzer in 1922, the "town censor" wrote the firm a warning that he would do the same to them.[34] After the 1928 raid on the Gotham, which netted more than eighty separate titles, Sumner noted the presence of Beardsley's *Venus and Tannhauser* in one of the shop's catalogs. During a series of negotiations with Frances Steloff and her attorneys, he informed both the lawyer and Steloff's husband, David Moss, with whom she managed the shop. "You will agree with us," Sumner stated, that the work, and any illustrations, were "obscene." Two days later Steloff drafted a letter to Sumner, saying she would withdraw the book until she had read it, and further stating that she "appreciat[ed] the way you have called this to my attention. I assure you that I shall always be eager to cooperate with you in this manner." She included copies of the books in question.[35] Clearly she would not necessarily have withdrawn any books the vice suppressor may have redlined for her. However, for lovers — and especially sellers — of literature to ignore Sumner's judgments was to ignore the nature of the world they lived in.

Vigilance Against Smut—and Foreign Subversion

In 1922, Sumner advocated the creation of a committee of responsible citizens, headed by a commissioner, that would decide if erotically explicit manuscripts (by D. H. Lawrence, James Branch Cabell, Sinclair Lewis, Ben Hecht, or Theodore Dreiser, to name a few targets) should be published: "Every one knows that many of the authors of the 'younger school' are lacking in literary merit and have made cheap reputations by turning to salacity after failing to command attention by legitimate work. Their vogue is largely the result of a conspiracy on the part of salacious writers of the new school to praise one another, and they have enlisted many critics in the log-rolling."[36] Paul Boyer, in his excellent study of the purity societies and book censorship, quotes journalist Henry F. Pringle to the effect that Sumner's polite demeanor was "synthetic," hiding puzzlement and annoyance.[37] Pringle suggests Sumner was like a middle-aged preceptor uncomfortably trying to work with young people whose passions and preoccupations he could never approve of or sympathize with. The vice suppressor's statement about the "younger school" suggests a defensiveness that comes from recognizing that one's own values are at odds, not with transparently venal scoundrels peddling smut, but with

writers of books taken seriously by ever increasing numbers of one's fellow citizens, despite their seemingly rank indecency and vulgar frankness.

The business of publishing was undergoing many changes. Owners of new
concerns, most of them young Jewish men (Horace Liveright, Thomas Seltzer, Ben
Huebsch, Max Schuster, Alfred Knopf), had begun to specialize in presenting
European writers to an American audience curious about their sexual frankness and
Marxist ideas. Established houses, such as Doran, Houghton, Appleton, and Doubleday, did not do so, and some of their executives resented their parvenu colleagues.[38] Modernist writers especially owed their exposure to Jewish firms.[39] One
"old guard" publisher feeling the pressure of Sumner's complaints about what he
considered the profession's lax moral standards blamed "those cheap little publishers who have been springing up from nowhere. . . . They're all goddamn
Jews!"[40] Books from their presses constantly crossed into those festering regions
where the one-hundred-percent American moralist saw the degenerate influences
of licentious sensuality, of sex for its own sake.[41] It was Sumner's lot in the Roaring
Twenties to help lead a doomed ideological struggle in days when the winds of
change were the only constant in the moral climate.

How necessary to preserving the integrity of America this crusade seemed to
be! In 1916, a member of the Authors League protesting the censorship of the first
edition of Dreiser's *The Genius* elicited this response from the society's new
secretary:

It is not for any limited group of individuals to attempt to force upon the people in general
their own particular ideas of what is decent or indecent. It seems to me that this is what your
associates are trying to do, as distinguished from our position which is based upon the
decisions of courts representing the sentiments of the people through a great number of years
up to the present day in every section of the country. . . . You stated that the people of this
country should assimilate the ideas of the foreign element coming to this country in the way
of art and literature. . . . We need to uphold our standards of decency more than ever in face
of this foreign and imitation foreign invasion rather than to make those things which are
vicious and indecent so familiar as to become common and representative of American life
and manners.[42]

Such a perspective was common, and long-enduring. Twenty-three years later, in
passing sentence on the Rebhuhns for their Falstaff Press publications, the federal
judge stated that First Amendment issues were irrelevant because the firm had no
right "to place in American homes all of the sordid details of the depraved sexual

conduct of a foreign people."[43] He was referring to French, and especially German, anthropologists and sex researchers congregated around Magnus Hirschfeld's Institute for Sexual Science in Berlin.

Just what "the color of the air" was like in interwar America is further exemplified by the fate of David Gordon, a DeWitt Clinton High School student, who published a poem titled "America" in the *Daily Worker* in March 1928. The verses "us[ed] obscene language in railing at the United States and the Statue of Liberty." The boy's assurances that the intent was metaphorical went unheeded by the arresting officer, a member of the bomb squad, and the three judges who convicted him of violating the state's Comstock Law. One of the justices, noting that the writer was born in Russia, and that his "real name was Goronefsky," regretted that "we cannot sentence you to Russia," presumably so that Gordon could contrast Red tyranny with American freedom. While Gordon's appeal was being considered, he entered the University of Wisconsin on scholarship. In April 1929, he left campus, keeping the reason to himself: he had to begin a term of thirteen months to three years in the New York City Reformatory. After news of his plight brought a vigorous protest from university supporters, and after he had served more than a month in prison, he was granted parole. The judge affirmed the correctness of the sentence, but declined "to make a martyr of an immature and inconsequential youth who has been guilty of writing a very bad and vulgar piece of poetry."[44]

Sumner had no hand in this particular case, but considering the ease with which he classified some of those he arrested as "young, radical, irreligious and overeducated," the judge's cast of mind mirrors his own. Due to the threat of communism, some moralists saw obscenity, subversion, and what Sumner termed the "foreign invasion" as a single force. Erotica dealers might have Red leanings; Russian agents might use pornography to undermine Christian values in America. In 1930, the fear was that irresponsible erotica dealers were importing materials that would corrupt the American character, and therefore weaken faith in democracy and religious discipline. That year, when the Senate debated revisions of the Tariff Act, Senator Reed Smoot of Utah (whom Ogden Nash exhorted: "Smite, Smoot, smite smut") spoke from behind a desk piled high with "beastly" books — *Lady Chatterley's Lover*, *My Life and Loves*, the *Kama Sutra*, Burns's poems, and Rabelais's works, among others. He argued for reinstatement of the provision in the Tariff Act that would allow Customs officials to bar importation of written materials that they felt advocated treason, threatened bodily harm, incited insurrection, or "offend[ed] the moral sense of the average person."[45] The phrasing echoes that of the Sedition Act of 1918, a spawn of the Red Scare: it declared unlawful "disloyal, profane, scurrilous, or abusive language." Each of these kinds of expression was demeaning to America, and thought to weaken her citizens' civic resolve. During the interwar period, the U.S. *Criminal Code* (title 18, section 334) specified "indecency" as "includ[ing] matter of a character tending to incite arson, murder, or assassination."[46] Smoot's phrase "the moral sense of the average person" indicates he linked "lewd" and "indecent," as closely as Comstock ("every obscene, lewd, lascivious, indecent, filthy, or vile article"). "Indecent" is a broader category than "obscene," including also scatology, as well as delineations of violent activities or those leading to public disorder. Indecency is assumed to attack the sensibility on a broader front than obscenity. Political as well as moral values are endangered.

When thoughtful conservative moralists championed decency, they did so because they believed implicitly that private desires should remain private. They were convinced that the bodily activities naturally evoked shame. To bring them into public view, as did writings about sex, violence, crime, and the bodily functions, confused the public sphere with the private in a degenerate way, even if these writings were scientific or naturalistic. For public order, taste, decency, and chastity of utterance were essential.[47] Indecency — of which obscenity, as we have said, was only one part — was the real cancer; if allowed to intrude in the public sphere, it would destroy civil discourse and empty the life of the nation of all but the coarsest sensationalism and self-indulgent sloganeering. This, thought Smoot, Sumner, and their numerous supporters, was just what shameless foreign subversives wanted.

These fears were shared by the Catholic Church's National Organization for Decent Literature (NODL). The NODL placed contemporary disrespect for marriage, religion, modesty, and sexual reticence "squarely on the red doorstep of communism."[48] Sumner was no Red-baiter, no more than the Church, which served so many Irish and Italian Americans, could be anti-immigrant. Despite Sumner's concerns about the behavior patterns of immigrants, he and the Church were allied in their concern to search out "dirt" wherever it existed. Obscenity and indecency were virulent species of dirt, hostile to red-blooded American rectitude. The full horror of indecent thought and action, in fact, lay not in its effect on sexual behavior. Sumner hated its presence in his country because it undermined the ability of secular and religious authority to influence how people thought about and used their bodies. He and other authority figures wanted to be assured that good Americans would restrain their impulses and frustrations in order to gain the trust of their fellow citizens as they went about running their businesses, buying what they needed to support their families, and preparing their children to be patriotic, decent citizens. They doubted that Europeans had such a realistic notion of the common good, or that their societies were as orderly, or as "decent."

In addition to his yearly ledgers, Sumner also wrote the NYSSV's annual reports, carefully digested into tables titled "Nationality and Religious Creed of Persons Arrested." Russians, Germans, and Italians, in addition to U.S. citizens (whether native or naturalized is unrecorded), predominated, as did the "Hebrew" religion. The ledgers from 1882 to 1930 list an approximately equal number of American and foreign-born offenders.[49] Sumner was far from being the only law enforcer to list those arrested by creed and country of origin. The New York Committee of Fourteen, for example, records information regarding prostitutes, bootleggers, saloon and taxi dance-hall operators and other offenders in terms of complexion, ethnicity, and race ("Jewess," "colored," "Irish American").[50] The 1909 U.S. Immigration Committee Report on prostitution categorizes women by "nationality" and "race" ("Hebrew," "Irish," "French," "Italian").[51] Reformist groups investigating urban social pathology commonly viewed such categories as a necessary method of analyzing social problems. Indeed, early twentieth-century movements for social reform, with their drives to raise standards of "social hygiene" by Americanizing the inhabitants of urban ethnic neighborhoods, saw the existence of racial and religious views brought to "the Golden Land" from Europe as ugly obstacles to progress. Sumner was no exception.

Social Reform, Social Control, and the Need for Americanization

The activities of the Committee of Fourteen are a strong example of a reformist society in action, and of the ways such a group was distinct from, and yet shared premises with, the NYSSV. In fighting the proliferation of brothels, it documented numerous cases of impoverished young women forced to become taxi dance partners, speakeasy "hostesses," and prostitutes. It had the backing of businessmen, social workers, and clerics, and received funding from Andrew Carnegie, John D. Rockefeller, Jr., and Jacob Schiff.[52] Through its political contacts, its donations of money, and its monitoring of police tactics and of magistrates' conduct, it encouraged reform of the women's prison system, more efficient public health legislation, the interdiction of hotels, dance halls, and "resorts" that served as houses of prostitution, and the incarceration of their operators. Its secretaries communicated closely with Sumner and found him very helpful in uncovering the resorts and numerous "indecent shows." But the Committee of Fourteen also encouraged sex education, whereas Progressive organizations felt that "social hygiene" would make it easier for the vulgar masses to ignore American traditions of genteel reticence.[53] The committee had cordial communications with sexologists, including Dr. Robert L. Dickinson in the United States and Havelock Ellis in England. Cooperating with Dickinson's Committee on Maternal Health, the Committee of Fourteen planned to publicize Margaret Sanger's teachings on birth control. It refused to support the Clean Books Bills of the mid-1920s.[54] Its decision was probably based on the opposition of these bills' sponsors to discussions of sexuality in general; they deplored, as Sumner put it, "books dealing with sex, medical, scientific, and pseudo-scientific subjects . . . regarding which there is a very pronounced opinion as to their harmfulness to the average lay reader."[55]

In many ways, however, the committee supported Sumner and his tactics. Besides using undercover agents, it agreed with him on which magistrates to support,[56] and felt, as he did, that obscene literature was a clear and present cause of lax moral standards in young people.[57] It encouraged, as strongly as did Sumner, the suppression of a whole book if any part of it was judged indecent, and felt that all obscenity cases should be decided by a jury's verdict, not by the judge.[58] As we have mentioned, it also charted offenders by ethnic and religious background. Finally, its seemingly progressive interest in the birth-control movement may have been motivated in part by support for the movement's eugenic concepts, which today seem racist. Committee Secretary Frederick Whitin wrote in a letter to Dickinson of the possibility of sterilizing individuals who constituted a social menace, and Dickinson responded with a flowchart that contained these desiderata of social hygienists' efforts: "Betterment of breed (Extinction of harmful varieties)" and "Restrictions on sensual sex excitants, books, pictures, dancing, plays, fondling." And yet Dickinson also called for "removal of [the] ban on wise, frank speech."[59]

The combination in one ostensibly philanthropic organization of harshly coercive methods of social control (implying contempt for that part of the population

needing help) with relief from physical and emotional bonds of poverty is characteristic of the era's reform movements, as is the equation of many sexually explicit
books, artwork, and plays with base prurience. This sort of zeal would have been
bolstered by what the newly developing social sciences presented as inductive
"evidence" of criminal indecency: an immigrant or poverty-stricken person's ignorance of law and custom, his or her lack of self-restraint, or the degenerate
influences of the public entertainments flourishing in his or her neighborhoods.
Statistics provided just the kind of objectivity these reformers were looking for:
disadvantaged people were of a certain race, religion, nationality, or "complexion," and needed special help to detach themselves from their backgrounds.

The frequent "Jew" listings in Sumner's ledgers did accurately document the
ethnic background of many dealers in erotica. If he ever made anti-Semitic statements, they have not been recorded. Rather, the entries show him acting within the
paradigm of privately supported reform activism, based on what were then accepted as reasonable and sociologically valid explanations of social phenomena.
Of course, this sort of research no longer seems objective or professionally acceptable; the kind of evidence gathered clearly implied that immigrants, including
Jewish ones, had character flaws that needed correction. Sumner, and Comstock,
tried to make reform come about not primarily through better jobs, shorter working
hours, and better chances at medical care, good food, lodgings, and schools —
although they did not oppose these measures. Rather, they sought to remove the
immigrants, whom they saw as too weak to discipline themselves, as completely as
possible from what they knew as inferior (because they were foreign or "imitation
foreign") values and habits. To reiterate: immigrants had to be Americanized. It
was imperative, therefore, to root out the degenerate and foreign influence represented by salacious-minded intellectuals and by those who profited by dealing in
sexually explicit materials.

To civil libertarians, and to others troubled by the seeming inability of vigilant
reformers to distinguish birth-control and sex-information manuals and sexually
explicit modern novels from publications created to be read "with one hand," this
focus on nationality and religion showed a bigoted hostility toward the foreign-
born. At the least, it encouraged chauvinistic attitudes about America's superiority
to other nations. Many journalists and academics, however, even during the period
of Sumner's tenure, concurred with those Progressives who had earlier asserted

that immigration diluted native strength and integrity. E. A. Ross used his academic training in genetics to describe the Hebrews of eastern Europe in America (in *Century Magazine*, September 1914) as a conniving race whose intellectual accomplishments were not in the service of aesthetic, social, or moral advances, but dedicated to making themselves economically secure. Their "race traits" were those of "moral cripples"; they hated authority; the "pleasure-loving Jewish businessmen" preferred gentile girls to Jewish girls. Ross evinces a fear of all immigrant groups of his time. "It is unthinkable," he concludes, "that so many persons with crooked faces, coarse mouths, bad noses, heavy jaws, and low foreheads can mingle their heredity with ours."[60] Progressive leaders saw evidence of beliefs such as Ross's, and those of Madison Grant as expressed in his *Passing of the Great Race* (1916), in the flourishing vice racketeering and flow of pornographic images and printed matter in the immigrant slums.[61] Its "promoters" were "foreign," parasitic infections of the social organism ("pestiferous evil" was the phrase of the Watch and Ward Society).[62]

In his 1931 report to the NYSSV, Sumner suggested that the statistics he compiled were "an argument supporting the demand for more stringent laws regulating the admission of immigrants to the United States and their distribution in the interest of assimilation."[63] Perhaps this statement can only be seen as bigoted. However, it was hard to classify as such, for the second part of the sentence was no more than a reiteration of the immigration policy, supported by Jews — albeit established and assimilationist-minded "uptown" groups — that had been in effect from 1881 to 1922.[64] Further, Sumner's statements might pass as a kind of reformism: such a policy might alleviate vice, and isolate the hardened degenerates who could not be reformed. But if it was not bigotry, it was part of a tidal wave of intransigent suspicion. Both in 1921 and, because the 1921 rules did not stop as much immigration as was desired, especially in 1924, the policy of unlimited immigration had been definitely abandoned. In 1929, limitations were set for different nationalities, in a manner that clearly favored applicants from western, not eastern or southern, Europe.[65]

As Walter Lippmann stated in 1927, censorship arises because the censor feels the need to exercise control over those whose loyalty to conservative institutions is assumed to be weak. He or she is concerned about the effect of indecent or obscene materials on the young, the undereducated, the poor, and women. Such people supposedly do not have within themselves, inherent in their characters, that interested loyalty to things as they are which makes men immune to subversive influences. In matters of this sort we must remember that the words "right" and "wrong" mean simply friendly or hostile to the purposes of the institution in question; that is why it is said that the outsiders do not have the interest of the institution sufficiently at heart to feel instinctively the difference between right and wrong.[66]

The danger seems heightened when the subversive material is distributed by those whose nationality and religion mark them as insufficiently "assimilated" into American values to know indecency when they see it. Throughout the interwar period, public-spirited people saw the work of the NYSSV as essential. "My own sentiments strongly coincide with the purposes of your organization," wrote President Harding in 1922.[67] In 1938, on the occasion of its sixty-fifth anniversary, the society received a message from President Roosevelt, congratulating it for its part in "the growing interest in law enforcement on the part of those not professionally engaged in this field — individuals and organizations of private citizens who are willing to devote their energies in the worthy cause of crime suppression."[68]

Sumner and the Intransigence of Authority

As Richard Hofstadter points out in *The Age of Reform*, immigrants and Yankees, whether progressive or conservative, were genuinely different from one another.[69] The former, and their sons and daughters, were too close to their Old World roots, too proud of their social rituals and ways of generating spiritual strength, and too involved in problems of immediate survival to accept what the "natives" were preaching to them. The cultural differences were real, and of course did not indicate anything inferior about the newcomers. But the racist essays of Ross and Grant show how deep the wellspring of xenophobia in the national psyche was by the 1920s. It had existed since before 1900, and did not go unexploited by the popular media. Beginning in 1902, magazines such as *Harper's Weekly*, the *North American Review*, and the *Independent* ran a series of articles on Jewish living conditions and dubious business dealings. An important series of articles in *McClure's*, beginning in 1907, on crime in the Jewish quarter declared that "the 'primitive peoples,' the immigrants, had 'suddenly' been handed 'the domination of American city life.' "[70] *McClure's* remarked on "the acute and often unscrupulous Jewish type of mind."[71] From various quarters came statements about the perfidiousness of "New Israel" and its supporters in corrupt (and Democratic) Tammany Hall.[72]

The Jewish community's long-range response focused not on condemning bigotry but on studying and eliminating the social and economic conditions in which "vice" had flourished.[73] There were the socialist unions and their mutual-aid societies, the Yiddish press and its encouragement of perseverance and political awareness, the "Americanizing" alliances that provided educational materials, and the settlement houses with their medical care and concern for improving the health and educational opportunities of ghetto dwellers.[74] The aforementioned Kehillah of Jewish organizations appeared in 1909, to identify Lower East Side criminals. It was a response both to the indisputable fact of Jewish influence in "white slavery" and to the anti-Semitic implications in the statements of other vigilance societies. The Kehillah's founders saw these implications made sensationally explicit by the muckraking journalists. In a sense, this Jewish-American organization was like those that existed in the Old World, which "mediated between the community and the authorities."[75] Far from fighting the media and the conservative establishment, or repudiating what the latter would term patriotic values, the Kehillah reminded them of the undeserved hate and fear that their elitist rhetoric might stir up in the public mind. The organization hoped that by showing that most Jews were law-abiding Americans respectful of the nation's institutions, it could serve as a bulwark against the lashing out at scapegoats that was a hallmark of public moral indignation, and of the one-hundred-percenters who instigated it. The members of this organization were not self-hating or servile; they were simply realistic. It should be noted that they were established, often German-American Jews, and thus closer in social class, temperament, and ideology to Yankees than were the recently arrived immigrants of the Lower East Side, who, proudly attached to their European habits and mores, suspected the motives of the Kehillot.[76] In the case of some dedicated and compassionate Jewish reformers of German descent—Jacob Schiff, Lillian Wald, Louis Marshall—the suspicions, however inevitable, were unfounded.

Not everyone who favored censorship of obscene materials in some form equated Jewish and other immigrant groups with political and moral degeneracy. Such an earnest reformer as William J. Schieffelin desired and worked for an improvement in existing conditions in poor areas. Head of the anti-Tammany Citizen's Union in 1909, and treasurer of the Committee of Fourteen before assuming that office, he later became a vice president of the NYSSV, at which time he gave lukewarm support to Comstock and later Sumner. In 1930, he responded to questions about whether Sumner could or did entrap by flatly repudiating the tactic. "I do not approve of inducing people to commit crimes," he said.[77] Schieffelin was also a sincere advocate of improvement of conditions in African-American ghettos, and an early protester against Nazism.[78] His support for the society was based on its work in preventing pornography from being thrust into the hands of school-children. His influence on Sumner is evident in the latter's *Smart Set* article, where the vice suppressor asserted, though with the crusader's typical us-them dichoto-mizing, that "the man who peddles dope to school children is no more vicious than the greedy wretch who places salacious literature in their hands or offers them some other form of vulgar amusement."[79] By the mid-1930s, the society's annual reports, under Schieffelin's influence, were stressing the dangers of minors' ac-cessibility to erotica. Schieffelin's tolerance for writings that advocated birth con-trol set him further at odds with Sumner; he told journalist Joseph Lilly that he had tried to convince the society's administrators that the issue should not concern it.[80]

With the encouragement of such men and the open-handed cooperation of local community leaders, the crime problem on the Lower East Side was effec-tively addressed, although crime and vice were endemic to ghetto life. The Kehil-lah's Bureau of Social Morals helped ferret out prostitutes, extortionists, thieves, and swindlers.[81] The streets became safer for legitimate businesses catering to the middle classes and for places of entertainment geared toward its bourgeois sense of decency. By the 1920s, upwardly mobile Jews had created, or were still agitating for, family-oriented community centers, "wholesome" popular amusements, good taste and propriety in entertainment, and self-censorship in the publishing and movie industries.[82] Many had moved up from the Lower East Side to the respect-able affluence of Washington Heights in Manhattan, the South Bronx, Pelham Park-way, the Grand Concourse in the Bronx, or Rego Park in Queens.[83] Out of sheer bourgeois respectability, most of these citizens would probably have approved of a clause the owners of the Irving Place Theater wished, on Sumner's urging, to have added to its lease in 1925. It stated that the lessee would produce no show deemed "objectionable" by Sumner's society or the police.[84] Many of the same class of cit-izens would also have joined in the Book Publishers Association and *Publishers Weekly*'s initial support for a Clean Books Bill, at least (perhaps) until they found, along with the publishing industry, that what its endorsers, including Sumner, had in mind went far beyond removing trashy erotic books from lending libraries. The Clean Books Bill would have created an official czar — or, in the language of the disapproving *New York Times*, a "pooh-bah" — to pass upon literary manuscripts before their publication.[85] However, that even this proviso would have compromised Jewish community support is doubtful. The Federation of Hungarian Jews of America had its own Clean Books Committee. In 1927, upset especially by Samuel Roth's serialization of Joyce's *Ulysses*, the Committee went to court to have his *Beau* and *Two Worlds Monthly* cited for obscenity. Leopold Bloom's prurience revolted them, ostensibly because *Ulysses* was "poisoning" people's minds, but possibly also because the figure of Bloom reinforced the stereotype of the Jew being preoccupied with unhealthy outlets for sexual frustrations.[86]

Sumner seems not to have acknowledged this burgeoning middle-class morality, judging by the charts and statements about immigrants in his annual reports written after 1929, when congressional legislation ended open immigration. In fact, nowhere in his annual reports or periodical letters to constituents does he acknowledge any accomplishments of respected Jewish artists or social reformers, or those of groups dedicated to civic improvements. Rabbi Stephen Wise often raised his strong voice against obscenity in print. Sumner did mention him once, in the 1942 annual report, but only because he and one other rabbi commended the work of the NYSSV. A double-edged, rock-solid, intransigence emerges, a hallmark of the one-hundred-percenter. From where he sat, of course, Sumner was correct to claim that the traffic in "pornography" was vigorous in the 1920s and 1930s, and that Jews were preponderant as distributors of gallantiana, avant-garde sexually explicit novels, sex pulps, sexology, and the most flagitious materials. He never stated that many of these materials would have been purchased by non-Jews, and some were available at prices most immigrants could not afford. As for the character of book people in general: for every notorious Sam Roth, how many Jewish booksellers or publishers were there who would not do business with him? But consorting with well-known smut merchants was only the most egregious of a bookseller's many possible sins. Since Sumner saw erotica of all types as equally pernicious, bookmen and bookwomen were equally culpable whether they published James Branch Cabell or Frank Harris, whether they sold Tijuana bibles or Boccaccio.

Another feature of Sumner's intransigence was his response to sexually explicit literature itself. Did editions of *Casanova's Homecoming*, *Women in Love*, *Ulysses*, or *Jurgen*, nudist magazines, or sexological treatises really lead to more "sex crimes" and hedonistic sloth? Was it impossible that *any* open depiction of sexual life might enlighten and harmlessly entertain, rather than debauch, the reader? The citizen truly committed to decency could not even consider this option: such distinctions let in the Devil.

In his outmoded single-mindedness, Sumner was loyal to the spirit, if not the heavy-handed methods, of Comstock's coercive efforts. Judges increasingly based obscenity rulings on evaluations not of isolated passages but of the book as a whole. They also attempted to assess the average adult's tolerance for nonprurient sexual explicitness. This, to Sumner, was simply "trying to explain away the appearance of admitted obscenity and filth." The 1934 decision permitting Random House to publish *Ulysses* in the United States especially frustrated him. Sneering at the "broad-mindedness" of the Second Circuit Court of New York, and realizing the precedent the case would set, he wrote to the attorney general's office, regretting its lack of resolve to pursue the case to the Supreme Court: "It seems to me that the good old American fighting spirit is lacking."[87] For a one-hundred-percenter like Sumner, such a ruling merely furthered the interests of "a rather reprehensible type of author and publisher." A few months earlier, he relished the conviction of a lending-library operator regarding a copy of D. H. Clark's *Female*, and the "setback" he had dealt to lawyers Morris Ernst and Alexander Lindey, as well as to the magistrate who had cleared the book for its publisher the year before. He hoped the victory over a work that had been sold in such stores as Macy's, Gimbel's, Womrath's, Dutton's, Scribner's, and Doubleday, Doran would lead to a reversal of the *Ulysses* decision. "Pride goeth before destruction, and a haughty spirit before a fall," he pronounced to his counterpart at the Watch and Ward Society.[88]

The NYSSV ledgers show that no incident of "indecent" cashing-in on a citizen's curiosity about the forbidden was beneath vigilant notice. Those arrested included many drugstore and bookstore clerks, "colored" porters, and peddlers (these four occupations involving the selling of spicy magazines, novelties, photos, readers, cartoons, and films), burlesque dancers, prostitutes, procurers, candy-store owners (because of their "obscene photographs"), as well as the occasional barber (exhibitor of "indecent business cards"). There was to be no compromise with anyone who was suspected of placing lust and sensuality in the way of the curious. That included the firms of Simon and Schuster, Thomas Seltzer, and Boni and Liveright. It was either/or, us versus them.

"The Virulence of Sex"

Contemplating the eroticization of leisure time, conservative reformers concluded that Americans had become susceptible to the "virulence" of sex. Since the print media were considered a potent carrier of "infection," reaching from the cities far into the heartland, they had to be quarantined. Charles Bodwell began his tenure as secretary of the Watch and Ward Society in 1927 by declaring that books containing "garbage" should be handled as solid waste is by city boards of health.[89] The disease metaphor was echoed by an editorial that year in the *New York American* (Figure 22). Comparing draconian enforcement of obscenity laws to strict adherence to codes preventing the "spread of infectious diseases," the paper called for "cities [to] follow the example of Boston and put their literary street cleaning departments to work."[90] At the time of the furor in Boston over the selling of *Lady Chatterley's Lover*, one of the city's religious leaders declared that "one who scatters cholera germs is less of a menace to society than one who sells an impure book."[91] In Chicago, Wirt W. Hallam, president of the Illinois Vigilance Association, observed a sensational case of a young girl's abusive relationship with an elderly man, who at one point asked her to read to him from Havelock Ellis's *Studies in the Psychology of Sex*. Hallam's conclusion: "Bad literature is a poison as ruinous as any drug."[92] He wrote to Sumner that his experience with "degenerate literature and stag pictures" instilled in him "a feeling of utter hopelessness." He was especially distraught about books describing "sensitive unusual people [homosexuals] who are born unfortunate. . . . Thirty or forty years ago American men would not tolerate the existence of such people in their towns, but as cities have grown larger and punishment more difficult, the festering sore has grown until now it is a horrible sickening mass of corruption."[93] Hallam here points his unsteady hand at the erotica dealer as a source of contagion, an anonymous urban stranger who vulgarizes the taboo subject of sexual desire for material gain.

It was this widely shared contempt for the vices of the metropolis that the American Civil Liberties Union (ACLU) found squarely blocking its path in 1929, when it lobbied against a proposed provision of the Tariff Act. This provision—

Figure 22. The virulence of obscene books: crime, disease, death. Source: Cartoon accompanying the editorial "Enforce All Existing Laws Against Unclean Literature," *New York American*, 11 Aug. 1927. Reproduced by permission of the Harry Ransom Humanities Research Center, University of Texas at Austin (JA Files).

defended by Senator Smoot in 1930, and opposed by Senator Cutting — would allow books suspected of political subversion to be detained summarily by Customs inspectors, without being submitted to judicial review, in the same way "obscene" books were at the time. The ACLU, which had been active for a decade, asked its man in Washington to parley with the lobbyist for the Methodist Board of Temperance, to see if he felt strongly about the revision. He found that the Methodist's "chief and only argument at the present time seems to be that . . . New York is not an American city, being constituted of only twenty-five percent Americans and seventy-five percent scum of the earth; since its courts are as corrupt as its politics are, that it will be impossible to effect any censorship through the courts of that district." The temperance man had one bit of advice for the ACLU, since it was based in New York: to see how Sumner felt about the matter.[94]

The supporters of the NYSSV, like those of the Women's Christian Temperance Union, feared their own language, schools, entertainments, and political leaders were becoming marginalized by the moral degeneracy, political apostasy, and atheism of city dwellers.[95] This made Sumner's energy in protecting innocent minds from lewdness and pornography all the more insistent. The same zeal guided the leaders of the temperance movement. In their case, the suspect middleman minority was not the Jewish population but German Americans, who had brought their brewery skills from Europe. Like the censors, advocates of Prohibition preached their cause as necessary to affirm American cultural values and social status at a time when urban ethnic immigrants had developed enough confidence in their enterprises, and political and economic viability, to weaken conservative mores and undermine entrenched advantages.[96] This meant the health of the American social system was failing. Sumner himself noted that "if we can't have public decency through a sense of decency, let's have it through fear of punishment."[97] The speakeasy owner and the nightclub "hostess," for the Committee of Fourteen; the rowdy barkeep, for the Anti-Saloon League; and the burlesque impresario, or dealer in contraceptives or pornography, for the NYSSV: such offenders had to be coerced, and frightened out of business, and their customers punished.[98]

In July 1930, publisher-distributor Adam Dingwall was importuned by a Sumner undercover agent for a copy of the ribald fifteenth-century French classic *One Hundred Merrie and Delightsome Stories* (*Les Cent Nouvelles Nouvelles*), a work inspired by Boccaccio and one of Rabelais' sources, which Carrington had published in 1899 and recommended as "the quintessence of the rollicking fun of the Southern nations."[99] The agent named a good customer of Dingwall's as having suggested Dingwall-Rock to him. An hour later Sumner and the police, without producing a warrant, were ransacking Dingwall's storeroom for copies of obscene books. As a duly deputized private citizen, Sumner exemplified a moral imperative for his community, with or without a warrant. Dingwall and his vice president, and later that day Alfred Risdon, president of the American Anthropological Society and the book's publisher, were arrested and held for hours at the police station, despite the presence of their lawyer with bail money. Eleven appearances in magistrate's court and four in special sessions followed. Eventually, Dingwall and his associates were fined and given suspended sentences for selling what they knew to be an acknowledged literary classic. The vice society, however, knew it to be "lewd" and "off-color." For Sumner, its virulence was confirmed by a complaint he received from a man who caught his daughter reading a Dingwall-Rock circular describing it, bawdiness and all, as a Renaissance classic.

Dingwall was representative of the most serious offenders, those who had to be most harshly dealt with, for he thought he was right. After Customs and the Post Office had interdicted his proposed unexpurgated edition of the *Arabian Nights*, he approached the ACLU's National Council on Freedom from Censorship (NCFC), stating that he would renew his efforts to produce a complete text if that organization would make a test case of the issue. His business sense soon led him to withdraw from that plan.[100] At Christmastime of the same year in which Sumner raided his premises, he had advertised the stories, with their "undulating forms of fair dancing girls and the coquettish glances of the generous-hipped women of the harem" as "belonging in every library where a truly sophisticated culture dictates the choice of books."[101] There could be no leniency for such self-assured litterateurs who used moral standards antipathetic to those of Sumner and his constituents in attempting to determine which books (and ideas) to distribute and how.

Left to his own devices, Sumner would attack anyone dealing in erotica, regardless of professional reputation — or lack thereof. By the mid-1930s, he faced definite constraints, but while he could do so, he was glad to arrange for any respectable publisher or bookseller who handled indecent works the treatment he meted out to the joyously irreverent Mae West. She spent ten days in prison on Welfare Island, New York, in 1926 after he closed her play *Sex*.[102] Vice, as Wirt Hallam saw, was indeed virulent, a clear and present danger when so many Americans, of various tastes, ages, and social strata, might indulge.

Boston's Watch and Ward and the NYSSV

Looking north to Boston, Sumner may well have felt himself especially burdened in fighting vice in Gotham. The New England Watch and Ward Society had, since 1915, a gentleman's agreement with the Boston Booksellers Association.[103] A joint board consisting of three Watch and Ward and three booksellers' representatives read and passed on polite, as opposed to blatantly pornographic, fiction. In the case of a tie, a municipal court judge was consulted. The gentleman's agreement produced a list of books with passages thought indecent, which was circulated to all bookstores, with notice that the joint board presumed that certain passages "will be held by our courts to be in violation of the statutes." Retailers accepted the edicts; the few who did not found themselves in court, where they summarily lost. In 1927, the district attorney decided to censor books unilaterally. By 1930, the Watch and Ward had its own board to advise the authorities, although by that time their judgments and tactics had been significantly discredited, as we will now see.

Boston was hardly an impregnable fortress against modern infatuation with impurity in books, magazines, and plays. During the later 1920s and 1930s, the Watch and Ward lost prestige, as did preventive societies everywhere. For years it worked quietly, and therefore was tolerated. But in 1926, H. L. Mencken successfully goaded the Watch and Ward into a futile and embarrassing attempt to suppress the issue of the *American Mercury* that featured Herbert Asbury's famous memoir of Fanny Fewclothes, or "Hatrack," a very thin prostitute.[104] The incident virtually ended the career of Watch and Ward's secretary. Then occurred the "Boston Book Party" of 1927, when the superintendent of police and the district attorney, having been asked by booksellers confused about the outcome of the "Hatrack" case to give their opinions, declared various titles, including the best-selling *Elmer Gantry*, obscene, without consulting anyone. This abrogated the gentleman's agreement. With booksellers, police, clergy, and other citizens now branding additional titles as "bad," the list of books banned in Boston — more than sixty, and perhaps one hundred, including works by Faulkner, Hemingway, and H. G. Wells — made the city a laughing stock. In 1929, citizens embarrassed by the stiff-necked righteousness of the censors directed near universal contempt at the Watch and Ward for its prosecution of Dunster House, the owner of which had procured copies of *Lady Chatterley's Lover* for five responsible customers.

In Boston throughout the 1930s fewer lists of bad books were circulated to dealers, but the practice did continue, focusing on lending libraries. A late-1930s list included serious novels from mainstream publishers, such as James Farrell's *A World I Never Made* and John O'Hara's *Hope from Heaven*.[105] Besides issuing lists, the Watch and Ward's agents scouted bookstores and the various retail locations that rented books, not to entrap them into selling copies but to speak earnestly to the owners.[106] In 1934, for example, three conferences with the proprietor of the Arcade Book Shop (the third included the owner's "representative in the legislature") resulted not only in the removal of the erotic book that had precipitated the discussions, but also in the distributor's promise not to handle any novels from William Godwin Inc.[107] Literary critic Bernard De Voto's prediction regarding the future of literary censorship in Boston, made at the time of the Dunster House affair, was dramatized for effect, but was in part accurate: "Nor does the [proposed] amendment [to the state obscenity ordinance] change in any way the system of espionage, multiple censorship, and extra-legal coercion which so interferes with the distribution of books in Boston. Officially, our community continues to suspect literature. . . . One would not be so exasperated . . . if this passivity were not part of a vast current."[108]

The Boston blacklist, both during and after the period of the official gentleman's agreement, and the cooperative conferences the Watch and Ward was able to arrange, must have struck Sumner as enviably genteel alternatives to the tactics he had to employ. Even when borderline fiction or sexology was at issue, he often needed to issue unsolicited warnings to publishers, and to entrap booksellers, or let his chief investigative agent Bamberger do so. At the least, he had to have a copy of a book purchased and then have the police make a noisy arrest. What followed were newspaper headlines, time-consuming prosecutions, legal quibbles regarding search warrants and impoundment of books, and the enmity of the entire book trade and intellectual community. The Dunster House case aside, Boston's tactics usually meant less notoriety, less contemptuous newspaper reports and editorials, and less need for defending the society's work to its membership. But New York was emphatically not Boston.

First, New York was a premier publishing center, and the books and magazines flowed to outlets and consumers faster than an intransigent crusader like Sumner could staunch; until legal precedents forced him to do so (see Chapter 4), he did not prioritize his targets. He attacked gallantiana, sex pulps, and readers indiscriminately. Also, no publisher would let Sumner dictate the house's choices.

When Sumner had proposed doing so in 1922, with his Boston-like plan for a committee to judge controversial manuscripts before publishing, he was soundly defeated.[109] As Paul Boyer points out, New York publishers could not tolerate this kind of interference.[110] It would have meant wasted motion and lost revenues, whereas banning in Boston a book published elsewhere meant only free publicity. The borderline and underground publishers were also New York–based. Boston had no shortage of underground distributors;[111] however, their own middleman sources were in New York.[112] Contrasting the two areas in 1937, Henry N. Pringle, law-enforcement director of the International Reform Federation, wrote: "In all of New England no erotic magazine is published and no habitual publisher of erotic books resides there. Cross into New York and you find 26 of the 28 habitual publishers of erotica in the United States, and 270 of the 374 magazines. This fifth seeps southward and westward, poisoning the youth of the nation."[113] New York's Sam Roth, Jack Brussel, Alex Hillman, or Samuel Curl would have pressured their wholesale customers, who included many respectable retailers, to stand up to Sumner. In many instances, booksellers would demur, but they did have to question whether the pressure from Sumner was worse than losing their middlemen suppliers.

Second, Sumner had to deal with the avant-garde intelligentsia of Greenwich Village and Fifth Avenue, whose advocacy of free dissemination of ideas and modernist literature was similar to, if more acutely expressed than, that of erotica dealers. Poets, novelists, and their wealthy sponsors, although widely suspected as social radicals, communists, and "free lovers," were far from powerless. Finally, liberal interpretations of censorship laws emanated from New York lawyers, and surfaced in decisions rendered in the Second Circuit Court of New York State, sitting in lower Manhattan. In contrast, the Boston Brahmins presented a staunch conservative front against "literary excesses," although the growing indignation against the Watch and Ward's literary tastes shows the old order was severely weakened by the late 1920s even there. Anticensorship sentiment led to a liberalizing revision of the Massachusetts obscenity statute in 1930 despite opposition from the Watch and Ward and from the powerful Catholic opposition.[114]

Of all the leaders of preventive societies, John Saxton Sumner was closest to the center of obscenity trafficking: printing, distributing, retailing. He had to immerse himself fully in the East Coast's capital city of the furtive, persistent, resourceful pariah capitalists who made their living from the business of forbidden

books. Yet Sumner epitomized the success of the moralists of the preventive societies and was highly respected by his counterparts in Washington, Boston, Chicago, and Cincinnati. As long as organizations such as his were able to make
themselves and their opinions indispensable to the book trade, politicians, legal
experts, clergy, and public-spirited leaders of church and civic groups, he was
effective. The winds of change felt in the later 1920s and especially after the Crash
altered the priorities of each of the constituent groups mentioned above. The reading audience changed; the economics of the book trade shifted; First Amendment
advocates became more militant; immigrant groups, as they entered the middle
class in force, impressed their manners and mores indelibly into the fabric of
American life. Finally, the intensity of Americans' need for knowing about, and
entertaining themselves with, sex was impossible for any concerned moralists to
regulate, even one with Sumner's common sense and acuity — especially one with
his grave intransigence.

4 "Fifth Avenue Has No More Rights Than the Bowery"
Taste and Class in Obscenity Legislation

Raids engineered by John Sumner during 1935 led to the seizure and burning of $150,000 worth of erotic books and photographs, as well as the plates from which the books were printed.[1] In mid-March Police Commissioner Valentine announced that twenty-five thousand volumes, when burned in the steam-heated headquarters, would produce two days' supply of heat, saving sixty dollars on the department's coal bill.[2] Sumner made his first public appearance at this kind of event in November of that year and helped janitorial staff stoke up the fire as cameras flashed (Figure 23).[3] Reporters noted that among the volumes were finely bound works, including copies of the rare *Immortalia* (a one-hundred-dollar item), and many items priced from five dollars to twenty-five dollars.[4] Indeed, these sorts of book burnings were fairly common in the 1930s. Five years earlier, the Sanitation Department allowed the New York Society for the Suppression of Vice (NYSSV) the use of its incinerator to burn five thousand books and circulars. Among the books destroyed may well have been *Fanny Hill*, Schnitzler's *Hands Around*, *Lady Chatterley's Lover*, Kuprin's *Yama*, Huysmans's *Là-bas*, and *Ulysses*; the latter was perhaps part of the inventory of Sam Roth's Golden Hind Press.[5]

The books committed to the flames ranged from leather-bound deluxe editions, flagitious or gallant, to sex pulps, bibles, and readers. Sumner and the police could, if they chose, have fed their flames with the stock of upscale "Fifth Avenue" bookshops and large department stores as well as of "Bowery" outlets, that is, the general and secondhand book- and specialty stores, back-date magazine outlets, and lending libraries. Anthony Comstock had proclaimed that "Fifth Avenue has no more rights than the Bowery."[6] In 1887, Comstock raided a Fifth Avenue art gallery and seized 117 photographs of contemporary French paintings. Accused of not knowing art when he saw it, he explained that the confiscated material was "lewd French art — a foreign foe," and

Figure 23. Sumner (center, wearing hat) aiding workmen burn pornographic magazines, pamphlets, postcards, and lending-library sex-pulp novels in the furnace of police headquarters. He and two workmen are holding copies of *Jack Ketch the Hangman*. Although the magistrate dismissed his libel suit against this satirical tabloid, and the publisher countersued, Sumner and the police still had possession of the publication three years after its seizure. Source: Photo accompanying "Obscene Tomes Fed to Police Bonfire," *New York Journal American*, 27 Nov. 1935. Reproduced by permission of the Harry Ransom Humanities Research Center, University of Texas at Austin (JA Files).

charged his sophisticated accusers with believing that obscenity was excusable if it represented the work of artists with respectable reputations. For Comstock — the quintessential one-hundred-percenter — any representation of the nude body was a sin, and art was just as lewd as smutty postcards, even when it was sold and enjoyed by people of wealth and education. Sumner reiterated these convictions. In 1921, he declared that the NYSSV would never "hesitate to act because the publisher is a wealthy corporation or because the author has previously published one or more reputable books. . . . It is just exactly this [wrongly] desired partiality . . . which gives ground for the frequent assertion that there is one law for this class and another law for that class and which breeds contempt for the law in general and breeds anarchists." In 1930, he wrote: "Of course it is not the law of obscenity which offends our opponents. It is the fact that the law is enforced and that in its enforcement no distinction is made between the push-cart peddler and the Fifth Avenue publisher. Why should there be? It is probable that the latter does more harm than the former. His apparent respectability gives his product entree to any unguarded home whereas the push-cart product must be handled with a certain degree of stealth and secrecy." Under questioning by Morris Ernst in 1931, Sumner reasserted that this was "the correct position to take."[7] Ernst then accused Sumner, correctly, of not practicing the principle. One example of this — although Ernst did not focus on it — was that by that time confiscated copies of erotic books were less likely to be from Fifth Avenue shops than from the Bowery outlets and mail-order publishing houses owned by the booksellers, distributors, and publishers who did business with international bookleggers, peddlers of spicy novelties, and Canal Street printers. By examining the reasons for this, we see what kinds of power Sumner was still able to exert, and how he had to adapt to changing times so as to avoid losing his raison d'être. Those in the financially secure and respected circles of the book trade had increasingly found means to defend themselves against his enduring influence.

"Bad Taste in Books Is, in the End, Bad Business"

In 1923, John Sumner's influence was at its height. That year, he and the outraged State Supreme Court judge John Ford, who threatened to manhandle a bookseller for lending his sixteen-year-old daughter a copy of D. H. Lawrence's *Women in Love*, proposed a "clean books" amendment to the New York State obscenity statute.[8] Ford, who three years later published *Criminal Obscenity: A Plea for Its Suppression*, defined unlawful books as those that appeared sympathetic to hedonism, particularly through stories about premarital sex, "inversion," or rejection of religious doctrine concerning the carnal instincts. His amended statute would prohibit expert testimony, and allow the prosecution to focus on any part of the indicted book.

Also in 1923, Sumner was able to convince some trade personnel, though not the National Association of Book Publishers (NABP), to support another proposal for cleaning up publishing: a committee to prejudge controversial manuscripts, headed by a right-thinking commissioner. Professional baseball had subjected itself to the iron hand of an external commissioner after the infiltration of the sport by gambling racketeers led to the 1919 Black Sox scandal. Sumner now wanted to take on a similar role for the book trade. He had reason to believe he could attain such status. Some publishers had been informally submitting manuscripts to him for his imprimatur; Broadway producers were known to have done likewise with some of their scripts. The value of such arrangements for Sumner was that if after a negative judgment the book were published or the show put on, conviction of producer, bookseller, or publisher would be easier than if the offenders had not been "warned." Such a commissioner could "divide those acting in good faith and those acting in bad faith."[9]

The clean books campaign enlisted a "league" of fighters for conventional mores — lawyers, legislators, clergy, the Boy and Girl Scouts, the Salvation Army, Fordham University. Members of these groups joined Ford, Sumner, Rabbi Stephen Wise, Reverend Anson P. Atterbury, and attorney Martin Conboy (who later presented the government's appellate case against *Ulysses*). The NABP could not countenance censorship, but the league's stature convinced them that Ford and Sumner were right in one respect: certain people from downtown were giving the book trade a bad name. If a mercenary group of publishers and booksellers was using sales tactics that blurred the boundary between decent and taboo experience, then this element, for the good of the industry itself, must be cut loose from the healthy body and taught not to expect protection.[10] The national association took a stern look at its own ranks and warned "some publishers" that they were joining other entrepreneurs of popular entertainment — managers of movie and burlesque theaters, dance halls, saloons, and amusement parks — in pandering to obscenity.[11] They pointed to two distinct practices: suggestive advertising and the distribution of texts that, whatever their literary value, stimulated interest because of their sexual content. One editorial in *Publishers Weekly*, another representative of the respectable mainstream in publishing, frankly stated that "many book publishers have felt so keenly the discredit on the profession by [prurient] selling methods that they have taken the position that . . . to line themselves with the opposition to [current censorship proposals] would be to bring false interpretation on their real attitude toward objectionable books." It moved on from selling methods to the merchandise itself: "A good motto . . . in dealing with debatable books, would be

'When in doubt, throw them out.' And throw out, too, those silly books and borderline magazines which avoid trouble-making sentences but whose intent is never
in doubt." [12] Another issue put the admonitions in anonymous doggerel:

> Another guy who seems to be
> On his way to the rocks
> Is the one who keeps on marketing
> His Balzacs and de Kocks.
> His Cabells and his Dreisers,
> Boccaccios and Symonds,
> Which, tho they're hardly decent
> Are as saleable as di'monds.
> But if he doesn't clean his house
> There isn't any doubt
> That the Comstocks'll get him
> If he doesn't cut it out.
> Stop the sale of shady stuff
> Or you all will get discredited
> And we'll never have a chance to buy
> A classic that's not "edited." [13]

Just which booksellers and publishers did *Publishers Weekly* feel might bring
"discredit" on everyone? Perhaps it meant newcomers such as Horace Liveright
and Thomas Seltzer. Older, established colleagues looked askance at the former's
successes with "privately printed," "limited" editions of *The Satyricon*, Louÿs's
Aphrodite, George Moore's works, and James Huneker's *Painted Veils*, a novel of
four women's love lives in turn-of-the-century New York. Neither the Authors
League nor the NABP backed Liveright in his early campaign against the Clean
Books Bill,[14] although later they vociferously fought its revised versions. Thomas
Seltzer had issued Judge Ford's bête noire, *Women in Love*, privately in 1920,
winning Lawrence's respect for being the first to dare issue a novel from the
maligned author of *The Rainbow*, which had been suppressed in Britain as obscene
in 1915. Amy Lowell, who knew well the conservative tastes of established literary
publishers, tried to warn Lawrence off Seltzer when she learned that he was issuing
the *Tortoise* poems as a separate volume. In them, Lawrence had expressed a

detailed interest in how the venerable, inelegant turtles handled the male-female dynamic. Lowell said, "Mr. Seltzer is getting a name for himself as rather an erotic publisher," and told Lawrence that if he wished to win an American audience, he would "not want to stress [his] sexual side to a public incapable of understanding it."[15] Perceptive about how literary reputations were made in America and deeply concerned about Lawrence's success, she did not want his chances ruined by the fear and misunderstanding that contempt for reticence about private, intimate matters occasioned. Her opinion, given in March 1922, probably echoed that of respected literati such as Henry Seidel Canby and John Farrar, as well as the established older generation of Boston and New York publishers.[16] This was just four months before Sumner raided Seltzer for *Women in Love*, *A Young Girl's Diary*, and *Casanova's Homecoming*. To at least some people of letters, then, as to spokespeople for the publishing industry, those responsible for what authorities alleged to be smut included not only those "who handle in a subterranean way books that are admittedly obscene,"[17] but also those whom we consider today to be pioneer champions of modernist writers. Seltzer was angry at Lowell when Lawrence relayed her opinion to him.[18] He knew he was risking Sumner's contempt; to have one of Lawrence's literary supporters think his business improper must have seemed ungrateful and elitist.

Just as Amy Lowell wanted D. H. Lawrence to establish for himself a positive impression among American readers as a novelist and not as one of the "younger school" whose shocking eroticism placed them in a special class and limited their appeal, *Publishers Weekly* wanted to warn book distributors not to give the "Comstocks" a chance to hinder new authors' efforts to reach as wide an audience as possible. What *Publishers Weekly* did not seem to recognize was that this method of fighting the moralists meant a weak commitment to newly emerging trends in sexual explicitness, and therefore to free speech in general. Modern authors such as Lawrence were victims of this line of thought, as were publishers such as Thomas Seltzer. It was infuriating to both to witness people in the publishing and bookselling trade being warned off important books so that they would be freer to circulate all the other books that did not allude to human sexuality. It amounted to a cash-driven sacrifice of whatever might be labeled "shady stuff." Perhaps *Publishers Weekly*'s main concern was that a bookseller called to answer obscenity charges in court should be able to declare his business free from prurient selling methods. However, the journal did not address the knotty problem of how to distinguish between "valueless" smut and "serious" literature. It would take liberal lawyers another decade to work that out as best they could. Advertising erotica without arousing prurient interest was an even thornier proposition. Meanwhile, regarding the Clean Books Bill, it was Senator Jimmy Walker who saved the day. His floor generalship as minority whip, and possibly his plainly worded speech, led to its defeat.[19] His debunking comment on the floor of the legislature is still remembered: "Why all this talk about Womanhood? I have never yet heard of a girl being ruined by a book."[20]

Magazine and newspaper publishers did more than the NABP to fight the Clean Books Bill. Some bookmen, notably George Putnam, were very critical of their organization. Putnam resigned from the association's Censorship Committee, because he thought he owed it to his authors and his counterparts in the magazine and newspaper business to do so.[21] Bad taste may be bad business, but as Theodore Dreiser and a few delegates at the 1923 convention of the American Booksellers Association articulated, serious publishers of modern works could not afford to have authors or customers see them as subservient to the censors.[22]

Still, even some well-known authors joined the association in lending credibility to the criticisms by Ford and Sumner. Local-color writers Hamlin Garland and Mary Austin saw a clear and present danger: the bastardization of the canon of "real" American literature, which their generation had struggled to legitimate, by a fascination with the "merely" erotic. Garland deplored the growth of Manhattan ("a city of aliens") as a publishing center. Austin, especially influential in the Southwest, saw "Anglo-American" romantic literature polluted by the "peasant" sex obsessions of writers from eastern Europe, especially "the Russian [and] the Jew."[23] Many figures in the literary establishment circled the wagons around the Fifth Avenue booksellers and long-established, sacrosanct publishers. They made little or no distinction of shadowy, foreign hack writers, itinerant peddlers of pornography, and younger publishers of modernist writers whose reputations were already established in Europe. Setting aside any concern for free speech in their zeal to protect "America," and setting aside any interest in innovative writing in their eagerness to protect "Literature," they played right into Sumner's hands.

From the beginning, Alfred Knopf engaged in a complicated dance to avoid being classed with those shadowy others. His strategy was not to challenge the censors, but to cooperate with them. In 1915, his first year of operation, he withdrew Przybyszewski's *Homo Sapiens* (translated, as it happened, by Thomas Seltzer) at

Sumner's insistence, stating that he "did not deign to satisfy the prurient demand which had been created."[24] This was an excellent business decision and one factor in his establishing the solid footing that Seltzer and Liveright lacked. The firm likewise withdrew its offer to publish Radclyffe Hall's *The Well of Loneliness* in 1928 when it found that advance orders were not from "the better type of book-sellers, but rather from dealers who expect a sensational demand for the book from people who expect something very salacious."[25] An obscenity case would be hard to win. Even if no one would label the Knopfs (Alfred and his wife, Blanche) as panders, the bad taste of the middlemen who would get the books to the public was a different matter. The Knopfs wanted no part of that tribe.

Publishers were aware that even liberal thinkers might show more deference to the smut hunter than sympathy for the erotic bookseller. The attitude of the *New York Times* was an example. Commenting on the police incineration of confiscated erotica in 1935, the editor reminded his readers that the Germans, and other "police states of Europe," ruthlessly suppressed free speech by burning books and im-prisoning dissenters; our own democratic system burned books not because they criticized the government, but to guard "public morals" from smutmongers.[26] The editor seemed to have forgotten that the Nazis also justified what they did in the name of public morals, and not to have seen it ironic that novelists and sexologists were significant victims of both German and New York book burnings.

The *Times* attitude toward "gutter literature" was even more revealing. Al-though the paper was often critical of Sumner's inability to distinguish serious literature from obvious smut, it would not give what community consensus as-sumed to be prurient trash the stature of speech at all. In 1929, the *Times* rejected not only Roth's advertising, but also that of Harcourt Brace, because of a book's title: *Kept Woman.*[27] The decision was prudent. If articulate advocates for purity, speaking in the name of a national moral consensus, could inflame citizens' doubts about sexual explicitness and its effect on young adult conduct, and find vigorous support from law-enforcement officials and politicians, a newspaper with a grave awareness of its stature in the community would consider carefully its respon-sibilities to represent and support that national consensus, even if this meant disap-pointing well-meaning advertisers.

Publishers Weekly's editorial position on erotic books suggests that the jour-nal felt as the *Times*'s staff did, and would have approved of the Knopfs' decision to abandon their plans for *The Well of Loneliness*. It assumed that responsible professionals knew, as venal bookmen and the crusading preventive societies did not, the distinction between fine literature and smut, and could be expected to shun those dark lanes and back alleys in the literary landscape where one ventured solely in search of ill-gotten gains. "If the circulating library, whose loaning system started this new discussion [the Clean Books Bill], is pushing this type of book regardless of the type of customer, its action would be recognized as culpable by any self-respecting bookseller. . . . If a bookseller has no way to increase sales except to use the whispered suggestion, he had better go into an occupation where his business standards will not do the public so much harm." [28]

Most members of the book trade could not afford to carry the weight of such an accusation. The respectable majority of the profession needed the myth of a clear, spatially marked dichotomy between the outlet for banned books (New York's Bowery and Fourth Avenue, Arch Street in Philadelphia, South Dearborn in Chicago, the Back Bay in Boston), and the respectable establishment (Fifth and Madison Avenues in New York, Chestnut Street in Philadelphia, Wabash Avenue in Chicago, South Street in Cambridge). Booksellers cultivated reputations for catering to those interested in antiquarianism, sporting books, scientific specialties, fine printing, or modern first editions, and not "porno." In fact, some well-heeled customers for some of these subjects were discreetly interested in curiosa and erotica, and their booksellers found it well worth their while to respond to their suggestions. The protective coloration made it a safe venture. Bowery booksellers were usually without it, and thus were subject to the moral indignation of clerical and lay moralists, and through them, of the community at large. They would find themselves subjected to serious business and personal risk: police raids instigated by undercover agents who had duplicitously gained their confidence; improper use of the search warrant during those raids; the double jeopardy of unexpected prison sentences for offenses previously punished by fines; the confiscation of stock, which might be kept by the police indefinitely or even publicly burned. Most booksellers had no stomach for such contingencies. The Bowery–Fifth Avenue dichotomy may have worked well for those who did, and who carried a wide variety of porno in their back rooms: reputed scarcity of outlets, and the aura of subversiveness, could have been good for their business. In the eyes of their disdainful colleagues, they were welcome to the troubles they courted.

For the Fifth Avenue bookman, bona fide credentials for publishing and reading "questionable books" were desired. The section of the city in which the bookshop was located, the shop's appearance, and customers' financial status, literary judgment about classical or modern writers, personal demeanor, and social background all had their place in creating a Fifth Avenue image or style that was good for business and for collecting erotica safely. People interested in sexually explicit "good literature" could pretend that they did not have prurient motives, and "proper" publishers and booksellers could deny using "whispered suggestion." This claim gained credence because upscale shops did not get involved with the readers and bibles. If booksellers recommended Cabell, Bodenheim, or Lawrence to customers, the sellers' whispers could concern the fact that such books might embarrass ladies, or that conservatives had denounced them. However, even when publishers' sales pitches were innocuous, and focused on literary value, curiosity always surrounded a taboo subject. Judge Learned Hand appears to have recognized the more complex reality, when he found Esar Levine guilty of pandering to prurience with the circulars for his Panurge Press books. He refused to admit into evidence the Panurge Press mailing list, with its "professors," "army officers," and "physicians." "Even respectable persons may have a taste for salacity," he wrote.[29]

The distinction between art and obscenity may have been clear to New York booksellers, but this clarity was mostly a matter of marketing convenience. An interesting example of the subjectivity of such criteria is that John Sumner was compelled by the mid-1930s to make similar distinctions. In 1936, he was forced to state, under cross-examination, that he found nude paintings and sculpture were often art, but that nude photographs were often lewd—because they were realistic, not "idealized," and presumably because they were found in magazines, newsstands, Bowery bookstores, and lower-class homes, not in centers of culture. The *World Telegram*, which six years earlier (as the *Telegram*) had run an excellent series of articles by Joseph Lilly exposing Sumner's extralegal tactics in book censorship, now jeered at the vice crusader's "fine distinctions between lewdness and purity."[30] Established booksellers may have shared the *Telegram*'s derision, but they continued to make a similar distinction between the "art" of what the uptown bookshops sold to their clientele and the "obscenity" of what was purveyed on Fourth Avenue and other secondhand shops with small back rooms.

The distinction was practical and comfortable. But by the 1920s so much modernist writing was sexually frank, and tolerances for it varied so widely, that even respectable dealers could cross a line without realizing it. This is what happened to the unfortunate individual who lent *Women in Love* to Judge John Ford's daughter. Ford identified him as "a local bookseller with whom my family has traded for many years." He had recommended the novel to Miss Ford, said the judge, "as a highly interesting love story. Upon discovering a vile passage in it, she showed it to her mother, who came running to me in high perturbation." Advice such as *Publishers Weekly*'s about keeping out of trouble by avoiding "whispered suggestion" would not have helped in this case. Had Ford's bookseller been given to whispering about erotica, he most likely would not have had the judge for a client, and in any event he would not have hinted that Lawrence was "hot stuff" to Ford's daughter; most likely he did not mean to imply any such thing. The Fifth Avenue–Bowery contrast was merely a public relations convenience, for which *Publishers Weekly* risked no charges of class snobbery. But the journal would hardly want to make lists of "safe" and "objectionable" books. Had it done so, it might have been seen as playing into the hands of the Philistines. So booksellers had to resort to discretion, and then keep their fingers crossed.

The Dirty Underside of the Publishing Business

Young avant-garde publishers and booksellers who stocked iconoclastic modern writing risked pariah status, but they were also capable of combating the moralists. The efforts of a Seltzer, Liveright, Covici, or Albert and Charles Boni to introduce American readers to European literature were admired by many literary reviewers, booksellers, and the reading community. Also, their finances, at least until legal fees came due, were considerable enough to command respect. When publishers who were convinced that their books had literary value engaged Sumner in legal action, he almost always lost. Examples include Seltzer (*Women in Love, Casanova's Homecoming, A Young Girl's Diary*, in 1922), Liveright (*Satyricon*, 1922; *Replenishing Jessica*, 1928), Covici-Friede (*The Well of Loneliness*, 1929), Simon and Schuster (*Casanova's Homecoming*, 1931), Random House (*Ulysses*, 1933), and Vanguard (*Female*, 1933).[31] A very real additional danger for Sumner was that the exonerated publishers could, and sometimes did, sue the NYSSV. Even if they were unsuccessful, the society could ill afford the legal fees. When the judge ruled in favor of Seltzer in 1922, he let it be known that the NYSSV was liable for countersuits, and Seltzer sued for false arrest. His lawyer hoped aggrieved publishers would "smother the Society with damage suits."[32] In addition, publishers occasionally offered, either in advance of publication or upon a bookseller's arrest, to pay legal expenses accrued while he or she was defending certain controversial titles. This ensured confrontations that might be damaging both financially and ideologically for the antivice societies.

Established bookshops, as well as publishers of books of acknowledged value, could embarrass the authorities. The trial of James A. Delacey, the proprietor of a Harvard Square bookshop, Dunster House, on charges of selling a copy of *Lady Chatterley's Lover*, dominated the headlines of Boston dailies in December 1929. Delacey had procured five copies of the novel from Samuel Roth meant for "three Harvard professors, a lawyer, and a book collector." How the Watch and Ward got wind of this is unclear; they may have heard rumors that this bookstore, no matter how highly reputed by professors (or possibly because it was so reputed, and thus a safe haven), had a back-room stock of erotica. Be that as it may, Delacey purchased an additional, secondhand copy of the novel from a Watch and Ward "plant"; this was sold to the society's undercover man, John Slaymaker. The trial was attended by "fashionably-gowned society women, a few members of the Harvard faculty, some of the students, and groups of the so-called intelligentsia."[33] Lawyers, jurists, and writers joined in deploring the society's presumption and extralegal zeal. Headlines read "Lash Watch and Ward at Book Trial," "Tactics Despicable," "Bookseller Says Leading Men Bought Lawrence Book," and "[District Attorney] Twits Watch and Ward."[34] Several faculty members attested to Delacey's reputation, including Robert Hillyer, whom the district attorney embarrassed when he extended his testimonial to include Lawrence. The professor was asked if *Chatterley* might possibly be used "in a course for young people." "I wouldn't even mention it in my class" was the reply.[35] However, the district attorney was much more agitated by the Watch and Ward's daring "to go into a bookstore of good repute and induce and procure the commission of a crime." The next time it happened, he thundered, the organization would themselves be on trial.[36]

Even when works of literary merit were at issue, moral entrepreneurs had much more success when the defendants were ill-reputed or obscure printers and publishers of pirated, banned erotica, bookleggers who supplied it, or those who also displayed prurient circulars and brochures for both borderline and officially proscribed materials. Sumner's raid on Samuel Roth's Golden Hind storeroom produced copies of other works of literary merit in addition to *Chatterley* and *Ulysses*, but no one came to Roth's defense. Middlemen such as Roth were, in the words of the scholar and publisher Temple Scott, Thomas Seltzer's onetime partner, the mere "colporteurs who furnish literary aphrodisiacs to debilitated gallants, and supply the textbooks for our modern Paphian sanctuaries of Artemis [whorehouses]."[37] Occasionally in the 1920s, and throughout the 1930s, their embarrassments peppered the pages of the New York dailies or the news-of-the-trade columns of *Publishers Weekly*. Sumner, having attained a search warrant from a magistrate who shared his view that a particular volume was obscene, searched the premises of people such as John Ruze (a stationery store owner who sold a "so-called medical work"); Hyman Mellstein, Harry Mishkin, and Nathan Pomerantz (arrested with Esar Levine for printing *My Life*); Isadore Lhevinne (entrapped by Bamberger at his publisher's office into selling a copy of his "indecent" novel); Moe Berg and Irving Plotkin (stationery store owners who lent copies of D. H. Clark's *Female*); the Loewinger brothers (printers of underground items such as *Anecdota Americana* and Roth's pirated edition of *Ulysses*); Earl B. Marks (for selling Louÿs's *Aphrodite*); the Nussbaum brothers and Alexander Costelito (partners in a scheme to send blatant pornography through the mails); and Benjamin Reisberg and David Brotman (distributors of readers and bibles).[38] Getting impounded volumes returned, which was often not possible even in the event of an acquittal, would involve filing an expensive civil suit, furthering public impression that the store, publishing house, or printing establishment was sleazy. The practical option was to plead guilty and get off with a fine.[39] That of course meant diminished public trust, already weakened in any event by the raid.

Those arrested and ordered to stand trial might be forced out of business by legal fees and fines. Expenses entailed in fighting Sumner in 1922 were one cause of Thomas Seltzer's bankruptcy just a few years later; unless a bookseller's financial resources were strong, that could happen to him or her even more quickly. Furthermore, if he or she had previous brushes with obscenity law, imprisonment was possible. This was the case with Christian Gerhardt. Police had caught him selling *My Life* in 1925, at which time they impounded one hundred copies of the book and more than one thousand "indecent photos."[40] In 1930, Sumner successfully prosecuted Gerhardt for obscenity on the basis of his having in his possession, when approached by a "detective disguised as a Bohemian," as the *New York Sun* put it, a flyer for Clement Wood's short-story collection *Flesh* daringly illustrated with a bare-breasted woman who had a bit of pubic hair showing (Figure 24). The stories described a variety of alternate styles of sexual gratification. The *Sun*'s coverage seems intended to give its breakfasting or straphanging readers a chuckle

Figure 24. Sample illustration (by Herbert E. Fouts) from Clement Wood's *Flesh and Other Stories* (New York: privately printed, 1929), reproduced for a four-page flyer advertising the edition. The book sold for twelve dollars and fifty cents, "35% discount to the trade." The flyer carries an order form from "Alex L. Hillman, Publisher." When John Sumner found a copy of this flyer on Christian Gerhardt's premises in 1930, he had him sentenced to six months in the penitentiary.

or snort at the bookseller's expense: "The book had been advertised in a four-page circular sent out to a chosen few of Village intelligentsia, which depicted the book as spicy stuff and which contained an illustration by Herbert E. Fouts not precisely of the kind which would look well in Sunday School literature. . . . Det. Wittenberg testified that Mr. Gerhardt . . . had promised to obtain for him another equally racy work entitled 'The Confessions of a Doctor.' " Gerhardt had accepted twelve dollars and fifty cents in advance for the book.[41] He was given six months in the penitentiary for "possessing obscene literature," though he was soon released on appeal, possibly because he was sixty-four years old.[42] He had shown "bad faith," and was to be taught a lesson.

There were other examples of the pariah capitalist's political vulnerability and weak capital. After the Vanguard Press successfully defended D. H. Clark's *Female* before a Manhattan magistrate, Sumner prosecuted the aforementioned Moe Berg, who had the book in his lending library. The work was "obscene, lewd, lascivious, and disgusting and nothing more, and intended to be so for mercenary purposes";[43] therefore, it was fair game to have it reviewed in as many jurisdictions as necessary until Sumner found a judge whose views mirrored his own. The NYSSV's lesson for Berg was that a bookseller had no reason to believe a book might be legal simply because it had been sanctioned by a single (too liberal) judge.[44]

A final example highlights the problems booksellers operating on the edge of insolvency faced when they had to answer for distributing obscenity. An aspiring actor and writer, Charles Chapet had been selling books for three years. His tiny shop on West 23rd Street, only a block from the NYSSV headquarters, had often been visited by Sumner himself, requesting specific titles. According to his account, Chapet habitually rejected the offers from peddlers to fix him up with banned erotica from which he could make large profits; buy for two dollars, sell for fifteen, they said. One day in July 1934, however, having taken in only thirty-five cents and being behind in his rent, he procured a copy of *White Stains* — either a set of pornographic short stories to which was appended a notoriously explicit manual on how to make love, or another book of the same title, a much sought-after collection of erotic verses by the iconoclastic mystic Edward Alexander (he preferred "Aleister") Crowley. The book was for a man who had tempted him with an offer of fifteen dollars for "spicy stuff." That customer turned out to be a NYSSV agent (probably Bamberger). Convicted, Chapet could not pay the one-hundred-dollar fine and had to spend twenty days in jail.[45] This is of course only the bookseller's side of the story; Sumner's ledgers record that he confiscated two books and ten readers, an indication in any event of the smallness of Chapet's store and his under-the-counter stock. In either case, circumstances had reduced Chapet to being a pawn in the "dirty books" game, as erotica peddlers and their prosecutors played it. With no resources or status in either community, his role was that of a sucker.

In one rare instance, in 1932, a high-spirited and irascible maverick bookseller won a sweet, momentary revenge for himself and his colleagues, shattering Sumner's self-possession, to the delight (on this occasion) of his West 23rd Street colleagues. Bernard Guibert Guerney, translator of Kuprin's *Yama* (an important Russian novel about prostitution) was the mustachioed, brawny owner of the Blue Faun Book Shop. His presence was emphatically a mixed blessing to his colleagues. According to one fellow bookseller, a large sign in Guerney's window read "Little Mags and Monthly Rags."[46] This referred to the strictly banned, small-format, under-the-counter pornographic readers and Tijuana bibles, and to his own satiric avant-garde tabloid-style newspaper, *Jack Ketch the Hangman* (subtitle: "What America Needs Is a Good Swift Kick in the Pants").[47] It was also a way of daring anyone — Sumner and his fellow bluenoses, or anyone of taste and refinement, especially Guerney's neighboring booksellers — to take offense at the public reference to sanitary napkins. It was Guerney who irritated Sumner with a *Jack Ketch* cartoon headed "John S. Smutrat: Vicesnoopia Filtheatia" (Figure 20). Sumner thought it enough of a likeness to file a criminal libel suit. He also had the police confiscate the entire print run of the magazine. But the magistrate refused to indict, and Guerney gleefully turned the tables, suing Sumner for having incited the magazine's distributor to breach his contract. The *World Telegram*, knowing the liberal segment of its readership would be amused, put feature writer A. J. Liebling on the story. He obviously relished the assignment.[48] When *Publishers Weekly* belatedly reported the incident, the iconoclastic Guerney, showing the spirit in which he had earlier founded the "To Hell With 23rd St. Association," took the occasion to upbraid "this flea-circus of a trade" for not standing up for themselves and their colleagues:

if booksellers would show a little "guts" when harassed by purity racketeers, instead of rolling over with their paws in the air and their tails dutifully tucked between their legs, the fight against censorship might really make headway.[49]

Belittling Sumner as a well-deflated prude was good sport. However, as Guerney intimated, eradicating his power would have required a united stand by the book trade against the much more widespread equation of the existence of sexually explicit books with publishers' venal exploitation of their readers' prurient furtiveness. That never happened. Various well-established segments of the trade worried about losing their reputation, and their clientele, if they protested too much against what seemed the conventional wisdom. Further, the members and board of directors of the NYSSV included powerful and respected New Yorkers, some in banking and finance; the older publishers — Doubleday, Doran, Scribner — knew them and probably either feared their influence or shared their civic-minded stance. Meanwhile, the Bowery segment of the book trade, whose exploitation of prurience was sometimes all too clear, felt legally and financially vulnerable. In addition, without the censor to publicize the "smut," what would happen to their sales? Sumner persisted with his searches and seizures at shops and lending libraries, and his closings of "indecent [Broadway and burlesque] shows." In the end, he kept the copies of Guerney's *Jack Ketch* he had taken for three years, and then tossed the lot into the police furnaces, lawsuit or no lawsuit (Figure 23).

High-Hat Booksellers and Erotica

The distribution of "shady stuff" was by no means exclusive to threadbare, recently established, ideologically radical, or unscrupulous booksellers. This is why it is important to contrast the public censoriousness toward Esar Levine, Samuel Roth, Ben Rebhuhn, Christian Gerhardt, and their colleagues to the deferential treatment given by journalists, academics, the publishing world, and even legal authorities to upscale, uptown literary bookshops such as the Argus (in Chicago) and the Gotham Book Mart (in New York). One glaring example occurred in the pages of *Publishers Weekly* in 1940, where cordial accounts of the Gotham's twentieth anniversary and Ben Abramson's relocated Argus contrasted with an unsympathetic account of the failure of Ben Rebhuhn's appeals of his, his wife's, and his nephew's obscenity convictions: the men were heavily fined and sentenced to two years' imprisonment.[50] In fact, some of the most reputable establishments were, according to Gershon Legman, "the main outlets for erotica."[51] No one was more in the know on behalf of his best customers than an affluent bookseller highly respected in the trade for his scholarship and open checkbook.

The best example is the most prestigious book dealer of the era, A. S. W. Rosenbach. As his biographers state, he "never had sold and would not sell pornography,"[52] although he did have it on hand, as a result of having purchased private libraries over the years. In 1951, near the end of the great bookseller's career, the Kinsey Institute Library was able to enrich its holdings greatly with some of this material, purchased by Rosenbach as part of a bibliophile's library in 1922 and kept in storage for thirty years.[53] In 1928 — in the United States, no less — Rosenbach was able to procure two copies of the "almost impossible to obtain" *Lady Chatterley's Lover*, one for the affluent collector of Renaissance literature William A. Clark, Jr., who could not find a copy in Paris, and one for himself.[54] In the previous year, he purchased fine editions of the *Decameron*, the *Heptameron*, and Rabelais's works,[55] and in 1933 he offered for sale the manuscripts of Beardsley's *Under the Hill* and Wilde's *Salomé* (the latter the original, from the library of Pierre Louÿs).[56] In 1928, Frank Harris, desperate for cash after his misadventures with the censored and pirated *My Life and Loves*, approached Rosenbach with an offer to sell two letters of Lord Alfred Douglas that purported, "in the crudest words," as Harris put it, to describe "what Oscar did to him" and to deny emphatically that he was a "sodomite." When Clark expressed interest in these letters, Rosenbach was able to get Harris to scale down his asking price considerably.[57]

Harry F. Marks was another uptown antiquarian dealer, known for sporting books and fine bindings; he first established his reputation, at 187 Broadway, with a large display of Dickensiana in 1923. Four years later, he negotiated the sale of Lord Byron's writing desk and bought a collection of Lincoln's letters.[58] Despite his access to some notorious erotica and curiosa — listed in several of his catalogs (Figure 25) — he was never arrested. In 1928, Marks contacted D. H. Lawrence, reporting the pirated editions he had seen of *Lady Chatterley's Lover* and requesting that Lawrence himself send him fifty copies of the legitimate first edition (he had not yet paid for a previously received six, Lawrence averred). "I don't trust Marks. . . . [American booksellers] take advantage of the Customs suppression not to pay for what they get."[59] What he did receive, Marks would have been able to sell at a handsome profit. His clientele was high-hat: affluent, sophisticated, and as eminently respectable. His sporting books attracted a nearly all-male readership; no better market existed for attractively printed, limited-edition erotica.[60]

Ben Abramson, of Chicago's Argus Book Shop, frequently issued extensive catalogs full of the most erotically oriented material. With his attractively printed,

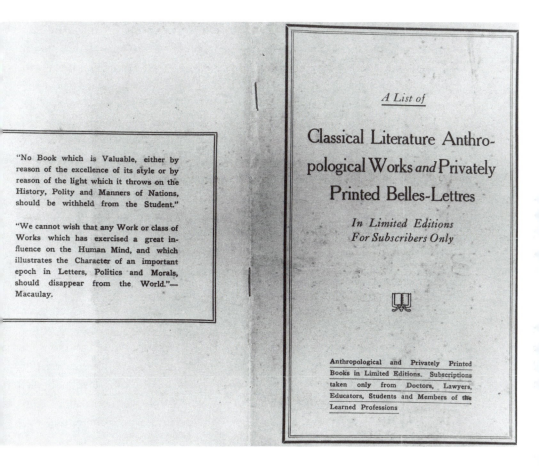

Figure 25. Catalog issued in 1923 by Harry F. Marks from his store at 187 Broadway. Listings include the unexpurgated *Arabian Nights*, *The Merry Order of St. Bridget*, *Opus Sadicum*, Stekel's books on homosexuality, Lind's on androgyny, and Louÿs's *Aphrodite*. These are all titles John Sumner interdicted, although not from Marks, with whom the NYSSV secretary may have had a special agreement.

unexpurgated "Nottingham edition" of *Lady Chatterley's Lover*, he joined Samuel Roth in supplying this famous erotic work to the prurient and to those simply curious, in defiance of Customs strictures (and of the Lawrence estate). Catalogs such as *Sixty-Six Sex Books* and *Ninety-Nine Unusual Books* featured borderline materials. Other lists, typewritten or multigraphed, included *Dialogues of Luisa*

Sigea, The Plague of Lust, Child Love, Fanny Hill, and more banned titles.[61] Abramson's daughter recalled that "everyone in Chicago who had anything to do with books knew that Ben sold pornography. He used to tell people that it was the pornography that paid for my private school education."[62] For most of his career, Abramson was based in Chicago, but from 1944 to 1953 he had a shop in New York.[63] In 1947, Sumner filed indecent literature charges against him, but astonished the presiding magistrate by requesting they be dropped. Abramson "had been very cooperative, . . . promis[ing] never to engage in the sale of indecent literature and pictures again and giv[ing] police permission to destroy everything of that nature in his shop."[64] In this case at least — and the Sumner of 1947 was not the Sumner of 1930 — Fifth Avenue had a great many more rights than the Bowery.

It is possible that the back room of Dunster House in Cambridge contained a variety of erotica, which Watch and Ward may have known, but did not mention during its prosecution of James Delacey for selling *Lady Chatterley's Lover*. The historian Francis Russell, a Harvard student in the late 1920s, wrote a sober, informative memoir many years later in which he stated that he saw, in a store near the campus that he calls "The Kelmscott," copies of Beardsley and de Sade, erotic prints, books on flagellation and homosexuality, and "poorly printed accounts of nearly every conceivable perversion." These items, he reported, were extremely expensive, purchased by prominent Bostonians, and a chief reason that the bookshop was able to keep open. Russell states that the "gentleman bookseller" who owned the Kelmscott became a "cause célèbre" when he procured copies of *Chatterley* and was arrested by a Watch and Ward agent.[65]

Sumner kept his ears and eyes trained on the Gotham Book Mart, but not because the store specialized in erotica. Just as younger publishers such as Thomas Seltzer, Horace Liveright, and the Boni brothers published avant-garde European writers in America, the Gotham brought them to the attention of New Yorkers by carrying as wide a range of their work as possible, especially including the little magazines they wrote for. Expatriate American poets and novelists made it a point to visit Frances Steloff when they returned to the United States; her kindness to them and her respect for their accomplishments is well known. Since the sexual frankness of these writers, and their American contemporaries, was integral to their work, the Gotham would have been a bookstore in which readers could find daring and intelligently conceived erotic materials and still exhibit respectable tastes. Gershon Legman states that the pioneering collection of bawdy humor *Anecdota*

Americana was first issued from there in 1927 (when David Moss was coowner), with a title page falsely identifying the date of publication.[66] David Moss, whom Steloff had made her business partner in 1920 and married in 1923, was a careful scholar rather than an ebullient rebel. However, he knew the market and convinced Steloff that good customers who wanted erotic material would get it somewhere (possibly against their better judgment) if not at the Gotham. *The Adventures of Hsi Men Ching* (sometimes referred to as *Chin P'ing Mei*), for which Sumner prosecuted Steloff in 1931 (her marriage and partnership with Moss had both ended in 1930), may have been a Moss publishing venture. Martin Kamin, Moss's friend, colleague, and eventual business partner, filed copyright for this title, as he did for *From a Turkish Harem*, *The Chinese Decameron*, *How the World Weds*, *Arabian Droll Stories*, and *Mademoiselle de Maupin*, probably all also stocked by Moss and Steloff.[67] The last of these was illustrated by Clara Tice, the so-called "bad girl of American art."[68] A friend of the editor and publicist Guido Bruno, the journalist Frank Crowninshield, and the poets Edna St. Vincent Millay and Mina Loy, she was a presence in the Greenwich Village of the 1910s and 1920s. Tice's skilled, playful paintings and line drawings, some hand-colored, often showed smiling naked or near-naked women whose pudenda were visible. Sumner told Steloff that he particularly disliked her work (Figures 15, 26).[69] So did his predecessor and mentor: Anthony Comstock responded furiously to a display of her artwork when, in 1915, he saw it gracing the walls of a Village restaurant, and had her arrested.[70]

Steloff herself may have been reticent, "almost prissy about sex,"[71] but like Charles Chapet, she was a businessperson trying to stay solvent during a time when only the keenest customers would purchase expensive books. Nor was she at all intimidated by Sumner, in spite of his occasional pointed harassment. Maurice Girodias, whose Olympia Press was a post–World War II reincarnation of the Obelisk Press of his father, Jack Kahane, reports Steloff as being Kahane's "single American trade client" for the Obelisk *Tropic of Cancer*: "streams of tiny orders . . . sometimes for six copies at a crack!"[72] One of Steloff's British sources for Continental works banned in Britain and America was probably London's resourceful William Jackson Ltd.[73] Legman and Jake Brussel's own New York–printed underground "Medvsa" edition of *Cancer* was distributed exclusively to the Gotham and the Argus in 1940.[74] According to Legman, the famous Gotham motto, "Wise Men Fish Here," was also sometimes taken to refer to the availability there of booklegged erotica (but only, of course, for trusted, affluent customers). Andreas Brown,

Love each other well in memory of me,
whom you have both loved.

close friend of Frances Steloff and present owner of the Gotham, states that Legman is wrong. Steloff would not have had that in mind when she added the phrase to the sign John Held, Jr., designed for her in 1923 — the Gotham was not selling erotica that early.[75]

Sumner kept close tabs on the Gotham through the 1930s, despite his diminished success in prosecuting literary classics issued by reputable publishers, and despite the store's ability to hire excellent lawyers, as he knew from its defense by Greenbaum, Wolff, and Ernst after the 1928 raid. He also knew that the store had strong public approbation, and "numbered among [its] customers some of the most prominent and distinguished people in the city."[76] Sumner risked both loss of legal fees and community tolerance. With his intransigent view of the virulence of sex, the Gotham must have symbolized all he hated, and against which he had to continue to battle, if he expected to be taken seriously, or to take himself seriously. The store housed a literate stock of new and used books. It did not feature a large scholarly inventory, like Dunster House, nor did it have the prestigious antiquarian or sporting books (devoted to gentlemanly pastimes like golf, tennis, or fishing) in fine bindings to be found at Temple Scott's, Harry F. Marks's, or Barnet Ruder's well-appointed shops. Nor was it, except in the early years, a general bookstore. The younger school of modernist writers was Gotham's special interest, especially after Steloff became owner.

By the late 1920s, Sumner needed to show the people — especially prominent politicians, law-enforcement officers, religious leaders, and jurists — that he could arrest, in the name of a "decent" moral consensus, the spreading influence of this school and its "imitation foreign invasion" of American life and manners. The 1928 raid had shown him that the Gotham carried the range of erotica, classical and modern, fiction, sexology, erotology, and flagellation. However, Marks also carried gallantiana and sexology; Sumner knew this, but took no action. Ruder, another upscale bookseller, was persistently rumored to have been a middleman between the millionaire Oklahoma collector and the combine of erotica writers revolving

Figure 26. Frontispiece, Théophile Gautier, *Mademoiselle de Maupin, or Double Love* (n.p.: privately printed for the Pierre Louÿs Society, n.d.), with frontispiece and illustrations by Clara Tice. Several copies of this edition and of the Pierre Louÿs Society's *Woman and Puppet* were confiscated by John Sumner during his 1928 raid on the Gotham. Reproduced by permission of Elizabeth Yoell.

around Anaïs Nin (see Chapter 2).[77] Perhaps Sumner thought Steloff and the writers she championed more vulnerable than these two booksellers, who had a smaller number of clients, a larger percentage of whom were wealthy and well respected. Perhaps, therefore, Sumner's distaste for the actors, dancers, and show-business impresarios who frequented the store, which was near the midtown theater district, was a factor. On 16 July 1931, the vice eradicator returned to 47th Street, giving the Gotham display area, cellar, and outbuilding a thorough thrice-over with the aid of a good flashlight and coming away with various books he thought indecent. Many of their authors were British (Lawrence, Radclyffe Hall), German (Schnitzler), French (Gauthier, Louÿs), or Chinese (*The Adventures of Hsi Men Ching*). On this occasion, according to Steloff, he required her to open her safe, so that he could assure himself that she had no dirty pictures hidden there.[78]

If Sumner thought he could regain by prosecuting a single bookstore what he had lost as a result of judicial decisions, he was mistaken. In December 1935, Sumner carried off from the Gotham copies of Random House's first American edition of Gide's *If It Die*.[79] At the ensuing trial, he compared the book's effect on the reader to that of Frank Harris's *My Life and Loves*.[80] He may have been hinting that the shop carried the Harris autobiography and other flagitious works. Otherwise, the statement is far-fetched; in fact, some critics say Gide's book suffered because, thinking it necessary to prevent the sort of comparison Sumner made, he was not explicit about sexual encounters. The book had been on sale at general bookstores, although some were sold out owing to the Christmas rush. *Publishers Weekly* sprang to Steloff's defense, vigorously deploring Sumner's censorship efforts.[81] Her establishment, unlike Rebhuhn's Falstaff Press or Christian Gerhardt's and Eugene Nussbaum's bookshops, was one in which the leading booksellers' journal could take pride, a bookstore in which professors, lawyers, physicians, and public officials would be pleased to be seen. Here was a store that, with a will to raise the cultural tone of its community, sponsored an "open-air art market," which brought to Manhattan a Parisian ambience complete with bookstalls replicating the Seine-side originals.[82] *Publishers Weekly* turned a withering scorn upon the NYSSV, noting that Sumner had singled out the Gotham, although a "long established shop," because it was "small" and could not afford to mount a strong defense. Such a strategy constituted a "grave injustice," and was "a poor way to carry on discussions about what the public should not read."[83]

The *Publishers Weekly* article was, ironically, titled "Picking On the Little

Fellow." Not only was the well-established Gotham capable of getting lawyers to defend the store, but it was patronized by sophisticated New Yorkers of the type who applauded the decade's liberalizing decisions regarding books challenged under the Comstock Law. It was hard to label their interest in sexually explicit literature as the kind with which people who patronized the Bowery outlets were burdened. Certainly the *Times* or *Publishers Weekly* would not do so, even though some of these customers arranged to purchase copies of Harris's *My Life and Loves*, *The Wild Party*, *The Flogging Craze*, or *Psychopathia Sexualis* (all available at the Gotham at the time of the 1928 raid), or *Lady Chatterley's Lover* or *Tropic of Cancer*. These were perhaps attractively bound and printed copies, as opposed to shabby, previously loaned-out, under-the-counter ones fished out from a secondhand dealer's back room. Novelist Christopher Morley's defense of the store emphasized that it catered to "artistic and mature clients. It deals not only in current books but in first editions, rare and out of print works, works on drama and the arts. Bookstores of this kind make generous contributions to public taste and culture. They are the last places likely to be visited by the callow hunter for tripe and smut."[84]

The true "little fellows" got some of their copies of *Chatterley* or *Tropic* from the same underground sources the Gotham tapped, including, possibly, Martin Kamin or Samuel Roth. They also dealt with the purveyors of salacious magazines, comics, and readers, but that was not the sole reason they constituted a different breed. They would not have thought of looking to *Publishers Weekly* for vindication, nor to Random House for lawyer's fees, as Steloff did when faced with defending *If It Die*. It is true that in 1929 the Vanguard Press, sympathetic to labor and socialist causes, sponsored the ill-fated Post Bill, which would have directed obscenity prosecutions at publishers equally with booksellers, and therefore would have relieved the latter of the costs, if not the dangers to their reputations, of having to fight alone in the courts. This would have helped some "little fellows," in the case of borderline items. However, as Sumner pointed out,[85] the smaller cigar-, book-, or drugstore operations and their lending libraries often got in trouble because of readers and bibles, and works "privately printed" or attributed to anonymous "societies." They also had trouble with the sex pulps; although they were good investments, their publishers, despite their promises, had little money to defend booksellers, and mediocre reputations at best. The sorts who sold these books, and mail-order publishers — the Nussbaums, Costelitos, Levines, Roths, and Rebhuhns — all had to live with the purple aura of "pornographers." They had to turn to colleagues, or to their own steady customers, for consolation, but would have found little financial or moral support from either quarter. Such were the facts of business for the pariah capitalist, among whose number, despite Sumner's efforts, Frances Steloff could not be counted, no more than could Harry F. Marks or Barnet Ruder.

Occasionally, when their business was successful and when the books in question had recognized literary value, distributors who did not shrink from aggressively prurient advertising or from tapping into the delivery system for obscene novelties and pamphlets could command the services of prestigious firms, in which such champions of free speech as Morris Ernst, Paul Blanchard, and Arthur Garfield Hayes were partners. This was true of Sam Roth, Esar Levine, and Benjamin Rebhuhn. Greenbaum, Wolff, and Ernst did win an acquittal for Roth's business manager in 1931, regarding Mirbeau's *Celestine*, and Esar Levine's 1936 conviction was overturned on appeal because the judge's instructions to the jury had been based on archaic "into whose hands" principles. However, even the most renowned law firms were less likely to win acquittals for such clients than for Fifth Avenue booksellers and established publishers. In fact, Levine and Rebhuhn eventually were incarcerated. To avoid such a fate, many erotica dealers humbly removed books from shelves, paid fines, and mouthed public apologies.

Sumner and the Booksellers: Cooperation—and Resentment

Although newspaper stories about erotica distributors and booksellers were often disdainful, by 1930 most of the New York dailies had become contemptuous of Sumner as well. The Hearst-owned *Journal American* always fulminated against obscenity,[86] but in the other dailies, the NYSSV was confronted with headlines such as: "Vice-Hunter Finds a Flaubert Book, Has Shop Owner Arrested — Is Chided for Failing to Return Volumes"; "Vice-Rakers Trap Woman, and Author Dead Centuries"; "Bookseller Wins $500 in Sumner Vice Suit"; "What's Sumner's Penalty? Boy Asks at Vice Trial"; "Sumner Criticized by Court for Picking On Little Fellow."[87] The stories themselves, and editorials, referred to his "myopic morality," characterizing him as a "sexpert," the "leading exponent of 'nude is lewd,' " and a "public nuisance."[88] Beginning 6 March 1930, the *Telegram* ran a series of articles on "Books and Bookleggers" by investigative journalist Joseph

Lilly, detailing the tricks of the undercover agents, the plight of the small book-sellers who did not know which works might offend Sumner, his refusal to admit that he was a censor, and the varying levels of support for him within the NYSSV. Lilly's conclusion questioned the legal basis for the society's actions.

Paul Boyer's *Purity in Print* carefully documents the way the vice-society movement, and Sumner in particular, gradually lost the ideological, political, and economic high ground during the interwar period.[89] Although throughout the 1920s, following the lead of *Publishers Weekly*, booksellers deferentially offered self-censorship, cracks in the moral consensus were ineluctably widening. After 1929, dwindling membership contributions were a special problem because, unlike his Chicago counterpart, Reverend Philip Yarrow, Sumner received no informant's fees from police.[90] Nonetheless, he must be credited with persistence against grow-ing odds. Even as contempt for him could be expressed more openly, he remained a potent foe whom one had to watch carefully over one's shoulder. Rumors among booksellers about dubious tactics on his part continued throughout the decade. Was this just resentful talk?

In an editorial titled "The Censorship Racket," the *New York Herald Tribune* opined, "It is a strange commentary upon the methods of our own Society for the Suppression of Vice that the publishers of *The Well of Loneliness*, after the court had cleared the book, received back from its secretary, Mr. Sumner, many fewer copies of the book than, according to the receipt signed at the time of the raid, they had seized."[91] In 1931, Sumner was required to submit to a pretrial interrogation by lawyers for Bernarr Macfadden's New York *Evening Graphic*, because he had sued the tabloid for a 1927 story in which it accused him of getting 50 percent of all fines levied against convicted booksellers he had arrested. Sumner testified that he held confiscated books in the society office. He would supply copies to the district attorney as needed. He returned some books after trial, if they were duly requested; others were destroyed. He was evasive about how many were returned, and could produce no records.[92] Perhaps a few of the confiscations went into what the *Sunday Mirror*'s feature writer described as "the staunch trunk" in which he kept "par-ticularly offensive examples of printed obscenity" (Figure 27).[93]

It was an advantage for Sumner to have custody of the books he impounded. After the case was settled in court, he might bargain with a bookseller or publisher or their lawyers for return of some and retention of others. This was the case after the 1928 raid on the Gotham: 367 volumes were at stake.[94] In his 1930 articles on

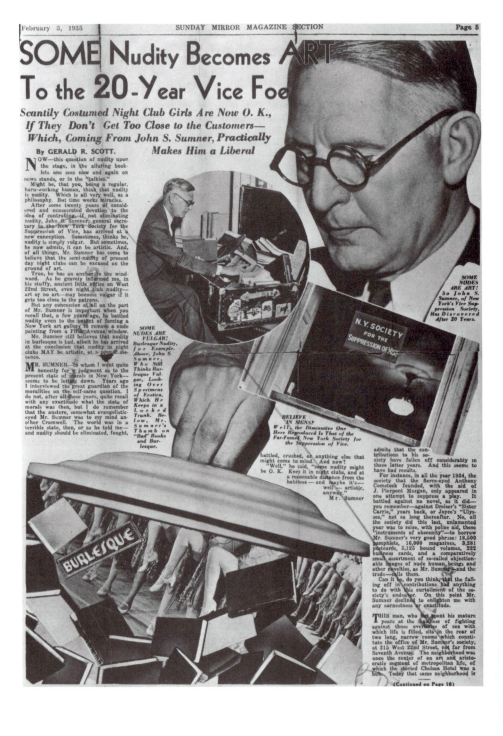

February 3, 1935   SUNDAY MIRROR MAGAZINE SECTION   Page 5

SOME Nudity Becomes ART
To the 20-Year Vice Foe

Scantily Costumed Night Club Girls Are Now O. K.,
If They Don't Get Too Close to the Customers—
Which, Coming From John S. Sumner, Practically
Makes Him a Liberal

By GERALD R. SCOTT.

NOW—this question of nudity upon the stage, in the alluring booklets one sees now and again on news stands, or in the "talkies."

Might be, that you, being a regular, hard-working human, think that nudity is nudity. Which is all very well, as a philosophy. But time works miracles.

After some twenty years of considered and consecrated devotion to the idea of controlling, if not eliminating nudity, John S. Sumner, general secretary to the New York Society for the Suppression of Vice, has arrived at a new conception. Sometimes, thinks he, nudity is simply vulgar. But sometimes, he now admits, it can be artistic. And, of all things, Mr. Sumner has come to believe that the semi-nudity of present day night clubs can be excused on the ground of art.

True, he has an anchor to the windward. As he gravely informed me, in his stuffy, ancient little office on West 22nd Street, even night club nudity—art or no art—may become vulgar if it gets too close to the patrons.

But any concession at all on the part of Mr. Sumner is important when you recall that, a few years ago, he battled nudity even to the extent of forcing a New York art gallery to remove a nude painting from a Fifth Avenue window.

Mr. Sumner still believes that nudity in burlesque is bad, albeit he has arrived at the conclusion that nudity in night clubs MAY be artistic, at a proper distance.

MR. SUMNER—to whom I went quite honestly for a judgment as to the present state of morals in New York—seems to be letting down. Years ago I interviewed the great guardian of the moralities on the self-same question. I do not, after all these years, quite recall with any exactitude what the state of morals was then, but I do remember that the austere, somewhat evangelistic-eyed Mr. Sumner was to my mind another Cromwell. The world was in a terrible state, then, or so he told me—and nudity should be eliminated, fought,

SOME NUDES ARE VULGAR! Burlesque Nudity, for Example. Above, John S. Sumner, Who Still Thinks Burlesque Vulgar, Looking Over Specimens of Erotica, Which He Keeps in a Locked Trunk. Below, Mr. Sumner's Thumb on "Bad" Books and Burlesque.

SOME NUDES ARE ART! So John S. Sumner, of New York's Vice Suppression Society, Has Discovered After 20 Years.

BELIEVE IN SIGNS? Well, the Diminutive One Here Reproduced Is That of the Far-Famed New York Society for the Suppression of Vice.

battled, crushed, or anything else that might come to mind. And now?

"Well," he said, "some nudity might be O. K. Keep it in night clubs, and at a reasonable distance from the habitues—and maybe it's—well— artistic, anyway."

M r . Sumner

admits that the contributions to his society have fallen off considerably in these latter years. And this seems to have had results.

For instance, in all the year 1934, the society that the fierce-eyed Anthony Comstock founded, with the aid of J. Pierpont Morgan, only appeared in one attempt to suppress a play. It battled against no novel, as it did—you remember—against Dreiser's "Sister Carrie," years back, or Joyce's "Ulysses," not so long thereafter. No, all the society did this last, unlamented year was to seize, with police aid, these "instruments of obscenity"—to borrow Mr. Sumner's very good phrase: 18,500 pamphlets, 16,000 magazines, 3,281 postcards, 5,125 bound volumes, 222 business cards, and a comparatively small assortment of so-called objectionable images of nude human beings and other novelties, as Mr. Sumner—and the trade—calls them.

Can it be, do you think, that the falling off in contributions had anything to do with this curtailment of the society's endeavor. On this point Mr. Sumner declined to enlighten me with any earnestness or exactitude.

THIS man, who has spent his mature years in the business of fighting against those overtones of sex with which life is filled, sits in the rear of two long, narrow rooms which constitute the office of Mr. Sumner's society, at 215 West 22nd Street, not far from Seventh Avenue. The neighborhood was once the center of an art and aristocratic segment of metropolitan life, of which the storied Chelsea Hotel was a hub. Today that same neighborhood is

(Continued on Page 18)

censorship, Joseph Lilly echoed the hostility of the book trade by hinting that Sumner did something quite different from using books as a kind of bargaining chip. He may have actually resold them: "the booksellers do not understand what becomes of [their books] after Sumner seizes them. But rather than antagonize him and rather than prolong their unprofitable publicity they do not ask him either for the books or what he does with them. He says that he destroys them."[95] If clandestine reselling occurred, surely the secretary himself would not have been present during the transaction, but would have operated through one of his agents. It is still bruited about the book trade that there was one designated shop, that of Harry F. Marks, to which the society's confiscated books were funneled. As mentioned above, Marks specialized in expensive sporting books, which he often rebound in blue morocco. Those he purchased from Sumner — the story has it — were similarly preserved.[96] Another report has it that confiscated books sometimes resurfaced when the libraries of deceased judges and public officials were auctioned off.[97]

By not pressing for information on the fate of their confiscated goods, booksellers themselves may have helped further their nemesis's goals. But the conditions under which one does business often preclude acting on one's resentments, however justified they are. After Sumner's threat to Simon and Schuster about putting them in jail, the firm could not afford to publish March's *Wild Party* in 1926. In 1925, Thomas Seltzer's financial situation made it impossible for him to fight for *A Young Girl's Diary* and *Casanova's Homecoming*, which three years before, he had had the resources to defend successfully. Faced with a grand jury indictment — Sumner had pursued the case after his defeat at the magistrate court level — Seltzer withdrew the titles from circulation and destroyed the plates. The assistant district attorney stated that there was no longer any reason to pursue the suit, and Sumner discontinued his complaint.[98] The threat posed by Sumner's

---

Figure 27. A Sunday supplement spread on Sumner and his work. The trunk contains collected "specimens of erotica"; the sign hangs in the window of the NYSSV offices on West 22nd Street. The article (one of several photo-essays of the period) is evidence that, however discredited for attempting to censor modern novels, Broadway plays, burlesque shows, popular movies, birth-control pamphlets, and anthropological tracts, Sumner was still a significant public figure "keeping the lid on" vice in mid-1930s Manhattan. From: "Some Nudity Becomes Art to the 20-Year Vice Foe," *New York Mirror*, 3 Feb. 1935, Sunday magazine section. Reproduced by permission of the Harry Ransom Humanities Research Center, University of Texas at Austin (JA Files).

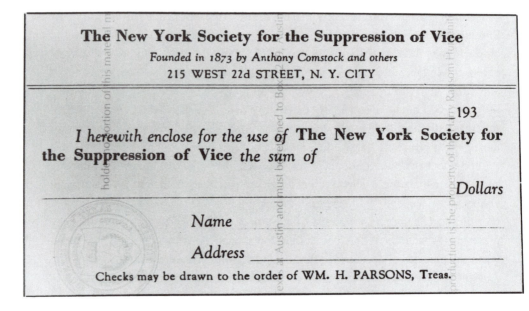

The New York Society for the Suppression of Vice

Founded in 1873 by Anthony Comstock and others

215 WEST 22d STREET, N. Y. CITY

_____ 193

I herewith enclose for the use of **The New York Society for the Suppression of Vice** *the sum of*

_____ *Dollars*

Name _____

Address _____

Checks may be drawn to the order of **WM. H. PARSONS, Treas.**

Figure 28. A form for contributing to the NYSSV. It is possible that the society's financial agent visited bookstores to solicit funds, and that some booksellers contributed because they felt it might prevent Sumner from focusing on items in their stock that he thought prosecutable. This particular copy was probably sent to the firm of Greenbaum, Wolff, and Ernst while Sumner and Greenbaum were negotiating over books confiscated during a 1928 raid on the Gotham Book Mart. Source: File box 391, MLE Papers. Reproduced by permission of the Harry Ransom Humanities Research Center, University of Texas at Austin (JA Files) and the Crime and Justice Foundation, Boston, Mass.

persistence was of course the motive for Seltzer's withdrawal, and there were other cases with this resolution. However, lest he be accused of restraint of trade, when asked at the 1931 pretrial interrogation, Sumner stated that his practice was to drop a suit only "on the advice of the District Attorney and the judge in the case."[99]

Another rumor about clandestine relationships between the vice society and certain booksellers suggests that Sumner and his troops ran what amounted to a "protection racket." In this case the organized effort to extort, if it actually existed, involved Sumner and his staff — that is, his "financial agent" — who would make rounds to bookstores, asking for annual donations to the society (Figure 28).[100] Sumner admitted that Baker and Taylor, a major wholesale distributor, not only was a contributor of between one hundred and one hundred fifty dollars a year, but would not handle any book Sumner had specified as obscene.[101] He also could remember, in the 1931 deposition, only one instance where he "ever proceeded against any book dealer, publisher, retailer or wholesaler who has contributed financially to the Society."[102] Perhaps those contributors included department stores. There is no record of a Sumner raid on any of them, although they carried the same borderline items as did cigar- and drugstores and lending libraries.[103]

Thunder on the Left: Morris Ernst and the National Council for Freedom from Censorship

An ominous sign of the disdain in which Sumner was increasingly held was the success of the brilliant young lawyer Morris Ernst, partner of the law firm of Greenbaum, Wolff, and Ernst. He was winning dismissals for publishers and booksellers, and taking a leading role in the activities of the ACLU (Figure 29). Ernst and Alexander Lindey were key figures in the National Council for Freedom from Censorship (NCFC), which the union organized in the early 1930s. The part of the council's platform that related to New York City specifically advocated "repeal [of] the special police powers of the New York Vice Society." Entrapment tactics were the council's chief complaint.[104] The NCFC also advocated excising from the Comstock statutes the bans on contraception as well as on "matter advocating 'arson, murder, or assassination.' " It thus aimed both to restrict the scope of obscenity legislation and to weaken the preventive societies' ability to operate, for the intransigence motivating their actions ensured an indiscriminate application of the statutes.[105] Realizing that the societies themselves had little power except what they drew from official agents of regulation such as Customs, the Post Office, and municipal ordinances controlling printed media, plays, theaters, and amusement parks, the NCFC vowed to challenge all these sources of interdiction: "to test in the courts all arbitrary censorship by administrative officers."[106]

After Sumner's scouring of the premises of the Gotham Book Mart in 1931, Greenbaum, Wolff, and Ernst defended the store. Ernst submitted copies of the books involved, and his brief described in detail the historical and literary importance of *Hsi Men Ching*, "a veritable source book of Chinese manners and customs" whose illustrations were not only appropriate to the text but "decorative, not realistic." The tales in *From a Turkish Harem* were described as "mild and in-

Figure 29. Morris L. Ernst, c. 1935. Courtesy of Stephanie G. Begen and the Harry Ransom
Humanities Research Center, University of Texas at Austin, Photography Collection.

nocuous"; the brief cited several precedents in which similar books were cleared of obscenity charges.[107] Several months passed while Sumner awaited Magistrate Louis B. Brodsky's opinion. He must have strongly expected a conviction; his own brief characterized *Hsi Men Ching* as "one continual sexual debauch," and he emphasized that a bookseller had been convicted for possessing a copy of it in a 1929 case in the Court of Special Sessions.[108] In November 1931, Brodsky cleared *Hsi Men Ching*, as well as *From a Turkish Harem*, on the grounds that the average contemporary adult would not be corrupted by them.[109] The former book included many discussions of lovemaking, but they were brief and allusive, without specific mention of sex organs. The English translation was, in fact, an abridged version of the original. Copulation, although often imminent, was not depicted in the text or in the illustrations, which, nonetheless, were typical of Clara Tice, and therefore, according to Sumner, grossly obscene (Figure 30).

Sumner simply could not accept this dismissal, particularly since Greenbaum, Wolff, and Ernst had won by stressing the book's literary and historical value. Referring in his brief to many sample pages recounting the numerous sexual adventures of Ching (described in the defendant's brief as a "Chinese Casanova") and various concubines, he had asserted, "If these passages do not bring this book within every judicial interpretation of the term 'obscenity,' then it would be difficult to find obscenity in any book or other print."[110] Here is a sample passage cited in his brief: "He then took off her shoes and undid her foot bands. These he tied to the woman's ankles and lifted her limbs by fastening the loose ends of the bands to the vines on the other side. Her marble columns, thus raised, revealed ineffable happiness to her lover. Hsi Men Ching reclined on the pillow, supporting himself on one hand, while with the other he gently stroked her velvety skin until Golden Lily writhed with tremulous delight."

Sumner published one of his periodical letters with the title "Something About Obscene Books and a City Magistrate."[111] Unlike his annual reports, which never identified specific books or distributors, this communication gave names, in this case Brodsky's. Sumner began by explaining that he was deviating on this occasion from his policy of accepting a magistrate's decision with equanimity. As he stated to Charles Bodwell of the Watch and Ward, "the Brodsky letter was a necessary publication in an effort to offset some of the newspaper comment suggested by his erroneous and misleading decision."[112] A year later, in his annual report to constituents, he made a special point of deploring newspaper publicity

Figure 30. Frontispiece to *The Adventures of Hsi Men Ching* (1927). Courtesy of Elizabeth Yoell.

about obscenity cases, because it advertised what "from a social standpoint was better ignored by the Press."[113] Specifically, this refers to the titles of books he challenged, upon which he would not want the public to whet its curiosity. But he also did not appreciate journalists who portrayed him as an ineffectual and self-appointed "sexpert." Increasingly, although by no means exclusively, this was the treatment he could expect, as opposed to stories debating his positions (Figures 5 and 27) or pictures showing him burning obscene materials shoulder to shoulder with police officials (Figure 23).

In January 1932, with the approval of District Attorney Thomas C. F. Crain,[114] Sumner sought a grand jury indictment against Steloff, submitting a copy of *Hsi Men Ching* and listing the passages he felt were obscene. Newman Levy, of Greenbaum, Wolff, and Ernst, wrote to the jury foreman, submitting a copy of Brodsky's decision and requesting that Steloff be allowed to testify.[115] Eventually, Sumner's request was rejected. Levy then requested that Crain direct Sumner to return six copies of *Hsi Men Ching* and thirty-four of *From a Turkish Harem*, confiscated during the raid the previous July. He deplored the fact that the district attorney had ordered that the books not be returned.[116] Sumner's use of the search warrant, and his refusal to return books, was now being effectively challenged. He may have been able to convince supporters that his 1929–31 deliberations with Gotham and its liberal lawyers resulted in a stand-off, but he was no longer able to convince the general public, the press, and the Fifth Avenue segment of the book trade that he commanded the respect in court or in the public mind that he had enjoyed a decade before. His power was eroding, even with the members of his own, increasingly cash-poor organization and shrinking constituency.

In 1929, Morris Ernst won an acquittal on obscenity charges for Covici-Friede and its edition of *The Well of Loneliness*. He took the opportunity to challenge Sumner's posttrial practice of keeping at least some of the books he confiscated, even if the defendant had been acquitted, or, in the case of a conviction, if the books detained were not those that had been judged obscene. Stating that the NYSSV had not returned to Covici 50 of the 865 copies taken despite months of formal requests, Ernst deplored the cavalier and self-serving manner in which the society used the search warrant. It did not bother to issue prior complaints, and then flouted the "sacred trust" under which an entity issuing a warrant was bound to return impounded property.[117] Sumner responded that he had told Ernst at the time that the number 865 did not represent "an exact count" and that Ernst "by some subterfuge or threat induced Mr. Bamberger to sign such a receipt."[118] The NYSSV's secretary knew Ernst was really questioning the propriety of allowing the society to assume police powers in obscenity cases. "This is nothing but a publicity scheme," groused Sumner.[119] In fact, it was a persistent campaign, against which the secretary struggled grimly. When Ernst won a case on behalf of Nathan Asch's *Pay Day*, he insisted, despite Sumner's denials, that the confiscated copies were on the vice-society's premises, and forced Sumner to admit it. Illegally, they remained there. Therefore, when the *Casanova's Homecoming* case was settled in Simon and Schuster's favor, Ernst "specifically asked the Court to direct Mr. Sumner . . . to return all copies."[120] Sumner still kept twenty-five books. After five more years of public protests, Greenbaum, Wolff, and Ernst were able to claim success. Sumner's unsuccessful complaint, in April 1935, against Flaubert's *November* was "the first literary censorship case," the firm's summary of facts stated, "in which every single copy was ultimately accounted for."[121]

In 1931, Greenbaum, Wolff, and Ernst defended Esar Levine when Sumner sent an agent to purchase a copy of Clement Wood's short-story collection, *Flesh*, from the Panurge Press, and had office manager Benjamin Levine arrested.[122] This was a new edition, without the daring illustrations that had gotten Christian Gerhardt convicted the year before. In prosecuting the case, Sumner did not mask his contempt for Morris Ernst's courtroom tactics. He wrote in reply to Ernst's brief, regarding the latter's inclusion of testimonial letters from physicians, that it was "only another instance, of which we have seen entirely too many, of the impertinent and flagrantly unethical methods of counsel herein to force upon the attention of the Court wholly irrelevant and specifically forbidden matter in an effort to cloud the issue and if possible to influence the Court in a hopeless defense."[123] For Sumner's part, testimony from experts was irrelevant, and the tolerance of scientists and other respectable sorts of citizens for sexually explicit materials was a red herring.[124] Greenbaum, Wolff, and Ernst's brief is in part a well-researched literary biography of Clement Wood and an argument for his being one of the most reputed contemporary writers of fiction, poetry, and social commentary. Was it not "utterly unthinkable"[125] that a man with such credentials would write to incite prurient interest? The judge must have answered in the affirmative, for the case against Panurge was "discharged."[126]

Sumner's contempt is understandable. The stories were advertised as concerned with subjects such as "prison eroticism," "teaser woman," "bestiality," and "sadism." However, the only successful strategy available to the anticensorship lawyers of the 1930s was to argue that the sex in books they defended was not there for its own sake but because it was intrinsic to the social and literary value of the work. Sexual content was "frank," not "prurient," and need not induce shame or guilt when it was part of a responsible writer's "serious" intentions. If this meant (as in the Wood case) overlooking the sly prurience of the publisher in order to defend the honorable intentions of the author, so be it. It was a matter of conviction: whether a work is obscene or has redeeming value can and should be determined in a way that does not allow a conservative construction of the moral consensus to dictate what adult Americans can read and think. Ernst proudly advocated this belief, with all his adversarial resources, in a period during which the liberalization of the Comstock statutes had to be fought for tooth and nail. In the "culture war" that pitted Ernst and the NCFC against the antivice societies and the Post Office counsels, each side saw the other as the Philistine camp. In each skirmish, the terrain was political, and the prize was community support. Clearly, in such a situation, absolute truth is not the only — and may not be the best — weapon at the disposal of liberal forces.

Sumner and his fellow vice suppressors were especially frustrated by Greenbaum, Wolff, and Ernst's success in 1936 in winning a reversal of Esar Levine's conviction for mailing obscene books and circulars. His arrest had been part of the postmaster general's campaign against mail-order "smut," especially directed against the very successful, and clearly prurient, circulars. Perhaps this is why the district judge assigned to the original trial was the conservative Charles B. Kennamer of Alabama. Kennamer's charge to the jury indicated that in his view of the law of obscenity, a book is to be condemned if any passage is obscene (i.e., if it stimulates "impure thoughts") and if, to use the 1868 Hicklin test, it might fall "into the hands" of those most susceptible to corruption, or, in the language of the test, "those whose minds are open to such immoral impulses." In their appeal, Ernst and three colleagues stated that the jury should have been told that criteria of obscenity do change, and that the circulars in question should be judged "against the literature, newspapers, movies, and other influences in the community today."[127] On appeal, Judge Learned Hand acknowledged that the three books involved might indeed have been obscene, but declared that this could not be decided on the basis of an absolute standard. "The problem is to find a passable compromise [the legal term Hand uses elsewhere is 'mesne'] between opposing interests, whose relative importance, like that of all social or personal values, is incommensurable." A jury must take into account the works' probable readership and whether their literary or scientific merit, and their possible positive influence, legally sanctions their publication, overbalancing a merely prurient appeal they might have for casual readers. The ruling was influential in establishing community standards and expert testimony as valuable evidence.

Thus, a foundation was laid for the basic rights of all citizens to read — and to disseminate — all sorts of material openly advocating various ways of conducting one's sexual life, even when this material departed from the views of established moral authorities and their plans for teaching people how to think and act. As Alexander Lindey stated a decade later, alluding to the Levine appeal in a letter to a client: "The Circuit Court was quite indifferent to argument on our part addressed to the *content* of the books; the reversal we secured was on purely technical grounds." [128] Lindey was using the phrase "technical grounds" in a broad, layman's sense. *U.S. v. Levine* helped greatly in abrogating the validity of the Hicklin test and thus significantly helped secure for the average citizen the freedom to read. Ernst's own retrospective comment underscores the principle involved: "*social* justice as opposed to *absolute* justice" was served. [129]

The most dramatic of Ernst's successes was as Random House's lawyer in the *Ulysses* case of 1933. Not only did he prepare an excellent brief, incorporating opinions from leading librarians, writers, and critics about the artistic originality and the lack of salaciousness of the book as a whole. He also engineered, with the cooperation of District Attorney Samuel Coleman, a series of postponements in the district court until the liberal judge Woolsey was sitting, instead of a "straight-laced Catholic judge." [130] That was the result not only of shrewdness and intimate knowledge of the court circuit, but also of collegial respect — from Coleman and Coleman's superior, George Medalie. [131] Lindey's sincere and unsolicited praise for Ernst's efforts is eloquent testimony to his partner's pioneering success: "he won the fight practically single-handed. . . . The tactics he devised were not only characterized by extreme resourcefulness and aggressiveness, but also by novelty." [132]

It is true that the government did not seem to prosecute the *Ulysses* case vigorously; it was at first not clear it would do so at all. Customs officers were so used to seeing copies of *Ulysses* in people's luggage that they often did not bother to confiscate them.[133] When the case moved forward, the government was represented by Coleman, a lawyer whom Ernst praised as more interested in justice than in getting convictions.[134] The influence of Robert Kastor, wealthy stockbroker and Joyce in-law, in preparing the way for overturning the ban on the novel is imponderable. Kastor encouraged Random House to initiate the legal battle.[135] If Martin Conboy, who became district attorney for the southern district of New York just months after the original trial, had been Ernst's adversary instead of Samuel Coleman,[136] or if the government had insisted on a jury trial,[137] the outcome might have been different. Of course, Ernst might have triumphed regardless: only he had all the credentials to liberate *Ulysses*. In the political and juridical arenas in which the fight for freedom of expression went on in America, he was uniquely effective. As he put it in his often reprinted foreword to the novel, "the precedent . . . will do much to rescue the mental pabulum of the public from the censors who have sought to convert it into treacle, and will help to make it the strong, provocative fare it ought to be." He may be forgiven his touch of sanguinity: "The first week in December 1933 will go down in history for two repeals, that of Prohibition and that of the legal compulsion for squeamishness in literature. It is not inconceivable that . . . sex repressions found vent in intemperance. . . . Perhaps the intolerance which closed our distilleries was the intolerance which decreed that basic human functions had to be treated in books in a furtive, leering, roundabout manner. Happily, both of these have now been repudiated." But if so, both bookleggers and smuthounds would have suffered more than they did.

Sumner never expressed animosity for Ernst personally. Instead, remaining true to his convictions, he regarded the aggressive young lawyer as he did all booksellers, publishers, and distributors of "indecencies." They were Philistines intent on enervating the American spirit with the virulence of sex. And their number, with Ernst in the vanguard, was becoming legion. Sumner's social views as well as his legal judgments were increasingly ignored. The vice crusader's contempt for the immorality of the city — as the NCFC writings suggest — was now considered as quaint as the "sunlight and shadows" genre of moral tracts about American Babylons. Thanks to popular novels, movies, musical dramas, and popular songs, the wised-up men and women of the metropolis — its streetwalkers, saloon habitués, gangsters, raunchy "pols," and hard-boiled business executives —

were considered glamorous, sometimes funny, sometimes even stout-hearted. Among academics, cities were being considered not hotbeds of vice but seminaries of "cultural pluralism."[138]

Sumner Perseveres

A signal indignity for Sumner occurred in 1936, when the newly elected president of the NYSSV, F. Bertram Elgas, responding to the string of liberal court decisions from *Hsi Men Ching* through *Ulysses* and beyond, instructed the secretary to confine his prosecutions to works of "flagrant" immorality, so "radically" had popular taste and judicial practice changed.[139] But Sumner was far from finished. In reporting the 1935 conviction of Greenberg Publishers for Jim Tully's novel of prostitution, *Ladies in the Parlor*, he attempted to show constituents that his efficacy continued to be significant. "Traffic" in such indecencies, he reported, had in recent years been stopped by "money loss, by confiscation of stock in trade and destruction thereof as a going business . . . particularly where such loss amounts to thousands of dollars. . . . There is also loss by disgrace to a book publisher, if of any standing, as in three criminal proceedings this year."[140] Actually, the fine in the Greenberg case was fifty dollars, and the three unnamed publishers were of little standing: William Godwin Inc. (owned by Alex Hillman), Phoenix Press and the Outlet Book Company (the Wartels brothers' concerns), and Louis Shomer's American Ethnological Press. The first two companies were fined five hundred dollars; Shomer received three years' probation.[141] Phoenix, Outlet, and Godwin published sex pulps and Shomer's was a mail-order house. No one criticized Sumner for moving against them, and he had the positive support of the Catholic Church.

In the early 1930s, the Church responded to the increasing volume of both under-the-counter smut and cheap sex pulps and magazines in the lending libraries of cigar and drugstores and on newsstands, campaigning intensively against obscenity from the pulpit and through lay spokespeople. One 1933 campaign in Brooklyn shows how Sumner and the Church complemented each other, and how effectively the Church could act independently of him, without drawing any of the belittling press coverage to which the NYSSV had become vulnerable. District Attorney William F. X. Geoghan's immediate call to action was a list of approximately thirty "indecent" passages gleaned from the wares of circulating libraries and bookshops by Rita C. McGoldrick of the International Federation of Catholic

Alumnae (IFCA) (Figure 19). Like Judge Ford a decade earlier, she had become alarmed by the contents of a book she had "inadvertently come across"; in her case it had been brought to her Long Island summer home by a young houseguest.[142] She was also concerned that since the decensoring of Mary Ware Dennett's *The Sex Side of Life* in 1931, "we have had unmitigated filth in books."[143] Since 1922, McGoldrick had reviewed new films in order to determine which could be recommended as decent for Catholics to patronize. She felt the lending libraries should be supervised, as the public library was, and obscene and subversive materials removed — a step endorsed by the police department's own chaplain, who further urged the licensing of all bookstores.[144] Geoghan sent his detectives out to inform any dealer whose shop contained any of the thirty or so books, pamphlets, or magazines McGoldrick deemed questionable that he or she must remove the material, and report his or her source of supply. These forbidden materials included some of the contemporary novels scrutinized disdainfully by the preventive societies, and characterized as "polite" by the Watch and Ward's Bodwell; an example is Hervey Allen's best-seller, *Anthony Adverse*, called by the rector of St. Patrick's Cathedral "the rottenest book I ever handled."[145] The district attorney's aim was the same as Sumner's: to prosecute the publisher or distributor.[146] However, McGoldrick proclaimed herself satisfied when the books themselves were taken out of circulation in the "several hundred [lending] libraries here carrying six or seven copies of each of the objectionable books."[147] As with her efforts to make theaters show respectable movies, she desired booksellers' self-regulation, rather than legal censorship.[148] This made her a different kind of moralist from Sumner. Like him, however, she refused to advertise the bad books by naming them; also like him, she felt "the law is clear."

In the considerable areas that fell outside the tolerances of the anticensorship lawyers, the NCFC, and the press, Sumner continued, shoulder to shoulder with the Catholic authorities, his muscular efforts to "keep the lid on" vice throughout the 1930s. Young, impressionable, underpaid folk who borrowed books and purchased newsstand magazines were just the type, political and religious authorities worried, who were most vulnerable to sexual promiscuity. This would lead to a general contempt for authority. If the young were lost to indecency, the mores and laws that directed their energies into respectable, manageable channels might become totally ineffectual. That was where Yarrow, Bodwell, or Sumner came in. In 1932, the NYSSV proudly alluded to the *Brooklyn Tablet*'s praise of the society as the most "necessary" and effective in the city, and the next year to Monsignor M. J. La-velle's commendation of the society as "a high minded, earnest, and hard working organization which deserves our high respect, and practical support." In 1934, the society's president called attention to the Church's campaign against films "cor-rupting public morals and promoting a sex mania," hoping that other faiths would emulate the Catholics and noting that the Church's efforts show "the necessity for such work as ours."[149] This enthusiasm, however, needs to be balanced against Sumner's recognition that the Church's program was different from his—it had "too many activities of its own,"[150] and was not likely to increase public support of the NYSSV sufficiently to stimulate much-needed contributions. Catholics would donate what they could to their parish. Wealthy Protestant conservatives who still supported the society would not contribute during the Depression as much as they had before the Crash. Catholic officials could not pick up the slack, no matter how much they praised Sumner's work.

In the mid-1920s, Sumner was respected by the wealthy bankers and indus-trialists who contributed to his society; heeded by politicians, who echoed his pronouncements; and regarded as a force to be reckoned with by the press and major publishers (who sometimes consulted with him). He even wrote a feature story for *Smart Set* magazine in 1928. By the mid-1930s, he had to content himself with whatever commendations the Catholics of Brooklyn chose to bestow on him. In his campaign against Frances Steloff, the media had made it obvious that he was the villain and she the innocent. His successes in the late 1930s were largely confined to ferreting out a few of the overwhelming number of publishers of bibles, readers, and flagellation pamphlets.

However diminished Sumner's public image by 1936, in that year the society provided him with a "rehabilitated" and "thoroughly modernized" office.[151] His power to empty bookstores of copies of *Lysistrata*, the *Decameron*, and *Casa-nova's Homecoming* had indeed passed by the early 1930s—although the Post Of-fice continued to make it difficult to circulate the same books through the mails—and a proposal for a censoring board to prejudge literary manuscripts would never be taken seriously now. Still, Sumner's persistence was as strong as his convictions. As late as 1944, he harassed the Gotham Book Mart about a window display created by Marcel Duchamp and André Breton for Breton's *Arcane 17*. The display included a prone female figure with a nipple showing; Sumner paid Steloff a visit, stating that "it would have to come out." Steloff pasted Sumner's calling card over

the offending spot, with a card beneath it that read "CENSORED." The display remained in the window, drawing larger crowds than ever.[152] Was it time for Sumner
to retrench? Apparently not. He commanded enough respect to be given serious
attention when proceeding against D. H. Lawrence's *First Lady Chatterley* and
Edmund Wilson's *Memoirs of Hecate County*. He lost the former case, although the
work could not be distributed in New York State for six months after its publication.[153] *Hecate County* contained explicit, almost clinical descriptions of the narra-
tor's techniques of arousing and enjoying intercourse with two women, but only in
one scene. Elmer Rice, lawyer and playwright, opined, "Mr. Sumner doesn't seem
to know when he's licked." But Sumner successfully had the novel banned.[154]

Whether in the 1920s, 1930s, or much later, as long as the book trade itself
maintained that there was a distinction between dirty books and world literature,
and between the smutmonger and the respectable bookseller, Sumner's influence
would linger. The last of Joseph Lilly's 1930 articles investigating book censorship
in New York concerns the plans of the year-old Book Trade Protective Association.
Lilly interviewed its spokesman, Martin Kamin, earlier a supplier of borderline
erotica to David Moss and the Gotham Book Mart. The association was planning to
fight Sumner's indiscriminate and totally unpredictable targeting of books as obscene by creating its own "blacklist." Kamin justifies the matter thus:

While I am unalterably opposed to any form of censorship, and while I take the view that
good taste and intellectual discrimination are the soundest way of weeding out worthless
literature, . . . because of the activities and spectacular raids of Mr. Sumner's society, it is
preferable to have within the organization a committee on letters, whose function will be to
make suggestions in reference to "doubtful" books. . . . The Book Trade Protective Association . . . maintains that there is a relative line of demarcation between good and bad letters,
and that it is a matter largely for persons of scholarship and culture to be the final arbiters,
rather than for the unlettered professional pornography hunters.[155]

In one way, this plan was reasonable, as was the U.S. Customs policy that
allowed a literate jurist to replace unskilled inspectors as arbiters of imported
books. It was also suitably hostile to Sumner's intransigence; no doubt *Hsi Men
Ching*, *The Chinese Decameron*, and *Arabian Droll Stories* — three borderline
books Kamin had a hand in publishing — would not be interdicted. But most likely
selected sex pulps, and of course readers and bibles, still would be — along with the
underground writings of the combines of aspiring writers in need of cash. Neither

would Kamin's arbiters sanction *Tropic of Cancer*, or *Lady Chatterley's Lover*, which had been characterized by the district attorney in the Dunster House case as the work of a "filthy degenerate with a sewer brain."[156] In the main, Kamin's proposal simply recapitulated the preventive societies' basic distinction between decent and indecent, and their us-them dichotomy, now placed at the service of book-industry profits. The plan was similar to that adopted in the 1930s by liberal lawyers when they advised clients specializing in mail order what they must expurgate in order to keep their books from being impounded. In its assumptions about the possibility of printed matter being infested with guilt and sin, the Protective Association symbiotically allied itself with Sumner in assuring that sex for its own sake would remain furtive and prurient — and thus lucrative, both for those with the chutzpah to write, produce, and distribute blacklisted materials and for those financially involved with tamer books and magazines that titillated by flirting with the boundaries of the forbidden. Lilly saw this quite clearly; he concluded his article by speculating that if the Protective Association blacklist were put in place, "booklegging, then, would become a business of the first order, and copies of books ordinarily procurable with the greatest ease would become an adventure comparable to night clubbing in Harlem dives."

Fishing out erotic books from their repositories, from the Bowery to Fifth Avenue, the Back Bay to South Street, or South Dearborn to Wabash Avenue could hardly be as glamorous as jazzing in nightclubs. That aside, if Lilly was right in what he saw, he was wrong to think he was describing something new. The mystique of erotica had always been maintained by ruling sex out of bounds, whether by a self-imposed blacklist, by a bookseller's lawyer accommodating himself and his client to Post Office censorship (see Chapter 5), or by a unilateral Sumnerian determination. This financial and psychological interdependence continued for the rest of the decade, and well beyond.

5

"Your *Casanova* Is Unmailable"
Mail-Order Erotica and Postal Service Guardians of Public Morals

"Will the Censor permit you to tell his story? . . . I hear that policemen in Boston and the chief of the letter carriers in Washington are the arbiters of literature and morals in the United States."[1] So wrote coauthors Paul Eldridge and George Sylvester Viereck in 1927, to fix in their readers' minds the audacity of their novel, the hero of which has to deal with shoe fetishists, odalisques, transvestites, and eunuchs. The censorship situation was familiar enough to anyone, especially since the Watch and Ward Society was at the height of its notoriety. However, the efficiency of the U.S. Postal Service as censor was longer lived. Unlike the preventive societies, the Post Office was not significantly hampered by the various social and legal developments that made sexual explicitness more generally acceptable during the interwar period. The legal, or quasi-legal, jurisdiction of the preventive societies was regional, whereas postal authorities had a countrywide group of alleged offenders to prosecute; they could call on the willing help of the police, conservative public officials, and clergy, as well as preventive-society personnel, from Maine to California. Post Office inspectors could not be called self-appointed busybodies: they could proudly point out that the mandate to purge the mails of obscenity came from Congress itself. As a federal bureaucracy, the Post Office employed a sizable workforce to interdict materials, and depended on taxes, not charitable contributions, to pay for the effort. Nor could skillful lawyers of the defendant's choice or liberal magistrates challenge obscenity rulings by the Post Office, because it had its own in-house adjudication procedure. Transportation of obscene materials across state lines was a federal offense; the Department of Justice, which did not demur from the postal rulings, stood ready to prosecute if postal officials themselves were unable to convince the promoters of mail-order schemes to desist by warnings and threats. It is true that federal prosecutors could not ignore the liberalizing trends in obscenity law. As time went on, the Post Office did have to consider, grudgingly, that the possible harmful effect of a book on a child could no longer be the basis for a federal prosecution. Nonetheless, postal inspectors continued to rule material on birth control, sexology, and even classical gallantiana unmailable.

Any mail-order bookseller who wanted to fight such a decision had a federal case on his or her hands, with the attendant threats of incarceration and loss of thousands of dollars in fines and legal fees. An erotica distributor could choose, perhaps, to defy the head-shaking of the established booksellers, the icy stares of respectable churchgoers, even the lightly veiled ridicule of the daily newspapers. No doubt it took considerably more strength to withstand the prying of the Post Office's inspectors and the attacks of postal solicitors and district attorneys. Most of the mail-order booksellers, once warned, did what they could to avoid skirmishes with the postmaster general, the Department of Justice, and the FBI. Only a few were willing to continue doing business in a way that dared such authorities to treat them as dangerous adversaries.

The Unfortunate Case of Martin Sugar

Martin Sugar of Manhattan learned the hard way about the postal inspectors' contempt for classical gallantiana. In the late 1930s, he was selling magazines, including the ubiquitous spicy ones. As a premium for large orders, he offered an eight-volume set of the abridged *Memoirs of Casanova* ("women with the red lips and white bodies of countless conquests"), the plates of which he had purchased from A. and C. Boni. The books proved popular, so in late 1938 Sugar began selling the volumes by mail, not only through circulars sent to his magazine customers but also directly to booksellers and mail-order distributors with extensive literature catalogs, such as the Union Library. Before doing so, however, he ascertained that the Boni edition had never been the subject of either Post Office or Customs prosecution.[2]

Having been so careful, Martin Sugar was dismayed when in March 1939 New York's postmaster, Albert Goldman, informed him that his *Casanova* circulars were unmailable. Sugar had sent them third-class, and it is possible that the local postmaster had lifted the unsealed envelope flap, inscribed "pull out for postal inspection" to check on their legitimacy, and then sent a sample to Washington for a ruling, meanwhile impounding any others he encountered. Looking for clarification, Sugar now sent a set of the books and sample circulars to Goldman. In reply, the Post Office refused to return his advertisements and temporarily revoked his second-class mailing privileges, until Sugar explained that this would cause him to lose all his assets (magazines were sent second-class). Later that year, the Union Library's proprietors had to paste a blank ticket over their listing of Sugar's edition in their Christmas catalogs before their mailing was accepted. Sugar went to Washington, ready to make whatever excisions in the text would sanitize the work in the eyes of the Post Office, which at the time, and especially in cases involving suspension of second-class mailing privileges, did issue advisory and advance opinions.[3] Sugar's willingness to cooperate did him little good. As was usually the case, he was granted an interview with the same assistant solicitor who had ruled his circulars obscene. Further, postal policy made no guarantee that when actually mailed, the material under discussion would not be subject to further prosecution, regardless of any changes made in compliance with the Post Office's recommendation. In Sugar's case, for example, private citizens' complaints might necessitate investigation by a postal inspector and a subsequent unmailable ruling by the general counsel's office.[4]

Sugar's case was being passed routinely through the Post Office bureaucracy. It was long-established procedure first to make an unmailable ruling ex parte,[5] without the publisher knowing that his business was being investigated or that his mail was being withheld while it was being analyzed.[6] The postal solicitors took it on faith that what they characterized as erotica, whether a literary classic or a pamphlet-size story of sexual gymnastics, was being circulated by smut peddlers to the palpable harm of the citizenry and that prompt action was as necessary as in cases of fraud. Only after the ruling on his *Casanova*, then, did Martin Sugar learn that he had a problem, and that he should plead his case before the same postal solicitor who had already made up his mind. "Due process" took place after the fact, and in a perfunctory manner. No suggestions about revisions were forthcoming during Sugar's interview with the postal inspector. Presumably, the department would not be fulfilling its congressional charge to purify the mails from fraud and obscenity if it suggested to publishers of books deemed pornographic how they could make just enough adjustments to text and advertisements to continue to do business by appealing to prurience. Sugar was simply asked to sign a statement to the effect that he would desist from mailing his *Casanova*.

For Sugar to file an injunction would have been pointless; the negative decision would have stood up in court. A postal solicitor could rest assured that his ruling would be backed by the third assistant postmaster general, and that the courts would uphold it unless it could somehow be proved "clearly wrong."[7] So there was no further appeal. Obscenity, the Post Office felt, was "largely a question of one's own conscience. The important question, then, is whose conscience it is, and what manner of man he is."[8] That one man was the employee to whom Sugar had been referred. In an appendix to the 1940 attorney general's report on postal procedures, the Post Office stated that the question was not to be left to a "panel of experts," for literary critics seem not to feel "there is any such thing as obscenity." Further, the appendix argued, to delegate such a determination to any group outside the postal bureaucracy would be an abrogation of the department's congressional mandate, one that might well lead to precedents far to the left of both the general counsel's office and the federal courts themselves.[9]

Frustrated, Sugar approached the American Civil Liberties Union (ACLU). They were very sympathetic to victims of this kind of summary refusal to respect First Amendment guarantees of freedom of expression and, with a view to using the decision as a test case, sent their representative Jerome M. Britchey to see the solicitor.[10] During a two-hour conversation, Britchey was informed that the general counsel's office considered the rottenness in Casanova's memoirs far too deep to be safely extracted. If Sugar persisted in selling his books, his case would be heard, not in too liberal New York, but in Washington, D.C. Sugar in fact did persist, but he used a commercial delivery system, Railway Express, for shipping and advertising books and held his breath.[11] The Comstock Law still applied: "whoever . . . knowingly uses any express company or other common carrier for carriage in interstate or foreign commerce" to publish and distribute any "obscene, lewd, lascivious, indecent, filthy, or vile article, matter, thing, device or substance" is subject to fine and imprisonment. The ACLU (perhaps Morris Ernst himself) stood ready to defend Sugar in court. Sugar himself did not want the situation to escalate that far, however. He was betting that whatever the obscenity criteria of the Post Office, it was not likely that the FBI would investigate nor that the Justice Department would indict on the basis of a single piece of gallantiana such as the Boni edition of *Casanova*. Many erotica dealers, mail-order specialists or not, did business on this basis.[12] Often, they were correct. When they were not, they were headed for disaster.

The Legal Basis for the Post Office's "Unmailable" Power

After 1930, the Post Office gained in stature as the federal agency entrusted with administering criminal penalties for obscenity violations. The Tariff Act of that year took away the right of U.S. Customs inspectors to determine unilaterally which books were to be impounded due to obscenity; thereafter, Customs abandoned any attempt at punitive measures and simply refused to pass on for delivery books or artwork it deemed obscene. Customs further pleased civil libertarians in 1934 by appointing a lawyer who was also a scholar of the fine arts, Huntington Cairns, to determine in an "enlightened" manner which these were.[13] The postmaster general and his force of inspectors and solicitors did not intend to abdicate their responsibilities in any such way.

As Ernst and Seagle pointed out in their important 1928 anticensorship tract, *To the Pure*, Congress had never set up a direct censorship, nor had it ever enforced the provision of copyright law that stipulates that protection cannot be granted to works considered obscene.[14] Rather, thanks to Comstock, it had taken an indirect route, delegating power of censorship to its postal system, which has always been fiercely protective of its right to determine what is suitable to circulate in the federal mail. *Ex Parte Jackson* (1877) was an important landmark for the Post Office's authority in these matters. The decision established that the Post Office could declare certain printed materials unmailable, notwithstanding the Constitution's guarantee of freedom of the press. Only printed matter of an explicitly political nature was protected under the First Amendment, the judges determined; other kinds of material could be liable to government control, and Congress could delegate one of its administrative agencies, the Post Office, to prohibit the distribution of fraudulent — and by later extension, obscene — material.[15] Freedom of expression was not restricted by these prohibitions; rather, public order was being preserved.[16] To this day, the Post Office has maintained the position that it fulfills its congressional mandate by protecting citizens from enticements that deceive or deprave.

Ex Parte Jackson was not an unmixed blessing for the Post Office. It also declared that first-class mail could not be opened, and that a full criminal prosecution had to be set up to determine if refusal to deliver mail was warranted; a postmaster's summary inspection and seizure of the mail itself — his personal and uncontested determination that it was obscene — was not legal. However, the Post

Office had often vigorously argued that it could not do its job of shielding citizens from fraud and obscenity in the mails if it was bound by this stipulation that full adversarial procedure should precede such determinations. Martin Sugar's case involving the *Memoirs of Casanova* was one minor example of this. Even his hearing was considered a courtesy, not a requirement. Jerome Britchey, Sugar's advocate from the ACLU, recognized the strength of the Postal Service's conviction that it served as an insulator of citizens from moral pollutants, and he further discussed the implications of this with his contacts in the Department of Justice. He reported to Morris Ernst's law firm what he had learned: "It is a long tale of politics . . . if you break down their machinery for stopping censorship you will also break down their right to issue cease and desist orders in fraud cases."[17] In the 1930s, the same ex parte procedures governed both kinds of violations. If those directed at obscenity were changed, the claim went, the safeguards protecting the people from all sorts of confidence swindles might crumble as well. As Representative William Ashbrook of the Committee on the Post Office asked Morris Ernst in 1935, "if there were no censorship of the mails by the Post Office Department, how would we prevent other frauds?"[18]

The Post Office as Enforcer of the Moral Consensus

Martin Sugar's travails help us understand the results most likely to occur in the 1920s and 1930s when authorities enforced the conservative moral assumptions incorporated in America's legal codes. One of these assumptions was that only a small number of bona fide scientists, physicians, lawyers, and clergymen could peruse erotic works without risk to their moral character. A measure of how important an instrument politicians, clergy, citizens' groups, and police felt this to be is the stubborn opposition to the liberal implications of the *Ulysses* decision and of the 1934 appellate ruling upholding it; this hostility was made forcefully evident to Britchey during his interview. The judges had declared that a book must not be denied publication on the basis of either isolated passages or its possible effect on the most weak-minded members of the community. The decision helped legitimize testimony by the literary expert, and postulated a criterion for decensorship based on the intentions of the author and the tolerances of the mature adult for sexual explicitness.[19] Opposition, however, lasted throughout the 1930s and well beyond.

As late as 1952, the U.S. House of Representatives' Select Committee on

Current Pornographic Materials, chaired by Ezekiel Gathings (Democrat, Arkansas), asserted that for the courts to excuse specific sexually explicit and scatological passages because a book as a whole had literary value was to encourage prurience, obscenity trafficking, and consequent moral degeneracy, and that such a legal precedent served only to line the pockets of middleman purveyors of newsstand and department-store smut. In the same vein, after listening to the concerns of religious leaders, police captains, high-school principals, and harried distributors, the Gathings Committee's majority report pointed out the urgency of controlling the spread of pornographic paperbacks and magazines and called for an exemption of the Post Office from the delays caused by the 1946 Administrative Procedures Act, which required a full adversarial hearing before the ruling.[20] Here is an example of ideological and administrative authorities working together to preserve a cherished moral consensus by justifying legal penalties and making them as swift and as strict as possible. Whatever law and the precedent on which it was founded might dictate, legal practice is always responsive to ideological and social pressure; therefore, the real world of bureaucratic regulation is sometimes excused from changes that in the abstract seem just. In the case of postal regulations regarding obscenity in the mails, the fervor of spokespeople for "decency" affirmed the rightness of what the bureaucratic enforcers did — even if they functioned ex parte and with relentlessly mechanical efficiency.

Faced with the spread of inexpensive erotic books, magazines, novelties, and movies during the Depression, private and office-holding advocates of a moral and social status quo forged a multilayered network of effective social control. The dubious constitutionality of what these moral entrepreneurs did was overlooked because their warnings about the crisis at hand and their call for a virtuous crusade against corruptors of the moral order found powerful echoes, and because the targets of their crusades had little social support.[21] As the Justice Department was able to send organized crime figures to prison through wiretapping and scrutiny of their sources of income and tax records, so the Post Office, with the sanction of elected officers and reformist societies, could use ex parte unmailable decisions to hamper middleman erotic dealers. For such bookmen, an interlocking series of obstacles emerged, each of which confronted the lawbreaker with moral censure, administrative constraints, or legal penalties.[22] Clergy and lay spokespeople for "decency" and "purity" presented themselves to both the faithful and the nonconformist as stern but loving parents or teachers. Others — the police, publishers' associations, the courts, Customs, and in 1930s America most especially the Post Office — were impersonal obstacles. As a matter of routine procedure, they could project shame and guilt on offenders through a series of legally sanctioned acts: loss of professional standing, the impounding of property, the return to sender of their incoming mail (marked "fraudulent" or "unlawful"), fines, and imprisonment.

The Scope of Mail-Order Erotica "Promotions"

The methods by which the Post Office fought the spread of mail-order erotica were either "tough" or "unconstitutional," heroic or mule-headed, depending on the observer. From where the postmasters general of the 1930s sat, they noted that booksellers had discovered a large middle-income audience for sex pulps, readers, and bibles, and were exploiting such individuals' preference for enjoying sexually oriented books in the privacy of their homes, without the embarrassment of having to ask for them in a cigar store or bookshop. An example comes from the autobiography of the comedian Lenny Bruce, who grew up to be a bitter enemy of all obscenity legislation. Sitting under his mother's sink in 1932, the boy observed her listening to a neighbor lady who began her conversations "in a pedantic fashion, using academic medical terminology" drawn from "the volumes of books delivered by the postman every month — *A Sane Sex Life*, *Ovid the God of Love*, *How to Make Your Marriage Partner More Compatible* — in plain brown wrappers marked 'Personal.' "[23] Such packages inundated the mails in the 1930s, and gave the postal bureaucracy the rationale it needed.

There were certainly mail-order dealers in the 1920s with extensive lists. The Chicago-based Hygienic Book Company, carrying forward the message of the eugenics movement, dealt in marriage manuals and educational tracts for adolescents and young women. Sexological tracts originally issued by Dr. William J. Robinson's Critic and Guide Company were reprinted by the daringly named Cosmopolis Press; since nineteenth-century publishers of clandestine erotica sometimes identified their place of publication as "Cosmopoli," this imprint made a direct challenge to postal inspectors who might declare its books obscene. Dr. Robinson openly deplored commercialized smut and insisted his writings were devoid of it. He likely would not have approved of Cosmopolis's modish and suggestive illustration for Ralcy Husted Bell's historical account *Women from Bondage to Freedom*; it included art nouveau vignettes of two bare-breasted females.

As we know, gallantiana that commanded high prices in finely printed limited editions was available in the late 1920s in cheap reprints by the Rarity Press. These books, with or without the Rarity imprint, could be ordered from firms such as the Arden Book Company, the National Library, Pioneer, Franklin, Garden City, and Mayfair Publications. Some of the books, by such varied authors as D. H. Lawrence, Richard von Krafft-Ebing, Jim Tully (author of racy fiction), Petronius, and Radclyffe Hall, may have been cheaply printed softbound impressions from the original plates.[24] One mail-order bookseller played a minor role in the liberation of Joyce's *Ulysses*. A. Heymoolen of Cazenovia, Minnesota, ordered copies from Paris in 1927; they were seized by Customs, and subsequent deliberations at the Customs Court established the legal status of the novel in America as obscene. It was this decision that Morris Ernst challenged on behalf of Random House in 1933. Other titles in Heymoolen's confiscated shipment were Beverland's *Law Concerning Draped Virginity* (a Carrington work), Louÿs's *Aphrodite*, and several works by Dr. Jacobus X, all of which were considered "offensive to chastity, delicacy, or decency" under the Tariff Act of 1922.[25] Heymoolen, and Joseph Lewis, whose Truth Publishing Company flourished in the 1920s, specialized in borderline materials: literary classics and sexology, as well as birth-control tracts. The federal penalties for interstate mailing of obscene matter usually kept notorious banned titles out of the mail, although there were exceptions: Esar Levine and Ben Rebhuhn, friends of Frank Harris, with their fixer Ben Miller, solicited mail orders for *My Life and Loves*; Ben Abramson mailed lists of banned erotica, reproduced by an early form of xerography; and Sam Roth sent copies of his piracies of *Lady Chatterley's Lover* at least as far as Boston.

From "Tillie and Mac" to Paris Flagellantia

With their chutzpah and ingenuity sharpened by hard times, post-Crash promoters violated the taboos of the postal inspectors even more aggressively than before. Cheap books on erotology, birth control, eugenics, "inversion" and other "sexual abnormalities," and the restoration of "lost potency" might seem certain to attract the attention of outraged clergy, concerned parents, and wary postal inspectors; still, these were commonly advertised in the classified sections of pulp, romance, movie-star, adventure, and humor magazines in the middle and late 1930s. Often, those who placed "get-acquainted" or "love-happiness-success" advertisements

in magazines and newspapers were not offering matchmaking services. Rather, they were purveying erotic materials: Tijuana bibles, spicy playing cards, joke books, "action" pictures of people copulating, and books such as *Seventy-Two Flappers Posing in Scanties* and *Confessions of a Bellboy*.[26] Not everything sold through the mail was what it appeared to be. The promoters of many "schemes" for selling both cartoons and books actually provided only innocuous or abridged materials. Deceptive advertising appealed to prurient interest; the goods themselves skirted the danger of prosecution for obscenity. To deal with these, the Post Office invented a new and rather ironic tactic: postmasters issued fraud orders against them.[27] Advertisements appearing in periodicals such as *Spicy Detective Stories*, *Movie Humor*, *Police Gazette*, *Ten Story Gang*, and *La Vie Parisienne*, for example, bore headlines such as "Tillie and Mac," "Fanny Hill," "Only a Boy," "Toots and Caspar," "73 and More Montmartre Type Action Photos, the Kind Men Like!" (Figure 31). Readers sending a dollar received seven sheets of small pictures of girls in lingerie, a sheet of small photos of fully dressed people embracing, or a single sheet printed on both sides with "witticisms" that incorporated the names mentioned in the advertisement. Caveat emptor. This scam was often repeated by the same "promoters," who, once caught, simply changed their company name. *Farley v. Simons* (99 F2d 343 [D.C. Cir.], 1938) speaks directly to these practices, which were widespread in pulp magazines except when, as the Clayton Group boasted on its masthead, "an intelligent censorship guid[ed their] advertising pages."

If fake "hot stuff" was common, so were advertisements for blatant pornography, direct from Paris. In the late 1930s, a catalog of "Parisian Erotic Photos and Booklets" reached a large number of men in this country (Figure 32).[28] The catalog itself carried a notice to the effect that it offered "REAL HOT STUFF . . . the fucking scenes are . . . described such as they are, in all their rawness, and not through the veil of decency." The photo sets offered showed men and women in various poses, described as "two young sisters," "two good boys who don't need women," "the captive woman," "a beautiful negro boy fucking a pretty Parisian girl," "a young

---

Figure 31. Classified ads from pulp magazines. "Gargoyle Press" and "Maggie & Jiggs" from *Paris Nights*, n.d., c. 1936 (vol. 13); "Fannie Hill" from *Spicy Stories*, Nov. 1934, 64; "Daring Book" from *Film Fun*, Feb. 1934, 58.

NEW
CONFIDENTIAL
CATALOGUE
OF
Rare and Genuine

PARISIAN EROTIC PHOTOS
AND BOOKLETS

NOTICE

THE wonderful collection of Lustful Books and Erotic Photographs offered in this catalogue is strictly unique in its kind.

It is the " REAL HOT STUFF " which you have been vainly seeking for so long.

The books are written in plain crude language : no hesitancy to call a prick a prick and a cunt a cunt : the fucking scenes are also described such as they are, in all their rawness, and not through the veil of decency ; this much said, all further comments become unnecessary.

The Photos are taken from actual life (in many instances the actors were taken unawares). The scenes of hysterical passion and extreme debauchery displayed in these pictures, will not only charm your eyes but also overexcite your sensuality. In this entirely exclusive line, we have the largest variety to select from, and we can therefore safely guarantee to give you full satisfaction.

Yours faithfully,
The French Publishing Company.

Price list n° 37.

Parisian boy of 19 with his three girl friends." One could also choose from seven photo sets on "Flagellation Among Women," or order a series of "Erotic Novelettes," including seven on flagellation. Finally, for three dollars, there was *Love's Encyclopedia*, a tract on intercourse positions (published c. 1910), the final section of which was about "how to fuck to conceive either a girl or boy baby, and other fucking hints of great value." For two dollars more, a "second copy can be sent direct to the address you give us." One's girlfriend, the publishers suggested, might like that.

Post Office investigators placed orders, using assumed names, to determine that often nothing at all was received in return for money sent. In any event, the circular itself was blatantly obscene by any contemporary standards, whether or not it was actually circulated in this country. Henry N. Pringle used his international connections as law-enforcement officer of the International Reform Federation to complain to the French ambassador, "who requested prosecutions by his government."[29]

Sexology: "Societies," "Libraries," and "Presses"

The most extensive mail-order booksellers in the 1930s incorporated themselves as "societies" or "libraries" if they distributed the texts of other publishers, and as "presses" if they printed new editions as well. They featured sexually oriented, but mainly educational and nonoffensive, fiction and nonfiction that presumably might be safely advertised, ordered, and sent by a common carrier. Distributors who made this presumption knew there were risks. I have defined sexology as a serious sociological or anthropological study of human behavior, and pointed out that prurient curiosities could be aroused by it, even in its most learned forms and austere formats. The promoters of mail-order sexology traded on those curiosities. The books themselves were usually informative and significant, but the publishers anticipated objections, and therefore sometimes excised the most explicit sections, or those most repugnant to established mores. Assuming they could then proceed

---

Figure 32. A catalog of photos and pamphlets from the French Publishing Company ("Hot Stuff," "Flagellation," *Love's Encyclopedia*), mailed from André LaCroix, 36, Allée Danton, Livry-Gargan, France, with introductory letter dated 8 Dec. 1937. National Archives, Records of the Post Office Department, Post Office fraud order 6585.

without legal objection, they assured themselves of the widest possible sales by writing advertisements that used the terms "sexology," "curiosa," and "erotica" interchangeably. In 1931, *Publishers Weekly* noted an increasing number of mail-order catalogs purporting to offer general literature but actually specializing in "esoterica, sexual books" offered at cut-rate prices that were "bargains" only if the prospective purchaser did not recognize how inflated the original price had been.[30] The advertisements made clear that many of the books offered were indeed erotic — as the trade names of the two largest, named after Panurge (Rabelais's "dissolute and debauched fellow") and Falstaff, underscored. Such cues were picked up not only by purchasers but by the Post Office, which could smell erotica even more acutely than *Publishers Weekly*. By the middle and late 1930s, it reported yearly investigations of more than two thousand cases of mailings suspected of being obscene.[31] Distribution of such material through interstate commerce was a federal offense, and carried a penalty of both imprisonment and heavy fine.

Mail-order erotica dealers compiled varied lists. The American Anthropological Society offered approximately five hundred works of history, travel and exploration, sexology, memoirs, psychology, and fiction, including Dickens, Aldington, Zola, and Maupassant.[32] The Anthropological Library specialized in "scientific" holdings exemplified by the following ten classifications in one of the catalogs:[33] "flagellation" (about 30 titles), "scientific sexualia" (about 70), "curious fiction" (about 70), "memoirs and biography" (13), "literature" (20), "phallic worship" (6), "curious poems" (5), "medieval tales" (9), "witchcraft" (2), and "anthropology" (5). The American Ethnological Press, directed by Louis Shomer of Brooklyn,[34] offered many titles from publishers such as Panurge, Falstaff, Faro, and Coventry House. The Eugenics Publishing Company, with which Joseph Lewis merged his Truth Publishing Company in 1927,[35] published as well as distributed its own books. The cover of a 1940 catalog titled "For the Good of the Race" lists the categories of its books: sex conduct in marriage, the art of love, sex disorders and abnormalities, birth control, morals. Esar Levine's Panurge Press (his brother Benjamin was office manager) published under three separate imprints: Panurge, Robin Hood House (some were later impressions of popular Panurge titles with limited first releases), and the American Anthropology Society, the stock of which Esar Levine purchased after the original owner declared bankruptcy.[36] Panurge's clients could order books on sexual customs in England, France, ancient Greece, the Levant, or during the Great War; they could learn about the perfumes exuded by the human body during coitus, about phallic cults, or about courtesans in various times and climes; they could also pursue esoteric studies of circumcision in men and women, bestiality, artificial insemination, bundling and sexual slavery in early America, and the preparation of excrementitious love potions. Motives for purchasing these books, which were often unavailable to general readers outside big cities except through the mail-order presses, must have varied enormously. The authors were some of the most significant anthropologists and sociologists working in the new but growing field of sexual science: Hirschfeld, Reclus, Niemoeller, Rohleder. The prurient interest, no doubt, made the business much more lucrative than otherwise would have been the case.

Benjamin Rebhuhn incorporated the Falstaff Press in 1932, with his wife, Anne, as president.[37] Its earliest imprints date from that year, three years after the earliest Panurge offering.[38] Eight of its works were later versions of Panurge titles. The Levines transferred their copyrights on these titles to the Rebhuhns, probably at the time of Esar's indictment for interstate commerce in obscene literature. Louis Shomer of the American Ethnological Press likewise transferred two of his titles to Rebhuhn.[39] Falstaff gave special prominence to the work of Iwan Bloch ("the father of sexology"), a Berlin physician and writer on sexual customs and behavior. It published five of his works, and a sixth under its Anthropological Press imprint. Three of these were translated by Solomon Malkin, the young scholar from New York University whose studies under Magnus Hirschfeld at the famous Institute for Sexual Science in Berlin had previously gained him employment as a translator for Panurge.[40] At Falstaff, Malkin supplemented Bloch's *Sex Life in England* with descriptive chapters on, and excerpts from, erotica that had been published since the first edition appeared, including Harris's *My Life and Loves* and Lawrence's *Lady Chatterley's Lover*. He also selected erotic artwork to accompany the text, and did the same for most of the other five titles he was contracted to work on by office manager Ben Raeburn, Rebhuhn's cousin.[41]

Other mail-order distributors included Jacob Brussel's Jul-Mar, the Julian and the Risus Presses,[42] the Biblion Balzac, the Pickwick and the Parnassus Book Shops, the Abbey and the Allied Book Companies, and Emerson.[43] Pioneer and Franklin also mailed sexology. As was common practice with other mail-order distributors, some of the books that Brussel and Samuel Roth published under imprints that can be traced to them were distributed by other mail-order firms as well. In turn, Brussel and Roth often distributed the books of other firms. Some, but probably not all, of these books were remainders.

The scale of Samuel Roth's operations, his motives, and the results, including the authorities' condemnations and prosecutions of him, were practically without parallel. Although he did advertise by mail, and put himself squarely in the way of federal convictions in 1928 and 1936 by mailing the most notorious banned books of the period, he was also able to place many of the innocuous titles in his William Faro, Black Hawk, and Coventry House imprints in bookstores. He was therefore not as exclusively involved in mail-order dealing during the 1930s as the other publishers and distributors described here. To the extent that his books reached not only mail-order but bookstore customers who either purchased copies or browsed the shelves, Roth's bookselling had a dimension of resourcefulness and daring only occasionally met by his competitors. He also featured a wider range of titles.

Attracting Customers: Circulars, Title Pages, Bindings, and Magazine Spreads

The circulars for mail-order erotica were seemingly ubiquitous, and therefore raised even greater alarm than the books themselves. A Justice Department spokesman noted in 1936 that the sophistication of Panurge's operations stimulated the activities of its competitors, especially Falstaff; he estimated the total number of circulars at six hundred thousand per year.[44] As for the appeals to prurience in these notices, it is fair to harken back to Shakespeare, as did Ben Rebhuhn: they are "gross as a mountain, open, palpable." What else can any reader think of a flyer for a study of corporal punishment that features a drawing of a trouserless child being held by hands and feet and caned, especially when the circular's headlined words are the title, *Tender Bottoms*, and the single word "Illustrated" (Figure 33)?[45] Equally self-explanatory is an advertisement of the usually staid Eugenics Publishing Company for a book on lesbianism; it depicts a nubile naked woman embracing a female statue while Cupid sits at its base and weeps (Figure 34).[46] Esar Levine's

Figure 33. Circular for a flagellation book published by the American Ethnological Press in 1934. Courtesy of Dr. C. J. Scheiner.

ILLUSTRATED

TENDER BOTTOMS

A Psychosexual Study in Modern Morals Based on Personal Experiences and Documentary Evidence

circulars attracted the curious with a volley of declarations, each the verbal equivalent of a large exclamation mark. Novels and memoirs of the Middle or Far East portray "adulterous and cruel" orientals and "the mad lust of black men for white women." Sexological tracts and histories of sexual customs proceed by anecdote and example, not by exposition, and make one "catch his breath" ("strange experiments," "sex horrors"). Abnormalities that give rise to the "blind fury of passion" are described, as is female "immoderate lust" that "degrades and humiliates" men. Homosexuality, pagan "obscene religions," and bestiality are analyzed in "historical, medical, literary and legal" studies. Promoting Panurge's *Praeputii Incisio*, Esar asks, "What can be as dry as a history of circumcision?" and need not pause for an answer.

This kind of advertising copy may now seem pathetically vulnerable to derision, or even quaintly charming. But the censoriousness of the moral entrepreneurs and the postal bureaucrats who supported them had resulted in the suppression of even explicit writings that everyone agreed were meant not to titillate but to soberly instruct people about their sexuality and its physiological and psychological effects. The mail-order dealers of the Depression period did have the moxie to publish their "sexology," with its unique mélange of scientific and prurient-interest appeals. They were gratifying eternally irrepressible curiosities that, for office personnel and salesclerks, physicians and professors, were as closely fused to prurience as two thousand years of secular mores and religious doctrine could make them. In their advertising, appeals to prurience coexisted in a near schizophrenic alliance alongside a shrill but seemingly sincere dedication to awareness of how responsibly to enjoy and control one's sexual nature: "The Good of The Race." Cogent observation revealed both to be good selling points.

Falstaff's circulars were crammed with quotations, synopses, lists of chapter titles, and statements of purpose. The "High Aim [or 'Vital Function'] of Falstaff Publications" (Figure 35) was to disseminate information about sexual customs in remote regions or in the past, with a view to decreasing sexually transmitted

---

Figure 34. Page one of a four-page circular ("copyright 1938") for Maurice Chideckel's *Female Sex Perversion*. Fearing Post Office interdiction because of the book's contents, illustrations, and advertisements, the Eugenics Publishing Company sought legal advice on how to market it. Reproduced by permission of the Harry Ransom Research Center, University of Texas at Austin. Source: File box 388, MLE Papers.

Figure 35. Full-page advertisement for the Falstaff Press, with a leering Falstaff, a statement of "high aim," and a coupon for a free catalog of "exotically illustrated Masterpieces." From *Hooey* (illustrated humor and girlie magazine), Dec. 1934, p. [1].

diseases and increasing "the health and pleasure of individuals" through education. Falstaff subscribers, the publishers asserted, comprised "a Who's Who of the Intellectual Aristocracy of America." Progressive parents joined scientists, nurses, physicians, dentists, philosophers, ministers, and certified public accountants. All clients were "registered in our specialized files" (the only real requisite for inclusion was being twenty-one or older) and "private announcements are sent only to our choicest collectors." Falstaff even offered a Book Guild that provided members with a book a month, each accompanied by a free volume or pamphlet. This erotic-book-of-the-month club was devised to increase sales not only by appeal to strong appetite for curiosa, but for its conspicuous consumption as a sign of the well-informed citizen.

Mail-order distributors of sexology provided frequent and heavy work for Railway Express. The books they sold were printed on quality paper and were between three hundred and five hundred pages long. Except for the pamphlets provided as free premiums, they were sturdily bound in cloth. They were usually quarto-size, but Eugenics, Pioneer, and Franklin produced octavo-size volumes, hoping to allay suspicion by imitating austere scientific tracts. Falstaff and Panurge had their own house styles of book design, attempts to produce an aura of exclusivity for that class of purchasers who could pay the five dollars for first printings. Ben Rebhuhn, however, seems to have decided that the customers for his Falstaff Press were uninterested in the ethos of aristocratic leisure reflected in the traditional style of gentleman's library erotica. Perhaps he was simply unaware of the way the components of fine printing ought to be combined to create a coherent style. His title pages, often in red and black, are crowded with varied typefaces and with long subtitles. The sheets of some volumes are tinted light green and deckle-edged; those of other books are glossy and thick with clay. Some title pages (Féré's *Sexual Degeneration in Mankind and in Animals*, for example) are printed on vellum and tipped in, as are some limitation statements. By conventional bookmaking standards then or now, genuine good taste counts for little; ostentation is all. Cloth bindings imitate watered silk or morocco, and one example carries color reproductions of a Blake painting on both boards — as if quantity of features in each and every case were a mark of distinction. Esar Levine, in contrast, deeply admired Charles Carrington's book design.[47] Esar and his brother Benjamin, his office manager, were fortunate to have the services of Samuel A. Jacobs, a talented typographer and designer. The binding and typography of their Panurge Press

Figure 36. First page of a four-page brochure for John Davenport's *Curiosities of Erotic Physiology*, published by the Panurge Press in 1930. Reproduced courtesy of McIlvenna Institute for the Advanced Study of Human Sexuality, San Francisco, California.

books created packages that could be advertised as worthy of a limited edition for an exclusive clientele of affluent professional readers (Figure 36). Panurge offered books to the taste of that ideal imaginary consumer of erotica and curiosa, the cultured gentleman of leisure — or his actual bourgeois descendants, whether scientists, amateur sociologists and anthropologists, physicians, or upwardly mobile dentists.[48] Falstaff had a different angle on what would appeal — perhaps more cynical, perhaps just heavy-handed.

Panurge took a unique and clever approach to cover design with a few of its Robin Hood House books. The upper cover of its edition of Reclus's *Curious Byways of Anthropology* carries only the subtitle: *Sexual Savage and Esoteric Customs of Primitive Peoples*. On the spine is only one word: *Anthropology*. Thus the volume makes a perfectly respectable display when shelved in a gentleman's library. When displayed on a table, it makes quite another impression. The same is true of Davenport's *Curiosities of Erotic Physiology*: the spine carries only the last word in the title, the upper cover only the first three. The "high aim" of this coy mixture of scholarly diction and overtly sexual signals — the unique ploy of the mail-order sexology publisher — was to make the books irresistible: it would take considerable willpower to keep from opening them and leafing through them.

Despite the highly developed portrait of the ideal well-educated purchaser, those to whom mail-order sexology was actually made available must have varied in age, sex, and income level, not to mention motive. This was especially true of the buyers solicited by Panurge and Falstaff, clearly the most sophisticated and best-financed operations. Initially, the Levines purchased a mailing list from a professional compiler, possibly one who specialized in serving erotica dealers.[49] This compiler, who maintained lists of customers for both magazines and books, may have been a list broker, although there were other firms providing this service: "People buy or borrow lists of people . . . in kindred lines of business."[50] On one occasion the Falstaff circulars were sent to Doubleday, Doran and Company's list of clients.[51] Possibly, general book publishers could profit from exchanging mailing lists with successful mail-order firms, and such trades may have been made directly by the interested parties. Another tactic was to locate and classify potential customers by profession. The secretary of the direct-by-mail firm Falstaff used explained that her organization maintained lists of lawyers and other professionals.[52] As Panurge grew and quite apparently prospered by employing some combination of these methods, its original mailing list expanded until it included approximately two thousand names.

In addition, prospective customers might express interest by responding to blurbs placed in the front or back of the books themselves, or by returning coupons found either in newspaper or magazine advertisements or in flyers either mailed or placed in bookshops. In 1923, Joseph Lewis employed the Sackheim and Sherman Advertising Agency, which also handled the accounts of Doubleday-Page, Nelson Doubleday, and the Little Leather Library Corporation, to place one of his advertisements in approximately fifteen magazines.[53] Falstaff's direct-by-mail agency beefed up the mailing list by placing advertisements in a wide variety of periodicals: *Scribner's*, *American Mercury*, *Gay Broadway*, *Spicy Adventure*, *Gentlewoman*, and *Modern Psychology* among them.[54] This eclectic group of steady newsstand and mail-order sellers suggests a diverse target audience: highbrow, middle- and upper-class intellectuals; conservatives; young men who enjoyed "dirty jokes"; men and women interested in titillating short fiction; rural housewives and their husbands; middlebrow seekers of explanations for unarticulated frustrations, sexual and otherwise. Clearly, some of the respondents might have been minors.

Besides collecting order forms, Samuel Roth resorted to using telephone books and other directories, at one point even acquiring for the purpose the membership list of the Harvard and Yale Clubs in New York.[55] Ivy League graduates had just the right blend of sophistication and ready cash to make them prime customers for esoterica and curiosa. A final, dubious way of adding names to the mailing list that many firms may have used, despite the risks if discovered, was the "obscene correspondence club." Such outfits put people in touch with prospective partners on the basis of preferences frankly stated in questionnaires the clubs circulated to those who wished to join. The clubs could have as many as three thousand members, some of whom would be promising candidates for mail-order sexology.[56]

Once the list was ready, potential purchasers had to be contracted. The actual mailing of the circulars could be contracted to a professional mailing service that would do the addressing and metering.[57] Falstaff's direct-by-mail advertising service sent its circulars using both first- and third-class metered mail.[58] As early as 1932, Falstaff applied for a permit to send out unstamped business reply cards and envelopes.[59]

Although most of Panurge and Falstaff's competitors were satisfied to place small classified ads in print media, those two concerns also ran more elaborate spreads in a variety of magazines. Eye-catching Panurge ads are found not only in *All Star Fiction* (a line of Broadway dancing girls points to a headline reading "Sex Life in America" [May 1935]) and *Love Fiction Monthly* (a languid bathing beauty points to the legend "Mail This Coupon Now! You'll Get the Surprise of Your Life" [November 1934]), but also in *Harper's* (July 1933) and the *New Yorker* (August 1931) (Figure 37). Falstaff's practice was similar. An advertisement in the January 1937 issue of the confession magazine *Modern Love* lists five works, each with the magic s-word in the title: *Strange Sexual Practices*, *Sex Life in England Illustrated*, *Magica Sexualis Illustrated Exotically*, *Illustrated Japanese Sexual Relations*, and *Sexual Relations of Mankind*; for novelty, there is also *Savage Arts of Love Illustrated*. These were not the exact titles of the actual books for sale, but for fans of spicy stories they were accurate enough. Small wonder that the Postal Service, the police, various journalists, John Sumner, district attorneys, and, eventually, Judge Learned Hand saw in Falstaff a ready-for-action pariah capitalist leering at men and women, young and old alike, whatever anthropological and eugenic motives he professed. Esar Levine's list of prominent and professional individuals (see Chapter 2) is undoubtably accurate, as are Rebhuhn's assertions about the number of highly educated customers Falstaff serviced. However, once the sale of newly released titles at five dollars per book to the professors, doctors, lawyers, and others who returned their coupons slackened, the firms spread their nets as widely as possible. "Price slashes" more than halved book costs.

How many replies did such advertising yield? The Post Office docket books of fraud and lottery cases summarize an August 1939 complaint against Metro Books, a company run by Esar Levine's brother Benjamin after Esar's 1935 conviction, and a 1937 complaint against Falstaff. According to these documents, at the time of the complaints Metro was receiving between one hundred fifty and two hundred pieces of mail a day, and Falstaff approximately two hundred sixty. These figures seem high; other case records show daily response rates of between ten and twenty-five pieces.[60] In any event, Panurge and Falstaff prospered during the hard times of the Depression. The 1939 *Annual Report of the Postmaster General* gave Falstaff's income for the year as one hundred thousand dollars.[61] The mail-order promoters had added a new and lucrative dimension to the distribution of erotica. As a

Figure 37. Full-page advertisement for the Panurge Press, possibly tailored for the kind of spicy humor magazine in which it appeared. Some of the spines of the books read "Bestiality," "Madame Sex," "Sexarians," "Sin and Such," "Merry Nights." From *Ballyhoo*, Dec. 1933, p. [30].

consequence, the Post Office, with a boost from the NYSSV, assiduously gathered evidence. Esar Levine's 1936 successful prosecution was a direct result; Ben Rebhuhn's 1939 imprisonment followed.

The Role of the Catholic Church in Post Office Obscenity Prosecutions

In a 1945 open letter to the British publishing historian Alec Craig, Gershon Legman reports that "it's common talk that the postmaster-generalship is the price the Democratic party pays for the political support of the Catholic Church,"[62] basing his statement on a decade of association with erotica distributors. The urban working class, with its large number of immigrants and Catholics, was an important voting block.[63] Further, Catholic agitation for decency was uniquely effective; it was thoroughly organized, and could address itself to a monolithic audience. Protestant sects were scattered across the entire economic spectrum, were geographically as well as ideologically diverse, and were often at odds with one another. Catholics, in contrast, stood uniformly for middle-class respectability, rather than aristocratic or fundamentalist values.[64] This helped make the boycott a powerful tool to use at the local level. Catholic spokespeople attributed the increase in pornographic magazines and books after 1930 on newsstands, in lending libraries, and in the mails to the moral laxness of judges and Customs officials who allowed the circulation of birth-control information, especially Mary Ware Dennett's and Margaret Sanger's books. Legman charges that as a result of Catholic-influenced Postal Service antiobscenity machinery, the Falstaff and Panurge Presses and other "publishers of sex-science translations . . . folded up in quick order," along with many of the "spicy story" magazines and "publishers of openly-distributed (and very nasty) flagellantia."[65] This statement needs some qualification. Panurge was out of business by 1936, and in that year Samuel Roth received a three-year prison term, but Esar Levine's brother and other parties continued — albeit on a smaller scale — to sell some sexually oriented books through the mails; it took until 1939 for the Justice Department to deal conclusively with Falstaff. Roth, Legman's employer at one time and frequent target of Post Office fraud and obscenity prosecutions over four decades, was equally convinced of the Church's influence. Years later he wrote a short story about "Plentipunda," a distant land in which "officials took turns in the several functions of the court so that all [officials] in the course of twenty trials when all were present, served in the several capacities of judge, juryman, master of ceremonies and tipstaff—an arrangement which resembles the departmental court of hearings of the United States Post Office except that the latter is run not as a court but as a parish of the Catholic Church."[66]

Any hard evidence for Catholic influence on postal policy is elusive, although a circumstantial case can be made. James Paul and Murray Schwartz, in their thorough study *Federal Censorship: Obscenity in the Mail*, observe that the ACLU always suspected the Church's influence, because many of the magazines declared unmailable in the early 1940s were those deplored by the Catholic-sponsored National Organization for Decent Literature (NODL).[67] The ACLU's National Council for Freedom from Censorship (NCFC)[68] noted that although the Post Office prosecuted materials dealing with sexology, birth control, and contraception, it tolerated information on the rhythm method, a point corroborated by testimony before the 1935 House Subcommittee on Offenses Against the Postal Service.[69] Paul Blanchard, lawyer, social critic, and onetime member of the State Department, also detected a Catholic influence on the Post Office. His trenchant criticisms of the Church's repression, wielding the snarl word "smut" and the shibboleth "decency," of liberal political and social ideas regarding divorce, sex education, family planning, and abortion include a discussion of the considerable 1938 success of the fledgling NODL in getting magazines removed from various points of sale. According to Blanchard, the NODL "is especially effective as a pressure group in dealing with small publishers and newsstand operators, and it has had the warm cooperation of many of our Postmasters General, several of whom have been Catholics."[70]

Catholic authorities saw the availability of erotic writings to children, and to adults of limited financial resources and aspirations, as a profound threat. The *Manual of the NODL* contains many statements to the effect that "sex is almost irrevocably linked to crime by youth" and that "filthy literature" accomplished the "dastardly job of destroying the moral fibre of many young boys and girls."[71] But this being true, the case for Catholic pressure on the Post Office to suppress mail-order erotica loses some force, at least as far as sexological books are concerned. True, the circulars could fall into the hands of children. The books themselves, however, were expensive—they started at five or six dollars, and even when remaindered or sold at bargain rates through advertisements in pulp magazines, cost two or three dollars per volume. Once in the home, of course, young people might find them, and since the books were sent in plain wrapper to one's home, rather than purchased in plain sight from newsstands and stores, the pledge to boycott obscene and indecent materials, which priests periodically exacted from their congregations, would potentially have had less effect. In any case, the NODL manual focuses on lending-library and newsstand material and the Tijuana bibles peddled in so many locations; the same is true of articles in the Catholic journal *America*, which focus on books sold in public places, not on mail-order materials.

The Role of Liberal Reform in Postal Policy

The Catholic lobby was not the only influence on postal policy. In fact, the Post Office was perceived by some observers, including First Amendment advocates, as being less repressive during the Roosevelt administration (1933–45) than previously. True, no liberal could accept the conclusions of the Attorney General's Report on Administrative Procedure, released in 1940,[72] that reform of the Post Office's procedures for interdicting obscenity was not needed. The report noted the ex parte tactics described above, but felt the postal authorities could be trusted to apply them wisely, and also discounted the value of a formal hearing (judicial review). This was completely unacceptable (a "shocking document") to the NCFC.[73] If Morris Ernst was nonplused, however, his public response was rather muted. In a letter to Dean Acheson, who chaired the committee that produced the report, Ernst asked Acheson to note that although he felt the Post Office deserved harsh criticism for its methods, he acknowledged that "the control of Literature by the Post Office during the past seven years has been carried on in a far more liberal manner than heretofore."[74] That at first blush seems a puzzling statement. Certainly Ben Rebhuhn and Esar Levine would have waved it off in disgust. Yet Ernst's opinion was shared by John Sumner and his fellow antivice secretaries, Charles H. Bodwell at the Watch and Ward Society and Henry N. Pringle at the International Reform Federation.

Bodwell and Pringle both looked to Sumner for aid and comfort, since most of the offending publishers were New York–based, and almost all of the circulars had been sent from there. These men had collected many pounds of flyers and coupons, especially from Eugenics, Falstaff, and Panurge. Some had been sent to them by angry recipients. Bodwell, who had been complaining since 1931, agreed with his colleagues that it was a special affront to find Falstaff notices appearing in the

World Almanac.[75] Writing to Postmaster General Farley and to one of his solicitors, Pringle had received only "formal acknowledgments. As far as I have learned, it appears that Mr. Farley, who as a Catholic, would naturally clean out these degenerate dealers, is for political reasons, perhaps, protecting them." He concluded by agreeing with Bodwell that the advertising in itself was actionable.[76]

Apparently the NCFC's legislative campaigns, and their efforts to inform their supporters about the restraints on free speech practiced by the antivice societies and the Post Office, had won the attention of the Roosevelt administration. In 1936, the NCFC aggressively campaigned to "Abolish the Post Office Censorship," as its pamphlet put in. The organization championed Senate Bill 3907, which would substitute Justice Department libel actions and jury trials for determinations of unmailability by postal counsel.[77] The NCFC had powerful allies, such influential figures as H. L. Mencken, Senator Bronson Cutting (Democrat, New Mexico), the physician Karl Menninger, the editor Maxwell Perkins, and the lawyer Arthur Garfield Hayes among them.[78] Samuel Walker, historian of the ACLU, remarking on the number of civil libertarians working in government agencies during the Roosevelt years, noted two results: the end of censorship by Customs agents and the reduction of the U.S. Postal Service's censorship of the mails.[79] This loosening of restrictions applied as much to politically oriented materials as to sexually oriented ones; the common denominator was a new recognition of free-speech principles. Ernst would have been especially sensitive to the salutary effects of the influence of liberal lawyers in the federal government, including the Justice Department, during the 1930s.

Perhaps this liberalizing trend is why his colleague Alexander Lindey could find only one case of postal prosecution of a mail-order bookseller in all of 1938 or 1939.[80] This was the trial against Falstaff that resulted in Judge Learned Hand's sending the Rebhuhns to jail. The Justice Department was determined to get a conviction in this case. But the NCFC may have shied away from becoming involved for two reasons. First, to do so would have embarrassed Farley, and made it harder for ACLU lawyers to gain the cooperation of postal counsels in other cases. But second, the NCFC would not have wanted its supporters, or the general public (let alone its enemies), to see it as protecting smutmongers. In 1932, Lindey had advised a bookseller that selling Hector France's *Musk, Hashish and Blood* (probably the Falstaff reprint of the Carrington edition) "involves considerable risk," and that the circular "is obscene as a matter of law."[81] One year later, Lindey advised Clifton Read of the ACLU that the case brought to its attention by the American Ethnological Press regarding three sexological texts was "not a deserving one" and that "the exploitation of the ACLU by cheap pornographers should be prevented."[82]

Ernst's political savvy — Walker tells us that he considered himself a "Washington power broker"[83] — may have led him to conclude by 1940 that progress had been made, and should not be jeopardized by too strident public condemnation of the Post Office, especially in the case of booksellers' obviously prurient circulars. The Postal Service was at the time advocating a bill that would allow it to prosecute the senders of materials deemed obscene at the place of receipt, where judges and juries were much more likely to convict than in New York. This was not just a tactic for stopping erotica mail-order businesses at the place where most were based, but also an unreasonable curb on dissemination of ideas, according to the NCFC. The council's memorandum in opposition pointed out that the proposed bill marked a federal usurpation of the states' prerogative, and would sanction the most puritanical criteria for rulings on obscenity and indecency.[84] However, there was a thorny complicating factor: the Post Office was also involved in strenuous efforts to stem the heavy influx of German propaganda. This situation presented free-speech interests with a painfully divisive dilemma.[85] Ernst, more than other ACLU lawyers who did not share his contacts or special status as writer and public figure, felt that the political climate called not for overt challenges but for careful discussions with the solicitors of the office of the third assistant postmaster general.

How Obscenity and Fraud Linked Up: The Unfortunate Cases of Esar Levine and Ben Rebhuhn

The administrative procedures for protecting the mails from fraud were the same as those used to stop obscenity: informing the purveyor (Martin Sugar, or someone advertising a shampoo that would cure baldness, for example) that he or she must desist using the mails for his or her scheme, after which items were returned to the sender as "unmailable," "fraudulent," or "fictitious." The latter designation meant the purveyor had not used his or her own name or that of a registered company.[86] In coupling obscenity with fraud, the Comstockian assumption was that Americans needed protection from offers of obscene literature in the same way they needed protection from schemes to restore one's "lost manhood" or cure incapacitating illnesses with elixirs, to increase one's breast or penis size with medicines, or to get rich quick by investing money with unauthorized speculators. One need not accept the idea that obscenity is a kind of fraud to see the Post Office's prosecutions in some of these other matters as legitimately necessary to serve the public. Nevertheless, the argument that their ability to stop the smut depended on the powers of the postal inspectors and their ex parte procedures was not easy to refute. Morris Ernst might well proclaim that the Post Office had "tried to translate a practice of fraud with relation to securities into the realm of the definition of a vague word like 'obscenity,' knowing this has to do with the remedy and not with the substance [i.e., the constitutional considerations]."[87] When such disturbances threatened, the postal officials would dig in their heels, and weather the ideological storm.

In 1939, the Post Office received aid and comfort from a court decision that clarified the relation between fraud and salaciousness. The immediate result of this clarification was that Falstaff Press lost its appeal of a previous conviction, and Ben Rebhuhn and his nephew were sentenced to the federal penitentiary. Learned Hand, renowned for his acumen in constitutional law and, later, for his belief in judicial restraint, was one of the appellate judges. His eloquent criticism, in 1913, of the Hicklin rule — he wrote that to censor books that might disturb the least mature community members would "reduce our treatment of sex to the standard of a child's library" — had been precisely twenty-one years ahead of its time. In the Falstaff matter, he reported that the books involved in the case, although sexually explicit, had their "proper place." However, the defendants had "woefully misused" them by willfully and indiscriminately appealing to "the salaciously disposed" (of any age and social status) in their circulars, thus purveying the books not to specialists but to the general public, and on the basis of their prurient rather than their educational or aesthetic value.[88] Because of the manner in which the circulars were written, the Rebhuhns clearly were aware — that is, they had "guilty knowledge" — that the books themselves could have been represented as having prurient instead of scientific interest.[89] Whether the prospective purchaser was a college professor or a sniggering schoolchild, selling him or her a book for purposes of sexual stimulation was inexcusable, even when the book itself was not a piece of smut but Iwan Bloch's *Sex Life in England* or even Joyce's *Ulysses*. The Bloch title was one of the books cited in the Falstaff prosecution, along with eleven others, including Cabanes's *Erotikon* and Mantegazza's *Sexual Relations of Mankind*. The promoter of such a scheme may or may not have transgressed the borders of obscenity according to the mores of the day; but even if the circulars were not obscene as such, the nature of the advertisements made him or her guilty of a kind of fraud: pandering. The latter was, in Hand's words, "the gravamen of the crime."[90]

There was a precedent for Hand's equation of prurient sales pitches with fraud: *Farley v. Simons* (1938), which concerned the widespread "Tillie and Mac" advertisements. These operations posed two problems for the Post Office. First, it would be hard to prove that the promoters were engaged in obscenity, since all the client received were innocuous materials, such as insipid, nonsnappy jokes attributed to people named Tillie or Mac. Second, the use of decoy letters had proved ineffective.[91] By the time an inspector's letter was processed, his quarry might have received many orders and have both changed the company name and discontinued the post office box, thus wiping out the paper trail.[92] Therefore, postal solicitors found it convenient to declare fly-by-night companies advertising erotic materials in pulp magazines and in personally addressed circulars to be frauds that did not deliver what they promised. The Post Office successfully argued in federal court that even the prurient-minded had a right to protection from fraudulent, unkept promises of nude pictures and bawdy stories.[93] The decision established a key principle under which the postal bureaucracy functioned: that material actually lacking any prurient interest, if advertised in a manner that enticed prospective purchasers with erotically stimulating suggestions, could be proscribed as a fraud.

Judge Hand did not cite *Farley v. Simons*, but his line of reasoning places the Rebhuhns in the same class of offenders as the promoters of Tillie and Mac schemes. Hand had overturned the conviction of Esar Levine, president of the Panurge Press, four years earlier, because the original trial judge had attempted to apply a pre-*Ulysses* "absolute standard" for testing obscenity instead of the tests of "community standards" and literary value (determined through expert testimony) that the 1934 decision had established.[94] Biographer Gerald Gunther underlines the importance of Hand's 1936 statement in codifying the association of obscenity only with material reasonable adults decide is unlawful, after weighing its likely audience and professed merit against the extent of, and rationale for, its emphasis on the erotic.[95] Hand frowned on the Postal Service's contempt for the *Ulysses* decision, and considered its interpretation archaic. However, he granted it the right to interdict the closely bound social evils of fraud and obscenity involved in pandering advertisements. Very significantly, his decision implicitly affirmed the postal administrative procedures by which these perceived evils were attacked: summary impounding of mail and ex parte adjudications of the postal inspectors, who had their own absolute standards.

Mail-order advertisers all over the country monitored the Rebhuhn case. Their trade publication warned, in reporting Hand's decision, that it "was important because a large number of reputable publishers sell at least some books dealing with sex." Some of the Falstaff books had been circulating unchallenged by the Post Office; now, there seemed to be no standards that one could use to determine the mailability of sexually oriented material.[96] Merchants could only look closely at their circulars and try to guess whether they might be offensive. The postal inspector was under no obligation to clarify where the borderline was, or to apply consistent standards; booksellers would be held culpable unless they took extraordinary care to try to prove the chastity of their sales pitches as well as their books. But the advertising copy that resulted might be so dull that their businesses would collapse. It is not amiss here to quote Felix Frankfurter: "The history of American freedom is, in no small measure, the history of procedure."[97]

Benjamin Rebhuhn faced two years of incarceration and a ten-thousand-dollar fine, for the sentencing judge had agreed with the prosecuting attorney that he was a hardened offender. In 1925, he had escaped prosecution as a friend of Frank Harris, but, as mentioned, he had been fined, given a suspended sentence, then jailed for selling pornography in the late 1920s, and several years later failed to heed warnings given him by the Post Office and the district attorney. The more than twelve hundred complaints from those receiving circulars from Falstaff included letters from the secretary of the California Probation Association, the chairman of the Marion County (Tennessee) American Red Cross, the secretary of the American Board of Commissioners for Foreign Missions, the legislative chairman of the Catholic Central Verein of America, and a retired U.S. army captain.[98] The moral indignation of such a large number of solid advocates of traditional American values, mirroring that of public officials and the clergy, convinced federal officials to act.[99] Rebhuhn and his lawyer had responded to repeated warnings by promising to discontinue third-class mailings, which they insisted had gone only to professionals in any case; but the mailings went on, and it seemed only a federal prosecution would stop them.[100] To bring a federal case — which would have to be based on the mailing of obscene circulars for obscene books — the postal authorities would have to convince the Justice Department. Only in cases the department thought exceptional would it respond to such requests.[101] The case of Falstaff, a one-hundred-thousand-dollar business ($1,190,000 in mid-1998 dollars) run by a clearly unrepentant offender, met the test. In late 1935, Rebhuhn was arrested.

The case was carefully prepared by a whole coalition of the enemies of indecency. In an instance of John Sumner's cooperation with the Post Office, one of his financial officers had successfully requested that several Falstaff circulars be sent to his Manhattan hotel.[102] Sumner's man had also gone directly to the Falstaff office to buy a copy of one of the advertised books. This was not the only instance of entrapment Rebhuhn suffered. The FBI also investigated Falstaff, on suspicion of transportation of obscene literature in interstate commerce, with a view to helping prepare the federal indictment. The Rebhuhns' credit ratings, bank balances ("medium high four figures"), reputation with their neighbors, and physical descriptions were noted. Writing his own "test letters," an FBI agent purchased five books.[103]

The legal basis of the Falstaff prosecution was as carefully organized as the investigation. Levine's 1935 conviction, and three-year sentence, had been overturned six months later on appeal, as stated above, and the NCFC had informed its members that the reversal was a landmark vindication of the whole-book rule, the validity of expert testimony, and the significance of "artistic value" in defending a book from charges of obscenity.[104] U.S. Attorney John T. Cahill, determined to win a conviction that could not be reversed on any such grounds, conducted the Falstaff case by adhering to a procedure more in keeping with the liberal criteria of the *Ulysses* decision. This proved a wise move. It took the jury less than three hours to find the defendants guilty on all fifteen counts of the indictment.[105]

Emboldened, the government now moved once more against Esar Levine, calendaring his retrial four years after his successful appeal.[106] Levine was desperate. In an impassioned letter to a congressman and personal friend, Representative Adolph J. Sabath, he stated that the tension he had endured for four years had exacerbated the intestinal problems incurred during his earlier six-month stint in prison (he had been denied bail while his appeal was pending). He noted that he was concerned by his wife's mental state, had abandoned his bookselling business after conviction, and hoped the Justice Department would not "be actuated by rancor or revenge." The congressman wrote to Cahill, stating Levine's case and requesting a *nolle prosse, prosequi;* but he was unsuccessful. The crusading attorney felt that Levine's tactics had motivated Rebhuhn and others to distribute obscenity more vigorously than would otherwise have been the case, and that his original sentence had not been harsh. "It is my objective to clean up the obscene literature situation in the Southern District of New York entirely."[107] At the second trial, Levine pleaded guilty and was given a suspended sentence.[108]

Perhaps the Rebhuhns had indeed felt they were on solid ground after the reversal of Levine's conviction. After all, they might have reasoned, their books were just as "sexological" as Levine's; many were merely reprints. If obscenity tests were now to be based on a book's value as a whole to adults, were they not safe? They might have had second thoughts if they had seen what Hand and the two other judges wrote in their pretrial memos regarding *U.S. v. Levine*. They would have learned that not just the Post Office and the vice societies disdained Falstaff and Panurge as venal and salacious outfits. All three appellate judges deplored the trial judge's confusing and archaic charge to the jury regarding obscenity standards, but even Learned Hand recognized the prurient appeal of the circulars. His brother Augustus actually voted to affirm the "mixed up" judges' decision, because he saw the books as "filthy" and the bookseller's intention as simple exploitation of prospective purchasers' sexual curiosities.[109] Augustus Hand seemed to feel not only that the *Ulysses* criteria were inapplicable in the Panurge case, but that to use the Panurge case as any sort of confirmation of recent legal precedent would grant that publisher a stature he did not deserve. The conservative judge's confusion, not the facts of the case, won Levine his freedom. Morris Ernst's law firm argued the case; he and his colleagues knew that the books were of "dubious literary value."[110] The situation was familiar to the NCFC. Not all judges were as perspicacious as Learned Hand. If they thought the books were bad, they would not consider First Amendment issues.

An ironic sidebar to these prosecutions, especially in view of Cahill's declaration of open season on dirty books in New York City, is provided by the open and unhindered sale by well-reputed publishers of such works as René Guyon's *Ethics of Sex Acts*, advertised by Knopf as "a discussion of onanism, incest, homosexuality, fetishism, and even such 'extraordinary' variations as necrophilia and coprophilia."[111] But the Rebhuhns were perceived as smutmongers, not people of letters. The Post Office campaign against obscenity in the mails had been well publicized, as typical headlines reveal: "U.S. Opens War on Ring Selling Obscene Books"; "U.S. Aims Blow at Risky Books"; "U.S. Nets Two Here in Drive Against Erotic Book Flood."[112] Crusades need scapegoats. Falstaff, with the "leer of the sensualist" radiant on every circular, played that role perfectly. Augustus Hand was as dismissive of the Rebhuhns' 1940 appeal of their convictions as the newspapers and book trade publications. Unlike his brother, he did not scruple to distinguish between the books and the circulars. "I cannot see how [the] defendants were justified in the dirt they put out on any theory."[113] Nor did anyone else. During early June 1939, the NCFC kept close watch on the court proceedings, Ernst and Lindey conferring with S. John Block, who had argued the case for the law firm of Arthur Garfield Hayes. Apparently, the council decided the books cited could not support an appeal on grounds that the defendants' freedom of speech had been violated.[114]

The Rebhuhn case set a rock-solid precedent for the use of pandering as a criterion in borderline obscenity cases. It was to protest this judgment that Samuel Roth, in the late 1940s, filed suits against "Dame Post Office": she had declared several of his books unmailable because he had circularized for their sale on the basis of a salaciousness that they did not possess. It was for pandering that the brash Ralph Ginzburg was sentenced to five years in federal penitentiary as late as 1965.[115] He tried to mail his stylishly designed *Eros* magazine — "devoted to the joys of love and sex" — from the Pennsylvania towns of Blue Ball and Intercourse (he settled for Middlesex). Justice Brennan, another judge famous for his progressive views and his sensitivity to freedom of speech issues, stated that although the contents of Ginzburg's publications themselves might be assumed to have merit, the fact that he "was in the sordid business of pandering" was a valid determining factor.[116] When salespeople appeal to prurience, the forces of justice become marshaled against them; the focus shifts from the work itself to the person doing the selling, who becomes a criminal exploiting the "widespread weakness for titillation by pornography." Brennan cited a contemporary study proposing a "progressive" set of obscenity laws that would effectively draw the line between the legitimate bookseller and the pornographer: Alfred Knopf, despite the way he advertised *The Ethics of Sex Acts*, would be an example of the former; Rebhuhn, Roth, or Ginzburg of the latter. The person, or the firm, not the product, was the "gravamen."[117]

Dissenting justices Black and Stewart stated that neither pandering nor titillation were part of the Comstock Law, and that people should not go to jail because a judge or jury found their way of making a living distasteful. The reality was that selling prurience presented a challenge that civil leaders could not leave unanswered. Spokespeople for morality, whether elected, appointed, ordained, or deputized, could not retreat from duties with which they were proud to be entrusted. If they did, they would become ineffective at what they most wanted to accomplish: protecting the moral character of the people. As for the Rebhuhns, Roths, and Ginzburgs — traders in prurience — they were damned if they did, and out of business if they did not. They could certainly have done without the political vulnerability that resulted from benchmark cases such as Ben Rebhuhn's. But that was a part of the territory, a high risk in pursuit of a high reward.

Postal Censors, Liberal Lawyers, and Publishers' Self-Censorship

Even when book dealers turned to their lawyers for advice, they might find them ratifying the criteria of the postal inspectors, despite their own personal convictions about free speech, due process, and full adversarial procedure. In this way, the system of authority extended itself even through its apparent opponents.

If a lawyer's clients requested practical advice, it was responsible practice to offer realistic guidance. Even Morris Ernst and Alexander Lindey observed this principle. Thus McBride and Company was advised in 1937 that if it published *Birth Control: A Practical Guide for the Married*, it should keep on file a statement from every purchaser as to his or her professional standing, since any municipal or postal authority who chose to prosecute would simply state that it was illegal to distribute books on contraception to the general public.[118] Brewer and Warren were advised that they should remove all references to homosexual liaisons and delete various incidents that possibly might strike Sumner as "indecent and disgusting" if they chose to publish Klaus Mann's *Alexandra*.[119] When Egmont Arens of the Vanguard Press requested Ernst to advise a friend of his who wished to sell by mail *Musk, Hashish, and Blood* and Mantegazza's *Sexual Relations of Mankind* (both probably Falstaff Press publications), the distributor was warned that the books were lurid and violent, that the circular was prima facie obscene, and that any prosecution would most likely succeed in the lower courts. "More than ordinary business risk" was involved.[120]

In autumn 1939, the Eugenics Publishing Company retained the services of Greenbaum, Wolff, and Ernst to advise it concerning its edition of Dr. Maurice Chideckel's *Female Sex Perversion: The Sexually Aberrated Female as She Is* (Figure 34; assessed by some contemporary booksellers as "dull book; great title").[121] The work had been published in 1935, and reissued in 1938 (the circular bears the earlier date); it was in 1938, with postal campaigns against erotica having shut down Panurge, and indicted Falstaff, that the lawyer's advice was requested.[122] The book had been circulating without interference, but Eugenics was uneasy. Chideckel's diction and style were unscientific and sometimes awkward, his attempts at humor were sometimes lubricious, and the illustrations featured nubile young women, naked or in underwear or low-cut gowns, cuddling up to lecherous old men, animals, or other women, admiring themselves, being whipped, or administering whippings. Lindey and Ernst discussed the work with Huntington Cairns. A copy Eugenics had ordered from London had been detained by Customs, its chapter on "Female Masturbation" singled out for special concern. Cairns felt the Chideckel book was a rather feckless work, but was willing to accept it on the basis of its learned (albeit brief) foreword by Dr. Samuel Wolman of Johns Hopkins. A few days before this meeting, Lindey had written to Cairns: "I suppose that if any question involving Post Office clearance comes up, someone from the Post Office will be available so that we can have a three-cornered huddle."[123] The firm's long memo to Eugenics, beginning "we have been assured a favorable Customs ruling on the book," advised that the postal authorities, at some future point, might not accept the judgment, but if they did not, "the favorable Customs ruling would be of tremendous help." Mark Jacobs of Eugenics was warned, however, that future circulation should be limited to people in medical and allied professions, with possible additional offers to "lawyers, ministers and social workers." Greenbaum, Wolff, and Ernst suggested revisions to the four-page circular so that the work would not be liable to prosecution for pandering, flatly stated that the illustrations should be eliminated, and recommended five categories of textual changes, involving approximately fifty pages. The most significant of these involved diction, and Chideckel's naive emphasis on the power of "lascivious" books to debauch, an insistence that a postal inspector could easily turn back against the doctor's own book. Finally, there was this flat warning: "all references that might offend the Catholic Church should be excised."

Lawyers who offered such services—it was probably a common practice—were merely doing their jobs. They opened themselves to criticism from clerical and lay officials for encouraging the distribution of smut, performing a kind of cosmetic surgery that disguised the beast of obscenity and allowed its essential villainy to circulate freely. But there was another, very different but equally caustic complaint: that members of the bar made "middlemen" of themselves and pandered to a sexually repressive zeitgeist, of which the Post Office was the official administrative authority. Gershon Legman makes this accusation, with the same kind of snarling "thus didst thou" he uses against the Catholic hierarchy. From Legman's *Love & Death: A Study in Censorship* comes an allusion to "the liberal lawyers who expurgate books beforehand for our pusillanimous publishers."[124] His open letter to Alec Craig deplores a "phoney set-up" in which a publisher who requests of a postal counsel an opinion about the mailability of a book is told that the Post Office is no censor and that he should consult a law firm with "lots of experience in obscenity cases."[125] The lawyer subsequently retained asks the postal counsel about the book and "the decision is retailed to the publisher as an 'opinion' for a stiff fee."

Despite Legman's methods of presenting a powerful message in a daringly hyperbolic style, his claim allows us to recognize that it was quite possible for legal advisors of erotica publishers to reinforce the approach of the Post Office solicitors in determining the kinds of erotic literature to which Americans could safely be allowed access. At least some influential and liberal-minded lawyers were doing so at the same time that their interpretations of the First Amendment were helping to shrink the boundaries of the obscene. This is an odd testimony to "the color of the air" during the 1930s, and to the power of the symbiotic network of administrative authority that protected the mails from the "pollutant" of "obscenity." It is also further proof of Legman's claim in *Love & Death* that "the American censorship of sex is internalized. The men & women in the streets carry it around with them in their heads."[126] Considering how closely sex and prurience are allied, the carriers included not only furtive readers of erotica but also U.S. district attorneys, postal inspectors, Augustus and Learned Hand, Morris Ernst, and Alexander Lindey. The basic equation of sex with prurience remained unquestioned, carried forward equally by the Levines and the Sumners, by liberal and conservative judges, by the Post Office censors and the crusaders of the NCFC.

The Two Worlds of Samuel Roth
Man of Letters and Entrepreneur of Erotica

In the 1920s Samuel Roth challenged John Sumner and delighted aficionados of pornography by publishing Charles Carrington's *Forbidden Books*. He gave James Joyce a "jawache" with his piracies of *Ulysses*, both in expurgated and complete editions: "Rothim! . . . With his unique hornbook and his prince of apauper's pride, blundering all over the two worlds . . . always cutting my phrose to please his phrase, bogorror, I declare I get the jawache."[1] He spent 1937, 1938, and 1939 in federal prison for mailing pornography on a scale only Carrington surpassed. He openly issued an "exposé" of Herbert Hoover that was taken seriously enough to occasion secret investigations of his income sources by the president's supporters. Throughout the 1940s and 1950s, Roth engaged the attention of squads of postal inspectors with circulars and books declared unmailable either for their obscenity or for their fraudulent promises thereof. He indignantly defended, before Senator Estes Kefauver's 1955 investigating committee, the titillating books and magazines he mailed in great numbers, denying that they reached or influenced teenagers. Rewarded with a federal indictment, he became absolutely identified with the virulence of sex. On one occasion, he was dubbed "the dirtiest pig in the world" for contributing to juvenile delinquency, on another, "the louse of Lewisburg" (he was an inmate there during 1936–39 and 1957–61). The Supreme Court's majority and dissenting opinions made his 1957 appeal of a five-year sentence and five-thousand-dollar fine a landmark case in liberalizing obscenity law. This was ironic, for Samuel Roth emerged from the adjudication with his status fixed as a pornographer, not as a free-speech advocate, and served the full term of his sentence in Lewisburg. A 1977 profile in *Hustler* hailed him for "pav[ing] the way." In a 1997–98 series of articles titled "The History of the Sexual Revolution" in *Playboy*, James R. Petersen describes Roth as the "last of the old-time pornographers" and claims, "for decades, Roth *was* the sexual underground."[2] These overstatements indicate the extent to which Roth has become a minor myth. He was the quintessential middleman erotica dealer as pariah capitalist. His career makes remarkably visible the talent needed to sell prurient sexuality effectively in the interwar years, the social pressures the erotica dealer encountered, and his or her public and psychic responses to these pressures.

Like other immigrants, Roth strove for emotional and financial security in America. The former would come if he found acceptance as a result of the efforts he made to improve the cultural life of his country — efforts that family and ethnic traditions had taught him to revere. He set out to be one of a number of young Jewish publishers, such as Alfred Knopf and Thomas Seltzer, who familiarized American readers with experimental European writing and the work of Americans influenced by them. As his only biographer, Leo Hamalian, has observed, Roth succeeded in becoming a literary celebrity. Hamalian did not have *Hustler* or *Playboy* in mind. No historian is "able to write about Céline, T. S. Eliot, André Gide, Ernest Hemingway, D. H. Lawrence, James Joyce, Friedrich Nietzsche, Frank Harris, Herbert Hoover, or Alger Hiss without at least giving Roth a long footnote."[3] This impoverished young man from eastern Europe wrote poems and monographs as well, in which he assumed other roles that as a boy he learned would inspire respectful attention. He saw himself as advocate for freedom of expression, social critic, creative artist, Zionist, denouncer of the sins of his own people.

The work of middlemen erotica dealers assured them of marginal status. The traders in sexually explicit books used their resourcefulness, perseverance, objectivity, and chutzpah to make good livings. Ironically, the ideals of free speech and sexual enlightenment to which they declared themselves committed as American intellectuals were undercut by the identification of sex with prurience that their borderline and under-the-counter publications epitomized. That this identification was "the color of the air" in between-the-wars America bears repeating because Samuel Roth's career is incomprehensible without understanding that his financial need to exploit the identification did not mean that he was not a complex and driven intellectual, a clever businessman, and a provider for his family. Self-justification, however, was a hallmark of his character: Roth the man of letters was punished for performing what close-minded folk would not acknowledge to be a public service. Most erotica dealers — then and now — cultivate this kind of self-image. The contradiction is clearer in Roth's case. He saw himself as a martyr, going so far by 1928 as to copyright under the name "J. A. Nocross" an anonymous memoir of "inversion" he arranged to have published while in prison — a Jewish Jesus without a cross.[4] In addition, his bookselling and publishing were uniquely extensive, and he wrote a lot about them in response to the authorities who, entrusted with upholding the decency of the community, furiously pursued him. He succeeded at times in convincing observers that he was an honest man, champion of avant-garde writers and victim of Philistines. But often such assertions, if weighed impartially, do not balance evenly with the facts, for in his advertisements he equated sexual passion with degeneracy and profited from its depiction. Roth and his colleagues did publish some informative and creative books that reached people for whom they were new and exciting. They were also middlemen between the moral authorities and the people, their identification of sex with prurience revealing them to be trading, unwittingly, in ideological as well as monetary capital.

The contradiction between these methods of attaining emotional and financial security was disorienting. Were erotica dealers venal smutmongers or humanist intellectuals with a social conscience? Into which efforts, honestly, were their efforts to shape their destiny, or *takhlis*, directed? What was the pose, and what the reality? We do not know enough about the private thoughts of Roth's fellow erotica dealers to determine how much these questions bedeviled them, but Roth's autobiographical work, and the material he had his assistants write about him, show that he suffered from, but lacked the self-awareness to come to terms with, the "spiritual instability, intensified self-consciousness, restlessness and malaise" that sociologist Robert Park has described as typical of American immigrants, and marginal people in general.[5] Nothing that Roth said or wrote suggests that he could look at himself objectively enough to be self-critical; he compulsively posed as a litterateur. The best example is a book he published when he was in his late fifties, a memoir ostensibly by Maxwell Bodenheim but surely edited by Roth or his assistants. Bodenheim's reputation, mind, and body were all badly tarnished by then but when he and Roth were young, Bodenheim had an absolute commitment to poetry and prose and burned with contempt for faddish versifying and conventional morality. In Roth's version of Bodenheim's memoir, there is a chapter in which either Bodenheim, or Bodenheim as "edited" by Roth, cites the publisher as "public bohemian number one," "a stormy petrel riding the seas of that outlawed world called Bohemia . . . an amphibious creature . . . who gravitates between the sacred waters of the arts and the dry land of cut-throat business activity."[6] For Roth to include or, more likely, fabricate this passage is the daring of the self-promoter, obsessively convincing others and himself that tough and practical as the profession of publishing has forced him to be, he has been true to what has been expected of him as a creative spirit.

The specter of the writer who had abandoned his art for financial security haunted Roth. In an afterword to the Bodenheim book, he mentions a "Poet-turned-Businessman . . . who had grown a little fat in his comparative prosperity" and who criticized Bodenheim for selling his poems to indiscriminate passers-by on the streets of Greenwich Village. The poet in question was Louis Grudin, and the incident Roth recounts is garbled. In fact, Grudin, an accomplished poet, artist, and writer on aesthetics, had another reason for criticizing Bodenheim. He did so because the latter had gotten involved with Roth, with whom Grudin had himself once been associated when Roth was a struggling young writer. The poet who had become, as the years rolled by, a businessman was Sam Roth. But he projected the behavior implied in such a change onto a person of whom he was jealous, a person with a solid and long-standing literary reputation, who was well liked, never fat, and never a businessman.[7]

Those who observed Roth's career often questioned who and what he actually was. So did he, but rhetorically, with a self-assured answer weakly hidden behind the apparent introspection. By 1931, Roth's reputation was that of a literary pirate and convicted, twice-jailed pornographer. That year, he wrote that in 1917, 1918, and 1919, people said "nice things" about him. "Could I have been the same Samuel Roth?"[8] He implied that he had never been other than a crusading literary editor, albeit lately much misunderstood. That would have elicited a guffaw from the editors of *Vanity Fair*. The magazine included Roth in its June 1932 photo-essay "We Nominate for Oblivion" (another profile was of Adolf Hitler) (Figure 38).[9] Behind the persona, *Vanity Fair* saw the base reality of the business he was in.

A few months earlier, the *New Yorker*, stating that Roth had used several personae, wondered if he had sorted them out. It would have been hard. In addition to his Hebrew name, Mishillim, as writer and editor he posed as "Francis Page," "David Zorn," "Daniel Quilter," "Norman Lockridge," "Joseph Brownell," and "Eric Hammond."[10] By the early 1930s, he had published under the aliases "J. A. Nocross," "William Faro," "Michael Swain," "John Henderson," and "William Hodgson." The *New Yorker* columnist noted that Roth's "name is always cropping up, of course, as the founder of this or that magazine, as the object of So-and-So's denunciations," and that he has "a variety of pseudonyms. Mightn't 'Samuel Roth' be a pseudonym too?"[11] After listening to Roth recapitulate his career and writing a

Figure 38. Samuel Roth's photograph in *Vanity Fair*'s June 1932 "We Nominate for Oblivion" feature. Roth was nominated "because he is reputed to be an active book-pirate; because, under the alias William Faro, he published *The Strange Career of Mr. Hoover Under Two Flags*, a scurrilous attack on the President; because he has served two prison terms for publishing pornography, but still poses as a great champion of fine literature."

thorough review of it, Hamalian concluded that this self-promoting man was a compulsive impostor who presented himself in assorted guises before a public whose gullibility he traded on, and did so outrageously, to invite the punishment he craved. Hamalian makes the situation oedipal, the guilt having arisen from Roth's knowing he had abandoned the moral and spiritual values by which his devoutly Jewish father lived.[12] Whether it was the standards of his father or of literary London and New York from which Roth deviated, the spiritual instability, narcissistic self-involvement, and need for the literary community's approbation certainly haunted him as much as his need for financial security. As the *New Yorker* columnist queried, "Then who would Samuel Roth be? Maybe he doesn't know himself." Another answer may be that he did whatever seemed effective at the time in providing him with financial and emotional stability, without immediately considering what the act would do to his reputation.

"Stop, Thief!" An International Protest

Sam Roth grew up poor, fending for himself on the streets of the Lower East Side by the time he was a teenager. But he was avid for knowledge and culture, ambitious to be a writer and a publisher. At first, he could not afford to rely on paid advertisements to promote his publications; possibly he could not or did not pay for some of those he placed.[13] The material he brought out would have to get itself talked about. He decided to include in the magazines he published, and the books he distributed, material with erotic interest, risking arrest, the indignity of newspaper innuendo, and the contempt of established booksellers. He knew he would be glibly accused of prostituting himself for money. But he intended to reduce such observations to the status of mere gossip. He was more discriminating than most in his choice of authors, and was willing, unlike his more conventional colleagues, to face fine and imprisonment. He well understood the smutmonger–respectable bookman dichotomy with which the interwar trade defined itself, and where he needed to take his stand. In an unpublished memoir, he recalled:

To improve his slim chances of success Mishillim limited his under-capitalized publishing ventures to books with a strong sex appeal, books such as sell by word of mouth rather than by advertising linage. He knew that Mrs. Grundy was never far off, that the censor searched for his prey only among the poorest of booksellers. Mishillim did not mind so much the arrests to which he was subjected, the resulting standoffishness of his stronger brethren in the trade, the deliberate newspaper lying that befogged his name — even in the most important American journal of the publishing trade — so much as he minded the need to deal with lawyers.[14]

The lawyers and newspaper stories came later. In his early twenties, Roth had established credentials for himself as a man of letters. Hamalian's essay portrays him rooming with social activist Frank Tannenbaum, winning a scholarship to Columbia University, publishing the literary magazine the *Lyric*, and founding the Poetry Bookshop, from which, using the Lyric imprint, he issued both his own and his friends' writings. With an acute sense for literary talent, he reprinted the work of leading contemporary European writers whose works were not under copyright owing to lack of international accords. In his bookshop he made the acquaintance of Frank Harris, Harry Roskelenko, Sholem Asch, Edna St. Vincent Millay, Floyd Dell, and Maxwell Bodenheim. He sold their works and, as did many others, sold or rented classics of under-the-counter pornography (*Only a Boy, Memoirs of a Russian Princess*). In 1919, Boni and Liveright published his polemic verses about Jewish concerns past and present, *Europe: A Book for America*, in which the speaker assumes the tone of an Old Testament prophet. In the 1920s, Roth's articles and poems appeared in the *Nation, Harper's Weekly, Poetry*, and the *Menorah Journal*. In England in 1921, he planned a history of contemporary American poetry, for which Ezra Pound was to supply margin notes.[15] *Now and Forever*, cast in the form of a dialogue with Anglo-Jewish writer and political activist Israel Zangwill on the future of Jewry and the nature of Zionism, was published by McBride in 1925.[16] In a preface, Zangwill admires Roth's "poetry and pugnacity," and refers to the young man as part of a "remarkable band of Jewish writers who have arisen to be the world's conscience."[17]

In 1925, Roth resumed a correspondence with Pound, which he had begun during his six-month visit to England in 1921. The thirty-one-year-old bookseller and writer made as many literary contacts as he could during that period, as correspondent for the *New York Herald*. He held letters of introduction from writers, including Edwin Arlington Robinson, who had been a customer in Roth's Greenwich Village bookshop.[18] With some capital in hand after three years as the administrator of an English-language school for immigrants, Roth wished to found a quarterly literary review, *Two Worlds*. He hoped to make a place for himself among other young Jewish publishers who had been sponsoring the style and ideas

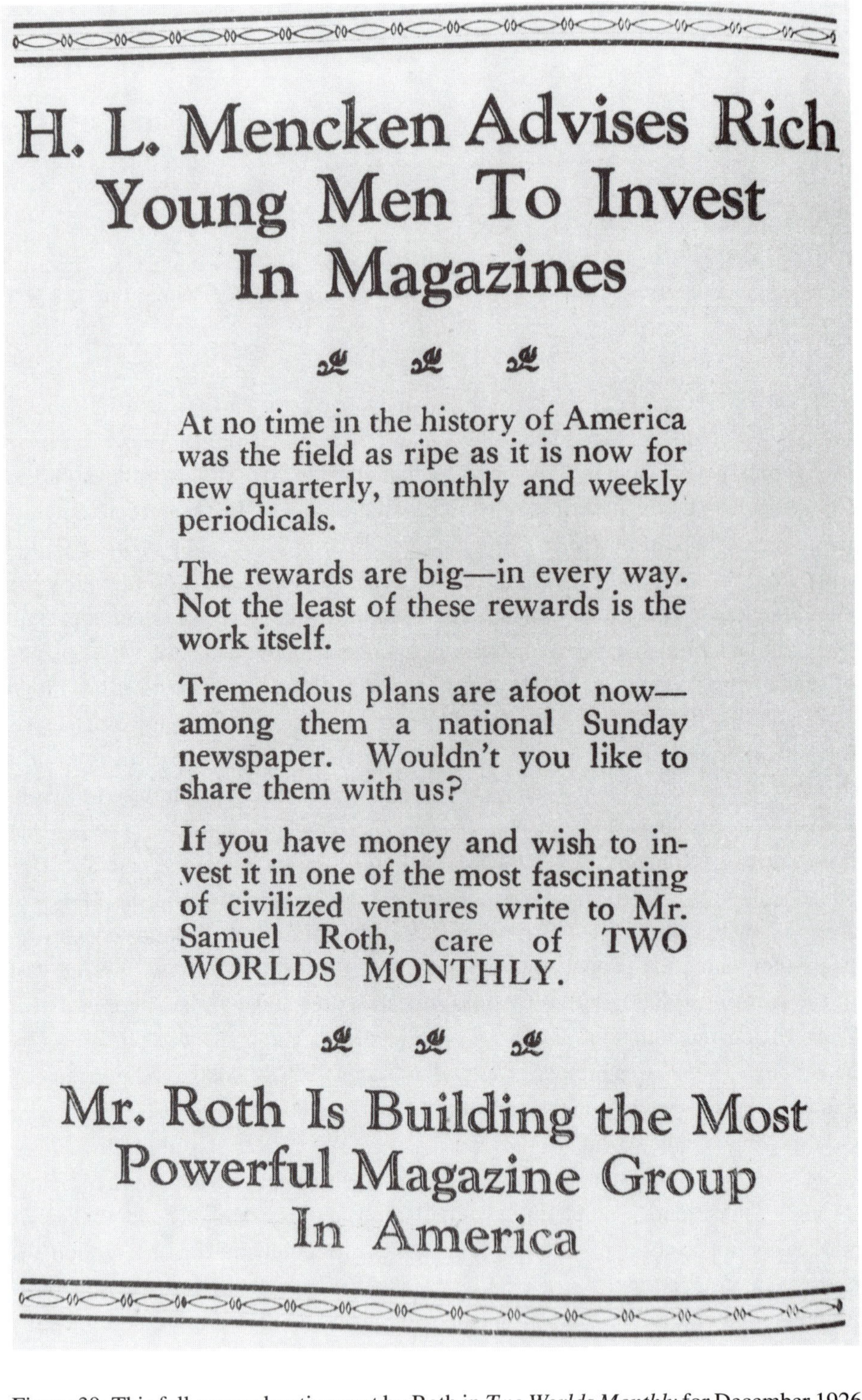

H. L. Mencken Advises Rich Young Men To Invest In Magazines

At no time in the history of America was the field as ripe as it is now for new quarterly, monthly and weekly periodicals.

The rewards are big—in every way. Not the least of these rewards is the work itself.

Tremendous plans are afoot now— among them a national Sunday newspaper. Wouldn't you like to share them with us?

If you have money and wish to invest it in one of the most fascinating of civilized ventures write to Mr. Samuel Roth, care of TWO WORLDS MONTHLY.

Mr. Roth Is Building the Most Powerful Magazine Group In America

Figure 39. This full-page advertisement by Roth in *Two Worlds Monthly* for December 1926 requests readers who "have money and wish to invest it in one of the most fascinating of civilized ventures" to help finance his "magazine group."

of the European avant-garde, and of their American enthusiasts. Thus he was lending himself to "the foreign and imitation foreign invasion" that incensed John Sumner. Having asked for Pound's assistance as literary editor (he made similar requests of Ford Madox Ford and Arthur Symons), he requested permission to serialize Joyce's *Ulysses*. The work was notorious; Roth's avowed aim, however, was not to appeal crudely to the curiosity generated by its suppression on both sides of the Atlantic. The magazine was to have "some merit of risqueness, gaiety," but not for the sake of prurient interest (Figure 39).[19] Readers might wonder about the inclusion of Twain's *1601*, or of Roth's own *White Streams* (the title reminiscent of Aleister Crowley's *White Stains*), advertised as included in the second issue.[20] In *Two Worlds'* fourth issue could be found Pierre Louÿs's "Leda," and work by and about Oscar Wilde, including Frank Harris's preface to Wilde's autobiography. If questioned, the editor would have asserted, correctly, that Twain, Louÿs, Wilde, and Harris were serious and irrepressible artists.[21] He would have made the same claim about himself.

In 1922, when Roth first requested that James Joyce send him publishable material, he included a copy of his prospectus for *Two Worlds*.[22] It was to be sold by subscription only, thus corresponding to the way privately printed books were circulated. These carried to a suitable audience poetry and prose that, if published for the general public, might be subject to censorship, and produce for their authors unsavory reputations. Privately printed books were thus a friend to the real artist, as Roth wished his magazine to be. Roth's daughter, Adelaide Kugel, has several letters indicating that Joyce, on the advice of Pound, responded favorably, and received some payment from the publisher. She also asserts that Roth had some sort of written permission through Pound for the Joyce item, which might conceivably have been excerpts from *Ulysses*.[23] Be that as it may, Roth was apparently able to convince Pound in 1925 that *Two Worlds* would reflect the vigor of defiant originality. The poet intimated as much in a letter to the *New Statesman* two years later,[24] saying Roth started out "not merely as a man on the make but as a man desiring to amuse both himself and others, and also to rebel against and satirize something more vile than any possible act of an individual." That would be the prudery and provincialism that had made so many American writers look to Europe for inspiration.

Pound's phrase is close to that which Roth himself used, much later, to describe his intentions. By that time, he had made news on both sides of the Atlantic.

His name, however, had become linked with terms such as "pirate" and "oppor-
tunist," and with worse epithets as well: "liar," "thief," "vermin," and (the title of
a December 1927 *transition* article) "King of the Jews."[25] That *transition* chose to
headline Roth's religious affiliation in an article about his way of conducting his
business speaks for itself, even though "King of the Jews" was a title Roth himself
had said proudly that he might one day lay claim to. The torrent of contempt did not
come from John Sumner or the police, nor from the New York newspapers. Rather,
the source was the literary avant-garde. The occasion was Roth's publication, in
1926 and 1927, of excerpts from *Finnegans Wake* in his quarterly *Two Worlds*, and
chapters from *Ulysses*, which he had expurgated, in *Two Worlds Monthly*.[26] More
than one hundred writers signed the international protest, written by Archibald
MacLeish and Ludwig Lewisohn, against what Roth did; Pound did not sign,
possibly because he had in fact led Roth to believe he could publish the *Ulysses*
selections. The possibility cannot be discounted because of the expurgations. The
selections Pound sent to the *Little Review* (he served as its foreign editor) were also
barbered, and the magazine's editors did some of their own trimming, albeit not
enough to please the Post Office and Sumner in 1920. Further, as Gershon Legman
has accurately observed, the work was never copyrighted in the United States, and
many American publishers printed the work of British and Irish authors without
giving them remuneration.[27] The point might well be made that Roth was not as
singularly villainous as the language of the protest asserted. However, after the
series of events the protest described, Samuel Roth was no longer known as a man
of letters. There had never been an international writers' protest before. Sam Roth
would never be the same in the eyes of his contemporaries.

The circumstances of his exile from the community of letters were unique.
Even more interesting is the defiance with which he responded to it; the chutzpah
and sense of purpose with which he planned not only this but also other phases of
his career; and his ubiquitous self-deception. Waverley Root, who later became a
Europe-based journalist, was hired by Roth as an editorial assistant in 1926 and
shortly afterward became his implacable enemy. It was Root who wrote the Roth-
bashing *transition* article. His prejudice notwithstanding, Root observed Roth well
enough to comment on the "superb self-contentedness that enables Mr. Roth to
make . . . a remark seriously and without ostentation and [which] also makes it
possible for him to survive absolutely alone."[28] It was a kind of psychic armor with

which Roth sheltered himself when he left behind "the sacred waters of the arts" and lost himself in "the dry land of cut-throat business activity."

A fine example of Roth's self-contentedness was observed by Joseph Freeman, a journalist (later a social activist) who encountered Roth during his stay in London. In his *American Testament*, Freeman writes of his dealings with a man he calls "Knox," who like Roth had attended Columbia University, run a bookshop, edited a poetry magazine, and been sent to London to write articles for a newspaper. Roth knew Freeman at that time, and Waverley Root, in his "King of the Jews" essay, clearly based his title on what Freeman told him.[29] This Knox cut "a tall, bizarre and impressive figure with his cloth cap, thick eyeglasses, J. M. Barrie moustache, fur-collared coat and heavy Malacca cane." "In the booming voice of a Yiddish actor," he deprecated such contemporaries as Dreiser ("a *potz!*") and Anderson ("a *shmok*"). The Zionist Jews in Palestine, Knox opined, would choose a king for themselves. Jewish leaders had always been men of letters; peering ten years into the future, Knox predicted that he would be that poet-leader.[30] Knox may be an amalgam of other men Freeman met in addition to Roth, but the congruences are unmistakable. And Roth may have had in mind the kind of mission Knox sets himself when his *Now and Forever* was published. His full-page advertisement in the *Nation*, headlined "On the Battlefield of the Ages," declared that "from the first word to the last you are caught up in a torrent of speech which sweeps you through the whole European realm of ideas and motives."[31]

From "Cosmopoli" to "the Workhouse," and Moyamensing Prison

On 15 June 1928, Roth was arrested at the Book Auction, the shop on East 12th Street near Fifth Avenue into which, he averred, pornography was smuggled in order to "frame him up." The business was in his wife's name, because Roth, both bankrupt and on parole, could not list himself as proprietor; she knew nothing, she said tearfully, of his involvement with banned books.[32] Roth was one of the "alleged dealers in obscene books, magazines, postcards, drawings and circulars" included in Sumner's "summer roundup."[33] The police and "Evic Rotacidare" found quite a cache on the premises: Sumner's ledgers for 1928 record 62 books, 1,393 magazines, 116 pictures, 11 plates and manuscripts, and 1,000 circulars. One of the most incriminating items was a reprint of *Forbidden Books*, a 227-page annotated compilation of Carrington's best-selling sexology and erotology.[34] In mid-October, Roth was sentenced to ninety days on Welfare Island ("the Workhouse").

The prison sentence was punishment for violating parole, on which Roth had been placed as a result of a January 1928 arrest for selling by mail order a complete edition of the Burton translation of *The Perfumed Garden*.[35] Jake Brussel and Roth had first published this work in 1923. The title page, a reset replica of the 1886 second edition, listed the "Kama Shastra Society," located in "Cosmopoli," as publisher of the edition.[36] Four years later, Roth had overextended himself with *Two Worlds Monthly* and a large-format review for men-about-town, *Beau: The Man's Magazine*,[37] so he arranged a mail drop in lower "Cosmopoli" to receive orders for a new impression of the Eastern sex manual. He later wrote that he really did not want to reissue the book, because readers who wanted to pleasure themselves by putting its teachings into practice would have to exhaust their financial resources in search of willing partners.[38] There is dry humor here, but also a sense of the publisher's influence over the lives of his customers. In any event, cash ruled conscience. Brussel provided an illustrated circular, and the project went forward. The price was thirty-five dollars per copy. If the three-hundred-copy edition sold out, Roth would have made about ten thousand dollars.[39] This probably did not happen, because it took only a month for the "Cosmopolitan" vice-society agents and postal inspectors to write decoy letters, receive copies, and arrest Roth. It does not seem that Brussel was apprehended. Roth's sentence was a five-hundred-dollar fine and six months in jail; the sentence was suspended.[40] He was also to return all monies sent to him for *The Perfumed Garden* and not to publish anything before approval by his probation officer.[41]

By this time, John Sumner had identified Roth as a man to watch, and did not have to wait long before putting him back behind bars. Raiding Roth's Golden Hind Press on 4 October 1929, the vice crusader found the stuff of any collector's dream. Its seizure was the nightmare of any dealer. *Ulysses*, *Lady Chatterley's Lover*, *Forbidden Books*, *Fanny Hill* — all proved Roth's heavy involvement with the distribution of erotica during his probation period. The *Ulysses* volume, printed two to three years later than the serialized chapters in *Two Worlds Monthly*, won him a dubious place in the authorized Joyce bibliography as the novel's first — and of course unauthorized — American publisher; Random House's authorized edition was inadvertently based on it.[42] Many of the copies in the possession of the New

York Society for the Suppression of Vice (NYSSV), "taken on search warrant," as Sumner indicated in a 26 February 1930 periodical letter to constituents, were destroyed in a city incinerator. Be that as it may, Roth never ceased to point with pride to the contribution he felt he had made to the cause of modernist literature with his edition of *Ulysses*, even to the face of the contemptuous Estes Kefauver in his 1955 testimony before the senator's investigation of his mail-order sales to juveniles. According to Roth, also found was "a translation of Boccaccio's *Pasquerella and Madonna Babetta* into which I had grafted a set of Aubrey Beardsley illustrations."[43] The edition of *Forbidden Books* introduced many American readers to erotic classics, and marked Roth as a dedicated purveyor of underground smut. Sumner's raid uncovered letters between bookseller St. George Best, "this individual in Chicago who apparently furnished the text," and Roth, indicating that the latter "was practically the publisher."[44] This was, and still is, accepted as the case by New York booksellers, Best having been credited with bringing Carrington's publications into the United States from Mexico and Cuba.[45] For internal evidence, they could point to the design of the spine label and the title page, and the American-style page layout, including the typeface.[46]

The eminently fair judge John Knox distinguished carefully between acceptable books and those that were "obviously obscene." He recognized in Roth "a man of some literary ability, . . . who, like many others, feels that any censorship law is unjust." But it was clear that Roth had violated the terms of his probation. His parole was revoked. After four months at Welfare Island (he was originally sentenced to six; the reduction was for good behavior), the State of Pennsylvania requested that he be remanded to Moyamensing Prison in Philadelphia. Waiving extradition, he served two months for selling a copy of *Ulysses* to a Philadelphia bookseller (Figure 40).[47]

None of Roth's procedures were especially original. Erotic books, even the most proscribed ones, could be and were sold through careful correspondence with trusted customers or telephone. If to circulate *Forbidden Books* was daring, Roth was no more so than St. George Best. Publishing the work, and *Lady Chatterley*, was certainly putting oneself at risk, but a few years later Ben Abramson did an edition of *Lady Chatterley's Lover* in Chicago, and the typographer Lawton Kennedy printed an edition equally as attractive as Abramson's for an unknown California distributor. If Roth had to tell a bookseller who ordered *Fanny Hill* that he needed a check or money order in advance, for he could not "keep such an account

Figure 40. Photographs from the Criminal Identification Files of the Philadelphia police, taken in June 1930, on Roth's reception there for a two-month term in Moyamensing Prison for distributing copies of Joyce's *Ulysses* in that city. Source: File of Roth materials prepared for Walter Winchell in the early 1950s.

with safety, to you or to us,"[48] other mail-order booksellers (as well as bookstore owners) would probably do the same: the Anthropological Library and the Gargoyle Press, for example, or Groves and Michaux in Paris, and "William Jackson Ltd." in London. But Roth, whose list of reliable customers for underground erotica was still in the formative stages (and possibly included Post Office inspectors), and who had little capital or prestige in the trade, did all these things at the same time, on probation, and under the careful scrutiny of John Sumner. This paid off. The Golden Hind sold more than seven hundred dollars worth of books per week in Chicago alone, and realized significant profits in cities in the Midwest and West Coast.[49] Furthermore, from prison in New York and Philadelphia, Roth continued to publish the kinds of books Sumner especially hated: a satire on the vice crusader himself, *Diary of a Smuthound*, in which the self-righteous diarist is given the name Hugh Wakem (imprint; Philadelphia: William Hodgson, 1930); and a novel of "inversion," *The Strange Confession of Monsieur Montcairn* ("privately printed"). It seems that he also profited from investing money in a "five-star thriller," Gaston Means's *Strange Death of President Harding* (1930).[50] His business arrangement was possibly with Maurice Fryefield, who published the book after serving as advertising manager for Nan Britton. In *The President's Daughter*, Britton asserted that her child was Warren Harding's daughter.[51] Fryefield, therefore, had experience with this kind of publishing. *The Strange Death* sold briskly. Means relates with gusto how Harding's attorney general got his job by blackmailing the president regarding the affair with Nan Britton. Harding's wife, Means opines, discovered "the truth" and, wanting to preserve her husband's reputation in the wake of the "Ohio Gang" scandals crippling his administration, poisoned the president.

Roth never tired of that kind of political sensationalism, and a few years later put out a smear book on President Hoover. However, in 1930, he was tired of serving time, and planned a set of books that could be sold openly, by mail order and in bookstores, and stocked in lending libraries. At last he had the capital to start his climb back to the respectability he had lost with the publication of the international protest.[52]

The Birth of William Faro, Inc.: A Barbered *Lady Chatterley*

After Moyamensing, it seemed time for Roth to have a legitimate business that allowed him to support his wife and children without imperiling them either by putting the business in their name or by having them help with the office work and bookkeeping required for the distribution of banned books. As Roth tells us in his partly autobiographical *Jews Must Live*, he had met in prison one William Paro, who had held an executive-level position in the Wall Street post office until he was caught stealing mail in 1929. Roth offered him the presidency of his newly conceived publishing house, which was to be incorporated in his name (presumably so that neither Roth nor his wife would have to bear direct responsibility for any prosecutions involving borderline erotic items). Paro demurred at the last moment, not being able to afford further legal problems. Roth changed the *P* to an *F* on the legal documents, and although disappointed, gave his former cellmate a job with the firm.[53] Roth was released from Moyamensing in August 1930,[54] by which time he had formulated plans to inaugurate his venture with "the Samuel Roth Edition" of *Lady Chatterley's Lover* (1930).[55] This was an expurgated and bowdlerized edition, although Roth's own descriptive term (appearing opposite the title page) was "revised." As a litterateur, and a hater of censorship, he believed himself to be incapable of rewriting a text to make it acceptable to conventional morality. He insisted on showing people who Sam Roth really was. Therefore he wrote letters to magazines and newspapers, and published his own apologia. The Faro imprint gave him that opportunity. In one statement, he explained that in accusing him of bowdlerizing, his enemies "lie in their throats, and they know it."[56] What they knew, by 1932, was that Roth had done very well in preparing a text that titillated the general reader, but that he or she was not ashamed to keep in the parlor. "You may now place *Lady Chatterley's Lover* on your favorite reading shelf, beside the best of the modern classics," read one dust-jacket blurb, a statement preceded by the frankest admission of abridgment Faro made: Lawrence was too ill "to do his own 'bleeding.' So the work of revision had to be completed by other hands."

Roth had an excuse for this piracy. Lawrence had abandoned his own expurgation and died, leaving the way open for someone with ingenuity, resolution, and a thick skin to capitalize on the book. Assuming — correctly, as it turned out — that a revision of so notorious a novel could "become one of the sensations of the publishing season," he had to move quickly, so that a larger, more affluent publisher might not anticipate his plan. "To have asked permission would have been to be refused, and to throw a ripe plum into the lap of any one of a dozen sanctimonious American pirates [i.e., established publishers] whose crimes against authors are protected against exposure by big advertising contracts with newspapers."[57] Roth's unpublished memoir "Count Me Among the Missing" records what had happened in 1929, when he attempted to follow the high road by securing a contract to publish *The Well of Loneliness*.[58] Alfred Knopf had aborted his plans for the American edition, noting the censorious British response and Sumner's likely prosecution, and using as an excuse a large number of early orders from booksellers he felt would exploit prurient interest.[59] Neither booksellers nor censors frightened Roth, but he could offer Radclyffe Hall an advance of one thousand dollars only. Covici-Friede was able to offer more, and got the contract. Therefore, he goes on to say in his memoir, instead of asking permission of the Lawrence estate for his "revised" Chatterley, or even advertising it, he set up a "ledger" in which to record funds in escrow until such time as Frieda Lawrence might authorize his edition,[60] which, he wrote in a letter to fellow bookseller Harry Schwartz, she almost did. This time Knopf offered a larger sum.[61] Roth did speak to the Lawrences' American agent, Curtis Brown,[62] and with Frieda Lawrence. He offered her one thousand pounds, but she did not want to do business with "an awful man."[63]

At this point Roth was showing no more bad faith than the reputable booksellers, including Ben Abramson and Harry F. Marks, who were selling pirated editions of the original version. Roth was after copyright and publishing rights to the title, both expurgated and unexpurgated editions, using as leverage his own dramatization, which he did copyright in his own name, possibly because he would have enjoyed getting the stage and screen rights to *Lady Chatterley's Lover*. As he wrote to Schwartz, Knopf himself had these in mind when he outbid Roth. But Frieda was appalled by the play ("so terrible I can't take his money").[64] He might have tried to impress on her the provocative, if self-serving, point he makes in "Count Me Among the Missing": that a highly respected and wealthy publisher like Alfred Knopf was too timid to skirmish with censors in the name of avant-garde literary expression, leaving it to men of chutzpah but smaller financial resources and shadowy reputation (and, in Roth's view, the unmixed motive of integrity) to introduce *Lady Chatterley's Lover* and *Ulysses* (he must have been thinking of his unexpurgated, underground piracies of both texts) to American audiences.[65]

The Faro *Chatterley* appeared in the fall of 1930: "Without as much as a newspaper announcement of my intention, [I] threw the book on the market where it became a favorite overnight. My best hopes for it were realized. For not only did the book sell rapidly; it was granted on all sides that I had accomplished my intention without real injury to the book either as a sustained story or as a work of art."[66] It is true that the book sold well. The reason for the "authorized" revisions of 1932 (Knopf brought out the American impression) might well have been Roth's success. The Faro edition did so well, in fact, that when Lawrence's British publisher, Martin Secker, published his "authorized" edition — noting, although only on the front flap of the dust jacket, that it was "abridged" — he and Laurence Pollinger, Frieda Lawrence's executor, based it on Roth's work.[67] There was no need to ask his permission; he had not asked theirs.

Not everyone was impressed by what Roth thought was unintrusive yet helpful editing. The *Nation*'s Henry Hazlitt wrote: "And recently one particularly unscrupulous publisher brought the book out openly, bowdlerized to get by the censors, but with no acknowledgment either of the theft or of the bowdlerization. It was sold in many of the so-called respectable bookstores, whose owners, presumably, would have indignantly refused to handle a book in which the organs of the human body, and the act by which children are conceived, were described in good plain English, but who thought it quite all right to act as receivers of stolen goods."[68] This is a review of the authorized edition, and yet Hazlitt directs his scorn not at Knopf, the guardian of culture, but at the pariah, Roth. Admittedly, Roth published without permission, but both editions were bowdlerized. There is, however, some grudging acknowledgment for well-rewarded cunning in the statement. In this it mirrors that of Knopf's own advertising department, and Frieda Lawrence's, which is evident on the dust jacket of the authorized edition. One of Roth's own dust-jacket blurbs stated, "Luckily, the few changes made do not impede at all the deep, torrential stream of the narrative." Browsers read on the front of the dust jacket of the Knopf edition that they held "the only authorized edition . . . after all the expurgated pirated editions . . . even in its revised form it has all the beauty of the original edition, and [suggests,] to the greatest possible extent, the original's strength and vigor." This statement is credited to "Mrs. D. H. Lawrence."

Harry Schwartz recalls that the Samuel Roth edition "sold by the thousands," although Roth himself claimed only a "modest trade success."[69] A publisher with his background had special problems placing books in legitimate stores. Perhaps some shops would not carry it, either because of the international protest or because there was no way for most purchasers to know from browsing through the volume that it was abridged. Brentano's, Roth said, had it on their shelves, though their customers did not buy it, Roth groused, because clerks would not recommend it, probably pointing out that it was barbered. Suspicious and persistent, the publisher one day sent six people to visit Brentano's to request copies, giving each one a different reason for wanting to make the purchase. Each of these "plants" was roundly discouraged.[70] Did other stores proceed similarly? If so, Roth had to tolerate an ironic situation, however begrudgingly. A retail outlet that snapped up some of his offerings, including under-the-counter "hot stuff" for discreet, loyal, and wealthy clients, might feel the need to carry, and then warn discriminating customers off, an expurgation or other exploitive item that they might feel cheated by. The Gotham, when Sumner raided it 1928, and Dunster House, which had on hand copies of *Lady Chatterley* purchased from Roth when the Watch and Ward Society investigated it in 1929, obviously needed to do business with him.[71] When a friend of Sylvia Beach asked Frances Steloff in 1931 about the pirate of *Ulysses*, she told him of Roth's 1929 printing of the Shakespeare and Company edition, but noted that "she [was] anxious not to be connected to this affair."[72] There were at least some other stores whose trade with Roth, and other erotica dealers as well, dictated comparable considerations. They would not offend him by refusing to stock his expurgated *Chatterley*, but might not participate in the ruse of pretending it was a complete text. However distasteful the trader in prurience to some of his colleagues, he was also too useful to hurt.

From Phallic Subversiveness to Pulp Romance

Mahlon Blaine, one of Roth's illustrators, stigmatized the Faro *Chatterley* as "the Louisa May Alcott edition."[73] The demure Lady Chatterley portrayed in the Roth frontispiece (Figure 41) seems calculated to generate sarcasm. Roth the pirate was following his society's parameters of what was allowable and easily comprehensible regarding sexual expression. This meant not only expurgation, but also a lack of sensitivity for feminine self-assertion, and the assumption that Lawrence's "phallic novel" could be read as a lending-library "sexer." Roth knew his audience. It was attracted to a good love story — the "deep, torrential stream of the narrative," the taboo sexual desires, the strong silent hero, and the curious and vulnerable heroine. Roth was the first to attempt to market *Lady Chatterley's Lover* to a mass audience. In 1960, Richard Hoggart, in his introduction to the newly decensored Penguin edition, felt the need to refute the criticism that the book was basically a pulp romance. The William Faro edition, due to Roth's advertisements and "revisions," initiated the process that encouraged this impression. Well-trained middleman erotica dealer that he was, Roth found a novel banned as virulently pornographic and molded it into a sex pulp.

The text as Roth revised it kept the narrative flowing so as to plant a variety of prurience-generating images in his readers' minds. At the same time, Roth was as strict with Lawrence's text as a Post Office censor ever was with him; the ubiquitous substitution of "love" for "fuck" is only the most obvious example of the kind of changes he made. He always signaled clearly to the reader that a "love-bout" was about to commence, by inserting rows of asterisks as well as judicious signals, even occasionally retaining a word such as "naked." Actually, Lawrence's language was discreet enough that nothing really need be taken out at the point the

LADY CHATTERLEY

Figure 41. The frontispiece of Samuel Roth's abridged edition of *Lady Chatterley's Lover* (New York: Faro, 1930). Signed A. K. Skillin. Mahlon Blaine, another illustrator of erotica (including Roth's) during the 1930s, described the Roth abridgment as "the Louisa May Alcott edition."

asterisks appear. Roth provided the titillation gratis. The convention was one some readers were accustomed to from years of reading borderline erotica; they probably not only enjoyed it but would have felt cheated without it. It is nearly impossible for the reader to confront any of Lawrence's iconoclastic message about the liberating effects of surrender to sexual instinct.

In its place, the Faro edition is suffused with a kind of teasing in which one is allowed to peek at sexual passion, but not to see it clearly or whole. In Chapter 10, for example, Roth will not allow the gamekeeper to be seen caressing "the curve of [Connie's] crouching loins" or "her flank," or, a bit later, with "his wet body touching hers." However, we do see Mellors and Connie walking through the woods together, after they make love for the first time — which Roth signals with Mellors's "You lie there," before substituting a row of asterisks for three paragraphs. Roth retains the passage in which Connie marvels, upon meeting her lover the next day, about his "touch upon her living body" and her "new nakedness." Late in the same chapter, however, Roth excises Mellors's yearning for "the sleep with the woman in his arms," and a paragraph later, in the same context, changes "sleep" to "rest"; the notion of a man and a woman sleeping together might have caught Sumner's attention. Throughout, Lawrence's descriptions of specific physical acts are replaced with tamer and more conventional ways men and women have of responding to bodily urges, and to one another. In this context, the excision process is mirrored by the bowdlerizations: "things" for "shit," "affair" for "intercourse," "love" for "cunt," "passion" for "penis." Roth, enemy of Sumner and the Post Office, and dedicated to bringing the boldest modern writing into American homes, did the Comstocks' work for them.

The transformation of Lawrence's novel into the stuff of pulp romance is clearest from the two sequels Roth published anonymously: *Lady Chatterley's Husbands* (1931; ghostwritten by Antony Gudaitis, "Tony Gud" to friends and acquaintances), and *Lady Chatterley's Friends* (1932; by the versatile and prolific Clement Wood).[74] Roth's instructions to Gud were simply, in the ghostwriter's words, "to make it dramatic with sensual overtones."[75] The dust-jacket illustration was of a shapely woman coyly inspecting a line-up of men; the frontispiece depicted a nubile nude inspecting her breasts (Figure 42) and the blurb asserted that readers would find the shocking Connie and Mellors "as delightful as ever to follow — and abuse."[76] The sequel describes Connie's drinking and dancing larks on the Continent with a reluctant Mellors very much in the background. Clifford,

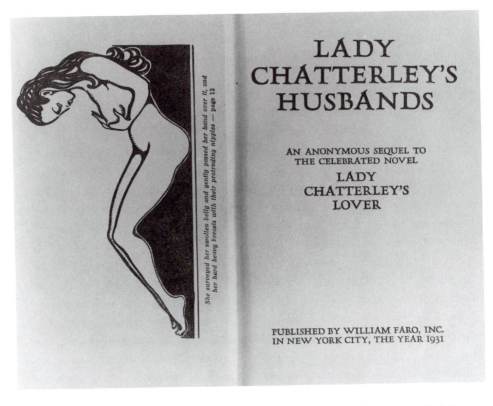

She surveyed her swollen belly and gently passed her hand over it, and her hard heavy breasts with their protruding nipples — page 13

LADY CHATTERLEY'S HUSBANDS

AN ANONYMOUS SEQUEL TO
THE CELEBRATED NOVEL

LADY CHATTERLEY'S LOVER

PUBLISHED BY WILLIAM FARO, INC.
IN NEW YORK CITY, THE YEAR 1931

Figure 42. Frontispiece and title page of the first of the "sequels" to *Lady Chatterley's Lover* (New York: Faro, 1931). Ghostwritten for Samuel Roth by Antony Gudaitis [Tony Gud]. The illustration is probably the work of Rahnghild [Susan Inez Aguerra?]. See Gershon Legman, *The Art of Mahlon Blaine* (East Lansing, Mich.: Peregrine, 1982), 22.

weakened by unrequited love, dies early and Connie's child is stillborn. Hilda emerges as a "tawny lioness" who marries a sugar daddy. Connie, before Mellors joins her, "wreak[s] havoc on herself with her hands"; together, their lovemaking carries a hint of sadism despite (or perhaps because of) the author's attempt to transplant some Lawrentian diction: " 'Some day,' she cried . . . 'you'll love me to death.' " She grows restless; thus begin her glamorous European adventures, the first of which is a Parisian orgy.

Clement Wood, one of the writers Roth relied on heavily through the 1930s, was best known for his *Poet's Handbook*, *Complete Rhyming Dictionary*, and

prize-winning early poetry, *The Earth Turns South* (1919). His work was anthologized in Braithwait's annual compilations, and he contributed to the *American
Mercury*, the *Liberator*, and the *Seven Arts*. Basically a freelance writer and editor,
Wood had also published with Haldeman-Julius and Macy-Macius. Among the
subjects of his biographies were Amy Lowell, Bernarr Macfadden, Lord Kitchener,
and Presidents Hoover and Harding — the latter three commissioned by Roth.[77] Besides the second Chatterley sequel, Wood wrote *Loose Shoulder Straps* under the
pseudonym Alain Dubois for the publisher.[78] He was Roth's friend as well as
confederate; the latter dedicated his *Private Life of Frank Harris* (1932) to "Clement Wood, The only man I know in America capable of turning this trick."[79] Wood
soon returned the dedicatory compliment ("To Samuel Roth who always enjoys a
good tale").[80]

Wood's sequel follows a beautiful, sexually active woman's adventures in
exotic lands (Paris, Cairo, the Egyptian desert). Connie vows to "not now refuse
any sensation that life offered her," and becomes an epitome of feminine generosity to her adoring travel companions: Tommy Dukes, Charlie May, and the author
himself, aka Alain Dubois. Mellors is there too, cast in the role of the malcontent
puritan. The climax of her Egyptian tour is dinner in a tent with the manservant
Mahmed, who bears the name and the muscular masculinity of the hero of E. M.
Hull's *The Sheik*, the novel upon which the Rudolph Valentino film was based. The
novel's end finds Mellors still in love with Connie but leaving Cairo for England, as
if he must put half a continent between himself and a pretty blonde leper (this, too,
is how he behaved at the end of the first sequel). His fall is paralleled by the
ascendancy of Clifford's old friends, whom Lawrence found to be unworthy "mental lifers" but who flourish in the sequels because they can live by the enlightened,
sybaritic rules of the game. If a serious moral is appropriate, one is implied (as a
respectable, however disingenuous, disclaimer) from the Roth camp: focusing on
sexual needs is decadent (the friends), self-destructive (Mellors), or both (Connie).

To Lawrence himself, this would be "pornography": "the attempt to insult
sex, do dirt upon it." Speaking of the "picture post-card," he says, "ugly and cheap
they make the . . . sexual act, trivial and cheap and nasty." Underground books, and
"dirty stories," he continues, are "just a trick of doing dirt on sex."[81] They are the
work of traders of prurience: the erotica dealers, and the moral authorities who
equate sex with sin. Lawrence — "the Priest of Love" — held both in contempt.
Samuel Roth earned his bread as one of the former, although he would rather have

thought of himself as a "bohemian," furthering the cause of "the truth of beauty." We now see that in his lucrative distortions of Lawrence he exemplified prurience's basic assumption — that sex is dirty and fleshly impulses verminous. In his self-contented autobiographical writings, Roth was not capable of admitting to himself that he reinforced this notion.

Disgust with sexual appetite is of necessity a subtext in Roth's advertising, expurgations, and choice of borderline texts to sell. That does not mean that it is a conscious part of his belief system, as far as can be assumed by reading his writings or from gathering reminiscences from his acquaintances. The latter do not recall a puritanical or prudish caste of mind. Speaking *in propria persona* in his short stories, essays, or poems, he expressed neither disdain nor enthusiasm for sexual openness and experimentation. He seemed not to be very interested in the subject, although he was extremely adamant about his right to publish books that were frank about sex. One short-story collection, *Body* (1931), does focus on erotic impulses. The male protagonists variously suffer from voyeurism, onanism, fetishism, pedophilia, and necrophilia. Roth may have been imitating Wood's exploration of similar themes in his short-story collection, *Flesh* (1929). In lieu of loving real women, many of Roth's characters attach sexual desire to bizarre, idealized images of femininity. They are the precise opposites of Lawrence's Mellors. Roth presents their psychosexual compulsions with insight, and unsympathetically. Of course, such subject matter sells books.

The Faro List

Between 1930 and 1933, when he filed for bankruptcy — an apparent casualty of the Depression economy — Roth published thirty titles under the Faro imprint.[82] The majority fall into four groups: gallantiana, pulp romance, sexology, and "exposés" of private lives or newsworthy current sensations or scandals. The first category's offerings included Sacher-Masoch's *Venus in Furs*, which stores carried openly and could include in display windows,[83] as well as the same author's *Venus and Adonis*. Octave Mirabeau's *Celestine*, about a beautiful chambermaid (touted as "the Frenchiest of all modern French novels") was an early Faro title that Sumner prosecuted unsuccessfully and that sold steadily.[84] Catulle Mendès's *Lila and Colette* was about French prostitutes; this was one of five items (with the two by Sacher-Masoch, a collection of poems by Ralph Cheyney, and Roth's dramatization of *Chatterley*) classed as "the Ardent Classics." Roth himself hacked up the important privately printed collections of American scatological and bawdy humor, *Anecdota Americana* (1927, 1934). He printed intact some of the non-scatological entries, and on the dust jacket described the collection aptly as "stories for the smoking car, stag, and the intimacy of your own parlor. . . . No obscene words are used, nor are any obscene situations described." He also offered *Body*, under the pseudonym Daniel Quilter. "This is perhaps the most revolutionary fiction published in English in many years," puffed one blurb. "The writing is cruel but beautiful." Roth's allusion to this book on the dust jacket of his *Private Life of Frank Harris* is equal in pretentiousness to the subtitle: *A New Study, in Narrative, of the Anatomy of Society*. The author, the dust-jacket copy states, "has served three short prison sentences for his services on behalf of the printed word. . . . His second sentence . . . was spent on a strange set of stories which eventually were published under a pseudonym."[85]

Roth did write *Body*, but he did not write more than the first third of the Harris book. In correspondence with a reader who stated that he did not see how the writer of the first and second halves of the work could be the same person, Roth admitted that he had been too busy to finish, so he let a ghostwriter do so.[86] The book's dedication, to the only other American writer who could "turn this trick," is yet another example of the protective coloration of supreme self-contentedness without which Roth could not face the public. It makes it clear that the author was his friend Clement Wood. Either Roth or Wood invents an old friend of Harris who knew him intimately in Nice. This convenient personage, Roth/Wood imagines, was privy to discussions between Harris and Lord Alfred Douglas about the nature of the latter's relationship with Oscar Wilde. He is suitably unspecific in reporting the conversations. Roth/Wood also invents for *My Life and Loves* a subject matter — sadism, pedophilia, a cacophony of fetishes — that it does not contain. It is inconceivable that either Roth or Wood had not perused each volume of *My Life*; with towering cynicism, and awareness of what attracted their audience's attention, they assumed that the Harris who wanted to write a book that would sell many copies would deliberately present himself as an Edwardian de Sade, despite his avowed aversion to fetishistic sex. The same reader who questioned Roth on the book's authorship questioned him on this, and on the need for mixing fiction with facts. The answer was, "I was so overcome with the bestiality of the love scenes that I forgot the good parts."[87]

Another answer might have been that Roth wanted readers to be overcome as well, so that the book would sell well enough for himself to claim recognition as Harris's biographer. The timing was important. Others, including A. I. Tobin and Elmer Gertz, whose *Frank Harris: A Study in Black and White* was soon to be published, were researching the infamous author's life in the year of his death. They were afraid that Roth had somehow gotten hold of their material. Mrs. Nellie Harris, planning her own account, was also concerned. She wrote to A. L. Ross, Harris's New York attorney, saying that Roth had met her husband only a few times and that the meetings were not amiable. She enclosed an unidentified newspaper clipping, which stated that Roth's forthcoming book was written "from material supplied by the late Mr. Harris in 1919, when he and Mr. Roth associated continually for several months. Plans for an autobiography were much on the mind of Mr. Harris at the time and he had asked Mr. Roth to help him map it out."[88] This clipping had the earmarks of a "plant" and was likely perpetrated by Harold C. Auer, a friend and admirer of Roth and at the time circulation publicity director for the Detroit Free Press. He was acting as American agent for Lord Alfred Douglas, and Roth was about to publish Douglas's *My Friendship with Oscar Wilde* under his Coventry House imprint, which he reserved during the period of his Faro business for editions as handsome as his resources would allow.[89] The rival biographers squirmed while *The Private Life of Frank Harris* — at least partly ghostwritten, more lurid fiction than fact, and well plotted to keep all sorts of curiosity aroused — sold briskly.

One of the earlier Faro pieces of gallantiana was Dr. Ralcy Husted Bell's *Memoirs and Mistresses: Colors and Odors of Love*. There was a later revision, slightly shortened, subtitled *Amatory Recollections of a Physician* (which suggests the Victorian pornographic classic *The Amatory Experiences of a Surgeon*). Roth's acquaintance with Bell predated the publisher's 1921 trip to England.[90] Notably, Bell remained Roth's friend despite the international protest, and published with Faro despite the *Lady Chatterley* expurgation. By 1931, Bell had retired from medical practice to write about his chief interests, which included poetry, travel, and protection of the country's wildlife and pastoral vistas. In reporting his death, the *New York Times* characterized him as a "well known nature writer and patron of the arts."[91] He had been an advocate of women's rights (*Woman from Bondage to Freedom*, 1921) and sex education, and had written on poetry, art, and travel. Bell's *Memoirs* are an elegy to the aging physician's many affairs with women. The reminiscences are a bit like Harris's in the way they treat the writer's mistresses: frank and sometimes unflattering about their character, and specific about their varying enthusiasms for having sex. Unlike the author of *My Life and Loves*, Bell limited his sexually oriented passages to descriptions of the naked bodies of his lovers. He did not mention Harris as an antecedent, but rather the *Decameron*, Theocritus, Casanova, Louÿs's *Aphrodite*, and Rousseau's *Confessions*: classical gallantiana. Bell had named the manuscript *A Few Leaves of Many Loves*. Samuel Roth, "a brilliant friend of mine," suggested the title of the published work; the original was "more likely to prejudice the reader before he . . . had a chance to learn that I am not a roué."[92] The publisher knew that the word "mistresses" would connote subversion of marital conventions while eschewing any equation of the good doctor with a notorious rake such as Frank Harris or the anonymous author of *My Secret Life*. He also knew that his erotica customers would recall that in 1929 he had issued the physician's essay in defense of masturbation, *Self-Amusement*, in a limited edition under his Golden Hind imprint. Roth also probably recalled that Bell's *Some Aspects of Adultery* (Critic and Guide, 1921) had been reprinted (for "students of sexology") by the Cosmopolis Press, and by Eugenics. Both works would be regarded as smut by conservative moralists, but could be legitimately defended as educational tracts.

In June 1931, Bell died at his home when a shotgun he had rigged to fire at a possible intruder killed him as he entered his house. Roth contacted police, theorizing that his friend had been murdered.[93] He apparently did not sully Bell's reputation by suggesting to them that *Memoirs and Mistresses* might have provoked jealousy or anger; he stated that Bell had made enemies adamantly protecting his grounds from loutish trespassers who were threatening him. But reading in the newspapers of the suspicion of foul play ("Scout Murder Hint in Gun Trap Death") made some people wonder. Juicy rumors spread in the book trade that one of Bell's mistresses had done him in. A listing of *Memoirs and Mistresses* in a mid-1930s mail-order catalog of the Anthropological Library stated, "So daring and open was he in his descriptions of his mistresses that there is no doubt, this was the cause of his murder in his country lodge three days after this book was published." Henry Pringle's 1934 list of prohibited books includes a privately printed version of *Memoirs and Mistresses*, although it records no prosecutions of the title, and repeats the story of its author being done in "after the disclosures of his book."[94] Roth's suggestion to the police that Bell was murdered need not have been the

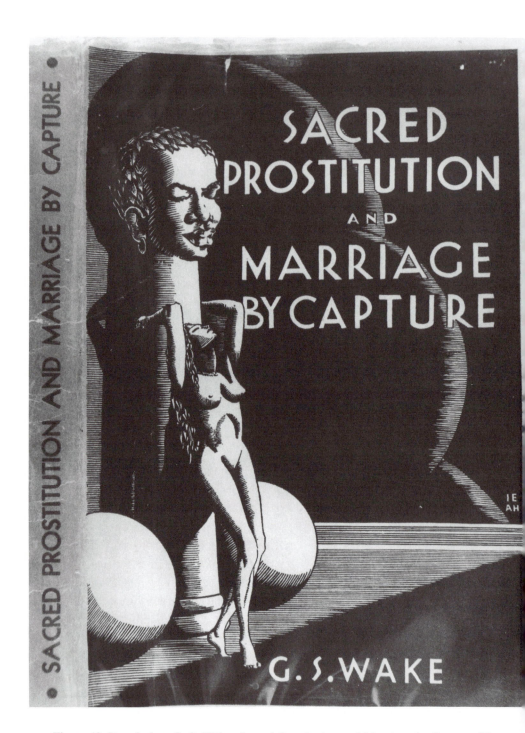

Figure 43. Dust jacket, G. S. Wake, *Sacred Prostitution and Marriage by Capture* (New York: Big Dollar Book Co. [Samuel Roth], 1932).

source of this gossip. However, much stronger evidence that the publisher was its cause is the blurb on the front flap of the dust jacket of the Faro shortened version: "He wrote gaily and honestly — so honestly that he was murdered in cold blood two weeks after the appearance of *Memoirs and Mistresses*." Perhaps the rationale for a shorter Faro edition — it must have been issued posthumously — was that Bell had expressed second thoughts about his revelations, and they had proved shockingly justifiable. Perhaps, however, it was issued both to prevent lawsuits (although news of such events would have helped sales), and, even more important, to fuel curiosity about Ralcy Husted Bell's tragic frankness with additional copies of his memoirs. The subtitle of the posthumous edition, with its suggestion of a comparison that Bell might not have allowed ("I am not a roué"), could only have helped accomplish the latter goal.

The Faro gallantiana was supplemented by sensation-seeking fiction and sexology. The former featured up-to-date themes and topics, such as are *Woman's Doctor* ("a story of the abortion of human life"), Alain Dubois's (i.e., Clement Wood's) *Loose Shoulder Straps, A Scarlet Pansy* ("the masculine counterpart of the picture painted in *The Well of Loneliness*"),[95] and *A Gentleman in a Black Skin* ("the story of the marriage of a rich, beautiful, cultured white woman to a colored singer in Harlem"). The sexology included Bell's *Self-Amusement*, and editions of *Padlocks and Girdles of Chastity* and *Sacred Prostitution and Marriage by Capture* (marriage, fertility rites, and customs among peoples of various cultures), sensationalized by a racist and titillating dust-jacket illustration (Figure 43). The latter two were issued as Big Dollar books. Roth used this imprint during the year he filed for bankruptcy as William Faro Inc., and they were sold, as were many books that year, at one dollar each.[96] Roth also distributed, possibly as a remainder, *The Sword and Womankind*, a misogynistic historical account of female machinations to influence events in periods of crisis, in an edition published by Esar Levine's mail-order operation, the Panurge Press. William Faro, as was common practice, routinely offered remainder copies of other publishers' books.

Roth Beats Sumner "Beautifully and Decisively"

The beauty of the Faro operation was twofold: Roth's net spread wide, and Sumner was pretty well stymied. "We agree with you," Sumner wrote to Bodwell of the Watch and Ward, that "the expurgated edition of *Lady Chatterley's Lover* would probably not sustain a prosecution." However, he went on to say that he had discovered a circular for the book that he thought would.[97] In February 1931, Sumner had Roth and his former Golden Hind confederate Julius Moss, now Faro office manager, arrested in the offices of William Faro at 96 Fifth Avenue, where he uncovered remainder copies of *Eastern Shame Girl* (an account of love and seduction in the Far East) and two Faro imprints, the expurgated *Chatterley* and Mirabeau's *Celestine*, as well as "thousands of copies" of a four-page circular headed "Books Banned in Boston," order forms, and envelopes. Nine women were busy preparing mailings.[98] The circular listed several borderline books (*Padlocks and Girdles of Chastity, Oscar Wilde Three Times Tried, The Sword and Womankind*) that Roth continued to advertise with his Faro imprints (the edition of the Wilde book was "privately printed," but its design and typography mark it as his own production), and at least one under-the-counter item, *The Strange Confession of Monsieur Montcairn.* This book was probably available to those who inquired about "Faro's Limited Editions." Information about the availability of such "limited and private editions" of "special books" (which may have included Roth's piracy of the unadvertisable, unexpurgated *Chatterley*) was cryptically noted in an order form appearing on some of the dust-jacket flaps of Faro offerings. The borderline books were intended as "window dressing" — they could be publicly displayed in stores or advertised through various media — and also to explain to authorities like Sumner, if necessary, a publisher's "otherwise inexplicable activity."[99]

Roth's Faro volumes, and their attention-getting dust jackets, gave him an edge in two directions. First, he could display in bookstores a broad range of openly sold offerings — without having to rely exclusively on newspaper or magazine "lineage" (as he termed it) or flyers sent through the ever vigilant U.S. mails. He did occasionally use both methods, placing notices in print media, including, for wholesalers, *Publishers Weekly*.[100] In addition, there was his extensive mailing list built up during his days as a magazine editor and from his Golden Hind Press activities. However, I have not found many advertising circulars for Faro titles in archives. Roth put advertisements for various books on the Faro list on the backs of the dust jackets of each title, but must have used circulars also, as Sumner's 1931 visit to Roth's offices attests. As Sumner's 14 April 1931 periodical letter states, "booksellers [who stocked Faro titles, or mailed them] have been deluging the community with objectionable circular matter using the name William Faro Inc."[101] But the presence of a dust jacket, rarely found on mail-order editions of erotica, is good evidence in itself that Roth was relying heavily, as were other general publishers of the day, on stores of various sorts as points of sale.

Although the Faro titles were much more than window dressing, they could have had that function for people who wanted the banned books. Roth had as strong a practical need to succeed, as much willingness to endure police action, and at least as much ideological defiance of authority as any of his colleagues. As we have noted, the five copies of *Chatterley* that precipitated the infamous prosecution of Dunster House in Boston were mailed from Roth's Golden Hind offices. That was before his specialization in material suitable for bookstore display, but it is unlikely that Roth completely stopped his dealings in banned pornography. According to one of his Faro authors, many mail-order customers and those who visited the press's office would pay in cash, not wanting a paper trail of their purchases of illegal goods. Some may have purchased the Faro titles by personal visit also. The practice aroused suspicion and was probably discouraged, for it was a modus operandi of Sumner's agents.[102] In any event, Roth was constrained to keep a great deal of paper currency in his office.[103] Although Sumner could not prove it in 1931, mail order continued to be a significant part of Roth's operations throughout the 1930s, especially after Faro ceased operations in 1933. The nine office workers indicate he must have had capital in 1931, and the sources of this must have included not only the barbered *Chatterley*, and other Faro titles, but also *Monsieur Montcairn* and interdicted works Sumner seized in 1929 but which his wife and brother might have been selling while Roth was in prison. The "Banned in Boston" circular attests that Roth would sell whatever and however he could, and as disingenuously as need be.

To return to the 1931 raid, the circular Sumner found listed fourteen books, and featured the Faro *Chatterley*. The latter was being fraudulently advertised in a pruriently suggestive flyer: "the chief of forbidden books," "the most daring of all modern novels," "the book as written by D. H. Lawrence."[104] Sumner charged Roth with mailing an indecent circular for books both obscene and purporting to be obscene. The defense's thoroughly documented brief, which Greenbaum, Wolff, and Ernst helped prepare, demonstrated that the advertising matter contained nothing obscene, and that the two books Sumner found and submitted as evidence were not obscene as a whole or by the mores of the current day.[105] The case was dismissed.[106] Roth's victory statement does not acknowledge the stellar legal talent arrayed on behalf of the defendants. He glories in a triumph purely personal:

"Defending myself and the books cost me over two thousand dollars. But I felt that it was fully worth it. Once and for all time it had to be proven to the vice crusader that the courts would not sustain him as a censor of literature. I was advised on all sides to sue him for false arrest, but I did not want that. I had beaten him beautifully and decisively. That was enough for me."[107]

To Roth's credit, some able and well-reputed writers joined Clement Wood and Ralcy Bell as Faro authors. Mark Hellinger, who rivaled Walter Winchell in popularity as a journalist, published *Moon over Broadway* with the house. Antony Gudaitis's *A Young Man About to Commit Suicide* showed him to be more than the hack writer who turned out the first *Chatterley* sequel. The novel is an interesting study of the anxieties and frustrations of a sensitive New Yorker physically satisfied but emotionally paralyzed by the promiscuous sex Manhattan offers. He becomes lost among the kind of urban sophisticates he himself had caricatured in the superficial *Lady Chatterley* sequels. The final book in Faro's series of Ardent Classics was Ralph Cheyney's poetry collection, *A Pregnant Woman in a Lean Age*, which included his "Bright Impossible Fox." Cheyney was a frequently anthologized poet, and editor of *Unrest: The Rebel Poet's Anthology*. Stung with reviews that decried *A Pregnant Woman*'s sexually oriented content, he wrote a spirited defense in the avant-garde review *Contempo*.[108] He is identified in that issue as "the winner of many national poetry prizes."

The presence of these authors, as well as the deference of the editor of *Contempo*,[109] is some evidence that despite the international protest and his bowdlerized, unauthorized *Chatterley*, Roth had some standing in the East Coast literary community as publisher and editor in the early 1930s. Nor were his own writings published under the Faro imprint inconsiderable. These included, besides *Body*, his account of his prison experiences (*Stone Walls Do Not*), his satire of Sumner (*Diary of a Smuthound*), and his lyric poetry (*Songs out of Season*). This measure of success as editor and writer, if modest, must have made the deprecation of the *New Yorker* ("then who would Samuel Roth be?") and *Vanity Fair*, which had nominated him for oblivion, easier to bear. The head of William Faro, Inc. may have taken such fashionable magazine stories as proof that he had become enough of a public figure to be satirized, and in the case of *Vanity Fair*, by sophisticated young women. With typical bravado, Roth told a friend that he cooperated with their "nomination" on stipulation that he might kiss the editor; he settled for the photographer.[110] The *New Yorker* had at least paid William Faro the compliment of a sarcastic nod in the direction of its *Chatterley* revision: "an edition . . . with all the censorable passages deleted and a good deal of the rest rewritten, apparently by someone around the office. It takes a pretty good book to stand being hashed up like that, but the firm of William Faro, Incorporated, had faith in the ability of D. H. Lawrence and was game to make the attempt."[111]

The Herbert Hoover Exposé

The Strange Career of Mr. Hoover Under Two Flags is one of the books for which Samuel Roth was best known. Leo Hamalian referred to it as the "pinnacle of his publishing career."[112] Roth's obituary in the *New York Times* devoted a paragraph to it, forty-two years after its publication.[113] Appearing in September 1931, the work, according to the publishing history on its copyright page, went through ten printings in four months. A recent Hoover biographer tells us that before year's end, it became a best-seller in several cities and appeared in sixth place on Macy's nonfiction best-seller list. During the presidential primary campaign, various candidates recommended it, as did Harry Elmer Barnes, a popular commentator on American history and culture with strong academic credentials. The *New Republic* and the *Nation* gave it serious attention, if not complete approbation.[114] In the first four months of its appearance, more than eleven thousand copies were sold. At that time, sales were projected at forty thousand. In mid-November alone, Roth received more than five hundred requests for copies, some from Scribner's, Macy's, Marshall Field in Chicago, and Gimbel Brothers in Philadelphia. Roth bank accounts did not show large profits, although his deposits during February and March 1932 totaled almost fourteen thousand dollars. However, it seemed that he might have been trying to hide the profits by having some of the monies realized for the book deposited in two other accounts, managed by his 1929 Golden Hind confederates.[115] Roth later wrote that with the money he made from *Strange Career*, he was able to publish a pet project, Voltaire's *Philosophical Dictionary*.[116]

    The Strange Career was written by an Englishman, John Hamill. Its title, which Roth may have chosen, suggests *The Strange Death of President Harding*; for readers this is also its pedigree as an exposé, because *The Strange Death* egregiously milked the sensationalism of Nan Britton's allegation that her daughter was Harding's child. Hamill approached Roth sometime in late 1930 with research concerning Hoover's career prior to his becoming president. It suggested that "the

Great Engineer" had been complicit in the abuse of Chinese mine workers in China and the Transvaal ("men are cheaper than timber"); had brought coolies into South Africa to work for slave drivers out of greed and a dislike for Caucasian laborers' concerns about working conditions; had manipulated stocks during the 1907 financial panic to the ruin of many innocent people; had profited from boondoggles involving the relief of Belgium that resulted in foodstuffs being sent to Germany, thus prolonging World War I; and had refused to save from execution the heroic British nurse Edith Cavell so that the Belgian relief dealings would not be discovered. He was also scored for falsely claiming credit for writing a treatise on mining, for timidity in the field, for heavy drinking, and for demonstrating greater loyalty to Britain and its colonialist entrepreneurs over a fifteen-year period than to his native country (the "two flags" reference of the title). It was the first of several smear books that had some part, however minor, in hindering Hoover's re-election bid.

Hoover certainly took the book seriously. His personal secretary dispatched three operatives to investigate Samuel Roth, where they found some powerful insiders who did not scruple to provide the president with confidential information. One such supporter, a collector for the Internal Revenue Service, was a colleague of Justice Salvatore Cotillo, who had been assigned to adjudicate a suit filed in the New York Supreme Court against the publishers of *The Strange Career*. The IRS employee obtained Cotillo's consent to allow Post Office inspector C. H. Saffell to copy the papers that Cotillo held relevant to the suit, and arranged for Saffell to pose as a "deputy tax collector."[117] With this cover, the inspector was able to gain information from the printer of *The Strange Career*. Then he called on Roth himself to inquire about his income tax return. He also gained access to Roth's bank account. What Hoover's investigators suspected was a secret Democratic underwriter of the project, but no such Hoover hater was found.[118] Nor was Saffell the only operative to visit Roth. Another of the president's men, Frank Hale, working independently of the president's secretary, pumped Roth for information and suggested that he might give the publisher financial help. Roth was suspicious that he might want to buy him out, and then withdraw the book from circulation. Hale, Saffell ascertained, was something of a maverick who offered to raid Hamill's office and remove his Hoover files.[119] What he did do, just a month after the publication of *The Strange Career*, was to suborn its author by signing him to a contract for another book, about Belgian relief.[120] Besides all these machinations, it has been suggested that Hoover himself requested the officer in charge of naval intelligence in the New York area to break into Roth's office.[121] At least in the sense that Roth gained the serious attention of the powerful, the Hoover exposé certainly was a craggy, perilous "pinnacle" of his career — until the 1950s when, with a book on the famous columnist's smears, libels, and "secret life," he gained the enmity of Walter Winchell. He later angered Estes Kefauver with belligerent testimony before his subcommittee (Figure 49).

Roth had long known the potential for disaster if a small publisher with little prestige were to challenge entrenched wealth and power with such explosive material.[122] There was something about that challenge, despite the additional disadvantage of his prison record, that was irresistible to him. "There must, under the circumstances, be someone courageous enough to publish such things. If not I, who?"[123] Nor would the shadowy history of Hamill's project have dissuaded him.

Hamill told Roth that he chose William Faro Inc. because every other publisher he had approached rejected the work, as had Democratic National Chairman John Raskob. Hamill and a dishonorably discharged policeman, a Tammany hanger-on who liked to engage in legal quibbles, James J. "Constitution" O'Brien, had originally planned the book; O'Brien may have been backed by a Tammany figure.[124] When O'Brien attempted to revise the manuscript in ways Hamill thought libelous, he broke with him.[125] Roth must have sensed, as did his friends, that there were good reasons the Democratic party leadership had turned Hamill down. He probably brought in a lawyer to check for libel before sending the manuscript to the printer.[126] The information Hamill had used, as he later confessed, was not false in itself, but the full evidence needed to prove his charges was not forthcoming. Hoover had, for example, been involved in mining operations in the Far East and South Africa that employed coolies, but he had been critical of their harsh treatment, at least at the hands of their "native" (Chinese) overlords. No one could show that he stated that men were not worth the price of the timber necessary to shore up the mines. Hamill in fact merely says that a report Hoover wrote replicated the statement; however, Hoover's report — the context of the entire piece is not stated, nor the text reproduced — could be more easily read as ironic rather than commendatory of such callousness.[127] To be sure, Hoover shared his colleagues' imperialist attitudes: the Chinese mine owners, he wrote, were dishonest, stupid, and suffered from "racial slowness"; the workers were "mulish" and "thieving."[128] To be sure, also, both Hoover and the British firm with which he was associated exploited indigenous peoples of China and South Africa. But Hamill does not systematically criticize British or American racism and paternalism; he is too interested in making a personal attack.[129] For example, Hoover did sell food to Belgians, and at a profit, but the fullest documentation available indicated that the sales were to those Belgians who could afford to pay, and that Hoover charged them only to defer costs of the project.[130] There was no documentation, but only a chain of inference, to suggest — and then only to the most partial investigator — that Hoover was in a position to control the events leading to the nurse Edith Cavell's death.

"You simply must not fail to read this great exposure," ran one blurb. Roth had a Faro imprint on the best-seller list, a book that was taken seriously. O'Brien sought an injunction against sale of the book, which he said was a pirated use of his property. In December 1931, Judge Cotillo issued a restraining order against its sale in New York State (later lifted, because O'Brien could not pay the required five-hundred-dollar contingency fee).[131] The only purpose of the book, he asserted, was for "persons of unsavory reputation" to make money by appealing to morbid curiosity. It was "unsportsmanlike" as well as immoral to take advantage of the president, who, given his position, could not file a libel suit.[132] As we have seen, so disdainful was Cotillo of Roth's behavior that he had allowed the Hoover men investigating the publisher to see and copy the papers filed relevant to the injunction.

Cotillo had cosponsored the Clean Books Bill in the New York State Legislature as Chairman of the Judiciary Committee in 1923. In granting O'Brien's request, he used language similar to that of John Sumner and others in referring to literature prosecuted for obscenity. He cast Roth in the role of the heartless promoter who would do anything for money. Cotillo, in contrast, was the defender of honorable men, even if it meant providing their agents with confidential information. At this point, Roth had some money and a readership. Cotillo and others would see to it that Roth did not have the other ingredients for power: public honor and credibility. And they were successful.

Roth's reply to his critics — "Seeing Mr. Hoover Through" — came in a lead article in *Plain English*, a magazine he seems to have published in June 1932 simply to showcase the essay; there was only one issue.[133] In his editor's introduction, he declared: "I will continue to publish what appears to me to be true or beautiful, if I have to make a barracks out of every jail in the United States."[134] His complex self-image is rooted in a powerful aversion from what he senses, at some deep level of his psyche, is his status as a pariah capitalist and of the political vulnerability to which it condemned him. Other middleman erotica dealers could accept these as conditions of being in business, and in their own minds rise above them, as did the idealistic Ben Rebhuhn, and the scholarly Esar Levine. Roth could do neither. These burdens he saw as vast injustices, and he refused to contemplate them with anything approaching objectivity. Whenever they reared their ugly heads, he responded publicly, in this instance as a crusading martyr, with moral indignation of his own, directed against a wide variety of individuals and institutions. Such a reaction made it inevitable that he would retain pariah status.

The Pirate Pirated

By late 1932, the effects of the Depression had forced Roth to liquidate William Faro, Inc. He was confident of an orderly procedure, for he had ample credit, books, and copyrights. His was a typical middleman enterprise, and its assets should have been easily liquidated. It is impossible to reconstruct what actually transpired; in his *Jews Must Live: An Account of the Persecution of the World by Israel on All the Frontiers of Civilization*, Roth casts himself in the role of martyr.[135] As he tells it, he approached his principal creditors, chief among whom were the wholesaler who had supplied him with book paper and the owner of a bindery. Arrangements were made to pay these men certain sums per month until debts were cleared. Because he owed more than four thousand dollars to the "paper house," Roth mortgaged to it the plates of eight of his "best books." The binder's lawyer suggested that instead of bargaining for terms with individual creditors, Roth should reincorporate William Faro under a new name, under which the lawyer would be the owner until the binder and the owner of the paper house were paid, after which, the lawyer promised, the business (stock, copyrights, linotype plates) would be returned to Roth. As an enticement, the lawyer also promised that new terms, more favorable to Roth, would have been established under which the rest of the creditors were to be paid off. But Roth was suspicious, so, on the lawyer's suggestion, he hired a financial officer (Roth creates for him the fictitious name "Lousse") to help him liquidate. All of these men, Roth asserts, led by the lawyer, were conspiring to cheat him of his business. The binder, whom Roth dubs "Parrach" ("parech" is Yiddish for an obscene, lowdown, brazen schemer) sold his plant to a party who refused to return the many books being stored on the premises, giving as an excuse Roth's failure to make good on his promissory notes. Some of these had been mishandled by Lousse, leaving the harried publisher hamstrung. The binder's agent, one "Ratte," promised to return Roth's books if he received notes for a certain amount; Roth had the checks ready but would not hand them over until the books were delivered to his warehouse. They were never delivered, and a few days later he was served with papers requiring that his business be put into receivership. Lousse had sworn an affidavit to the effect that William Faro Inc. was unable to satisfy creditors because the owner was misappropriating funds. Just before Roth received these papers, he learned that the Faro stock, thanks to the machinations of Ratte, had been ordered sold to Parrach as an equivalent to the amount of money Roth was unable to pay him. The evidence for Roth's inability to satisfy creditors was a summons served by an unscrupulous bookseller with whom Parrach and Lousse had conspired to complain that Roth had defaulted on a promissory note that Lousse, not Roth, had issued in the first place. Roth was able to solicit many other creditors to vouch for him and obtained a restraining order, but the binder and paper wholesaler were already selling his property. The bankruptcy court judge — through political influence, Roth believed — denied the publisher any of the legal safeguards of voluntary bankruptcy.

Roth had, at the time of the Hoover exposé, been secreting monies in surreptitious accounts, so perhaps there is some basis for Lousse's affidavit. Indeed, we can hardly take the publisher's account at face value. On the other hand, four of Roth's Faro titles were issued from 1933 throughout the rest of the decade under two imprints seemingly unauthorized by him. The titles were the expurgated *Lady Chatterley's Lover*, *Anecdota Americana*, *A Scarlet Pansy*, and *Venus in Furs*; the imprints, Nesor and Royal.[136] Gershon Legman — who by the late 1930s was acutely observing and participating in New York erotica dealing — says that "two remainder publishers" were involved, one the owner of a Canal Street bindery named Rosen or Rose ("Nesor" is "Rosen" spelled backward). Legman notes that Roth had contracted with a man named Rose to bind his underground publications during this period. Perhaps this was Roth's "Parrach." In 1929, there was a Rose Bookbinding Company at 200 West Street, near the Hudson River, south of Canal Street.[137] The Nesor texts are identical to the Faro editions, but reset. In physical appearance, therefore, the books differ, although the front panels of the dust jackets for Nesor editions of *Anecdota Americana* and *Chatterley* are identical to Faro's. Also, some of the paper spine labels on the Nesor volumes of *Lady Chatterley* are the same as those Roth used; perhaps these were an overrun of the labels Rosen (or someone else) had printed for Roth, which were used simply because they were on hand, as part of the stock Rosen (or someone else) appropriated without Roth's consent. Roth told Leo Hamalian that Nesor became Crown Publishers, an opinion Gershon Legman shares. Crown was founded in 1934 as a remainder house by Nathaniel Wartels and his brother Emmanuel. Nathaniel was a graduate of the Wharton School, and over the years he made of Crown one of the most successful of American publishing operations. In 1935, Crown started its own publishing, under the imprint Phoenix: the successful publisher of lending-library books, two of whose titles were challenged by Sumner in 1935.[138] Crown also issued titles as Arcadia House.

Whether Nesor cheated Roth will never be ascertained. Surely many publishers of erotica who could not pay the printer's bill when the books were ready for distribution did not receive them. This was established cash-and-carry practice. The property of William Faro, Inc. would have been desirable for young businessmen at the height of the Depression, if it could be had cheaply. Booksellers could fall into traps set by lawyers, political fixers, judges, politicians — and fellow bookmen. Far more important than how it came about is the effect that losing his assets in 1933 had on Samuel Roth. It damaged his ability to project himself as a respectable publisher, and put him back in the dangerous occupation of underground erotica production. This meant weak capital, lack of security, reliance on the untrustworthy protocols of the trade, pursuit by the law and the vice society, and the need to watch for informers and entrapment tactics. In short, after a period breathing the air of an *alrightnik*, Roth found himself back where he had been after the collapse of *Beau* and *Two Worlds Monthly* in 1927: thrown back upon surreptitious scheming and confronted by a new round of legal troubles.

Jews Must Live

Jews Must Live began as a sheaf of notes on people who had mistreated Roth in the course of his business. He elaborated them into the work published under his Golden Hind Press imprint in 1934. Its immediate motive was to recount the circumstances — as he saw them — under which he had lost his Faro assets to the likes of Parrach, Ratte, and Lousse. The vulnerability of his situation inspired a neurotic identification with the aggressor, with those who had been prosecuting him: the Christian moral authorities who spoke for decency. He internalized their contempt, and to exorcise it wrote an anti-Semitic tract demonizing the ethnic middlemen with whom he had worked and lived. *Jews Must Live* is an ultimate consequence of pariah capitalism, of the vulnerability and ambivalence about personal identity that accompany it, and of the strange symbiosis with authority that lives at its heart. The importance of this unique work for us lies in what it shows about erotica dealers of the interwar period and the nature of their enterprise. No other Jewish person did what Roth did. His actions, however, are those any disturbed man of his trade and time might have undertaken.

Jews Must Live is still kept in print by anti-Semitic groups. Today, fascist and white supremacist groups in cyberspace sell books by Jewish authors that they hatefully misread to support their attitudes about "the Jew World Order," as well as Roth's, which openly condones such intolerance. Roth's old friend the poet Charles Resnikoff recalled that at some point in the 1930s a California fascist group hired an airplane to advertise the book in sky-writing. Julius Streicher quoted it at Nazi rallies.[139] It earned its author the hatred of his fellow bookmen everywhere; many of them were rumored to have burned any copies they could get their hands on. It reiterated Jewish stereotypical traits such as hatred for gentiles and desire to remain isolated from them, prioritizing of wealth over patriotism, total lack of compassion for those with whom they deal, sexual neuroses, fear of physical labor, shyster lawyering, heartless real estate swindling, and control of prostitution. *Jews Must Live* also perpetuated Jew-baiting declarations about the dilution of American art forms by clever but vapid, tasteless, and vulgar popular songs, films, and novels. Surely, the established publishers of New York and Boston, the editors of *McClure's* or the *Century Magazine*, and vice crusaders like John Sumner and Charles Bodwell would, if pressed, have responded to such a book with gestures of sympathy for the American Jews subjected to its scurrilities. It was such individuals, however, who deplored the books issued by newly founded, Jewish-owned publishing houses, and who had brought to their fellow Americans' attention the assertions in academic books about furtive and sinister Jewish "race traits." In popular magazines alarms were raised about immigrants capturing the businesses and financial institutions of the cities. In reports to their constituents, and in newspapers, directors of the purity societies described Jews and other immigrants as possessing character flaws that only thorough Americanization would eliminate. Among the people most animated by such condemnations were those to whom the disdain was directed, those who felt their dreams of moral and professional respectability strangled by them — especially Samuel Roth.

The final chapter of *Jews Must Live* is titled "Do Jews Emit a Peculiar Odor?" The book is illustrated with caricatures, captioned "The Shadow over Main Street," "I Must Eat," "Always Take," depicting sneering, black-garbed Jewish men with long noses, beetle brows, pot bellies, bald heads, and cold sharp eyes. The lettering on the title page is designed to look like Hebrew script. Most riveting is the author's obviously Jewish name on the title page and dust jacket (Figure 44). Other Jewish writers of the period — Jerome Weidman, Samuel Ornitz, Michael Gold, Meyer Levin, Budd Schulberg — had presented to the nation negative portrayals of Jews as sharp businessmen or heartless politicians. But these occurred in serious novels addressing important social issues. What Roth did was completely sui generis. And this from a man who had so impressed Israel Zangwill with his Zionist resolution in *Now and Forever* just nine years earlier.

According to William F. Ryan, a journalist who befriended Roth and his wife during the last two years of Roth's life, the publisher regretted what he had done, and he and his wife at one point destroyed many copies of the book themselves. In federal prison in 1937 on an obscenity conviction and applying for parole, the author pled for "a chance to revise that tragic book of mine."[140] Many people had told him not to write the book.[141] But Roth had had to do it, with the same compulsion that had made other challenges — publishing *Ulysses*, sending copies of banned erotica through the mail while on parole, writing a satire on John Sumner while in prison, and taking on Herbert Hoover ("if not I, who?") — irresistible, despite the chances for disaster. He states in his prologue that writing the book was a spontaneous response. "What I have set down here I had to or go out of my mind. It struck me like a tidal wave. . . . Everything I had ever felt, heard and learnt was being welded into artillery and commandeered into action in this new battle of my blood [mein Kampf?]. Writing the book was really something of an organic necessity."[142] Perhaps Roth's decision, not just to write, but to publish and sell his book-length jeremiad, displays something of what Waverley Root called "superb self-contentedness."[143] Root, however, was no impartial observer; a compulsion to justify oneself, even if that means taking a perversely self-destructive revenge, goes well beyond self-assurance.

Once the "tidal wave" of inspiration was past, the project became painful. Jewish faith and tradition were very important to Roth. His reference to himself by his Hebrew name, Mishillim, in his unpublished autobiography, which he began well before *Jews Must Live* and continued writing for most of his life, is one sign of

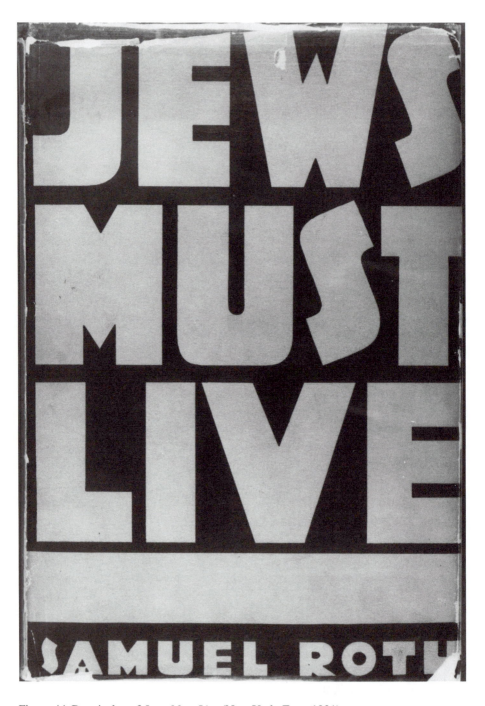

Figure 44. Dust jacket of *Jews Must Live* (New York: Faro, 1931).

that. Immediately after the passage excerpted above, Roth states that reading the proofs and preparing the book for publication was "a metamorphosis I am still agonizing through." But the transformation was more complex than a simple conversion from committed Jew and Zionist to anti-Semite. Milton Hindus has suggested that Nietzsche was a seminal philosophical influence on Roth's thought and behavior. Indeed, early in Roth's career, he had planned to publish a book about the philosopher; given Roth's business sense, it is not surprising that the work was an account of Nietzsche's "unnatural relationship" with his sister.[144] When the book finally appeared, the dust-jacket copy praised Nietzsche's "intellectual and moral revolt against the bias and stupidity of centuries." Hindus notes that Roth's title for a collection of his poetry, *Songs out of Season* (1932), is an allusion to Nietzsche's *Thoughts out of Season*. It is possible to see the author of *Jews Must Live* as breaking free, like Nietzsche, from all restrictions on human behavior, in order to become a different order of creature than anyone thought possible. At least, it is possible to imagine that the author believed he was doing so. This metaphysical commitment to growth and metamorphosis was what Israel Zangwill admired in Roth: it may have had its roots not only in Nietzsche but in the Jewish belief in *takhlis*, or destiny.

Either *takhlis* or Nietzsche, or both, had been much on Roth's mind four years before, in his prison memoir, *Stone Walls Do Not* (1931). The book carries one of the world's strangest limitation statements: "for himself the author will keep one copy in the hope that it may some day grow into a good book." At one point its author ruminates on Josephus's betrayal of the Jews when he surrendered to the Romans and joined their forces, even adopting a Roman surname. The ultimate result of this was his "magnificent history" of the Jews under the Romans. Roth imagines that the writer's motive was Roman citizenship, and the leisure "to write a history of [his] people that would live as long as the works of Livy." And so his people in the end honored him, rather than immortalizing him as a traitor.[145] Roth was fascinated by apparent paradoxes working themselves out over time.

Often Roth's writings focus on an irremediable sadness at the heart of existence, and sadness is what his prophetic note most often calls forth. Perhaps Nietzsche was an influence here, or the Old Testament; Samuel was its first prophet, admonishing, excoriating, and judging. Prophecy was evident in Roth's early poetry, especially in *Europe: A Book for America* (1919). Zangwill approved of the stance of Hebrew prophet that Roth and other young Jewish writers had taken.[146] In

Europe the future is sometimes envisioned as bright. However, there is also a long poem ("Thus Saith the Lord") in which an angry God speaks to Roth of his vengeance on American Jews for their materialism. In *Now and Forever* the writer foresees an America that, discovering "her subconscious character," will embrace the ideals of the Ku Klux Klan. "I expect to be living when they will be roasting Jews alive on Fifth Avenue."[147] This sentence is repeated in *Jews Must Live*. In *Stone Walls Do Not* there is a vigorous passage of misanthropic assessment: "I see no reason for being glad that I am alive. If there is any significance in my existence, it has been very carefully hidden from me. . . . Man? He is no better than a fox, a louse or a cucumber. . . . At least if a bed bug bites, it does not do so with a mouth used in invoking holy prayers."[148]

The despair is visceral, more potent than expressions of self-assurance or faith in ability to intuit the future. It occurs in relation to the Jewish experience. In *Jews Must Live*, if not before, it is rooted in self-hatred. For a Jew to write an anti-Semitic book in order to show the world how fellow Jews have abused his confidence in them is certainly that. It is as if the writer were willing to forfeit everything, including an honest, realistic view of the world, and the respect of peers, to escape the life experience that has raised the specter of total vulnerability, of being nothing but a victim. Thinking himself betrayed by his neighbors and colleagues, by consanguineous enemies with whom he had a lot in common from business methods to religious practices to shared history, Roth may have been unable to assess the reasons for his misfortune objectively, and especially unable to acknowledge his own share of responsibility. Instead, he wished heart and soul to deny that he was one of them, and it became an "organic necessity" to ignore the similarity.

The path Roth took was masochistic: it forced its victim to cleanse himself of an illusory "infection" that he accepted as somehow genetic. The concept of spiritual infection of "decent" society by alien carriers of the virulence of sex was central to the thought and action of the law-enforcement officers fighting the ethnic middleman erotica dealer. Roth, the victim, wanted to exorcise in himself "Jewish" motives and feelings. These in fact are — to people not deluded, as he was — familiar American desires for status, security, leisure, beauty — the enjoyment of which native elites would not wish to share with immigrants whom they could not trust to assimilate with them. For the self-hater who had internalized the majority's contempt, the American Dream became skewed — when expressed by members of the minority group in which he did not want to be included — into greed, deception, laziness, and ugliness. Roth did not look, act, or talk like his Lower East Side neighbors. He affected the clothing and haberdashery of the 1890s dandy. Observers remarked on his broad-brimmed hats, cane, bow ties, and, occasionally, lemon-yellow gloves and even spats (Figure 45).[149] Lyle Stuart, a fledgling journalist when he published with Roth in 1953, notes that Roth affected an English accent, a remnant of his six-month visit to that country thirty-two years before.[150] He viewed himself as of a conservative, "Tory" cast of mind; disliked modernists' experimentation with language and narrative; distrusted utopian experiments ("man [is] doomed eternally by the Beast within him"); and feared that leftist politics would gravely damage the polite civility he saw as essential to the cultivated, contemplative life of the library, café, and literary bookshop. Beauty alone was truth, and worth preserving.[151]

With *Jews Must Live*, Roth became a pariah to his own people and existed "absolutely alone." At least he could fancy himself to have undergone a "metamorphosis." Now he was the master of his fate, and (at least in his imagination) was relieved of the "foreigner-radical-pornographer" status with which secular and religious authorities were wont to stigmatize his colleagues, and especially, from 1926 onward, himself. Roth's detachment is epitomized by a vision he says he had at the time he was being "swindled" out of his business. Dazed and despairing, he writes near the beginning of *Jews Must Live*, he wandered into a flophouse in the Bowery to bed down for the night. A ghostly figure appeared to him (Figure 46), to give him its blessing to write about his fellow Jews as he was about to do.[152] That apparition was of the holy spirit he had first read about in the boat which carried him to America from his native Galicia. He had picked up an evangelical pamphlet which an indignant rabbi saw in his hand and immediately threw overboard. The pamphlet was about "Yehoshea" (the Hebrew name for Jesus). Roth claims here to have felt Yehoshea's presence at significant moments throughout his life. He actually lists Him among the men and women whose visits to the Poetry Book Shop were important to him.[153]

The Christian savior, not the Jehovah his father had sent him to Hebrew school to honor, and not any tyrannical rabbi, sanctioned *Jews Must Live*. As Roth tells it, the beloved figure of Jesus compelled him to isolate himself from his fellow Jews. But why specifically was it such a visceral necessity for Roth to escape from in 1933? It was the experience of the pariah capitalist, and specifically the characteristic way of life of the middleman erotica dealer, including

Figure 45. Sketch of Samuel Roth used to decorate a biographical essay, appended to his first (and only) novel, *Bumarap: The Story of a Male Virgin* (New York: Arrowhead, 1947). Note the jutting chin; determined, pugnacious expression; vest; striped pants; and the walking cane. Roth dressed well, and the cane was one of the publisher's habitual affectations.

The Vision

Figure 46. Illustration from Samuel Roth's *Jews Must Live* (New York: Golden Hind, 1934), titled "The Vision," showing Roth, seated on a bed in a Bowery flophouse, being visited by a ghostly presence who encourages him to tell of his unfair treatment by colleagues and the law.

himself: those hard-driving, relentless, amoral, devilishly successful disseminators of the virulence of sex.

Now that his own ingenuity had failed, perhaps the blessing of the God of the mainstream American community would save Roth from the risks involved in advertising and selling "obscene" material; the clannishness of its producers; the "weakness" of the capital and the way it could therefore be stripped from its owner by authorities; the constant frugality, long hours, and employment of one's own family in the operations; the habitual furtiveness; the enticements one's colleagues offered to make money with dangerous schemes; the pressures of entrapment, police confiscation of stock, court appearances, and creditors, including lawyers. Also demoralizing was the contempt of the citizenry, as orchestrated by John Sumner, various newspapers, and one's own "uptown" colleagues; the way judges and juries could join with Sumner in ostracizing the erotica dealer as a seducer of the innocent and as a panderer, and the way the guardians of culture — writers, critics, publishers, and booksellers — also made common cause with Sumner in demonizing those who sold books by appeals to prurience.

This segregation of the erotica dealer from the rest of his profession, from "decent" people in general, and specifically from the intellectual elite, must have been especially hard to keep from seeping into a middleman's self-image. This would have been true for Roth in particular, who — despite his bravado — did not deal well with vulnerability or culpability, and who had hoped to make his mark as a man of letters. Ben Rebhuhn and Esar Levine could point to their sacrifices for Frank Harris. Levine wrote scholarly introductions to his Panurge Press gallantiana and sexology; Rebhuhn, under federal indictment for Comstock violations, could count on First Amendment crusader Theodore Schroeder for legal advice and moral support. Joseph Lewis was a freethinker and champion of Tom Paine, with books on such subjects to his credit. Sol Malkin was a multilingual scholar, a student of the most renowned sexologist in Europe. David Moss was identified with the prestigious Gotham Book Mart. And Jack Brussel, a knowledgeable book scout and dealer himself, was just as highly respected and well liked by antiquarian bookmen as was his brother I. R. Brussel, a bibliographer and literary scholar. Roth was well read in both world literature and Judaic doctrine and ritual. He had his admirers, including many of his Faro authors. He could look back fondly, even in *Jews Must Live*, to the meetings with poets at his Poetry Book Shop, before any questionable publishing or bookselling ventures could be traced to him.[154] But after

1927, he lacked any practical or psychological support system similar to that the others enjoyed. He had accumulated unprecedented opprobrium, due to the international protest of February of that year. For a time, William Faro Inc. had lent some weight to his claim to be a serious writer and publisher. Then came the Depression economy, and the Nesor disaster.

The only truth *Jews Must Live* embodies is its author's dependence on the authority figures who identified him as a pariah in the first place, and who were in reality responsible for his woes. Roth allowed them to define him. His book took the shame they foisted on the erotica dealer as venal, duplicitous, and prurient and magnified it into a condemnation of not only his colleagues, but his own people as a whole. It would be hard to find a more complete display of the kind of authoritarian control that makes its victim so devoid of self-worth, and so submissive to its will, that the beliefs of its advocates — moral entrepreneurs, postal inspectors, federal district attorneys, the "uptown" book trade — completely override any individual analysis by the victim of specific cases, including his own. If Roth had no compassion for his business colleagues, he had none for himself either. If there was a reward for this kind of submission, it was that Roth could delude himself into thinking he was free from the sensibilities and actions of "his own kind," whom he saw as rats and lice. And yet, he continued to publish material for which he was cited for obscenity. He may have believed himself a different order of human being than other erotica dealers, but he continued to play the part of smutmonger, and to be punished for it. He played compulsively according to the rules the one-hundred-percent Americans set up for him.

Explaining himself in public or in print, Roth seems incapable of balanced judgment. He could, however, be honest about the rules of the game and the consequences of trading in prurience when he could objectify the situation by writing fiction. On one such occasion, he specified the bleak consequences of prurient fantasizing, both for the masses who indulged in it and for those who benefited materially from providing the fantasies for them, in a startling manner. In the title story of the pseudonymous *Body* (1931), a wealthy movie producer is devastated to learn on his honeymoon that the beautiful seventeen-year-old starlet he has fallen in love with "was completely debauched." She has never been with a man, but, as a psychologist explains to him, "when a man lusts after a woman something happens in his body and communicates itself to hers. It is simply a yet undiscovered branch of anatomy." Roth draws on Jesus Christ for the ultimate

Figure 47. Frontispiece to Daniel Quilter [Samuel Roth], *Body: A New Study, in Narrative, of the Anatomy of Society* (New York: Autographed Editions Club, 1931). Signed Anton K. Skillin. The drawing is especially relevant to the first story in the collection, about a movie magnate whose films titillate the multitude with fashionable sexual fantasies.

unraveling of the mystery: "whosoever looketh on a woman to lust after her hath committed adultery with her already in his heart." The psychologist can only advise that the producer forget his bride, whom he has "set in the midst of a brothel as wide and populous as the world, mak[ing] her precious body available to every lout with the price of an afternoon paper." Further, the bridegroom is reminded that his wife is already "wedded to her public," and that he should consider the wisdom of the orientals, who require their wives and daughters to be veiled. They do not do this to enslave them, but because they know "the power of the imagination," and "how much more damage a man can do with his eyes than with that ridiculous organ whose power of evil has been so grossly exaggerated in our society." [155] The frontispiece to the first edition illustrates this credo (Figure 47). Roth's little parable has an acute "moral," and it is emphatically not that sex is evil. Instead, it asserts that repression of sexual desire and its exploitation diminishes the capacities for love and commitment of normal adults, making voyeurs out of everyone. He carries this insight further, into the most severe cynicism, directed at those whose business it is to provide the prurient entertainments that substitute for "natural" sexual fulfillment. Such people debauch themselves, those they serve, and even their loved ones, when the loved ones are part of the business.

The implications of Roth's story seem to epitomize and reinforce his cynicism and self-hate, and his attempts to escape the psychic wounds that gave birth to them. These neuroses lead directly to the self-justifying and equally self-destructive vengeance that inspired *Jews Must Live*. He never escaped either the neuroses or the symbiotic dependence on contemptuous authority.

"I Went to Prison That Year"

In December 1936, Roth and his wife, Pauline, were convicted of distributing obscenity through interstate commerce and of conspiracy to do so. The works were among the most strictly taboo of the era. In 1934 and 1935, the Golden Hind Press had used the U.S. mails to publicize, and Railway Express to ship, a wide range of materials, including erotic playing cards and photograph sets. District Judge Grover Moscovitz sentenced Roth to three years and twenty days, and fined him two thousand dollars, the payment of which was suspended, to be enforced when and if he violated parole. The judge also suspended Pauline's three-year sentence, because of her two teenage children. She had to post a five-thousand-dollar bond, to be forfeited if there were a violation of her probation; Samuel was to post an identical amount upon his release. Both were to be on probation for five years.[156] The sentence seems extremely severe for a misdemeanor, although if maximum sentence had been enforced on all twenty-four counts of the indictment, Roth could have faced 117 years in jail and a fine of $125,000.[157] One reason for the severity was the publisher's previous record, which was certainly damning. There were the convictions of 1928 (*Perfumed Garden*), 1929 (the Book Auction, *Forbidden Books*, magazines, pictures, violation of parole), and 1930 (*Ulysses*, *Lady Chatterley's Lover*, and other officially banned titles, including *Fanny Hill*, mailed and delivered from the Golden Hind Press while Roth was on parole). In 1934, in an action initiated by John Sumner, he had been fined one hundred dollars for distributing books, including his (expurgated) *Anecdota Americana* and other borderline materials.[158] Roth's previous record may have been one of the reasons that the jury needed no time to deliberate before declaring his wife and him guilty;[159] his wife was deeply involved in the 1929 and 1930 cases. But there were other factors. Judge and jury seemed particularly shocked to learn that the Roth children had helped with office tasks.[160] Moscovitz told Pauline Roth that if he heard of any future family activity with nonmailable matter, either during or after Roth's prison sentence, he would revoke her parole.[161] Roth had also committed perjury during the trial; in what connection is not clear.

In May 1937, Roth petitioned unsuccessfully for reduction of sentence. He reminded the judge that his sentence was the most severe handed down for the specific offenses; that, as testimony from customers proved, he had confined sales to "doctors, lawyers, financial and business men," whose average age was about fifty; that he had cooperated in revealing the procedures by which "the obscene book business is being operated in this country and district"; that he kept his children from any knowledge about obscene books; that he would never again distribute such books (the work had left him a pauper);[162] that his physical health had deteriorated and he was experiencing extreme anxiety about dying while in prison. The prison's chief medical officer provided a supporting document stating that Roth's physical problems were not significant but that "his psychoneurosis has become more magnified."[163] Hugo Pollack, Roth's lawyer, argues in his memorandum in support that the judge should be merciful on the basis of his client's poor health and his posttrial cooperation with postal inspector Chester A. Battles in detailing the procedures of erotica distribution. Pollack also discusses the perjury.

The publisher at first apparently testified that he had not actually marketed the flagrantly obscene books for which he had been cited, but had only given his mailing list to another distributor. Later he confessed that these books had been left for him in a subway locker. The unnamed printer or distributor who left them there had given Roth the key. Very early in the morning, Roth took the books out of the locker and wrapped them himself for mailing with the others, finishing the task by 8 A.M., when his office staff reported for work. He did this, his lawyer said, to keep his wife out of danger of involvement.

Roth was not granted parole. The district attorney assigned to the case, Lamar Hardy, stated that the authorities had heard at least some of these pleas before; this was the publisher's fifth offense. It was altogether likely, therefore, that he and his wife would continue their erotica dealings. Furthermore, Hardy was not convinced, after conferring with Battles, that Roth had given genuinely helpful information.[164] The publisher remained in the Lewisburg, Pennsylvania, penitentiary until the middle of 1939.

Many of the books for which he served his sentence must have been expensive: the various counts of the indictment state only one price, $12.50 (about $148 in mid-1998 currency). They probably brought Roth lucrative returns, which of course was his reason for risking their sale. They represent a range of erotic specialities. Some were readers: *Loves of a Sailor*, *Memoirs of a Hotel Man*. *Pageant of Lust* (illustrated) and *Amatory Experiences of a Surgeon* (the underground counterpart of Dr. Bell's gallant reminiscences) present the physician as sexual athlete. *Episodes of Life* and *Wide Open* were as explicit in their illustrations as in their texts. *Nirvana* was the journalist Gene Fowler's work, as uninhibitedly scatological and erotic, and as suitable for reading at smokers, as was his *Lady Scatterley's Lovers*. *The Horn Book* was a classic of erotology, as was the manual appended to *White Stains*, if that work was a set of short stories and not Aleister Crowley's decadent poems of the same title. Other fiction included *The Lustful Turk*, *The Romances of Blanche La Mare* (illustrated with drawings of various positions of copulation, and part of a rare Carrington publication), and *Fanny Hill*. *Annabel's Education* might have been a version of the lubricious, and graphically illustrated, memoirs of *Annabel Fane*.[165]

Lamar Hardy's indictment accused Roth of circularizing by U.S. mail, as well as distributing, such books. Just what kind of circulars is not specified, but we can use what is on record regarding Roth's photo sets, pamphlets, and books to guess the nature of his post-Nesor erotica distribution. There are three sets of circulars: for sexological material and realistic fiction, for spicy but familiar gallantiana and erotology, and for truly underground books whose existence was shared with only the most trusted readers. Roth did prepare conventional, slyly suggestive advertisements for four titles that carried his Black Hawk Press imprint. These were serious books about sexual intimacy, seduction, and syphilis by James Hanley, Rhys Davies, Norman Davey, and Havelock Ellis. Neither the circulars for the four Black Hawk books nor the books themselves were cited in the indictment, but the FBI provided federal investigators with copies of the advertisements for them that it found during its investigation, as it did with two other circulars stressing the "sex angle" (May–December, rape, venereal disease, adultery).[166] These two circulars show Roth offered his own editions of "Two World Famous Suppressed Books," Twain's *1601* and Lewisohn's *Case of Mr. Crump*.[167] The six books circularized were offered at $1.25 to $1.98, and could have been considered only marginally "offensive."

Of a different nature was *The Secret Places of the Human Body*, Roth's spicy title for the *Ananga Ranga*, offered at six dollars, and identified opposite the title page as published by the Golden Hind Press (Figure 48). Neither this book nor its circular, a copy of which the FBI provided the federal attorneys, was made part of the indictment. However, both further exemplify the nature of Roth's business in the mid-1930s. The circular described the book's contents and was illustrated — ironically, given the work's description of lovingly mutual pleasure — with a reclining nude female watching apprehensively as a large and decidedly phallic sword held by a disembodied hand approaches her pelvic area. This edition contains pasted-in photographs of seminude women on otherwise blank pages scattered throughout the book. However, it is abridged. Chapter 10, delineating coital positions, is almost completely exercised, as are words for the sex organs throughout. In short, the book manages to leave out the "secret places" of the title, just as the illustration on the circular distorts the author's philosophy of lovemaking. This *Ananga Ranga* was expurgated and deceptively marketed, and the pasted-in photographs were much like those found in girlie and humor magazines — flirtatious women, not quite wearing their costumes. However, by sending ten dollars, those in the know could receive a version with photographs more like those found in the aggressively pornographic readers of the period, showing copulating couples or threesomes, with special powers of muscular contortion.[168]

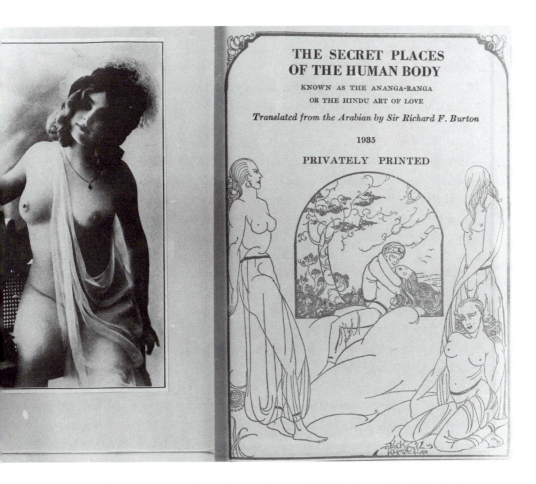

Figure 48. One of Roth's privately issued books of the mid-1930s ("copyright 1935, by the Golden Hind Press"), an expurgated version of the *Ananga Ranga*. This was not one of the books Roth was sentenced to three years in prison in 1936 for distributing. He may also have circulated an unexpurgated version.

Possibly these special customers were wised up through yet another set of advertisements in the form of simple xeroxed lists, without illustrations or salacious descriptions, these being superfluous anyway for the carefully selected, steady customers for the underground pornography to whom they were sent.[169] Roth wrote such circulars under the names of "Eric Hammond," the Fifth Avenue

Book Shop, or the Golden Hind Press, and sometimes warned prospective purchasers: "as an added precaution, please send your order in the Eric Hammond return envelope enclosed."

In a gesture of either desperation or reckless defiance of the Post Office and the publishing establishment, Roth sent through the U.S. mails copies of *Fanny Hill* and *Wide Open*, using as a return address "Alfred A. Knopf, Publisher, 730 Fifth Ave., New York."[170] Roth particularly disliked Knopf, as we have seen, because the latter backed away from publishing books that might be challenged for obscenity, and because he thought Knopf had outbid him at the last minute for authorization to publish the abridged *Lady Chatterley*. The use of Knopf's name may be read variously as further evidence of Roth's irascibility, resentment, arrogance, or masochism. Knopf was pleased to publish sexology and anthropology that, because of the nature of his advertisements, wholesalers, and retail customers, were safe from the stigma of erotica. In Roth's mind, this emperor had no clothes. The basic reason for his mailing such banned books, of course, was not to tweak Alfred Knopf. It was Depression-era insolvency, the result of his inability to liquidate the Faro assets satisfactorily. It was a risk the circumstances made a necessity — a very unpleasant and lonely one, especially if the perpetrator needed to hide it from his wife and loyal helpmate.

The man who left the books for Roth in the subway locker may have been one of the most significant printer-distributors of European erotica from the 1880s through the 1930s: H(arry) S(idney) Nichols, an English bookseller expelled from France in 1908. Among his U.S. customers were J. P. Morgan and Henry Huntington. After leaving France, Nichols settled in New York City, where he lived until his death in 1941. My conjecture that he was the middleman from whom Roth received texts (sheets or bound books) of the clandestine titles for which Roth was prosecuted in 1936 is based on evidence generously provided to me by Nichols's grandson.[171] At the time of the Roth trial, Nichols wrote to his children, asking that they deposit with his attorney testimonials of his loving attention to family responsibilities.

Whoever Roth's confederate in the subway locker gambit was, the hapless publisher gave the postal inspector the man's name in his posttrial confession. The district attorney admitted that "Roth did furnish [postal inspector Battles] the name and address of one person, a dealer in obscene matter, which information resulted in the apprehension of said person."[172] That person might have been Nichols, and if so, it might explain Nichols's requests for character references from his children. But there is no record of Nichols's arrest or conviction in connection with Roth's operation. If the latter had informed on him, he might have taken advantage of his earlier association with the late J. P. Morgan, by asking the industrialist's son to help him avoid involvement. That could have afforded him the political protection that was emphatically not available to Roth.

Whatever cooperation Roth was forced to give to authorities, there was one indispensable key to his business he must have protected from them: his mailing list. We know he must have held onto it somehow, because he still had it and made use of it again in 1940, to considerable profit. Gershon Legman tells us that when Jack Brussel arranged to distribute his "Medvsa" edition of *Tropic of Cancer* (printed in Mexico), Roth helped pay expenses, in exchange for additional (over-run) sets of sheets (from two hundred to five hundred in all) that he would distribute, in small quantities, to customers on his mailing list seeking banned erotica.[173] This was the list of business and professional men that he had used to advertise the books that had sent him to prison four years earlier. But where would Roth have gotten the money? As his attorney had stated, he had taken a pauper's oath before entering prison. If Legman is correct, Roth must have found a way before entering prison to do what he failed to in 1933: transfer assets to someone he could trust, as he had tried to with "Richard Ross" (an account set up by two colleagues into which Roth deposited money earned during the Hoover exposé).

An additional possible explanation for his 1940 capital is that Roth may have been supervising the distribution of other strictly banned books — specifically, some of those for which he was indicted in 1936 — while incarcerated. Legman and C. J. Scheiner believe an edition of *White Stains* that they date to approximately 1940 was his production. This, they feel, was not the notoriously rare and scabrous volume of poems by Aleister Crowley but a set of six short stories with the same title, falsely attributed to the poet Ernest Dowson, to which was appended *Love's Encyclopaedia*, an Edwardian-era erotological manual. Scheiner suggests Roth may have found and collected copies of these tales, which were written for the Oklahoma millionaire who enjoyed masturbating to erotic stories he had not previously read (see Chapter 2). Since these erotica writers kept carbon copies of their work, it is plausible that Roth could have obtained them, and so produced his *White Stains*.[174] If Roth had collected these stories as early as 1935, the *White Stains* cited in count 8 of the 1936 indictment may have been this book.[175]

Roth had been also dealing in borderline erotica during this period, despite his promises to Judge Moscovitz, and had been using the mails to circularize selected Faro and Black Hawk titles under the imprints Wisdom House, Coventry House, and Broadway Bargain Counter.[176] Curiously, one of these titles, *A Scarlet Pansy*, bore the Nesor imprint. Roth might have ended the decade purchasing remaindered copies of books published by his 1933 Nesor nemesis. A warrant was issued for his arrest, and his term of probation was extended until the end of 1944, but somehow he avoided being remanded to prison.

The End: Back to Lewisburg, and a Sequel to *Jews Must Live*

After World War II, Roth found that bookstores would not stock items otherwise sold by mail order. As he stated in his unpublished memoir, "a complete immersion in mail order advertising became inevitable"; he estimated that during this phase of his career, he had sent out ten million pieces of mail.[177] By doing so, he ran afoul of Senator Estes Kefauver, who in 1955 became chair of the Senate Subcommittee to Investigate Juvenile Delinquency. Organized in 1953, the subcommittee focused on the role of the mass media in using sensational movies, magazines, comic books, and cheap novels in hard and soft covers to entice the nation's youth from the guidance of the home, school, and church. Especially under Kefauver's aggressive leadership, it popularized on a national level the supposedly clear equation between media exploitation of sex and violence on one hand, and youthful rebellion against moral and social conventions on the other. An effective moral crusader, Kefauver's logic of cause and effect was typically facile, and tailored to capture the attention of a mass radio and television audience. His staff did present convincing evidence that entrepreneurs of popular culture were getting rich by appealing to the postwar teenager's irrepressible prurient curiosities. The senator won considerable praise from historians for showing the variety of contemporary erotic materials, the extent of their appeal, the number of people they reached, and the amount of profit to be had by distributing them.[178] Roth proved to be an interesting object of study on all four counts.

In 1956, Roth faced a federal indictment. The Post Office had received so many complaints about Roth's mailings — it claimed their number had reached five thousand — that a special form letter had been devised to answer them.[179] His circulars got progressively bolder and more suggestive, and some of them contained sneering references to the "blue noses" who repressed "vital" novels and magazines, and who told his customers their reading matter was indecent. "Don't let them worry you," one of his circulars assured his customers, "your morals are all right."[180] Roth requested hearings regarding unmailable rulings against his books and flyers; he kept a list of the names the inspectors used in decoy letters. At one point he told the presiding officer that postal inspectors had ordered so many of his materials that they were paying his postage bill. The scope of his business is reflected in his postal meter bill for 1952: $32,930 (equal to $202,800 in 1998). In 1947, fraud orders had been issued against two of Roth's books, one of them his own novel *Bumarap: The Story of a Male Virgin*.[181] The circular promised the excitement of the hero's first sexual encounter, which he starts by kissing a certain "Countess's" toes; by the next morning, he has reached her face. In the actual book, however, the toe-kissing starts only a few lines from the end of Chapter 25 and, after a brief reverie by the lady, the narrative recommences with Bumarap kissing the lady's eyes. "YOU MUST BE THERE IN PERSON," stated the circular. "The book sweeps you right into it as if you were actually there."[182] But one could not be, and "Dame Post Office" was not amused. Foreseeing a good sale for his *Bumarap*, Roth filed an injunction against her. At the hearing, he made the excellent point that many commodities other than books were sold by appealing to sexuality, and that no one saw any harm in that. Nor, he felt, had any harm been shown to result from getting people to buy books by appealing to their interest in sex.[183]

Roth could get away with selling and advertising books under one or another of his trade names until the postal inspectors had ordered, read, and issued interdictions against specific books or circulars sent under that particular name. This is why the number of his "presses" or "book services" totaled sixty-two by the mid-1950s. Business was obviously flourishing; he could not have filed for injunctions unless he could have afforded the lawyers. Journalist John J. Makris reports that Roth's gross income in 1954 was $270,000 ($1,638,900 in 1998 dollars).[184] Roth published new titles, purchased many remainders, and also peddled the new digest-size paperbacks, which by the late 1940s had saturated newsstands nationwide. Faro and Black Hawk staples from the 1930s were also sold. Under his Joy Bookery trade name, he offered framed stereoptic pictures of women whose lips, thighs, or breasts moved when the picture was touched ("a sweetheart for your bedside!").[185] He also sold "strip sets" of photographs of women undressing, which, when one flipped rapidly through them, gave the illusion that the women were moving.[186]

Dirty-Pix Probers Entangle 3

obscene

By JAMES DESMOND

The Kefauver Senate subcommittee closed its New York pornography hearings yesterday by setting up three asserted dealers in dirty books and pictures for contempt charges. In addition, the citizenship of a publisher, who denied he is a pornographer, was challenged.

The subcommittee is dedicated to proving that the circulation of filthy pictures is a major cause of juvenile delinquency and is boosting violent crime among the young.

Sen. Estes Kefauver (D-Tenn.), the chairman, masterminded the contempt attack on three dealers who clammed up under the refuge of the Fifth Amendment.

Kefauver required the clams to invoke the Fifth up to 35 times each before releasing them from the stand.

The multiple questioning was designed to pile up indictable contempt counts and thus make prosecution easier.

King of the Pinups

The three who took the Fifth were: Irving Klaw, self-styled King of the Pinups, who assertedly does a business of $1,500,000 a year from offices at 212 E. 14th St.; Edward Mishkin, asserted partner of three Broadway area book shops—the Times Square Book Bazaar, the Little Book Exchange and the Kingsley book

(NEWS foto by Frank Castorai)
Samuel Roth holds one of his advertising leaflets as he answers Sen. Kefauver's questions about it.

store — and Abraham Rubin, alias Al Stone, of 1639 41st St., Brooklyn.

Rubin - Stone set some kind of a record by

Irving
Klaw

Edward
Mishkin

claiming the Fifth when asked by Sen. William Langer (R-N.D.) whether he could name the President of the United States or identify Abraham Lincoln.

Abraham
Rubin

The publisher involved was Samuel Roth, of 110 Lafayette St., who puts out a monthly magazine called Good Times and a quarterly called American Aphrodite.

Kefauver wondered out loud just how valid Roth's citizenship was after the publisher, who said he derived citizenship from his father's naturalization in 1915, admitted to seven arrests and four jail terms, ranging from 60 days to three years, for dealing in obscenity.

Roth was a truculent witness. "Anyone who places me among the publishers of pornographic books should be compelled to take a literacy and an intelligence test before being allowed to perform public duties," he told the subcommittee.

One would not know it from studying Roth's blatant advertisements, but in the late 1940s and early 1950s, publishers of mass-market books and magazines in general, and especially erotica dealers, were well advised to be careful. Not only Kefauver's subcommittee, but also Representative Ezekiel Gathings's Select House Committee, formed in 1952 to investigate obscene and pornographic newsstand paperbacks, were identifying antisocial teenage behavior, adultery, "sexual perversions," rape, promiscuity, and rising divorce rates with "sex exciting" books sold at newsstands, in drugstores, and through the mails, as well as with comic books and films. Kefauver, the Post Office, a national climate of suspicion of political and moral unorthodoxy: it was only a matter of time (Figure 49). Roth was sentenced to five years in prison and fined five thousand dollars in 1956. Appeals to the district court and the Supreme Court failed. The original indictment totaled twenty-six counts,[187] of which all but four were dismissed. These four cited the indiscriminate circularizing for books and magazines; the stories and advertising matter in certain issues of the pocket-format pictorial *Good Times* and the clothbound periodical *American Aphrodite*; the "strip sets," "NUS" (albums of nudes), and, most tellingly, the appearance of Aubrey Beardsley's *Venus and Tannhauser*, with his illustrations, in *American Aphrodite* (vol. 1, no. 3).[188] The government attorney, George Leisure, who defended the Post Office's ban on *Lady Chatterley's Lover* four years later, brought a dozen recipients of Roth circulars to court to express the government's indignation. Referring to the photos and strip sets of nudes as having no artistic value, he reminded the jury, "we know who buys that." Turning to *American Aphrodite*, he remarked on the "boring" stories that served as cover for the sexually explicit pieces, including Roth's own dictionary of erotic expressions. Finally, Leisure read out passages from Beardsley's "filth." In his summation, he warned the jury that if Roth were acquitted, the Post Office inspectors would not be able to keep back the pornographic flood: "this stuff will sell.... I can assure you the sewers will open."[189]

Figure 49. Roth defending his advertising methods before the Senate subcommittee investigating the effect of pornography on juvenile delinquency. He told the senators, "Anyone who places me among the publishers of pornographic books should be compelled to take a literacy and an intelligence test before being allowed to perform public duties." Photo accompanying James Desmond, "Dirty-Pix Probers Entangle Three," *New York Daily News*, 1 June 1955, JA Files, Harry Ransom Humanities Research Center, University of Texas at Austin.

At the district and Supreme Court levels,[190] the decisions revolved around whether the Comstock Law was too vague and subjective to be enforceable, and whether the harm obscene writing did could actually be specified. Whether or not the materials for which Roth was to serve five years were obscene was never in question. To Justice Brennan and the majority of his colleagues, as to Morris Ernst when he defended *Ulysses*, it was still necessary for the authority of the state, and the bureaucratic structure that supported it, to set boundaries on legitimate sexual expression by maintaining the concept of prurience. To Justice Warren, as to Learned Hand in the 1930s, the crime lay in pandering; "the 'conduct of the defendant,' " Warren declared, "should be made 'the central issue' in each case."[191] And Roth's tactics revealed what kind of man he was.

Within a few years, Barney Rosset of Grove Press was able to market *Lady Chatterley's Lover* and *Tropic of Cancer* in such a manner that they were no longer considered obscene works. It was the marketing — "the format and composition of the volume, the advertising and promotional material . . . [with] no attempt to pander to the lewd and lascivious minded for profit"[192] — that allowed the books to leave the bogs of smut for the pastures of literature. These novels were the work of two writers whose philosophies of the relationships between the social order and the individual were so subversive as to border on the sexually anarchic. They were liberated as a result of legal decisions in the best American traditions of tolerance for free thought and expression. Ironically, the Supreme Court case on which these decisions were based sent Samuel Roth back to Lewisburg Penitentiary — the Sam Roth whose business tactics succeeded to the extent that they reinforced the most traditional of notions about the guilty furtiveness of sexual desire.

As had happened at other times of humiliation and abandonment, Roth had visions. He wrote a 628-page treatise, *My Friend Yeshea*, which was a mixture of self-reproach (especially regarding *Jews Must Live*), Job-like questioning of divine purpose, and messianic prophecy. If *Jews Must Live* gave aid and comfort to Nazis, *My Friend Yeshea*, in a gentle and elegiac manner (as far as Roth's prose is capable of these qualities), did the same for Christians and Jews desirous of respectful cooperation. On the eve of his actual transportation to Lewisburg, Mishillim finds himself magically transported to Israel at the time Yeshea (Jesus) is beginning to make his way to Jerusalem. His "friend," whom he addresses as "rabbi," tells him to observe and record the events the four gospels do not. He will thus complete for mankind in his own time the message of Jesus. Yeshea tells him that he (unlike

Waverley Root and his fellow scoffers at *transition*) had not laughed when Roth declared twenty years before (in *Europe* and *Now and Forever*) that through his literary gifts he could offer his people visionary guidance: "it was a long time since anyone like you had appeared in the world." Therefore Yeshea had decreed for Roth the destiny of "publish[ing] books of such a degree of sensitiveness that they would be sure to bring you condemnation by the ignorant and prurient."[193] Roth would be imprisoned, and have the leisure to write. After his earthly mission is completed, the risen Yeshea gives Roth prescriptions for the salvation of Russia and the United States (arms control, civil rights, self-determination for subject people and minorities, wage controls), and for Israel (normalization of relations with neighboring countries). Yeshea turns out to be as much a Zionist as Roth: "Moses and I are two servants of one master, Israel."[194] The book ends with Roth's renewed faith in himself to instill in Judaism a reverence for "the prophetic wisdom of its greatest son," and to impress Christianity with a "crying need of a return to the sources of its original inspiration."[195] The result will be "truth and universal brotherhood."

Roth was again reaching out for security and self-acceptance. The consequences of his pursuit of the American Dream were the stresses and stigma of being a middleman in the erotica business. *Jews Must Live* was an attempt to shed these burdens and assimilate himself to Christian "morality," insofar as that could be effected by demonstrating the perniciousness of Jewish venality and turning his back on Old Testament Judaism. In *My Friend Yeshea*, this Roth of many aliases forged another, sunnier path to spiritual and nationalistic identity. Posing, once again with Christ's blessing, as prophet and patriot, he claimed status as free-speech advocate, Hebrew scholar, and quintessential American, ideally situated to reconcile Jew and Christian in the modern world.

Samuel Roth made good use of the considerable capital that his 1950s enterprises brought him. For several years after he left prison he remained in publishing, then retired. He died on 3 July 1974, at the age of seventy-nine. After his interview with Roth, Leo Hamalian reported that Roth had "only an occasional twinge of regret about the past."[196] One conclusion is certain: Samuel Roth had a strong, persistent, and certainly idiosyncratic sense of personal, social, and spiritual mission. With his iron-clad sense of purpose, his moxie and his mailing list, his sensitivity to both good literature and prurient salesmanship, he stands out because, up to a point, he is a representative figure, and, paradoxically, an American original as well. His passing was mourned by his loyal wife, Pauline; his son, Richard; his daughter, Adelaide, four grandchildren, and close friends. His autobiography remains unpublished. It begins with an account of the old offender's appearance before the James Joyce Society at the Gotham Book Mart. Those present may have been prepared to judge him harshly, but he immediately amused and impressed them, and not only because of his physical resemblance to Joyce. He began his address with a remark that was hard to forget. He said that he felt "like a lion in a den of Daniels." [197]

Epilogue

Whatever stage of a sexual revolution America may be in, prurience is just as powerful a catalyst to action now as it was in the 1920s and 1930s. Witness the Clinton scandal and its parasites: the prattlers on *Eyewitness News*; the talking heads and the jackals who hosted them; the sleuths from the independent counsel's office. Oral sex and semen-stained dresses are too provocative to refrain from publicizing, regardless of the age and sophistication of the viewer, just as sex pulps, Tillie and Mac cartoons, and sexological texts with salacious titles were three generations ago. The independent counsel himself, with broadcast issuance of his report, became a distributor of erotica as well as a crusading moral entrepreneur, exemplifying the symbiosis between the two in a startling way. The events foregrounded, for me at least, the power of prurience. William J. Bennett, whose book about Clinton's enduring popularity despite the scandal was entitled *The Death of Outrage*, insisted that Clinton's perfidy "wasn't about sex." Certainly it was, as was the intensity with which the media attended to it. Just as certainly, the controversy — not fired by the outrage Bennett wished — was about decency, who was worthy of the status the word bestowed, and the kind of behavior the law should most severely censure. In this epilogue I show how endemic prurience has been in American discourse about sex since the interwar period. What follows is in no way meant to serve as a history of postwar censorship.

When Samuel Roth left prison in 1961, many of the erotica dealers he had known over a twenty-year period were still at work, although some had entered more "respectable" occupations. Jack Brussel was still publishing, under legitimate imprints such as Brussel and Brussel, New York Medical Press, and United Book Guild. His wife, Mina, was a successful publisher of silkscreen prints, and he had built a first-rate collection of assorted editions of *Aesop's Fables*. Sol Malkin had purchased from *Publishers Weekly* the magazine *Antiquarian Bookman*, of which he was founding editor; he had made it the premier medium of communication in the used- and rare-book trade. Joseph Lewis was still writing on atheism and Thomas Paine, and had begun editing *Age of Reason* magazine. Benjamin Rebhuhn had taken to selling books and magazines devoted to bodybuilding, using slogans such as "I can make you commando-tough" to earn a loyal following.[1] Esar Levine, under the name Evan Esar, had assembled several steady-selling anthologies of wit and humor, and become a frequently consulted authority on the subject.[2] Louis Shomer had published the "Nofkeh [Yiddish for 'prostitute'] Publications," illustrated editions of classical erotica, side-stapled and paperbacked, which appeared circa 1950. He was also distributing erotic films and tiny pulp booklets of ethnic jokes.[3]

Many younger erotic booksellers, including some who had known and worked with Roth, were prospering and extending the scope of the trade. Lyle Stuart, author of Roth's Winchell exposé, was beginning to use innovative mass-market advertising, strengthened by his connections to popular entertainers and journalists. He successfully and widely circulated books on sexual behavior and erotology by mail order. Later, he claimed to have "started the sex revolution in [trade] publishing." Albert Ellis's *Art and Science of Love* (1960) was one of the earliest books about birth control that the Post Office allowed in the mails, although *Esquire* would not run Stuart's advertisement for it. Stuart followed up with Eichenlaub's *Marriage Art* (1961) and Ellis's *Sex and the Single Man* (1963). In the mid-1960s, the publisher confronted Customs by importing editions of *Roma Amor*, an extensively illustrated treatise on Roman and Etruscan erotic art, and the work on Hindu erotic sculpture *Kama Kala*. *Sun-Warmed Nudes* successfully challenged New York City's police interdictions on photographs of women's pubic hair. *The Sensuous Woman* (1970) was a signal success, a kind of how-to book by a female ("J") as adept at satisfying male fantasies, including oral sex, as any harem odalisque. The hoax *Naked Came the Stranger* (1969), supposedly by a respectable housewife and radio cohost who becomes a sort of serial seductress, was a best-seller.[4]

Arnold Levy's clever and successful mail-order catalogs for his World Wide Book Service included many Roth books, purchased from Pauline Roth while her husband was in prison. Inimitably touted in nugget-size blurbs, they included the kind of underground classics for which Roth had served three years in Lewisburg in the late 1930s. Some of these — *The Lustful Turk, A Night in a Moorish Harem, With Rod and Whip*, Poggio's *Facetia [sic] Erotica, Fanny Hill* — Levy published with illustrations ("cut-and-paste jobs") in his own trade paperback editions as high spots for the catalogs.[5]

Barney Rosset was also about to liberate old banned classics: *The Pearl*,

Justine, *My Secret Life*, *The Way of a Man with a Maid*. Recent court decisions, brought about by Roth's own unsuccessful challenge to the obscenity statutes, had redefined obscenity so that only materials deemed "hard-core" by contemporary standards would be banned. Rosset had purchased a closetful of these under-the-counter books from Radio City Books, one of the older lending libraries, which went on specializing in erotica through the early 1950s, until publicity attending the Kefauver hearings forced many of their owners to close their doors.[6] Rosset eventually sold millions of the pornographic classics through Grove Press and (more recently) Blue Moon paperbacks. Roth himself wondered whether publishers like Rosset had not gone too far toward liberating sexual energy from legitimate restraints by publishing such material, *Lady Chatterley's Lover*, and the *Tropics* for the masses.

But there was even more chutzpah to come.[7] In 1968, Al Goldstein and Jim Buckley founded the scurrilous *Screw* magazine, an "up the establishment" weekly for anyone interested in any kind of sexual expression and practice. It was intentionally and proudly written in outrageously bad taste. Marvin Miller, released from prison in 1951, set his sights somewhat later on the most notorious and rare relic of Victorian pornography, *My Secret Life*; Grove Press had to pay Miller well to make it worth his while to stop issuing the work in magazine-format installments. But soon Milton Luros's Brandon House was offering most of the volumes of this title, as well as *Grushenka*, *Luisa Sigea*, *Teleny*, *The Merry Order of St. Bridget*, and many others, and other paperback houses, such as Midwood/Tower, Pendulum, Star, Magenta, and Lancer, were pushing back the borders of sexual expression.

When Roth left prison, William Hamling was publishing Nightstand Books: lurid, fast-moving stories of sexual gymnastics with narrative frameworks, sex pulps for the "swinging" 1960s. Later, Hamling's rather special edition of the 1970 report of the National Commission on Obscenity and Pornography, with an introduction commissioned from an ACLU executive, was adjudged by the Supreme Court to be egregious pandering because the publisher had illustrated the text with hard-core pornographic photos. Sanford Aday's line of Sabre and Fabian Books, like Hamling's, went farther than Roth ever had: *Sex Life of a Cop*, for example, was a highly unflattering story of both the professional and private activities of the police. But Roth (the victim of a brutally aggressive police raid on his home and office in 1954),[8] would have found the consequences of its publication sadly familiar: Aday's Fresno office was raided and the furnishings, as well as his files, were carried off. The FBI reportedly sought out Aday's customers, editors, writers, and distributors for "interviews." The enraged U.S. attorney for western Michigan arranged a "show trial"; Aday, although ill with heart problems, had to stand trial in Grand Rapids. He was sentenced to three consecutive five-year prison terms in 1963.

A similar draconian punishment awaited Ralph Ginzburg for *Eros* magazine, published in 1961–62, and mailed from Middlesex, Pennsylvania. Ginzburg was as unashamed of his advertising ploys as Goldstein was of his bad taste. Perhaps Roth thought that *Eros*, and especially its photo-essay depicting a black man and white woman together in provocative poses (though they were not having intercourse), was also going too far. But Ginzburg was a Sam Roth of his generation, and *Eros* clearly had an antecedent in Roth's *American Aphrodite*. In its third issue, Ginzburg published a perceptive article titled "Sam Roth, Prometheus of the Unprintable."[9] The old offender must have read it; it is too bad that no one has recorded his opinion. Perhaps he found its breezily ironic style irreverent or even unjust. The title, however, must have been deeply satisfying, with its suggestion of the heroic martyrdom of a crusader for honest sexual expression, on a cross labeled "king of the smut-mongers," erected by enemies of Olympian strength: Sumner, Lewisohn, Joyce, Eliot, Hoover, Knopf, Winchell, Brennan. To Roth, they all had one sin in common, the same one of which they accused him: the inability to distinguish between courageous liberation of the masses from fear of honestly expressing their sexual needs and exploiting prurience for the sake of venal opportunism.

Ralph Ginzburg did not seem to be haunted by Roth's hubristic visions nor did he carry his emotional baggage. But like Roth, he knew his material had literary value, declared that the Post Office had no constitutional basis for interdicting obscenity, and saw nothing wrong with frankly selling sex in his flyers. He went further, expressing pride in their prurience and taking a defiant stance toward his prosecutors.[10] This Roth-like self-contentedness biased several Supreme Court justices against him, as it did Attorney General Robert Kennedy and several of his closest aides. For the latter group, the photo-essay depicting the black man with the white woman was also crucial, both for sober political reasons involving orderly desegregation in the South and because, apparently, they were just plain shocked. Eventually, Ginzburg spent eight months (of a much longer sentence) in prison. To ensure that his arrogance would be put in its place, his original trial, in June 1963, was in Philadelphia, not far from two small towns from which he had tried (un-successfully, for their facilities were inadequate) to get his circulars mailed: Blue Ball and Intercourse, in Pennsylvania Dutch country. Ginzburg felt that Brennan's Roth case opinion, and the *Lady Chatterley* decision, protected him from charges that his materials were without value, patently offensive, or merely prurient. He was wrong, especially about the last. Not only in Philadelphia, but also at the Supreme Court, where Brennan himself was repulsed by the exhibits, Ginzburg was convicted of pandering.

During the early 1960s, Philadelphia's mayors and district attorneys assidu-ously tracked down distributors of erotic books and films. Confiscated materials were burned on the steps of churches; in one case, a superintendent of schools watched approvingly. The crusading Billy Graham warned Americans that God would punish them for the alarming increases in racial strife and alcoholism, and for the "obsession with sex that we see all around us."[11] In downtown Philadelphia in June 1960, a "raiding party of five county detectives" and an assistant district attorney — followed closely by TV reporters and their cameras — visited my uncle Benjamin Gertzman's Bookazine bookshop at 1528 Market Street, seizing five hundred books. The owner had named his business, with permission, after the large New York City distributor. Bail for the clerk — his brother Isadore, my father — was set at five hundred dollars.[12] Isadore was seen on the local news that night trying to move the NBC microphone far enough from his face to wave the police off the premises; he said they were "hurting his business." He remembered the tensions endured fifteen years earlier by Uncle Ben's close friend and partner Samuel Mas-over, who with four other Philadelphia booksellers was raided by the vice squad for carrying works by writers such as Erskine Caldwell, William Faulkner, James T. Farrell, Harold Robbins, and Jack Woodford. The booksellers were eventually cleared, thanks to a brilliant and influential opinion written by Judge Curtis Bok. My father recognized that the book business had become no safer because of Judge Bok's sharp criticism of the connection between sexually explicit books and antiso-cial conduct, and that the decensoring of *Lady Chatterley's Lover* may somehow have made those who carried such books more vulnerable. The assistant district attorney stated that "the books sold at Bookazine would arouse any man, unless he were made of stone." Bookazine was Philadelphia's biggest outlet for the sex-pulp novels of Jack Woodford, distributed by Citadel Press in New York. The case never came to court, since the New York distributors agreed not to circulate the Woodford line in Philadelphia (in the near future).[13] Plenty of copies were available in any event, and could always be safely purchased at the local department stores. Eventually, the anonymous phone calls — warning that the decor of an establishment owned by "dirty Jews" might be improved by detonation of a firebomb — ceased. A few years later, my father opened a "clean and respectable" book and card store a few blocks away. By the mid-1960s, the paperback editions of *Lady Chatterley's Lover*, *Candy*, *Lolita*, and *Tropic of Cancer* that my father sold were no longer under-the-counter dirty books. They had stylish covers, sometimes featuring abstract or posterlike designs, or "sensitive" paintings, devoid of prurience. They carried blurbs from literary critics and college professors, who ordered them for their students' class assignments. Isadore, therefore, in his own way followed the path of Esar Levine or Sol Malkin. My uncle Ben, with his moxie, years of experience, and contacts, which dated from wholesaling discarded newsprint and magazines during the Depression, had a career more like Jack Brussel's.

The erotica dealers discussed in this book were a hardy bunch; several live proudly and well today. The paradox of prurience has been equally hardy. America still has a taste for furtive entertainments, on the printed page as well as in newer media. America also still has a taste for moral outrage, whether it emanates from the pulpit or from secular activists fighting social "ills" from political rostrums, on school boards, and in police stations. True, sex for its own sake is now much more fully integrated into mainstream media, for example, in mass-market erotic novels featured in large bookstore displays, trade paperback anthologies of erotic stories and poems by classic, contemporary, and minority authors, and in the lusty Hollywood movies. The borderline of the sexual taboo has been pushed farther into the middle distance. The materials themselves may be much more explicit, rougher, rawer. But the mechanisms of social control and the dynamic interaction between the indignant moral entrepreneurs and the erotica dealers they strive to marginalize are surprisingly familiar.

It is also true that the industry has taken on a new organization: promoters of erotic material are often consortia producing all sorts of entertainment in various media, or large companies that distribute videotapes and films. But the situation of the pariah capitalist has survived. Moralists, finding it impractical to go after large corporations and mainstream cultural activities, still target individuals whose social background, personal goals, business methods, and political vulnerabilities make them kin to the earlier traders in prurience. As the "bad taste," indecencies, and lack of propriety of ethnic immigrants of the interwar period made them targets of the purity crusaders, advocates of "traditional standards" today avail themselves of similar language to discredit the prurience in popular music and films by black, gay, and working-class artists, writers, and distributors. The ethnic flavor of prewar erotica distribution is still with us, although, except for extreme right-wing hate groups, critics of sexual explicitness do not overtly exploit the fact. Many distributors of erotica are Jewish, even though very few sons and daughters of the people whose careers are surveyed here have adopted their parents' careers.

David Hebditch and Nick Anning, researching the pornography business in the mid-1980s, report that "some industry insiders claim that porn in the United States is essentially a Jewish business."[14] If this is so, it is because Jews have for a very long time cultivated the temperament and talents of middlemen, and they are proud of these abilities. The attitudes and techniques of resistance we saw in Roth, Guerney, Rebhuhn, and Brussel survive in the psyches of Ralph Ginzburg, Marvin Miller, Al Goldstein, and Milton Luros, but also in successful coreligionists in many fields of popular entertainment. Such traits helped Lenny Bruce and Howard Stern, for example. And they have also helped non-Jews whose families had no history of middleman activity: Larry Flynt, Bob Guccione, and Hugh Hefner.

Pariah middlemen ripe for social stigma can now be found most readily in the hard-core pornography industry, in paperback book or X-rated film distribution, or more recently in cyberspace. The most notorious case is that of Robert and Carleen Thomas, who operated a Bulletin Board System (BBS) in California. Warning browsers about the contents of their offerings, they collected pornographic images of all kinds for adults who paid for their service. They ascertained, from an acquittal in a San Jose court, that none were illegal by the standards of that community. In business strategy, the Thomases were not very different from erotica dealers such as Samuel Roth, Jack Brussel, or Louis Shomer. Their announcements, pictures, and captions pandered to prurient tastes, in this case including those of people interested in seeing images of bestiality, violent sex, and boys and girls in sexual poses and acts. The pictures the Thomases provided worked like the postal circulars of an earlier age: they were basically enticements, but for purchasing videotapes instead of books. A postal inspector stationed in Memphis, Tennessee, subscribed to the service in 1993 under an assumed name and, using a strategy similar to Comstock and Sumner's agent Charles Bamberger, gained Robert Thomas's confidence with many e-mail messages. Eventually, the inspector offered Thomas illustrated magazines loaded with child pornography that he and his wife could scan into their computers. He had successfully trapped BBS operators with this ploy in the past. He had waited until the magazines were in the suspects' possession and then had had them arrested. So it was with the Thomases. The inspector warned the couple that their sentences would be more severe if they revealed his alias, for he was using it for other ongoing investigations. They were tried in Memphis, the location in which the images were received, not in the more liberal atmosphere of San Jose. Portrayed as "monsters," subjected to the moral standards of that conservative community — although the concept of community standards is illogical in cyberspace, where anyone can access a site without its creator's knowledge — and convicted of selling obscenity and accumulating child pornography, Robert Thomas was sentenced to three years in federal prison, his wife to thirty months. Their sons are now carrying on the business. "There is something incongruous about the family life of the Thomases," conclude the authors of *Sex, Laws, and Cyberspace*, "a seemingly secure, financially comfortable, stable, nuclear American family where the family business, eventually taken over by the sons, trades in images of rape, bondage, and torture."[15] It is incongruous, but, with its vertical structure, political vulnerability, and required chutzpah, the Thomases' business is hardly unprecedented, no more than the methods used to trap its owners, and the language used to characterize them.

A brief historical summary of the accusations used to stigmatize erotica dealers shows a surprising lack of change between the 1920s and today. Erotica dealers were thought to be agents of the communists in weakening the moral courage and self-control necessary to achieve the American Dream, and to defend God and country.[16] As pornography itself is a drug, so its purveyors are just as sinister as narcotics dealers;[17] each crime plunges the victim into bitter, antisocial self-absorption. Booksellers and publishers who display erotic literature on newsstands and in drug or candy stores are human detritus making "quick dirty dollars,"[18] neither understanding nor caring about the harm they cause. They "deserve neither sympathy nor regard of any kind from their fellow men."[19] Indignant parents might eventually take the law into their own hands; since the authorities cannot cope with the growing emergency or are too corrupt to do so, public contrition or "voluntary book-burning" is sometimes called for.[20] If booksellers cannot exercise prudent self-censorship, they can be boycotted into insolvency. People without the "good taste" to distinguish between literature and smut hardly deserve to be in the book business in any event.[21]

Crusading politicians and clergy attempted to heal society from this infection by preventing those responsible from using the flexibility of democratic legal codes to protect themselves. The Clean Books Bill of 1923 proposed mandating jury trials in obscenity cases (so that the prosecution could bring to bear the indignation of the average citizen) and barring testimony from so-called expert witnesses. In 1947, Governor Dewey, with brave conviction, vetoed the McGowan Bill, which would have made anyone who writes obscenity guilty of a misdemeanor.[22] A 1959 California law banned possession of an obscene book in any place of business where books were kept. A Los Angeles bookseller was sentenced to thirty days under the ordinance.[23] Eventually, the unconstitutionality of these measures hindered the antismut crusades. But the threats they produced continue to be ubiquitous, constantly assuring that the erotica distributor is accorded the status of a pariah.

In fact, the language of the preceding decades is echoed quite precisely in today's culture wars. On 31 May 1995, Senator Robert Dole, speaking to Republican supporters a short distance from major Hollywood studios, angrily considered sexually explicit and violent films and song lyrics. His remarks sounded the same notes of disgust and full-hearted concern for the effect of such entertainment on the young that John Sumner and Catholic spokesmen had voiced regarding books and magazines in the 1930s, or that Senator Kefauver and Postmaster General Summerfield expressed in the 1950s. Dole spoke of the "marketing of evil through commerce," as had Judge John Ford in 1923; the "debasing of America," as had Senator Smoot in 1930; the "mainstreaming of deviancy," as did Father Francis X. Talbot and Rita McGoldrick of the International Federation of Catholic Alumnae in 1933. Though he called "not . . . for censorship," but "for good citizenship," Dole attempted, like the executives just mentioned, to focus universal public contempt on those who made money by pandering to prurient fascination with sex and violence. The goal was to make them ashamed of crassly reducing love and respect for others to sex and naked aggression ("putting profit ahead of common decency").[24] In an essay in the *New York Times* a few days after Dole's speech, William J. Bennett, who was head of the Department of Education during the Reagan administration, and C. Delores Tucker, chair of the National Political Congress of Black Women, characterized the films and music they deplored in the same way the moral entrepreneurs of the early twentieth century described the "indecent" books and magazines of their era: as an infection of the country's soul, undermining religious faith and the ability to make moral judgments. Bennett and Tucker's phrasing for the effect of the virulence was "the death of conscience, corruption of the spirit and ultimately the destruction of the individual and community."[25]

Bennett, in a televised debate with actor James Woods, stated that anyone who could not tell the difference between the now classic novels that were the targets of 1930s moralists and present-day lyrics callously (he thought) describing rape, murder, and mutilation was "a moron."[26] Certainly, the culture wars of the 1930s and of the 1990s are very different. Criticism of entertainments that pander to prurience is now largely directed at broadcast media and telecommunications, for these media reach many more people, especially young people, than do books. Today's creators of pornographic images have the opportunity to use electronic media to engross people more completely than could the purveyors of blue cartoons and Tijuana bibles. Furthermore, although the erotica distributors of an earlier period could point with pride to their role in enriching the lives of the common people with contemporary literature, and improving their knowledge of sexology and erotology, they had no empathy for same-sex lifestyles, little interest in gender equality or in giving women awareness or control of their sexual impulses, and no sensitivity to how they stereotyped the sexual customs of racial minorities as "exotic" or "primitive." Although conservative moralists who opposed them believed in parents who took care to teach their children "good taste," love of God, respect for adults, and control of sensual extravagances, they did not have to fight against successful, widespread challenges to conventional sex roles (including gay and lesbian alternatives) or to definitions of the family unit. Dole, Bennett, and the ideologues of the Christian Coalition, Family Research Council, and American Family Association would describe the sex and violence of today's popular entertainment as an attack on the traditional nuclear family and cultural values presented by gay, feminist and "alternative sexuality" activists, and by spokesmen for racial and ethnic minorities. They cannot afford to lose their fight against what they see as the Philistines of the 1980s and 1990s. They were stunned by the sympathetic treatment given Larry Flynt in Milos Forman's 1996 film about his struggles for free-speech rights against Jerry Falwell, Charles H. Keating, Jr., and the moral entrepreneurs of Cincinnati's Citizens for Decency Through Law (who included Keating's brother). Their attitude toward Ellen DeGeneres's coming out as gay on her prime-time TV sitcom is well known.

Equally repulsed by *The People vs. Larry Flynt*'s portrayal of the owner of *Hustler* magazine as a constitutional hero are feminists who believe that the meaning of Flynt's career is that he has gotten rich demeaning women. This would be especially true of those who believe, with Andrea Dworkin and Catharine MacKinnon, that the presence of commercially produced images of women sold for male sexual stimulation is a crime against the civil rights of women. The way conservatives from Comstock to Pat Robertson and procensorship feminists think about sex and its effects could not be more antithetical. The former deplore sexually explicit materials because they incite shame and result in irresponsible prioritizing of bodily pleasure over manly self-restraint and spirituality, and over patriarchal responsibility to the family a man should head and the community a man should serve. Feminists who see pornography as discrimination against women do not really seem to care if it induces prurient feelings or not. They identify it as an act of shamelessly thinking about, and instinctively treating, women as objects, silencing and enslaving them, and as such, as a manifestation of an inherently autocratic patriarchal zeitgeist. They want to destroy root and branch the form of male sexual release that pornography represents to them.

Despite the antithesis in their conceptions of what sex is and what it does, the two groups act similarly. First, both believe untrammeled sexual expression goes beyond offensiveness to palpable harm, psychological as well as physical.[27] They point to white slavery, or to discrimination, harassment, and assault. They deplore the harm to one's secular and religious convictions, and to the common good — or to what should be women's inalienable right to think of themselves as, and to be treated as, equal to men. "The social harm of . . . pornography," states a feminist constitutional lawyer in words that echo John Sumner's rhetoric, "is that it brutalizes our moral imagination, 'the source of that imaginative possibility by which we can identify with others and hence form maxims having a universal validity.' "[28] Second, both groups target representative materials. The moral entrepreneurs of the interwar period campaigned against the "invasion" of avant-garde European literature, and against lending-library sex pulps and mail-order sexology; today, the Eagle Forum and the Family Research Council focus on school texts that advocate "values clarification" or "occultism." Women Against Pornography makes much of "snuff films" and depictions of female-submissive sadomasochism. Third, both groups are uncomfortable with the concept of literary, artistic, political, or social value; they fear the concept allows the social evil of pornography to continue, and to be legitimized in ways that ignore its demoralizing, or antiwoman, essence. Finally, the rhetoric of the extremists in both groups is shot through with moral indignation.

Not only is American discourse about sex complex and sensational, but — and this is its most distinguishing feature — the discussants line up in keen, binary opposition to each other. It is the social order, and common good, that is in question: who is clean and trustworthy and who is dirty and delinquent. More important, at stake is how a man or woman responds to his or her deepest needs, what his or her peers and partners think about him or her, and what he or she thinks of them. It is, and has been, a debate in which each side focuses on what its supporters find outrageously immoral and repressive in the opposition. The combatants of the 1980s and 1990s are Patrick Buchanan, Pat Robertson, William Bennett, Senator James Exon of Nebraska, Phyllis Schlafly, and Women Against Pornography, on one hand, and Oliver Stone, Robert Mapplethorpe, Karen Finley, Allen Ginsberg, and the Feminist Anti-Censorship Task Force, on the other. The same burning antagonism resonated throughout the 1920s and 1930s: John Sumner and his colleagues, Senator Reed Smoot of Utah, the Catholic Church, and the Post Office versus Morris Ernst, Margaret Sanger, Senator Bronson Cutting of New Mexico, Samuel Roth, and Frank Harris. Anthony Comstock and Sumner, and their supporters throughout earlier twentieth-century America, were vigilant against what to them was an unprecedented assault on decency and purity, in which smutty photographs, books by writers from Apuleius to Schnitzler, birth-control manuals, and free-love and nudist tracts were all "demoralizing." It was more practical, however, to focus on what very few would defend: the incontestable (thus constantly titillating) obscenities sympathetically displaying the enemies of home and family life: libertines, adulteresses, "inverts," "foreign" sexologists, and sexually anarchistic adolescents, as celebrated in *My Life and Loves*, *Lady Chatterley's Lover*, *The Well of Loneliness*, books from the Falstaff Press, and Tijuana bibles. Similarly, today's purists find rap songs, Madonna's videotapes, Karen Finley's performances, and Robert Cormier's novels for young adults all worthy of shock and outrage. But as alternative sexualities like sadomasochism, bisexuality, and gay and lesbian sex become public, openly celebrated, and confusing to the average person, conservatives like Pat Robertson and Senators Jesse Helms and Mitch McConnell focus on these behaviors, identifying them with random, barbaric degeneracy. Linda Williams asserts that the 1990s version of the "scapegoatable deviant sexuality of the other" is the sadomasochistic homosexual, often imagined to be the child molester.[29] For Comstock, Sumner, Catholic boycotters, and the Protestant fundamentalists, it was the atheistic, communistic pornographer of indeterminate eastern European, Russian, Italian, or Spanish background.

At both ends of the century, the most visible enemy was and is not the radical ideologue himself or herself, but the businesspeople ("smutmongers," from Roth to Hefner, Ginzburg, and Flynt, not to mention film and cyberspace distributors) who disseminate the ideologue's lifestyle to the curious masses. The purity society activists of the interwar period, when they found it difficult to prosecute the Fifth Avenue booksellers of erotica, focused attention on their Bowery colleagues. The latter could not expect protection from entrapment tactics, abuse of the search warrant, or the posttrial return of confiscated goods. Had Senator McConnell's Pornography Victims Compensation Act passed in 1993, the person who sold an erotic book or tape to someone who committed a sexual assault would have to pay compensation to the victim, although the criminal was a third party over whose behavior the merchant had no control. Moral entrepreneurs constantly acknowledge the dangerous power of the erotica distributor, making sure that he or she pays harshly for his or her influence. That influence is strengthened, not weakened, as a result. Prurience popularizes and sensationalizes sex, which therefore continues to sell. Furthermore, its aura of subversion attracts promoters. From Roth to Flynt to Annie Sprinkle (a performance artist arrested for distributing "pornographic" literature in the late 1970s), there is something about the status as scapegoat that some people find attractive, whether they crave money, fame, or both.

Specific incidents of scapegoating, involving "cyberporn" rather than dirty books, are resonant of much earlier purity crusades. In Cincinnati in 1995, the same sheriff who prosecuted the exhibition of Robert Mapplethorpe's photographs headed a SWAT team that pounced on five unfortunate owners of BBSs and took computer equipment, e-mail, phone lines, and personal papers, including financial and tax records.[30] In Arizona, the operator of a BBS had his computer confiscated when local police suspected that some of the pictures on his system were of girls younger than eighteen and others showed bestiality. The owner had not seen the latter and had warned subscribers not to upload these kinds of materials, for it is impossible to view every text and image that someone may subsequently download from an operator's system. The police ascertained that the girls were underage not by the naked eye but by use of a scale of physiological characteristics of which the BBS operator was unaware. He was eventually acquitted of violating his state's obscenity laws, but was fired from his full-time job and for six months lost access to his computer and therefore his service. Meanwhile, many of his local competitors voluntarily closed down their systems or their adult sections rather than risk loss of respect, employment, financial resources, and liberty.[31] A similar police action a year later in Texas resulted in confiscation not only of the computer equipment of the operators of an erotica-purveying web site, but of all their office furniture. These actions, reminiscent of Sumner's sweeping confiscation policies, may violate the Constitution's search and seizure provisions, but the police attained their goals. They shut down the web sites and raised the issue of "guilty knowledge"—the distributors' responsibility for knowing whether or not each of the thousands of images they collected was illegal.[32]

The crusade against child pornography has caused other, even more legally dubious actions. The government agreed not to prosecute under the 1996 Communications Decency Act (CDA) until after federal adjudication of the bill, which banned any "indecent" or "patently offensive" speech online accessible by a person under eighteen. However, while the federal court was considering the CDA, the Justice Department "reviewed" (since it could not "investigate") the sexually explicit material on the Internet Service Provider (ISP) CompuServe. The department had received the same kind of complaints it had in the 1930s about the underage being debauched, in this case not by books on how to make love but by web sites featuring, according to the American Family Association, obscenity and child pornography. Like the Post Office in the interwar period, the Justice Department wanted to see and judge for itself.[33]

In Oklahoma in 1997, Oklahomans for Children and Families (OCAF) got an Oklahoma City judge to declare distribution of the videotape of the film *The Tin Drum* illegal; one scene suggested oral sex between a boy of six and a teenage girl and thus was actionable because of the way the municipal ordinance was phrased (the fundamentalist group has complained of approximately twenty segments of the award-winning film). Police confiscated copies of the videos, used the store's records to ascertain which customers had rented the tape, and, in a replay of

Anthony Comstock's brand of vigilance, went to the people's homes to collect the tapes. Among the various basic rights violated were due process, unreasonable search and seizure, and the Video Privacy Protection Act. Free speech would also seem to have been violated, but child pornography law does not take into account the literary, scientific, artistic, or political value of a work.[34]

Nor did the University of Oklahoma, where, as of a 1997 ruling, professors need special permission to view sexually explicit sites blocked from the university's computers. The "family-friendly" OCAF found that students using the university server could access pornographic sites on the Internet. One professor sued, saying the ruling hindered certain kinds of scientific, political, or literary research, but a federal judge ruled that he had not been harmed.[35] At the University of Virginia, credentials are also required, for that state has passed a law prohibiting any state employee from accessing sexually explicit sites using state-owned computers.[36] Concern about the disorienting effect of sexually explicit materials has a long history, as we have seen. When presenting bona fide credentials could be assumed to be an effective deterrent to keep the general population—especially children and adolescents—away from them, the dangers of society as a whole being "debauched" were assumed to be minor. Until the 1930s, erotica dealers could legitimately use disclaimers on brochures and title pages regarding conditions of eligibility for viewing and purchasing their books. However, technology has made this restraint increasingly less effective, making moralists nervous about availability not only in the workplace and library but in the privacy of one's home. One of the reasons the Panurge and Falstaff presses were vigorously prosecuted was that their widely available coupons verifying age and professional status were mere formalities, excluding no one and thus no check on distributors in establishing a large and indiscriminate customer base. OCAF's president made the point heatedly: when people access pornography by computer, instead of having to visit "a sleazy sex shop," the result is that "we have taken shame away from people addicted to this stuff." This implies that either all should suffer for the weakness of a few or the "stuff" is so potentially addictive that only the elite can be trusted to come in private contact with it.

While the constitutionality of the CDA was being decided, some of the most concerned parties were those with the heaviest liabilities, the ISPs. The free-speech rights of their subscribers were secondary to the consequences of being prosecuted for accommodating prurience, and risking the loss of millions in fines and legal fees. In 1995, America Online (AOL) created a list of taboo words that might suggest vulgarity or pornography and had employees view many of the sites posted on its service. When they located a word on the blacklist, the material was deleted, regardless of context. For a while, one of the taboo words was "breast." Others were "defecation," "submissive," and "sexual devices." The owner of a gay video store advertising on AOL was informed that the titles of many of his videos did not "reflect the image we would like to project."[37] This kind of word hunting reached its nadir about a year later, when the filtering software created by Surf-watch blocked the word "couples" as indecent. The word occurred in several sexually oriented sites, but also, referring to the Clintons and the Gores, on the White House's own web site, which Surfwatch's subscribers were therefore prevented from viewing.[38]

"Indecency" — the airing of subjects at variance with conventional standards of morality — is the focus of initiatives targeting not only the Internet but also cable television, phone sex, and radio programs. Communications in these media do include hard-core pornographic images and statements. But they also include, for example, information on sex education, prison rape, contraception, abortion, AIDS prevention, alternative forms of sexual expression, and music and literary readings with both scatological and sexually explicit content. People who believed in reticence in sexual expression deplored open expression of similar topics in the 1920s and 1930s, and long before. From a practical standpoint, it proves impossible to censor sexual openness without also censoring indecency, as the above examples show. In addition, some of those who believe in sexual reticence have actively targeted indecency. We saw this with the moral reformers of the 1920s and 1930s, and even earlier with the language of the Comstock Law stipulating that all sexual material is immoral. The present-day moral entrepreneurs, like Representative Henry Hyde of Illinois, have a similarly inclusive view. Hyde wished to have all sexually oriented web sites declared indecent, and proposed adding a clause to the CDA stipulating that information on abortion be interdicted, lest the underage read about it.[39] Indecent expression is granted constitutional protection (most recently in *Sable Communications v. FCC*, 1989), as obscenity is not, for the First Amendment of course protects citizens' rights to express ideas that anger or upset their fellows. However, words and images that describe "sexual or excretory activities or organs" in a manner considered "patently offensive as measured by contemporary community standards" may easily reach children through broadcast media regardless of parents' attempts to control what their children can access. In such a case, a variable standard is applied.

What is not indecent for adults may be so for children and adolescents. There is no better example than a set of instances in which text and books, not pictures and electronic media, have been subjected to censorship. The increasing restrictions on school library and classroom reading material started in the early 1980s. In 1992–93, there were 395 incidents of books assigned to public schoolchildren being decried as unfit ("pornographic," "offensive," "negative," "anti-Judeo-Christian"); 41 percent of the challenges were successful. The supposed vulnerability of children to sexual gratification, violent impulses, and irresponsible rebellion against authority has restricted their freedom to read in ways that adults could and would fight off as backward and dangerous. The number of incidents has been rising since the early 1980s; it is estimated that many more are unreported.[40] This phenomenon is as much a hallmark of the New Right's ascendancy under Ronald Reagan, and its way of waging its culture wars, as is the report of Reagan's attorney general Edwin Meese's Commission on Pornography (1986), which listed four categories, ranging from "mere nudity" to "sexually violent material." The commission found all four kinds to be harmful, relying on anecdotal evidence, especially from law-enforcement personnel, much more fully than on the evidence of social scientists.[41]

What restrains public schoolteachers also restrains producers of electronic communications. In 1978, the Supreme Court ratified the Federal Communications Commission (FCC) ruling that children should be protected from hearing George Carlin's "Seven Dirty Words" comedy routine; therefore, the commission was correct to penalize a radio station for playing it in the afternoon.[42] The supposed moral welfare of children took precedence over the tastes of adults, who in any event could go to a club or buy a tape to hear Carlin's satire, just as the Virginia professors could use their home computers to access sexually explicit material, or just as readers of the 1930s could purchase sexological texts at bookstores rather than at lending libraries or newsstands.

The FCC takes just as seriously its responsibility to protect the underage from indecency on the airwaves as the Post Office, with its mandate to purge the mails of fraud and obscenity, once did. The "seven dirty words" criteria were an objective measure of indecency, but at present the commission applies the Miller test for both obscenity and "programming contain[ing] sexual or excretory references that do not rise to the level of obscenity."[43] (Miller interdicts material the community finds prurient, lacking in value, and patently offensive.) Because they are held responsible under subjective "community standards" criteria, many broadcasters no longer risk readings of Allen Ginsberg's poetry, discussions of AIDS, or the playing of popular songs outside the "safe harbor" time period, rather than face suspension of their licenses and fines. Many distributors of compact discs and tapes featuring a wide variety of rap and rock music have made a similar self-imposed restriction on the circulation of popular culture: since Wal-Mart department stores support the cause of clean-cut youth by stocking such music only in versions that eliminate indecent lyrics and violent or sexually explicit album covers — or those suspected of depicting devil worship — special versions are prepared for this vast chain. K-Mart and Blockbuster Video have similar requirements.[44]

Congress wrote the CDA with the FCC's concern for the effect of indecency on children (i.e., people under eighteen) in mind. In the summer of 1997, the Supreme Court solidly thwarted this attempt to make the well-being of the least mature members of the community the determining factor in what was legal to publish on the Internet. Cynics would say the decision was good for the communications business, but there are better ways of protecting children from indecency, and the Court followed the principle that the least restrictive way is the most desirable. President Clinton now supports these alternatives, though his administration's stance is far from consistent: his Justice Department vigorously advocated the CDA before the Supreme Court, and at one point, the government suggested all contested sites should be shut down until the material could be reviewed, even if it took months to do so.[45] This was a distant echo of Comstock's dictum: morality mattered, not art or literature.

The fact that the CDA passed in both houses of Congress by wide margins shows that moralistic zeal has not lost its effectiveness. Nor is it limited to our most conservative public figures. When House Speaker Newt Gingrich remarked on an increasing concern about the hedonistic values projected in music popular with teenagers, and the resulting need to teach spiritual and ethical values within the American family, he attributed this new awareness to former Vice President Dan Quayle's criticisms of single mothers and other women who work outside the home. Vice President Gore was quick to counter, pointing with pride to the First Lady's efforts on behalf of family values, and to his own wife's book *Raising PG*

Kids in an X-Rated Society and her advocacy in the mid-1980s of warning labels on popular music albums.[46]

When Robert Dole was asked about ratings systems, he noted approvingly the swing in Americans' mood regarding the country's moral balance: it is now of greater concern to parents, he said, and thus "more family-friendly programming" is needed.[47] President Clinton agrees, but advocates parental supervision, not government action, as do the ACLU and other organizations fighting the CDA. Meanwhile, the vice president has introduced a new Web site instructing parents on ways of limiting Internet access.[48] To facilitate this process, television, recording systems, and the Internet are being requested to have their programs, presentations, and sites rated by prurient content. One rating system, used by Microsoft and Cyber Patrol, is based on the "tried and tested system used for computer games." It allows subscribers to choose from five levels of tolerance for "violence, nudity, sex, and language," including a zero level ("harmless conflict," "no nudity or revealing attire," "romance, no sex," and "inoffensive slang; no profanity").[49] The industries themselves are likely to comply, but if they do not, it is possible that the FCC, and congressional legislation, in loco parentis, will do the rating for them. Either way, some musicians, performers, writers, and producers will find themselves, as rock musicians do at present, with smaller audiences, and more institutionalized disapprobation. If legal censorship will not be the source of their frustration, what is already being called "censorware" (V-chips, Netnannies) will be. Citizens who choose to use it will find that many varieties do not allow the purchaser to edit what the vendors have preset. Some computer software blocks sites that offer unconventional viewpoints on sexuality, and therefore on social and political issues as well.[50] It is questionable whether power to control what comes into homes will rest with the individual owners of the TV and computer, or with the corporations that manufacture the blocking tools.

In the mid-1930s, John Sumner found his power waning as cultural conditions changed: he was no longer as effective or as publicly respected as he had been ten years previously. Does the failure of the CDA mean that advocates of government censorship are in the same position today? Has official censorship become the recourse of fringe elements? Such an assumption would certainly have been premature in June 1991, when the Supreme Court upheld Indiana's right to ban nude dancing (*Barnes v. Glen Theatre, Inc.* 115 L. Ed. 2d 504). Judge Antonin Scalia wrote that the state could prohibit "expressive conduct," at least a version of it not essential to express an idea, if it had a "rational basis," for example, "public order," for so doing. It is easier to prove essential significance in the case of historical or political expression than in the case of fiction, poetry, artwork, or popular entertainments. Thus flag-burning merits First Amendment protection; nude dancing does not. The court considered such goals as the maintenance of a "decent society" and of a "traditional moral belief" in the demoralizing effect of nudity or obscenity to provide a "rational basis" for state interdiction — even when the proof of the expressive act's harm is not solid.

But the legislative and judicial background may not be the most important now. As the cyberspace examples show, calls for a return to decency by religious and family-oriented organizations have effectively influenced such corporate entities as the ISPs, chain stores, and radio and TV programmers, encouraging certain kinds of commercial activity and discouraging others. Resourceful conservatives like Pat Robertson, Donald Wildmon, and Billy Graham appear to understand that they can regain control over American mass culture by influencing the increasingly centralized corporate providers of that culture. Advocates of reformed cultural perspectives on gender, ethnic, and gay issues have also had success in persuading ISPs, TV and radio programmers, and entrepreneurs of goods and services from clothing and perfume to automobiles and tourism that their businesses can thrive by accommodating left-wing constituencies. But the conservatives have an advantage, apart from pointing out that each of their enemies in the culture wars can be counted as a minority. Many Americans still recognize and respect the power of prurience. They still agree that sexual experiences pose dangers, that it is wiser not to discuss them openly, that both the experience and the discussion leave one morally conflicted and place one's physical and moral health at risk. "This culture," writes anthropologist Gayle Rubin, "construes and judges almost any sexual practice in terms of its worst possible expression. . . . Virtually all erotic behavior is considered bad unless a specific reason to exempt it has been established."[51] Psychologist Ira L. Reiss, reviewing problems with AIDS, date rape, teenage pregnancy, and sex abuse, criticizes the widespread support for abstinence instead of discussion and understanding as the best solution for young people. He calls for "an end to shame" in order to effect "our next sexual revolution."[52] Columnist Ellen Goodman summarizes the poignant stories of pregnant teenagers and young unwed mothers who ignore their conditions and abandon their children; she explains that these women feel so much "guilt, dread and desperation" that they simply cannot bring themselves to face the obliquity of pregnancy and nurturing without the social sanction of a husband. "Shame," she concludes, "is making a much applauded comeback."[53]

Some of these liberal commentators would also deplore the activities of merchants who sell "sleazy" books and pictures by prurient teasing, rightly understanding that furtive and self-consciously wanton expression buys into, and underwrites, the association between sex and shame. Others see that in a cultural environment restricted by shame, one person's sexual enlightenment is another person's dangerous pornography, and one cannot chastise or restrict any explicit materials without appearing to shame or taint them all. Either way, through legislative channels or by appeals and threats to business and media powers, the available range of sexual images and expression is artificially narrowed. Innocent people suffer.

The most radical opposition to the power of prurience today is that of feminists who find hard-core books, magazines, and films potentially liberating rather than evil. They do so regardless of the psychosexual fetish or the amount of aggression or submissiveness displayed. In *Caught Looking* (1986), a magazine-format collection of papers issued by the Feminist Anti-Censorship Task Force, Lisa Duggan, Nan Hunter, and Carole Vance concede that pornography "exaggerates the fantasy of male power" but explain that the purposes it serves are incongruous. The uses of hard-core pornography include sneering at the association of sex for its own sake as indecent or as off-limits to women, familiarizing the audience with a bizarre potpourri of orgasmic satisfactions, and sanctioning whatever urges are identified with male or female desire. The subversiveness of erotic expression is attractive to the "postporn" feminist because it is a medium for demonstrating that women are free to find the pleasures they uniquely desire, whether those are reached through nonpatriarchal erotica (i.e., romantic love and mutuality, with women initiating the contact) or through single-minded carnality (which has been characteristic of the way hard-core pornography has been sold to men).[54]

Postporn feminists such as performance artists Linda Montano and Annie Sprinkle are remarkably nonjudgmental. Sprinkle's "Anatomy of a Pin-up" poster (1991) includes comments about her false eyelashes and eyebrows, and the "mandatory fake beauty mark." She remarks how uncomfortable her boots, corset, and bra are, and how she needed assistance to climb into her outfit; is she showing the pathos of the male-dominated female as sex object? Although this could occur to the viewer, especially since the bottom-line comment is "In spite of it all, I'm sexually excited AND feeling great," Sprinkle's stated intent, as the rest of her work shows, is to relieve the male from guilt because he might require a getup and pose such as the one Sprinkle displays. She functions as a nurturing instructress, creating a variety of scenarios in which she "feels great" exploring her own impulses. These include many kinds of taboo sexual expression—gay, bisexual, transsexual, and heterosexual—involving dildos, female ejaculation, paddles, restraints, anality, and cross-dressing. The conventional male is brought to believe that sexual desire is polymorphous but that none of it is perverse. He learns what various women may need and how powerfully their imaginations can work. He may learn, despite himself, that his sexuality has a lot in common with that of women, gays, and transvestites. Sprinkle's art drains the mystique of shame from all forms of sexual expression, treating it as an everyday experience to which people should have unregulated access.[55] It would be tempting, and hopeful, to label her artwork as "postprurient." However, to separate prurient interest from any other motive for viewing, and even being aroused by, sexually explicit representations may be impossible at this (early?) stage of the sexual revolution, or "New Freedom."

It is not surprising that in the midterm election year of 1990, several feminist performance artists holding grants from the National Endowment for the Arts had their funding revoked. They included Holly Hughes, who styles herself a "lesbian scientist exploring the polymorphous perverse."[56] That year, Senator Jesse Helms campaigned to prevent federal funds being given for projects deemed obscene or indecent, "including but not limited to depictions of sadomasochism, homoeroticism, the exploitation of children, or individuals engaged in sex acts, or material which denigrates the objects or beliefs of the adherents of a particular religion or nonreligion." His legislation failed, but federal funding for projects involving the "obscene" was interdicted. Specifically at issue were the so-called deviant sexualities Hughes and Sprinkle celebrated.[57]

Given the basic fears and needs we have reviewed, it is inevitable that attempts to regulate sexual expression and behavior will persist. It is also inevitable that they will fail to stop anyone who wants to express him or herself in this way, but the social disapprobation, and the power of authority to impose it, is what matters. A list of otherwise liberal public figures who have approved of some restrictions in this area might begin with Morris Ernst and Learned Hand, and would extend through Franklin Roosevelt, Justice Brennan, Attorney General Robert Kennedy, and President Jimmy Carter down to the Clintons and the Gores. Shame and guilt, and the political capital that can be made from them, survive American new freedoms and sexual revolutions. For many of us, they remain "the color of the air." Thus the erotica dealer prospers. And so does the moral entrepreneur.

In fact, very little is new about our present-day culture wars, or the cycle of moral indignation that drives them. When *Lady Chatterley's Lover* was decensored in 1959, critics of the decision predicted that it would open the floodgates to a new and irreverent wave of cheap scatological and lubricious pornography, of both the soft-core drugstore and the hard-core adult bookshop varieties. Business being business, they were correct. Any liberalizing move against the advocates of sexual restraint unleashes both a moral panic and a spate of material in which it is difficult to ascertain anything apart from a direct appeal to guilty curiosity about what D. H. Lawrence called "the dirty little secret." This is not what the liberalizers had wanted. Nor was it what Morris Ernst had wanted in the 1930s, when a by-product of the efforts of the ACLU's National Council for Freedom from Censorship was the appearance of prurient sex pulps and mail-order erotica. But conservative activity also had unintended effects on both occasions: following the inevitable dynamics of antismut legislation, the campaigns of moral outrage by district attorneys, private citizens, and organized groups only publicized and made more desirable the stigmatized books, playing into the hands of the pornographers and leading to much hand-wringing by the forces of decency.

Another sufferer from the paradox of prurience has been the serious artist who wishes to explore the vitality of sexual energy — from D. H. Lawrence to Annie Sprinkle. When outraged conservatives attack, a wall of detached, bemused incredulity is built around this artist, who is viewed as deviant or mad. Thus, when the advocate of the moral consensus loses a battle, our society's taboos may be relaxed or redefined, but that does not mean that the artist's message has taken deep root in the popular imagination. The material beneficiaries are publishers and distributors who load the market with mediocre but lucrative material, solidifying the popular association of sex with guilt and shame, or with conventional and restrictive romantic norms, or both.

And yet, even the most crowd-pleasing genres of mass entertainment can claim a significant place in American cultural history. Sexually explicit popular entertainers and writers have been and still are regularly labeled time-serving sellouts or pornographers responsible for "nightmares of depravity." Looking back, however, we can see that some who survived long enough can claim to have been pioneers of social reform and imaginative expression, however outrageous that statement would have seemed at the time. As we have seen in the case of the eroticization of leisure time, "mere" entertainment can be just as iconoclastic, just as world-shaking, as the most ardent, single-minded artistic statement — if not more so.

The stories told in this book may be of interest, though for different reasons, to diverse players in today's struggles over prurience, from Ralph Reed to Madonna to Holly Hughes, from Henry Hyde to Andres Serrano to Howard Stern. The message is sobering, but need not be depressing: no one has ever succeeded in controlling sexual discourse in America, because no one has succeeded in defeating the perverse dynamic of prurience, or moved outside the unhappy symbiosis between those for whom it has meant "letting oneself go" (and in some cases making a good living) and those for whom it has been a perversity against which to campaign publicly. But whoever succeeds, from either side, in opening the minds of individuals to how taboos are relevant to his or her own life has done something important, even though not every such exploration will be beneficial to every explorer.

To many Americans — both those who purchase erotica and those who hate it — the intentions of its authors and distributors are irrelevant. Erotica speaks frankly and in detail about human beings and their irrepressible sexual selves. Some find this useful; others find it dangerous; many are indifferent. But behind these easily consumable words and images, even as marketed by impersonal corporate enterprises, are human beings with complex motivations and real lives. The traders in prurience whose stories I have told were men and women who needed a particular combination of self-possession and single-mindedness, shrewdness and combativeness, idealism and chutzpah to survive. To the charge that they were responsible for the spiritual degeneracy and emotional bondage of their fellow citizens they responded variously. In at least one case the rejoinder was replete with self-destructive, delusional denial. More typical responses were anger, fear, compromise, defiance, contempt, cynicism, and supremely spunky Yankee determination. Personality traits giving rise to these sorts of emotions have been survival strategies for figures like Larry Flynt, Al Goldstein, Lyle Stuart, and Ralph Ginzburg. Today's erotica writers and distributors, raunchy humorists, filmmakers, and their cyberspace incarnations, persevere in their work, and carry the same stigmas as the Roths, Rebhuhns, Levines, Shomers, Brotmans, and Costelitos. If we cannot understand the distinctively American backgrounds of the erotica dealers of the 1920s and 1930s, and of the moral entrepreneurs who carried the burden of suppressing them, we cannot recognize that we live today in essentially the same world that they were instrumental in shaping when the eroticization of leisure time first caught everyone's attention and it was "sex o'clock in American literature."

Notes

The following abbreviations appear in the notes.

ACLU Archives   Archives of the American Civil Liberties Union, preserved at the Mudd MS Library, Princeton University, Princeton, New Jersey.
Gertz   Papers of Elmer Gertz (1906–). Manuscript Division, Library of Congress.
Harris-Ross   Correspondence relevant to the works of Frank Harris, once in the possession of Harris's American lawyer, C. L. Ross. Arents Library, Syracuse University, Syracuse, New York.
HH-Misrep   "Misrepresentation Files" at the Herbert Hoover Presidential Library, West Branch, Iowa.
JA Files   Research files (the "morgue") of the *New York Journal American*, preserved at the Humanities Research Center, University of Texas at Austin.
KI Files   Vertical Files at the library of the Kinsey Institute for Sex Research at the University of Indiana, Bloomington.
Ledgers   Names and Records of Persons Arrested Under the Auspices of the New York Society for the Suppression of Vice. Manuscript Division of the Library of Congress.
MLE Papers   Letters, trial transcripts, legal briefs, and personal papers of Morris L. Ernst, preserved at the Harry Ransom Humanities Research Center, University of Texas at Austin.
NA   National Archives, Washington, D.C.
NYT   *New York Times* All *New York Times* and *Herald Tribune* articles are from the late city edition.
PW   *Publishers Weekly*.
RA   Rebhuhn Archive   In the possession of Dr. Ronald Rebhuhn, Westbury, New York.
Scheiner Archive   Archive of clippings, catalogs and brochures (1929–31) related to the Panurge Press, in the possession of antiquarian bookseller Dr. C. J. Scheiner, Brooklyn, New York.
WW Papers   Papers of the New England Watch and Ward Society, in the Special Collections Department of the Harvard University Law Library, Cambridge, Massachusetts.

Introduction

1. Richard A. Posner, *Sex and Reason* (Cambridge, Mass.: Harvard University Press, 1992), 351–52.

2. Laura Kipnis, *Bound and Gagged: Pornography and the Politics of Fantasy in America* (New York: Grove, 1996).

3. Brochure for the Falstaff Press's *Sex Life of the World Photographed* (actually either Robert Meadows [Solomon Malkin], *A Private Anthropological Cabinet*, or Iwan Bloch, *Anthropological and Ethnological Studies*) included as exhibit in the trial transcript of *U.S. v. Ben Rebhuhn, Anne Rebhuhn, and Ben Raeburn*, C97-410, U.S. District Ct., So. District of N.Y. (1939).

4. These terms are used in a full-page notice for La Forest LaRue, *Strange Loves: A Study in Sexual Abnormalities*, offered by the Robert Dodsley Company in *Love Fiction Monthly* (Nov. 1934).

5. Brochures for Felix Bryk, *Voodoo-Eros* (privately printed, 1933), one in KI Files and one found laid into an unexpurgated pirated copy of *Lady Chatterley's Lover*, in private collection of the author.

6. Brochures for the Panurge Press editions of Jean de Villiot's *Black Lust* (1931) and Hector France's *Musk, Hashish and Blood* (Robin Hood House, n.d.), in KI Files and MLE Papers, respectively.

7. Circular for the Robin Hood House edition of France's *Musk, Hashish and Blood*, in KI Files.

8. Brochure for *Black Lust*.

9. John Cameron Grant, *The Ethiopan* (New York: Black Hawk, 1935), vi.

10. Brochure for the Panurge Press edition of Esar Levine's *Chastity Belts*, in KI Files.

11. Blurb for Clement Wood, "The Uncut Loaf," in his *Flesh*; from brochure in MLE Papers.

12. Described in blurbs for several of the stories in the Panurge edition of Remy de Gourmont's *Colors*; brochure in Institute for Advanced Study of Human Sexuality, San Francisco, Calif.

Chapter 1. Traders in Prurience

1. Jack Biblo, personal interview, Brooklyn, N.Y., 8 Dec. 1991.

2. Jacob L. Chernofsky, "Louis Cohen and the Argosy Book Store," *AB Bookman's Weekly*, 15 Apr. 1991, 1508–12.

3. The following pages in *U.S. v. Samuel Roth*, C53-79, U.S. District Ct., So. District of N.Y. (1929), stenographer's minutes, refer to the events and facts relevant to this arrest: books at 122 Fifth Avenue: 77; at 160 Fifth Avenue: 26, 28, 86; Pauline Roth's ownership of Golden Hind: 10, 19–20; order forms: 27, 86–89, 93; circulars: 91, 93; mailing *Yama* and *Chatterley*: 17; arrest of Roth's brother Max: 22–26, 91. The circumstances of the arrests themselves are detailed in a letter from W. K. Halliday and Chester A. Battles (Post Office inspectors) to George Daly (Roth's probation officer) dated 10 Oct. 1929. The letter is included in the indictment. See also "Seize 3,000 Books as 'Indecent' Writing," *NYT*, 5 Oct.

1929, 22; "Max Roth Raided," *PW*, 2 Nov. 1929, 2176; William F. Ryan, "Samuel Roth: A Lion in a Den of Daniels" (unpublished essay, 1977), 43–47.

4. On Apr. 5, 1952, the *Saturday Review of Literature* published a letter from Margaret Meehan, apparently an editor at Roth's Seven Sirens Press, regarding the controversy over the authorship of *My Sister and I*, which Roth had published, declaring it to be a lost manuscript by Friedrich Nietzsche. Meehan stated that the manuscript had been taken during Sumner's raid on 160 Fifth Avenue, "along with our entire Carrington collection," which probably included the pictures. The letter is reprinted in a 1990 edition of *My Sister and I*, published by Amok Press of Los Angeles.

5. Adelaide Kugel (Samuel Roth's daughter) to the author, 7 Sept. 1988. He is mentioned, but not so identified, in a typed sheet headed "The Strange Career," HH-Misrep.

6. *U.S. v. Samuel Roth*, 23.

7. Samuel Roth, *Stone Walls Do Not: The Chronicle of a Captivity* (New York: Faro, 1931), 1: 117–18.

8. Samuel Roth, *Jews Must Live: An Account of the Persecution of the World by Israel on All the Frontiers of Civilization* (New York: Golden Hind, 1934), 150–52.

9. "Summary of Report in the Case of Samuel Roth," 2, HH-Misrep.

10. Ibid.

11. Roth, *Stone Walls*, 2: 191.

12. Charles Rembar, *The End of Obscenity: The Trials of* Lady Chatterley, Tropic of Cancer, *and* Fanny Hill (New York: Random House, 1968), 21; Heywood Broun and Margaret Leech, *Anthony Comstock: Roundsman of the Lord* (New York: Boni, 1927), 128–44.

13. The Comstock statutes are incorporated in title 18 of the *U.S. Code*, secs. 1461 (characterizing the various unmailable materials), 1462 (forbidding importation of obscene matter and its interstate transportation by common carrier), and 1463 (prohibiting obscene wording on wrappers deposited for mailing). Sec. 1464 covers obscene radio communication. Also relevant to Post Office concerns are secs. 1341 (frauds and swindles), 1342 (fictitious name or address), and 1717 (unmailable letters; opening letters). Title 19, sec. 1305 deals with confiscation and destruction of imported materials deemed obscene. Title 39, secs. 3001–10 deal with the Postal Service and its procedures regarding unmailable matter. In the interwar period, the Comstock statutes were found at title 18, secs. 334 and 335. Title 39, sec. 259 a, b, and c (now title 49, secs. 4006–7) describe mail blocks. See Frederick F. Schauer, *The Law of Obscenity* (Washington, D.C.: Bureau of National Affairs, 1976), 172–89; Dorothy G. Fowler, *Unmailable: Congress and the Post Office* (Athens: University of Georgia Press, 1977), 61–63; James N. Paul and Murray Schwartz, *Federal Censorship: Obscenity in the Mail* (New York: Free Press of Glencoe, 1961), app. 4. The contemporary Post Office manual, *Postal Laws and Regulations of the United States of America* (Washington, D.C.: GPO, 1932), contains these statutes, using its own reference system.

14. Richard Hofstadter, *Anti-Intellectualism in American Life* (New York: Vintage, 1961), 118–34.

15. Joseph Gusfield, *Symbolic Crusade: Status Politics and the American Temperance Movement* (1963; Urbana: University of Illinois Press, 1969), 9; Paul Boyer, *Urban Masses and Moral Order in America, 1820–1920* (Cambridge, Mass.: Harvard University Press, 1978), 218–19. Sumner's statement is from his "Truth About Literary Lynching," *Dial*, July 1921, 65.

16. The term "moral entrepreneur" is described by Howard S. Becker, *Outsiders: Studies in the Sociology of Deviance* (New York: Free Press, 1963), 147–63.

17. Boyer, *Urban Masses*, 214.

18. Sylvia Beach, *Shakespeare and Company* (New York: Harcourt Brace, 1959), 180–81.

19. The sociological concept of "pariah capitalism" was inspired by such classic statements about outsiders as those of Georg Simmel ("The Stranger," in *The Sociology of Georg Simmel*, ed. Kurt H. Wolff [New York: Free Press of Glencoe, 1950], 402–8) and Max Weber ("Judaism, Christianity, and the Socio-Economic Order," in *The Sociology of Religion* [1922; Boston: Beacon, 1963]), 246–61. Weber analyzes the responsibilities of the diaspora Jew toward those with whom he is engaged for economic survival. Simmel discusses the behavior of, and the nature of hostility toward, "the stranger" who arrives to carve out a living for himself in a society that views his arrival and activities as outrageous. Irwin Rinder's "Strangers in the Land: Social Relations in the Status Gap" (*Social Problems* 6 [winter 1958–59]: 253–60) asserts that transactions between elite and dependent social groups are often carried out by "middlemen" who, loyal to the elite, are willing to absorb the community's hostility by setting prices, collecting revenues, or dealing in desired but officially stigmatized commodities. Rinder builds on the work of Weber, Howard Becker, and Robert E. Park.

In "A Theory of Middleman Minorities" (*American Sociological Review* 38 [Oct. 1973]: 583–94), Edna Bonacich develops a "model" of the behavior of various ethnic groups who, having immigrated to a land as either permanent settlers or "sojourners," organize themselves economically and ideologically in a way that perpetrates their status as strangers even as they begin to become assimilated. Hostility is occasioned by economic as well as cultural habits. See also Bonacich and Jonathan H. Turner, "Toward a Composite Theory of Middleman Minorities," *Ethnicity* 7 (1980): 144–58. The persistence of middleman status in cultural groups is discussed by Marlene Sway in *Familiar Strangers: Gypsy Life in America* (Urbana: University of Illinois Press, 1988), 17–21. Gary Hamilton's "Pariah Capitalism: A Paradox of Power and Dependence" (*Ethnic Groups* 2 [1978]: 1–25) explores the dynamics between the elite and pariah groups, showing the political dependency of the latter on the former as a key factor in the ongoing symbiotic relationship, and stating that the ethnic identity of the pariahs is important in that dependence. Jack Nusan Porter's "The Urban Middleman: A Comparative Analysis" (*Comparative Social Research* 4 [1981]: 199–215) discusses marginality in the context of the middleman and uses Jews in the United States as an exemplar of middleman minorities in modern societies. See also Walter P. Zenner, "American Jewry in the Light of Middleman Minority Theories," *Con-*

temporary Jewry 5.1 (spring/summer 1980): 11–30; and Zenner, "Middleman Minority Theories: A Critical Review," in *Sourcebook on the New Immigration*, ed. Roy S. Bryce-Laporte (New Brunswick, N.J.: Transaction, 1980), 413–25. The Zenner essays appear in expanded form, with much new material, in his *Minorities in the Middle: A Cross-Cultural Analysis* (Albany: State University of New York Press, 1991).

20. The concept of commercialized outlets for repressed instincts in modern societies, and of these outlets as themselves a kind of social control, is reminiscent of Herbert Marcuse's "surplus repression." See *Eros and Civilization* (1955; rpt., Boston: Beacon, 1974), 37–48, 87–91.

21. Bennett Cerf to Robert Kastor, 22 Mar. 1932; and Cerf to Morris Ernst, 20 Oct. 1932, preserved in file box 270, MLE Papers. In the letter to Ernst, Cerf identifies the "notorious pirate" as Joseph Meyers, of the Illustrated Editions Company. To Kastor, he writes that "there are three or four firms now in New York that are today boldly pirating anything that they possibly can without running afoul of the law."

22. For Brussel and *Tropic of Cancer*, see Gershon Legman's introduction to Patrick Kearney's *Private Case: An Annotated Bibliography of the . . . Erotica Collection in the British (Museum) Library* (London: Landesman, 1981), 54.

23. Ledgers, 1927, s.v. "Lewis, Joseph." Robinson, a socialist dedicated to freeing the working classes from ignorance of family planning, was the first American physician to advocate teaching the average citizen about contraceptive devices; thus he was a chief nemesis of Anthony Comstock. See Peter Fryer, *Secrets of the British Museum* (New York: Citadel, 1966), 197–98; Leslie Fishbein, *Rebels in Bohemia: The Radicals of* The Masses, *1911–1917* (Chapel Hill: University of North Carolina Press, 1982), 109–11.

24. Records of the Post Office, Office of the Postmaster General, Office of the Solicitor (archive 52 of the *Preliminary Inventories*), "Transcripts of Hearings on Fraud Cases, 1913–45," box 2, in re Truth Pub. Co., NA, Hearing of 16 Dec. 1921, 7–8.

25. Ibid., 4.

26. Nat Schmulowitz, preface to *The Legend of Joe Miller*, by Evan Esar [Esar Levine], Anecdota Scowah 2 (San Francisco, Calif.: privately printed for members of the Roxburghe Club, 1957), 8; Lawrence Van Gelder, "Evan Esar, 96; Wrote Books on Jokes and Humor," *NYT*, 5 Jan. 1996, D21.

27. Fra Poggius, *The Trial of Hus: His Sentence and Death at the Stake* (1523; New York: Carl Granville, 1930). Rebhuhn's son Ronald told the present writer in a 23 Dec. 1993 interview that his father's ideals led him to distribute the copies.

28. Ronald Rebhuhn, personal interview with the author and C. J. Scheiner, 12 Aug. 1992; C. J. Scheiner, personal interviews with Esar Levine, undated but c. 1978–82. Dr. Rebhuhn has many letters that passed between his father and Harris, Schroeder, and Wright. He kindly showed me extensive notebooks his father kept during the Mexican stay.

29. For analysis of the organizational structure of middlemen minorities, and their group solidarity, see Bonacich, "A Theory of Middleman Minorities," 585–90. It should be pointed out that the erotica dealers of the 1920s and 1930s were not sojourners but perma-

nent settlers in America, and the hostility they engendered in the community had little to do with their being perceived as preventing native businessmen from competing with them or driving down the wages of artisans in the general book trade.

30. Another potential, but incomplete, source of information are the docket books of the magistrates' courts. These contain records up to 1930. However, although the docket books record the defendants' "residence, sex, age, color, and nativity," they do not mention religion or nationality. Further, no obscenity arrests seem to be listed. See the Microfilm Finding Guide for the *New York City Department of Records and Information Services, Municipal Archives Division, Records of the Criminal Justice System* in the Municipal Archives on Chambers Street in lower Manhattan.

31. Ronald H. Bayor, *Neighbors in Conflict: The Irish, Germans, Jews, and Italians of New York City, 1929–1941* (Baltimore, Md.: Johns Hopkins University Press, 1978), 23.

32. Thomas Kessner, *The Golden Door: Italian and Jewish Immigrant Mobility in New York City, 1880–1915* (New York: Oxford University Press, 1977), 57.

33. Ibid., 59–65.

34. Kessner, *The Golden Door*, 171.

35. Ibid., 86–90.

36. R. Whitley, special agent in charge, to FBI director, 31 Dec. 1936. This document is part of the voluminous FBI files on Samuel Roth, obtained by Patrick Kearney of Santa Rosa, Calif. I am grateful to Mr. Kearney for sharing the material with me. See also *NYT*, 4 Sept. 1936, 7.

37. *U.S. v. Samuel Roth*, stenographer's minutes, 23–28, 52, 64, 91.

38. "Seize Obscenities Worth $70,000," *New York Evening Sun*, 10 Apr. 1934, JA Files. Books mentioned include *Randiana, Crimson Hairs*, and *Anecdota Americana*. The Loewingers were also responsible for printing Samuel Roth's piracy of the ninth impression of the Shakespeare and Company *Ulysses*. See John Slocum and Herbert Cahoon, *A Bibliography of James Joyce* (New Haven, Conn.: Yale University Press, 1953), 18.

39. Jacob and David Brotman of the Bronx and Brooklyn were cited for pamphlets, playing cards, pictures, and comic strips. "Raid Nets Two," *Brooklyn Eagle*, 18 July 1939; "Obscene Library Raided by Police," *NYT*, 28 Mar. 1936; "FBI Smashes Ring of Obscene Booklet Sellers," *New York Herald Tribune*, 24 Nov. 1942, JA Files.

40. *U.S. v. Ben Rebhuhn, Anne Rebhuhn, and Ben Raeburn*, C97-410, U.S. District Ct., So. District of N.Y. (1939) trial transcript, 314; *U.S. v. Rebhuhn et al.*, 109 F2d 512 (2d Cir. 1940), point 8 (p. 515); "Two Publishers Get Prison Sentences," 8.

41. *U.S. v. Levine*, 83 F2d 156 (2d Cir. 1936), trial transcript, 50–51.

42. The KI Files contain numerous letters, catalogs, and brochures related to the selling of erotic books. Some of the brochures are identical copies of each other, except that the address of the bookseller or distributor differs, and the price has been reduced.

43. *Post Office v. Metro Publications* (1939), brief for respondent, 1–3, Scheiner Archive.

44. John S. Sumner to Ellis W. Meyers, 13 Mar. 1930, file 388, MLE Papers.

45. Greenbaum, Wolff, and Ernst to Ellis W. Meyers, 25 Mar. 1930, file 388, MLE Papers.

46. A list of books Sumner confiscated as evidence during the 1928 raid is in file box 391, MLE Papers, in the folder titled "Gotham Book Mart vs. Sumner, legal papers and draft."

47. On 12 Aug. 1992, antiquarian bookseller Dr. C. J. Scheiner and I visited the son of Benjamin Rebhuhn, Dr. Ronald Rebhuhn, at his Westbury, Long Island, home. Dr. Rebhuhn, who was born in 1942, spoke at length with us about his father, whose activities he was able to describe in extraordinary detail. He showed us the editions of *My Life and Loves* and other Harris works lovingly inscribed to his father by the author. In addition, he very graciously allowed us to photocopy a sheaf of approximately seventy letters (mostly typed transcriptions of holograph originals) from Frank Harris to Ben Rebhuhn dating from 1923 to 1929. There was also a journal kept by the latter during the 1920s, several telegrams relevant to *My Life*, and a few brochures published by the Frank Harris Publishing Company. This is the material cited as RA. Dr. Scheiner and I are most grateful to Dr. Rebhuhn for his generosity and concern for our research.

At least some of this correspondence has been seen by Harris scholars. Vincent Brome (*Frank Harris: The Life and Loves of a Scoundrel* [New York: Yoseloff, 1960], 238) cites among his "letters consulted" the "correspondence between Harris and R. and Mrs. R, 1923–26. Largely unpublished." A. I. Tobin and Elmer Gertz had access to some letters, courtesy of Levine or, as is most likely, Rebhuhn, for they quote several, using "X-" or initials of surnames, in their *Frank Harris: A Study in Black and White* (1931; rpt., New York: Haskell House, 1970), 323–37.

The RA greatly supplements a series of six letters, four telegrams, and one attorney's memorandum regarding the printing and publishing of *My Life and Loves* that exists at the Harry Ransom Humanities Research Center, University of Texas at Austin. They are cited with the abbreviation "Harris letters, HRC." Other important materials include the Harris-Ross archive of legal papers and correspondence at the Arents Research Library, Syracuse University; the materials at Fales Library, New York University, in folder 83.3, "Harris, Frank. Corresp. to Ross, Arthur L." (Fales also has a scrapbook of clippings about Harris compiled by A. I. Tobin, and galley proofs of both vols. 3 and 4 of Harris's Niçois edition of *My Life*, and of the first [pirated] American edition of these two works, published in one volume); and the Elmer Gertz Papers at the Library of Congress, which contain voluminous correspondence and newspaper clippings.

C. J. Scheiner, who interviewed Esar Levine on several occasions in the 1970s and 1980s, is another source of information about Levine and Rebhuhn's relationship and an important supplement to the evidence of the letters and published works for the Levine-Harris dealings.

It should be noted that the RA does not contain the complete correspondence regarding *My Life*. Other letters may have passed between Rebhuhn and Harris, and certainly there were quite a few between Esar Levine and Harris that have not come to light.

48. "Paid 'Fixer' Publisher Testifies," *New York Journal*, sports extra ed., 24 Jan. 1931, 2.

49. "Mysterious $65,000 Traced to Two Police at 'Fixer' Hearing," *NYT* 25 Jan. 1931, 1, 2; "Miller Under Fire as 'Fixer' Today," *NYT*, 26 Jan. 1931, 1; "Indict Six in Failure of Clothing Concern," *NYT*, 28 Mar. 1931, 3; "Book Case Suspect Defiant on Alleged $2,000 to Simpson," *New York World*, 25 Jan. 1931, 1; "Book Case Fixer Accused of Asking $2,000 for Judge," *New York Herald Tribune*, 25 Jan. 1931, 1; "Swears 'Fixer' Demanded $2,000 for Judge," *New York American*, 25 Jan. 1931, 1. The last three of these articles were found in box 412, Gertz.

50. "Raid Plant, Seize Book as Obscene," *NYT*, 27 June 1925, 3. According to the newspapers, the police had taken only books, not the heavy metal plates from which the sheets were printed, in the raid. The 1926 annual report of the NYSSV, written by Sumner, reports that plates and "unbound printed sheets" were seized. Sumner may simply have been putting the best interpretation on events for his constituents.

51. Benjamin Rebhuhn to Frank Harris, 16 May 1926, 3, RA: "Then after much contention and $1000 we managed to get the books and plates then withheld by the printer."

52. Esar Levine to Frank Harris, 20 July 1925; Rebhuhn to Harris, 18 July 1925, Harris letters — HRC.

53. Rebhuhn to Harris, 16 May 1926, 4.

54. Rebhuhn to Harris, 3 Feb. 1926 and 16 May 1926, 5.

55. "Jail for Selling Frank Harris," *PW*, 27 Mar. 1926, 1136. Harris to Rebhuhn, 30 Mar. 1926, RA: "Thanks for . . . the good news that [Levine's] imprisonment at Queens City prison 'is really not a prison' except for the confinement."

56. *U.S. Criminal Code* 211.

57. "Court Denounces Harris' 'My Life,' " *NYT*, 21 Aug. 1925, 15; "Harris Book Denounced," *PW*, 5 Sept. 1925, 750.

58. Rebhuhn to Harris, 25 Aug. 1925, RA.

59. "Raid Plant," 3.

60. Harris to Rebhuhn, 11 Oct. 1925, RA. On 25 Sept. the judge reserved a decision on Leibowitz and Sidowsky, arrested in the June raid at 195 Canal Street, until 19 Oct. ("No Decision on 'My Life' Publishers," *NYT*, 25 Sept. 1925). See also "Jail for Selling Frank Harris," 1136.

61. Rebhuhn to Harris, 16 May 1926, 3–4, 6.

62. In May 1926, when Miller tried to stop Levine, Rebhuhn, their partner Raymond Thomson from advertising by mail the expurgated edition of volume 1 on their own, he was himself advertising, under a fictitious name, as distributor of the edition (Rebhuhn to Harris, 1 Nov. 1926, RA). Harris was told, no doubt on advice given to his American friends by his New York attorney, Arthur L. Ross, to write to Ross, being careful not to mention Rebhuhn or Levine (who would not wish to testify in court about whatever deals they might have made with a court fixer). He was to state that he had assigned copyright in *My Life* to his wife, Nellie (so that his creditors could not attach royalties), and to start proceedings against

Miller for violation of copyright. He was also to authorize Ross to start any action necessary against the Davidson Press, 161 Grand Street, to enjoin it from turning over to Miller the books and plates of the expurgated version (Ben Miller to Frank Harris, 1 Dec. 1925 and 2 Sept. 1927, Harris letters — HRC).

63. Rebhuhn to Harris, 16 Sept. 1925, RA.

64. Rebhuhn to Harris, 27 Mar. 1926, RA. Letter incomplete; only first page present.

65. Rebhuhn to Harris, 16 Sept. 1925, RA.

66. Harris to Rebhuhn, 14 Apr., 25 June, and 6 July 1926, RA.

67. Raymond Thomson to Elmer Gertz, 6 Sept. 1927, Gertz. For a detailed account of the first American printings of these volumes, see my "Trap for Young Book-leggers: The First American Printings of Frank Harris's *My Life*, Volumes Three and Four (1927)," *Papers of the Bibliographical Society of America* 89.3 (Sept. 1995): 316–38.

68. As for who the pirates may have been, Sumner's ledgers for 1927 contain an entry for "printing and publishing Harris Vol. III." The Publix Printing Company is named, as are Morris and Gus Picker and Jacob Brotman. The latter was prosecuted, several years later, for printing readers and comics. These may of course be other pirates than those who cheated Levine and Rebhuhn. H. S. Nichols, a notorious and resourceful printer and publisher of erotica in Britain and France before immigrating to New York in 1909, might have been involved in printing one or more volumes of the work. See Peter Mendes, *Clandestine Erotic Fiction in English, 1800–1930: A Bibliographical Study* (Aldershot: Scolar, 1993), 19.

69. Another impression has a different title and place of publication: *The Love Life/* OF/FRANK HARRIS/AN AUTOBIOGRAPHY/"Magna est veritas, et prevalebit."/Truth is mighty, and it will prevail — /Privately Printed — Sold by Subscription Only./London — 1931

70. Mary Ann Malkin, telephone conversation, 30 Nov. 1992, and Oscar Chernovsky, telephone interview, 1 Dec. 1992.

71. Courtenay Terrett, "Smut Racketeers Flourish Dealing in Forbidden Books," *New York World*, 22 Nov. 1929, JA Files

72. These character traits are described by Bonacich, "A Theory of Middleman Minorities," 585.

73. See Simmel, "The Stranger," 404.

74. Sol Steinberg, *Yiddish and English: A Century of Yiddish in America* (University: University of Alabama Press, 1986), 60–61; Gene Bluestein, *Anglo-Yiddish: Yiddish in American Life and Literature* (Athens: University of Georgia Press, 1989), 36–37; Alan Dershowitz, *Chutzpah* (New York: Little, Brown, 1991), 18. See *Oxford English Dictionary*, 2d ed., s.v. "chutzpah." For "moxie," see Lester V. Berry and Melvin Van Den Bark, *The American Thesaurus of Slang*, 2d ed. (New York: Crowell, 1956); and Harold Wentworth and S. B. Flexner, *The Dictionary of American Slang*, 2d supp. ed. (New York: Crowell, 1975). The latter's earliest recorded usage of "moxie" is in novels published in 1943.

75. "Swears 'Fixer' Demanded $2000 for Judge," *New York American*, 25 Jan. 1931, 1, 17; "Mysterious $65,000 Traced to 2 Police at 'Fixer' Hearing," *NYT*, 25 Jan. 1931, 1, 2; "Book Case Suspect Defiant on Alleged $2000 to Simpson," *New York World*, 25 Jan. 1931,

1. The NYSSV ledgers for 1926 list two arrests and convictions regarding *unexpurgated* editions of *My Life*. A Greenwich Village book and art dealer (Joseph Kling?) is stated to have received a sentence of one hundred dollars or thirty days for selling the book; a West 15th Street dealer (Henry Klein) was penalized fifty dollars or thirty days for "giving [a Sumner agent] obscene circular 'My Life' "; 136 such advertisements were taken from his shop. See "Frank Harris 'Life' Case," *PW*, 17 Apr. 1926, 1334.

76. In addition to *NYT*, the *World*, and the *American*, the following papers carried front-page stories about Simpson and Miller in 1931: *Evening Graphic* ("Book Racket Under Vice Fire," 24 Jan.), *Herald Tribune* ("Book Case 'Fixer' Accused of Asking $2000 for Judge," 25 Jan.), *Evening Journal* ("Cite Simpson In Love Book Deal," 24 Jan., Sports Extra Ed.; "Probe $10,000 Simpson Case," 24 Jan., City Ed.). Clippings of all but the last two of these are on file in Box 412, Gertz. Only the *American* specifies a date of Simpson's decision: 21 Jan. 1926. However, both *PW* ("Frank Harris 'Life' Case," 17 Apr. 1926, 1334) and the *New York World* have stories in 1926 about the decision, and the advertisements of the Frank Harris Publishing Company, when Simpson legalized their expurgated edition. Both give the date as 1 April. The *World* for 2 April 1926 ("Frank Harris Book Not Obscene, Court Decides") states: "A salesman, arrested last January . . . was discharged in Tombs Court yesterday by Magistrate Simpson." Patrolman Louis Friedman is mentioned as having made the arrest. This article is preserved in the Fales Library, New York University, in a large scrapbook of clippings regarding Frank Harris kept by A. I. Tobin. The *World*'s three-star edition for 2 April 1926 carries the story on p. 3 under the headline "Court Holds Harris Book Is Not Obscene."

77. "Book Case Suspect Defiant," *New York World*, 25 Jan. 1931.

78. "Court Holds Harris Book Not Obscene," *New York World*, 2 April 1926, 3.

79. "Harris Book Expurgated," *New York World*, 3 April 1926, p. 3.

80. "Frank Harris 'Life' Case," *PW*, 17 April, 1926, 1334.

81. Levine mentions, and (in retrospect, or for Harris's satisfaction) regrets the inclusion of, this incident in a letter to Harris, 10 July [1926?] (Harris letters, HRC). Harris was annoyed because he saw that it hindered his plans to have the expurgate published in England. Levine's expurgated text retained the passage (pp. 153–54; pp. 152–53 in the unexpurgated edition) which described the cowhand Charlie's gentle but ineffective method of determining whether or not a "girl" was "ill," and the chancre which indicated that he had contracted syphilis. This was the single passage Simpson has ordered expurgated before he "passed" on the book. Rebhuhn expressed enthusiasm to Harris about the expurgation in a letter to Harris of 16 Sept., 1925, RA, stating that the advertisement for the book (and a planned expurage of volume 2) were to be headed, "the frankest and boldest book every written."

82. Sumner's ledgers for 1928 record the following regarding Rebhuhn: 6 Feb.: "11 E. 42nd St. Atheist. Books by mail. Moorish Harem. Vio Sec. 211, USCC. Bail $1500. 2 yrs prob. $150 fine." 4 Nov.: "505 5th Ave. bookdealers [Benjamin and David]. ind. books. US Vio 221. 24 books, 39 photos in album. 1 yr 6 mo."

83. "Two Publishers Get Prison Sentences," *NYT*, 14 June 1939, 8.

84. Ronald Rebhuhn, personal interview, 12 Aug. 1992.

85. Rinder, "Strangers in the Land," 257–58.

86. Leo Rosten, *The Joys of Yiddish* (New York: Washington Square, 1970), 388. See Moses Kligsberg, "Jewish Immigrants in Business: A Sociological Study," in *The Jewish Experience in America*, vol. 5, *At Home in America*, ed. Abraham J. Karp (Waltham, Mass.: American Jewish Historical Society, 1969), 254–60. See also Mark Zborowski and Elizabeth Herzog, *Life Is with People: The Culture of the Stetl* (1952; New York: Schocken, 1962), 409–11; James Yaffe, *The American Jews: Portrait of a Split Personality* (New York: Paperback Library, 1969), 252–57, 262; and Jacob Lestchinsky, "The Position of the Jews in the Economic Life of America," in *Jews in a Gentile World*, ed. Isacque Graeber and Steuart H. Britt (New York: Macmillan, 1942), 402–16. Another analysis of the Jewish character, discussing the solidarity of Jewish culture over the centuries as a result of "cultural hybridity" and resilience of the unique marginality they have internalized, is Everett V. Stonequist's "The Marginal Character of the Jews," in *Jews in a Gentile World*, ed. Graeber and Britt, 296–310. For other incisive comments on marginality, the emotional strains of living on the edge of both the majority culture and the ethnic value system, see Robert E. Park, *Race and Culture* (New York: Free Press, 1950), 352–56. The concept of marginality, stressing the anxiety of the minority individual as well as his or her unique skills and in-group support system, acts as a useful complement to the middleman minority theories. A review of these relevant to the Jewish experience is Walter P. Zenner, "Middleman Minority Theories and the Jews: Historical Survey and Assessment," Working Papers in Yiddish and East European Jewish Studies 31 (New York: YIVO Institute for Jewish Research, 1978).

87. Hamilton, "Pariah Capitalism," 2–3, 9–11.

88. Rinder, "Strangers in the Land," 256–57. In "Theory of Middleman Minorities" (589–92) and "Toward a Composite Theory of Middleman Minorities" (151–56), Bonacich states that the hostility of the majority population toward the ethnic middleman is not a matter of irrational ethnocentric response to difference, but to the facts of the success of the minority group, their monopoly of a particular area of endeavor, and their lack of charitable concern for those who, although long-time residents, find themselves less well-off. It is possible to sense in these statements an unintentional racism, perhaps because they imply that native entrepreneurial groups evince more fellow feeling for those less fortunate than do the ethnic middleman. See Zenner, "Middleman Minority Theories and the Jews," 17.

89. Joseph Brownell [Samuel Roth], ed., *The Telephone Directory as a Guide to American Culture* (New York: Coventry House, 1929), n.p.

90. "Seizure of Books Upheld," *NYT*, 18 July 1925, 8.

91. "Books Barred as Evidence," *NYT*, 24 July 1925, 2; "Court Denounces Harris' 'My Life,' " *NYT*, 21 Aug. 1925, 15; "Harris Book Denounced," *PW*, 5 Sept. 1925, 750.

92. "Use of Harris Book as Evidence Barred," *NYT*, 30 June 1925, 12.

93. Alexander Lindey to Clifton Read, 14 Apr. 1936, ACLU Archives, 878: 9–10. *Immortalia* is a collection of erotic anecdotes, now considered a classic compilation of American humor and folklore.

94. Undated memo headed "The National Council for Freedom from Censorship," bound vol. 394, MLE Papers.

95. Alexander Lindey, "The Bad Book Bill" (letter to the editor), *Bowling Green*, 18 July 1936, 9–10. Clipping preserved in the ACLU Archives, vol. 878. See also National Council for Freedom from Censorship, *Brief in Support* [of the 1929–30 Post Bill], ACLU Archives, 503: 221; "Albany Hearing on Censorship," *PW*, 22 Feb. 1930, 983–94. Correspondence regarding the 1936 Bad Books Bill exists in the ACLU Archives, 878: 9–10.

96. Nan Britton, *Honesty or Politics* (New York: Elizabeth Ann Guild, 1932), 105–10, 122–25, 145–46.

97. Britton, *Honesty or Politics*, 152, 153, 243–45, 257–58, 276.

98. New York Society for the Suppression of Vice, *Annual Report* (1928), 12.

99. J. Owens Smith, *The Politics of Racial Inequality* (Westport, Conn.: Greenwood, 1987), 50–54, 68–71; Nathan Glazer and D. P. Moynihan, *Beyond the Melting Pot: The Negroes, Puerto Ricans, Jews, Italians, and Irish of New York City*, 2d ed. (Cambridge, Mass.: MIT Press, 1970), 217–38; Kessner, *The Golden Door*, 62–64.

100. Bonacich, "A Theory of Middlemen Minorities," 591.

101. John Higham, "Social Discrimination Against Jews in America, 1830–1930," in *At Home in America*, ed. Karp, 356–64.

102. Gerald M. Lacy, *D. H. Lawrence: Letters to Thomas and Adele Seltzer* (Santa Barbara, Calif.: Black Sparrow, 1976), 254.

103. Howard M. Sachar, *A History of the Jews in America* (New York: Vintage, 1992), 408–20.

104. See Hannah Arendt, *The Jew as Pariah: Jewish Identity and Politics in the Modern Age*, ed. Ron H. Feldman (New York: Grove, 1968), 18–19, 67–69. Arendt uses the term "conscious pariah" to reflect the radical independence of the few Jewish intellectuals who, shunning the parvenu values, avoid identifying themselves with moral conventions and economic strategies that ensure material status.

Chapter 2. "Sex O'Clock in America"

1. Leopold von Weise, *Systematic Sociology: On the Basis of the* Beziehungslehre *and* Gebildelehre, adapted and amplified by Howard Becker (1932; rpt., New York: Arno, 1974), 340. See also Becker, *Man in Reciprocity* (New York: Praeger, 1956), 215–17.

2. Harry Schwartz, *Fifty Years in My Bookstore, or A Life with Books* (Milwaukee, Wisc.: n.p., 1977), 50–51.

3. Leslie Fishbein, *Rebels in Bohemia: The Radicals of* The Masses, *1911–1917* (Chapel Hill: University of North Carolina Press, 1982), 74. Fishbein attributes the phrase to the journalist William Marion Reedy (1862–1920).

4. John D'Emilio and Estelle Freedman, *Intimate Matters: A History of Sexuality in America* (New York: Harper and Row, 1988), 172–73, 181–85, 195–99, 277–84; Kevin

White, *The First Sexual Revolution: The Emergence of Male Heterosexuality in Modern America* (New York: New York University Press, 1993), 57–79.

5. Fishbein, *Rebels in Bohemia*, chap. 5. Rochelle Gurstein's *The Repeal of Reticence: A History of America's Cultural and Legal Struggles over Free Speech, Obscenity, Sexual Liberation, and Modern Art* (New York: Hill and Wang, 1996) reviews challenges to obscenity law as an example of erosion of the concept of civility. She finds the belief in silence about sexual matters to be rooted in the conviction that private feelings about bodily functions should not be brought into rational, public discourse. Not to feel shame is to replace a high level of civilization with a narcissistic one.

6. Paul Boyer, *Purity in Print: The Vice-Society Movement and Book Censorship in America* (New York: Scribner's, 1968), 66–72.

7. [Federal Writers' Project, N.Y.], *New York City Guide* (1939; rpt., New York: Octagon, 1970), 167, 171.

8. New York Society for the Suppression of Vice (NYSSV), *Annual Report* (1937), 10–11. The annual reports are pamphlets printed by the society. The Research Libraries of the New York Public Library hold a complete run.

9. "Book Censorship by Licenses Urged," *NYT*, 14 Feb. 1933, 21.

10. "Broadway Filth Fought by Priest," *NYT*, 12 Feb. 1934, 17.

11. Richard Maltby, " 'To Prevent the Prevalent Type of Book': Censorship and Adaptation in Hollywood, 1924–34," *American Quarterly* 44.4 (Dec. 1992): 557.

12. D'Emilio and Freedman, *Intimate Matters*, 280–82; Francis G. Couvares, "Hollywood, Main St., and the Church: Trying to Censor the Movies Before the Production Code," *American Quarterly* 44.4 (Dec. 1992): 584–615.

13. Paul W. Facey, *The Legion of Decency: A Sociological Analysis of the Emergence and Development of a Social Pressure Group* (New York: Arno, 1974), 34–37, 77–85; Gregory D. Black, *Hollywood Censored: Morality Codes, Catholics, and the Movies* (Cambridge: Cambridge University Press, 1994), 149–50, 184–92.

14. John F. Noll, *Manual of the N[ational] O[rganization for] D[ecent] L[iterature]* ([Huntington, Ind.: Our Sunday Visitor], n.d.), 42–45.

15. Frederick Allen, *Since Yesterday* (New York: Bantam, 1965), 105–10; D'Emilio and Freedman, *Intimate Matters*, 239–74; Lewis Erenberg, *Steppin Out: New York Nightlife and the Transformation of American Culture* (Westport, Conn.: Greenwood, 1981), 237–38, 258–59.

16. D'Emilio and Freedman, *Intimate Matters*, 239–48, 256–71.

17. Emanuel Haldeman-Julius, *The First Hundred Million* (New York: Simon and Schuster, 1928), 290–304.

18. Walker Gilmer, *Horace Liveright: Publisher of the Twenties* (New York: David Lewis, 1970), 62–63.

19. Frank Harris to Benjamin Rebhuhn, 10 Oct. and 30 Nov. 1923; Esar Levine to Rebhuhn, 8 Oct. 1926; Harris to Rebhuhn, 9 Oct. 1926, RA; "Probe $10,000 Simpson Case," *New York Evening Journal*, 24 Jan. 1931, city ed., 2.

20. D. H. Lawrence, *A Propos of Lady Chatterley's Lover* (London: Mandrake, 1930), 5–7.

21. The offices of bookseller Ivan Stormgart of San Francisco kindly sent me two of Marks's catalogs. The order form of one is dated 1923.

22. John Tebbel, *A History of Book Publishing in the United States* (New York: Bowker, 1978), 3: 502–3.

23. Thomas Cochran, *The Great Depression and World War II, 1929–1945* (New York: Scott Foresman, 1968), 2.

24. KI Files contain copies of several catalogs of erotica issued by Abramson from the Argus Book Shop in Chicago. There are also a few letters and invoices for the notorious banned books of the era, apparently mailed to trusted clients.

25. Several catalogs of the Anthropological Library are in the KI Files.

26. "Erotica Dealer Blames Sumner," *New York Evening Post*, 6 July 1934, JA Files.

27. The MLE Papers (bound vol. 87) contain mailing lists, brochures, briefs, and news clippings regarding Esar and Benjamin Levine's 1931 and 1935 prosecutions for distributing obscenity through the mails.

28. Brochures in KI Files show the reductions ("price slash"; "seasonal discount") rubber-stamped; sometimes as many as three reductions are stamped on the same circular, one over the other.

C. J. Scheiner (personal interview, 14 Nov. 1991) spoke with Esar Levine of the Panurge Press several times c. 1978–82 and learned that after the initial sale, remaining books were discounted severely.

29. Tebbel, *A History of Book Publishing*, 3: 427–40.

30. Tebbel, *A History of Book Publishing*, 3: 458–59.

31. Tebbel, *A History of Book Publishing*, 3: 209–10.

32. Alexander Lindey to Morris L. Ernst, 17 May 1933, file 388, MLE Papers. Advertisements in *PW* (for example, the two-page spread in the 30 Apr. 1932 issue, 1855–56) bragged that "the general public can and does dig up money to buy these books." The Rarity Press published this set of erotic classics in the late 1920s; their imprint appears on title pages as late as 1930. The Godwin versions were later impressions, identical in format and binding style. Rarity either sold the copyrights or merged with Godwin.

33. Alan Devoe, "Erotic Books and the Depression," *PW*, 5 Aug. 1933, 344.

34. Devoe, "Erotic Books," 344.

35. Chester A. Battles (postal inspector) to Lamar Hardy (U.S. attorney), 13 Aug. 1938, U.S. Dept. of Justice, Central Files, file 33 S 251-1, NA.

36. The press's proprietor, Maurice A. Fryefield, had hired a "mail-order specialist," Sidney Abelson, who devised the circular, which cost him his job when the Post Office acted on several complaints from organizations whose sense of decency was offended. (The New England Watch and Ward had sent a decoy letter to receive the books.) Abelson was arrested by John Sumner of the NYSSV when he raided the Dingwall-Rock offices in 1930 to seize *One Hundred Merrie and Delightsome Stories* (Battles to Hardy, 9 Sept. 1938).

37. NYSSV, *Annual Report* (1933), 10.

38. Bob [Robert Carlton] Brown, *Gems: A Censored Anthology* (Cagnes-sur-Mer: Roving Eye, 1931), 18–19.

39. Mr. Porter's statement is in a questionnaire returned to the present author, 29 Sept. 1991. Mr. Biblo's was made during a personal interview on 8 Dec. 1991. The author is grateful to both gentlemen for their helpfulness, and to Bernard Conwell Carlitz, antiquarian bookseller in Philadelphia for many years, who was interviewed on 15 July 1992.

40. "Bonserk Theater Corporation v. Paul Moss, as Commissioner of Licenses," in file 391, MLE Papers. See Morris Ernst and Alexander Lindey, *The Censor Marches On* (1940; New York: Da Capo, 1971), 67–68.

41. Gershon Legman, *The Horn Book: Studies in Erotic Folklore and Bibliography* (New Hyde Park, N.Y.: University Books, 1964), 12.

42. Charles H. Bodwell to Lillian Block, 6 Mar. 1930, Paige box 2, WW Papers.

43. The WW Papers, in Paige box 2, contain two such lists, one fourteen typed pages and dated 1931, the other sixteen typed pages and dated 1934, with annotations regarding contents, publishers, booksellers, and prosecutions. They were "for the use of mature persons, trying to restrict or abolish erotic or crime literature at the sources of publication, distribution and sale." "Protested" means cited as, not adjudicated to be, obscene.

44. Correspondence between Sumner, Pringle, Bodwell, and Yarrow of the Illinois Vigilance Association reflect this stubbornness. See, for example, Yarrow to Bodwell, 8 Feb. 1930, re Robie's *The Art of Love* (Paige box 1, WW Papers); Bodwell to Yarrow, 1934 (otherwise undated), re Louÿs's *Woman and Puppet* (Paige box 2, folder I-1934, WW Papers). In a 13 May 1931 letter to Bodwell (Paige box 4, WW Papers), Sumner writes that of all the "borderline books" in a mail-order catalog of the Union Library, *Woman and Puppet* is "the worst of the lot." He recommends Post Office prosecution.

45. For a survey of contemporary fiction and nonfiction subject to censorship in the 1920s, see Irene Cleaton and Allen Cleaton, *Books and Battles: American Literature, 1920–30* (Boston: Houghton Mifflin, 1937), chap. 3.

46. Peter Gay, *The Bourgeois Experience, Victoria to Freud: Education of the Senses* (Oxford: Oxford University Press, 1984), 366–67.

47. These and others are among the 754 items listed in *First Editions, Press Books and Finely Illustrated Editions: The Property of the Artist Miss Clara Tice Including Selections from the Library of Mr. William Stanley Hall with a Few Additions* (cover title; auction catalog) (New York: American Art Association, 1929).

48. Lindey to Ernst, 17 May 1933.

49. G. Thomas Tanselle, "The Thomas Seltzer Imprint," *Papers of the Bibliographical Society of America* 58 (1964): 396; "Censorship Beaten in New York Court," *PW*, 16 Sept. 1922, 802.

50. Henry S. Canby, *Definitions*, 2d series (New York: Harcourt Brace, 1924), 108.

51. Esar Levine to Nellie Harris, 6 June 1930[?], box 1, Harris-Ross.

52. The letter, in file 388, MLE Papers, is signed W. J. Kelleher. It gives the address of

Art Studio Books as 15 West 44th Street, New York City. A memo from Lindey to Ernst, 19 July 1930, notes that the Art Studio is "undoubtedly one of the disseminators of expensive erotica."

53. See "Seize Obscenities Worth $70,000," *New York Evening Sun*, 10 Apr. 1934, JA Files. The article names two brothers, Vincent T. and Joseph Smith, and a wholesale distributor from Philadelphia, Max Montgomery. The brothers were arrested at the offices of Art Studio Books and the Treat 'Em Square Publishing Company, 24 Water Street. Titles found on the premises included *Randiana*, *Crimson Hairs*, and *Anecdota Americana*, vol. 2. Four hundred bronze plates, from which illustrations could have been made, were taken. The plates were made by the Loewinger brothers, printers of Roth's pirated *Ulysses*, who were also arrested at their place of business. Sumner's ledgers note that the books taken included the rare *My Secret Life*, and record Vincent T. Smith's sentence as sixty days in the workhouse, sentence suspended. C. J. Scheiner thinks that Martin Kamin and mail-order distributor Alex Field were involved in Art Studio Books' plans to distribute these titles.

54. Grete Meisel-Heiss, *The Sexual Crisis: A Critique of Our Sex Life*, trans. Eden Paul and Cedar Paul, 4th ed. (New York: Eugenics, 1933), 27.

55. Brown, *Gems*, 22.

56. Tebbel, *A History of Book Publishing*, 3: 573–74.

57. Ibid., 3: 580.

58. Groff Conklin, "Results of a Survey of Manhattan Rental Libraries," pt. 1, *PW*, 27 May 1933, 1686–88; *How to Run a Rental Library* (New York: Bowker, 1934), 119–27. Conklin stated that the office library system developed "in recent years"; the earliest instance he found dated from 1914.

59. Gershon Legman, "Sex Censorship in the U.S.A.," *PLAN: Organization of the British Progressive League* (London) 2.1 (Jan. 1945): 3.

60. Geoffrey Perrett, *America in the Twenties: A History* (New York: Simon and Schuster, 1983), 156, 323.

61. Curl's and the Wartels' associations with Godwin are noted in Sumner's ledgers (1933, 1935). For Hillman's and Curl's affiliations with Arcadia House, see Peter Dzwonkowsky, ed., *American Literary Publishing Houses, 1900–1980: Trade and Paperback* (Detroit, Mich.: Gale Research, 1986), 15. Hillman was investigated by the FBI in 1939, due to the detective magazines he published. His dossier reveals he served as manager of Rarity Press; resigned and founded William Godwin Inc. in 1931; continued to act as president and treasurer of this corporation in 1939; and incorporated Hillman Curl in Apr. 1935 (FBI Investigative Report, 5 Sept. 1939, U.S. Dept. of Justice, Central Files, file 97-51-20, NA).

62. Hendrik W. Van Loon, "Uplift Journals Please Copy!" *Commonweal*, 31 Dec. 1924, 202–3; Ernest W. Mandeville, "Gutter Literature," *New Republic* 17 Feb. 1926, 350–52.

63. Noll, *Manual of the NODL*, 207.

64. "Publishers' Output in 1937," *PW*, 15 Jan. 1938, 208–9.

65. *PW*, 24 Mar. 1934, 1196.

66. George Orwell, *Keep the Aspidistra Flying* (1936; New York: Harcourt Brace Jovanovich, n.d.), 202.

67. Ibid., 18.

68. Ibid., 227.

69. Legman, *The Horn Book*, 30–34; H. Montgomery Hyde, *A History of Pornography* (New York: Dell, 1966), 188–90; Peter Mendes, *Clandestine Erotic Fiction in English, 1800–1930: A Bibliographical Study* (Aldershot: Scolar, 1993), 31–40, 463–65; Rod Boroughs, "Oscar Wilde's Translation of Petronius: The Story of a Literary Hoax," *English Literature in Transition* 38.1 (1995): 13–17. An interesting essay, partly fictional, is "Richard Manton" [Francis Selwyn], "Charles Carrington: The Man and His Books," in *A Victorian Sampler*, ed. Manton (New York: Blue Moon, 1992), 1–24.

70. Peter Fryer, *Secrets of the British Museum* (New York: Citadel, 1966), 60–66. As I discuss in Chapter 5, chief American distributors of these books, besides Panurge and Falstaff, were the Eugenics Publishing Company, the American Ethnological Press, Dingwall-Rock Ltd., and the American Anthropological Society.

71. Paul Blanchard, *American Freedom and Catholic Power* (Boston: Beacon, 1950), 167.

72. James J. Kirkpatrick, *The Smut Peddlers* (New York: Avon, 1960), 148–51.

73. Henry H. Huntington of the International Nudist Conference wrote to Charles Bodwell (21 Sept. 1933, Paige box 1, WW Papers) regarding his possible condoning of newsstand sale of *The Nudist* magazine. Bodwell replied (22 Nov.) that he would bring the matter before his board of directors and that he did distinguish such publications from "many serious matters" the society felt required interdiction.

74. Ilsley Boone to Charles Bodwell, 27 Jan. 1934, Paige box 1, WW Papers; Bodwell to John Sumner, 27 Jan. 1934, Paige box 3.

75. Sumner to Bodwell, 29 Jan. 1934, Paige box 3, WW Papers.

76. NYSSV, *Annual Report* (1933), 12; Sumner to Bodwell, 29 Jan. 1934; "Sumner Averse to Nudist Book, But Not the Cult," *New York Herald Tribune*, 12 Nov. 1932 (clipping preserved in file 388, MLE Papers).

77. NYSSV, *Annual Report* (1938), 10; (1939), 11–12.

78. "Druggist Bookseller Arrested," *PW*, 21 Oct. 1933, 1429.

79. This information was given to me by C. J. Scheiner, who has spoken with several of the publishers and booksellers of the interwar period. During the 1970s, he was able to locate more of them than I have been able to since.

80. These catalogs are in the KI Files.

81. Gargoyle applied for copyright to *[The?] Strap Returns: New Notes on Flagellation*, giving their address as 69 Fifth Avenue. The person paying the fee was Samuel Wegman; the book's editor was listed as Sidney Frank.

82. Legman, "Sex Censorship," 5.

83. Eric Dingwall, *Very Peculiar People* (London: Rider and Co., n.d.), 132–42.

84. Courtney Ryley Cooper, *Designs in Scarlet* (Boston: Little, Brown, 1939), 241.

This book is a hysterical and often racist diatribe intended to show that juvenile delinquency, theft, prostitution, and other social evils are the result of a single evil force: the purveying of cheap amusements to common people. The evil can be eradicated by modesty in women, discipline within the family, restriction of sex to the marriage bed, and stricter law enforcement. To her credit, however, the writer had access to Post Office records and conducted interviews with postal inspectors, resulting in a compilation of evidence not elsewhere recorded. A revised and (posthumously?) edited version of the book, *Teen-Age Vice!*, was published by Pyramid Books in 1952. The blurb about the author states that "FBI Director J. Edgar Hoover inspired [Cooper] to dramatize the truth about our shocking vice problem." Pyramid records six impressions of the Little, Brown edition of *Designs in Scarlet* between 1939 and 1941.

85. Havelock Ellis, "Love and Pain," in *Studies in the Psychology of Sex* (1942), 1: 131, quoted in Ian Gibson, *The English Vice: Beating, Sex and Shame in Victorian England and After* (London: Duckworth, 1978), 45.

86. NYSSV, *Annual Report* (1937), 12.

87. Memorandum dated 19 Jan. 1932, Paige box 2, WW Papers.

88. The publisher was Louis Shomer, president of the American Ethnological Press.

89. C. J. Scheiner is the main source for this information, obtained in a personal interview with him on 5 June 1987. Some of this was corroborated by Richard (now deceased) and Adelaide Roth (Samuel Roth's son and daughter) in a personal interview on 3 July 1987, by Allan Wilson in a questionnaire returned 27 July 1987, and by Tony Gud, who published with Roth in the 1930s, in a questionnaire returned to me on 7 July 1987.

90. Douglas H. Gamlin, ed. *The Tijuana Bible Reader* (San Diego, Calif.: Greenleaf, 1969), 1–2, 9–10; Joseph W. Slade, "Pornography," in *Handbook of American Popular Culture*, rev. ed. (Westport, Conn.: Greenwood, 1989), 2: 967–68. "Special Catalogues," nos. 2 and 3, issued by Ivan Stormgart of San Francisco in 1992, contain several examples of the genre, informatively annotated by Patrick Kearney, bibliographer of Maurice Girodias's Olympia Press and author of *A History of Erotic Literature* (London: Macmillan, 1982). I am indebted to the bookseller Chris Eckhoff of Brooklyn, N.Y., for showing me varied examples of these readers.

91. C. J. Scheiner has seen many of these booklets and has a store of information regarding them, some of which he shared with me in a personal interview on 3 June 1987. In his introduction to Patrick Kearney's *Private Case* (London: Landesman, 1981), Gershon Legman attributes to Gene Fowler certain pornographic novels, which he and other Hollywood-based writers penned for about a dollar a page (53).

92. R. G. Holt, *Little "Dirty" Comics* (San Diego, Calif.: Socio Library, 1971), 11–35.

93. Cooper, *Designs in Scarlet*, 237.

94. Bob Adelman, *Tijuana Bibles: Art and Wit in America's Forbidden Funnies, 1930–1950s* (New York: Simon and Schuster, 1997), [2], 5; Holt, *Little "Dirty" Comics*, 35.

95. Bernard Wolfe, *Memoirs of a Not Altogether Shy Pornographer* (New York: Doubleday, 1972), 19.

96. The term is used frequently in his 1931 and 1934 lists of protested books.

97. "Protested Books, 1931," [1].

98. See memos headed "To Collectors of Customs, Appraisers and Other Officials Concerned," 16 Apr. 1929 (2 pp.) and "To Customs Officers," 27 Aug. 1928 (9 pp.), ACLU Archives, 503: 50–60. There were 379 titles in Spanish, 231 in French, and 114 in English (Max Bogart, "A Study of Certain Legally Banned Novels in the United States, 1900–1950" [Ph.D. diss., New York University, 1956], 247). Paul Boyer (*Purity in Print*, 210) states that Customs and the Post Office composed a "blacklist" of some seven hundred works in Aug. 1928. James Paul and Murray Schwartz (*Federal Censorship: Obscenity in the Mail* [Glencoe, Ill.: Free Press of Glencoe, 1961], 43) refer to a 1929 list, never published and now "lost," and state that neither Post Office nor Customs officials would "disclose to the public, even upon request, the titles of the books they have banned."

99. Cutting obtained a copy through the Committee on Military Affairs, of which he was a member (ACLU Archives, 503: 50).

100. A. B. Shiffrin, *Mr. Pirate: A Romance* (New York: Mitchell Kennerley, 1937), 25–26, refers to "a high, dim den where the proprietor found it convenient to snatch an occasional nap or to conceal an equally occasional piece of incunabula or otherwise rare item, erotic or Elizabethan."

101. Stated by Mrs. Lorraine Wilbur of Gramercy Book Shop, Union Square, during a personal interview on 21 July 1993. Mrs. Wilbur clerked in various bookshops, including that of Joseph Kling in Greenwich Village, during the period.

102. Gerald R. Scott, "Some Nudity Becomes Art to the 20-Year Vice Foe," *New York Mirror*, 3 Feb. 1935, Sunday magazine section, 6, JA Files. These books, if thirty thousand words, may be readers of ninety-six, as opposed to thirty-two, pages, or even twice as long, depending on the number of words on the page. C. J. Scheiner, the most knowledgeable scholar in this field, has seen some pornographic works consisting of single thirty-two-page gatherings bound in soft covers. He has seen very few soft covers of 100 to 150 pages from the interwar period (e-mail to the author, 26 Nov. 1996).

103. In describing for reporters the books and photographs taken at one warehouse, Sumner stated that the books were sold at one or two dollars and the pictures for twenty-five cents. "Obscene Literature Checked: Three Held in Raids of Sixth Avenue Bookshops" *New York American*, 9 Mar. 1937, JA Files.

104. Sumner to Bodwell, 19 and 24 July 1933, Paige box 3, WW Papers. The 24 July letter mentions books of both 32 and 196 pages.

105. "Obscene Library Raided by Police," *NYT*, 28 Mar. 1936, 3.

106. "Obscene Literature Checked."

107. Sumner to Bodwell, 30 Mar. 1936, Paige box 3, WW Papers; Ledgers, 1937: "books, booklets, cartoons, playing cards . . . about 1500 unbound printed sheets." One of those arrested was "salesman and publisher" Andrew Zinns. One book is mentioned: *Forbidden Passion*.

108. Sumner to Bodwell, 30 June 1934, Paige box 3, WW Papers.

328 ☞ Notes to Pages 83–87

109. Bodwell to Henry Pringle, 17 Apr. 1936, Paige box 2, WW Papers.

110. "Seize Obscenities Worth $70,000."

111. Cooper, *Designs in Scarlet*, 235, 237, 248.

112. Names of those arrested include Robert Fairberg, Joseph and Andrew Zinns, Benjamin Reisberg, Jack Brotman, Joseph Levine. One such raid was recorded in Sumner's ledgers for 1936.

113. Sumner to Bodwell, 30 June 1934, Paige box 3(?), WW Papers.

114. Sumner to Bodwell, 24 July 1933, Paige box 3(?), WW Papers.

115. See Cooper, *Designs in Scarlet*, 232, 235–36, 248–49. C. J. Scheiner corroborated the information in Cooper, and added the fire brigades and fraternal organizations (personal interview, 24 July 1992).

116. George E. Worthington [secretary of the Committee of Fourteen] to John S. Sumner, 19 May 1931; Sumner to Worthington, 20 May 1931, Committee of Fourteen Archives, box 14, New York Public Library, MS Division, New York, N.Y.; "Sumner Averse to Nudist Book."

117. C. J. Scheiner, Introduction to *White Stains* by Anaïs Nin and Friends (London: Delectus, 1995), iii–xi. C. J. Scheiner is a physician, collector, author, and antiquarian bookseller specializing in erotica, curiosa, and sexology. He is also a professor of erotology and sexology at the McIlvenna Institute for the Advanced Study of Human Sexuality in San Francisco. He used interviews and letters as well as printed sources and an intimate knowledge of the New York book trade in his research.

118. Legman, introduction to *The Private Case*, 53.

119. Ibid., 53–55. Legman says that the stories written for the Oklahoma collector, not by Henry Miller but by another group of writers, including Nin, were later published as *Sexus*, attributed to Miller.

120. Wolfe, *Memoirs of a Not Altogether Shy Pornographer*, 281–85.

121. See Scheiner, introduction to *White Stains*, viii, for a list of fifteen names.

122. Jacob Loft, *The Printing Trades* (New York: Farrar and Rhinehart, 1944), 61–63.

123. Sources for this are C. J. Scheiner, interview of 24 July 1992, and Gershon Legman, interview of 17 June 1990.

124. The author is grateful to Mary Ann Malkin of New York City for suggesting this possibility (interview of 6 Mar. 1992).

125. "Obscene Library Raided."

126. "Obscene Library Raided" states that the Police Confidential Squad prepared for the raid. "Obscene Literature Checked" indicates that undercover work was done by a member of the Illinois Vigilance Association.

127. Benjamin Rebhuhn to Frank Harris, 27 Mar. 1926, RA.

128. See especially the NYSSV ledgers for 1905.

129. Recorded in the ledgers for 1931, 1934, and 1935. The annual report for 1937 mentions the American Legion Convention.

130. Diana Rice, "Literary Booklegging," *NYT*, 6 Aug. 1922, Book Review section, 1, 24.

131. Louis Sobol, "A Slap at Some Books," *New York Journal American*, 25 Feb. 1956, JA Files.

132. The Cabanes is listed by Art Studio Books, New York City, in the 8 Mar. 1930 issue; the Harris, by Austin Book Company, also of New York, 5 July 1930. When *AB Bookman's Weekly* was conceived in 1949 to relieve *Publishers Weekly* of the chore of making these listings, Solomon Malkin was chosen as editor. Malkin's comprehensive knowledge of the book trade included awareness of each such code word, for he had been a clerk in Jack Brussel's Ortelius Book Shop ("More Books Seized by Sumner in Raid," *NYT*, 27 June 1928, 26; "Sumner Drive Traps Five as Obscene Book Dealers," undated newspaper clipping, file 391, MLE Papers). He was also a colleague of many Fourth Avenue booksellers, and a translator for the leading mail-order erotica firms in the 1930s. I am indebted to the late Mr. Malkin's widow, Mary Ann Malkin, for information regarding her husband. See also Jacob L. Chernofsky, "*AB Bookman's Weekly*: The First 50 Years," *AB Bookman's Weekly*, 5 Jan. 1998, 14. Esar Levine's advertisements appeared in the 16 and 23 June and 21 July 1928 issues of *PW*.

133. "Harry Marks, 78, Dealer in Books," *NYT*, 23 Aug. 1958, JA Files. In 1938, the Harry F. Marks Galleries and Bookshop moved to 280 Park Avenue. The 1935 *Directory of Booksellers in the United States* lists Marks's address as Rockefeller Center. The 1925 edition places him at 31 West 47th Street.

134. Hugh Ford, *Published in Paris* (1975; New York: Pushcart, 1981), 28, 85; Harry T. Moore, ed. *The Collected Letters of D. H. Lawrence* (New York: Viking, 1962), 2: 1104.

135. "Prosecutor Raids a Philadelphia Book Store" (Townsend's), *NYT*, 25 Jan. 1930, 1. The information about erotica being available at the famous five-story Leary's in midtown Philadelphia comes from interviews conducted by C. J. Scheiner.

136. The Dunster House proprietor was entrapped by Watch and Ward agents into selling them copies of *Lady Chatterley's Lover*; the trial and its appeal (*Commonwealth v. Delacey*, 271 Mass 327, N.E. 455 [1930]), resulted in the fining of the owner. See Tebbel, *A History of Book Publishing*, 3: 407, 420. For the variety of "private stock" at Dunster House, see Francis Russell, "Arty Crafty and the Beginnings of the Joyce Cult at Harvard," in *The Great Interlude: Neglected Events and Persons from the First World War to the Depression* (New York: McGraw-Hill, 1964), 160–61. Russell names the store he describes as the Kelmscott, but the location given, off Harvard Square at the edge of the campus, is that of Dunster House.

137. Legman, introduction to *The Private Case*, 55; D. B. Covington, *The Argus Book Shop: A Memoir* (West Cornwall, Conn.: Tarrydiddle, 1977), 48–50; Tebbel, *A History of Book Publishing*, 3: 408–11; C. J. Scheiner, personal interview, 24 July 1992.

138. Schwartz, *Fifty Years in My Bookstore*, xv–xvi, 34–51, 92–95. The 1891 ledgers

of the NYSSV, compiled by Anthony Comstock, describe Caspar as "an old and sly offender. Said to have received his [erotic] pictures from Rome, Italy."

139. Michael Squires, *D. H. Lawrence's Manuscripts: The Correspondence of Frieda Lawrence, Jake Zeitlin and Others* (New York: St. Martin's, 1991), 161, 168, 173.

140. The MLE Papers contain correspondence dated December 1929 between Greenbaum, Wolff, and Ernst and Charles Katz, attorney for the Satyr Book Shop. Covici-Friede had accused the bookshop of selling pirated copies of March's *Wild Party*. N. M. Gordon, the proprietor, sent one hundred copies to the Argus Book Shop in Chicago and sold fifty more to individual customers.

141. Some specific stores Sumner raided (not necessarily resulting in convictions), date and owner/manager listed in parentheses: Abbey, 61 East 8th (1933, Nathaniel Kaplan); Alladin, 45 East 17th (1928, Henry Klein); Book Auction, 28 East 12th (1928, Samuel Roth); Chelsea, 365 West 15th (1926, Alfred Fisher); Gerhardt's, 25 West 42nd (1925 and 1930, Christian Gerhardt); Golden Hind, 41 West 46th (1934, Samuel Roth); Inman's, 47 East 44th (1923, Maurice Inman and Max Gottschalk); International(?) Book and Art Shop, 3 Christopher (1926, Joseph Kling); Knickerbocker, 124 West 45th (1929, Max Gottschalk); Ortelius, 134 East 8th (1928, Jake Brussel); Reingold's, 42 Broadway (1920, Jacob Reingold); Renaissance, 131 West 23rd (Eugene Nussbaum, Alfred Nussbaum, and Alexander Costelito); Schulte's, 80 Fourth Ave. (1929, Thomas Schulte). Joseph Kling's was one of the most important literary book shops in Greenwich Village; he was a poet and novelist, and editor of the avant-garde magazine *The Pagan*. Sumner discovered he was selling copies of *My Life*.

142. Lamar Hardy (U.S. attorney) to attorney general Robert H. Jackson, 6 Jan. 1937, U.S. Dept. of Justice, Central Files, file 97-51-44, NA. Hardy requested $7.40, which suggests that the agent purchased not Roth's privately printed edition of the *Ananga Ranga* but books that carried his Black Hawk imprint: Havelock Ellis's *Kanga Creek*, Norman Davey's *Passion Before Death*, or Rhys Davies's *Bed of Feathers*. In 1929, the coowner of Schulte's, Philip Pesky, was arrested for intending to sell Schnitzler's *Hands Around* (Felice Flannery Lewis, *Literature, Obscenity, and Law* [Carbondale: Southern Illinois University Press, 1976], 81). For Pesky, see Manuel B. Tarshish, "The 'Fourth Avenue' Book Trade," pt. 2, *PW*, 27 Oct. 1969, 51.

143. Roth himself discovered that Brentano's, although it did stock his bowdlerized version of *Lady Chatterley's Lover*, would warn off prospective purchasers. Samuel Roth, "By Way of Explanation," in *Lady Chatterley's Lover: A Dramatization*. Ardent Classics 2 (New York: Faro, 1931), 8–9.

144. Tebbel, *A History of Book Publishing*, 3: 109–10, 440.

145. "Sumner Loses Damage Suit," *PW*, 18 Apr. 1936, 1608.

146. Rarity's advertisements in *PW* appeared on 30 Apr. 1932.

147. For Joseph Meyers's Illustrated Editions, see Kenneth C. Davis, *Two Bit Culture: The Paperbacking of America* (Boston: Houghton Mifflin, 1984), 48; for the Three Sirens Press, see Tebbel, *A History of Book Publishing*, 3: 463.

148. Simon and Schuster, three-page list of "Stores Who Purchased *Casanova's Homecoming*," n.d. (part of a response to an 11 Aug. 1930 request of Greenbaum, Wolff, and Ernst for documentation in preparing a defense of the firm against charges brought by Sumner), file 386, MLE Papers.

149. *People v. Irving Plotkin, Memorandum by American Civil Liberties Union*, Amicus Curiae, 20 Jan. 1934, 4, file 389, MLE Papers. Sumner wrote about his victory in this case to Charles H. Bodwell, 24 June 1934, stating that the man he had convicted was Moe Berg, not Plotkin. Plotkin also ran a lending library.

150. NYSSV, *Annual Report* (1939), 10.

151. NYSSV, *Annual Report* (1937), 13.

152. "11,744 New Magazines Seized as Indecent," *NYT*, 10 Oct. 1934, 24.

153. These are in the KI Files, s.v. "Erotica Dealers, Twentieth-Century." The Esoterika Biblion Society takes its name from the Erotika Biblion Society, founded in 1889 in England by Leonard Smithers and H. S. Nichols to publish gallant and pornographic books.

154. This information was supplied to the present writer by C. J. Scheiner, who has spoken with the coowner of Radio City Books, Sy Gaynor. The 1935 edition of the *American Booktrade Directory* lists this concern (1227 Sixth Avenue) as specializing in old and rare books. Its proprietor was Max Feingold. Gargoyle Press advertisements appeared in many pulp magazines in the 1930s, for example *All Star Fiction*, May 1935, 126.

155. NYSSV, *Annual Report* (1931), 13; (1932), 9; " 'Bad Books' Scanned by Geoghan and Police," *Brooklyn Eagle*, 1 March [?], 1933 (misdated by clipping service), ACLU Archives, 503: 64.

156. NYSSV, *Annual Report* (1932), 9.

157. Conklin, *How to Run a Rental Library*, 17–23.

158. Conklin, "Results of a Survey of Manhattan Rental Libraries," 1688; *How to Run a Rental Library*, 115.

159. See NYSSV, *Annual Report* (1931), 13. Sumner wrote, "Two of the prosecutions involving books related to the loan of such books in drug stores having loan libraries at 25 cents to $1.00 per day. In one instance the book business was carried on independently and in the other the druggist and his clerk were the offenders."

160. O. H. Cheyney, *Economic Survey of the Book Industry, 1930–31* (1931; New York: Bowker, 1965), 295–96.

161. Conklin, "Results of a Survey," 1688.

162. President of the American Civil League to Franklin D. Roosevelt, 1 Aug. 1936, U.S. Dept. of Justice, Central Files, file 97-0, NA.

163. Francis X. Talbot, S.J., "More on Smut," *America*, 25 Feb. 1933, 500–501.

164. He may have meant the Rarity Press reprints or similar books, and older privately printed editions, which would have been for sale, not for rent. The older editions, with their limitation statements that specified an audience of mature collectors, would have been purchased as remainders by the libraries.

165. Ellis Parker Butler, *Dollarature or the Drug Store Book* (Boston: Houghton Mifflin, 1930), 22.

166. Butler, *Dollarature*, 4–9, 22.

167. Groff Conklin, "Suggestions for the Ideal Circulating Library System," *PW*, 17 Feb. 1934, 757–61; Conklin, *How to Run a Rental Library*, 39–41. Some extant copies, with lending-library stamps, have the dust-jacket flaps pasted to the front and back paste-down endpapers.

168. "Purity at the Port," *Nation*, 22 Feb. 1933, 194.

169. "Detroit Circulating Library Raided by Police," *PW*, 15 Dec. 1934, 2146.

Chapter 3. "Hardworking American Daddy"

1. *Jack Ketch the Hangman*, July 1932, 7.

2. [James] Branch Cabell, "The Genteel Tradition in Sex," in *The American Spectator Year Book*, ed. George Jean Nathan et al. (New York: Stokes, 1934), 219–20.

3. Henry F. Pringle, "Comstock the Less," *American Mercury*, Jan. 1927, 58.

4. Ibid., 56. For other descriptions of Sumner's personality, see Paul Boyer, *Purity in Print: The Vice-Society Movement and Book Censorship in America* (New York: Scribner's, 1968), 30; Pringle, "The Genteel Crusader," in *Big Frogs* (New York: Macy-Macius, 1928), 258–59, 270–71. It is possible that Sumner wrote an autobiography. According to C. J. Scheiner, the publisher Ralph Ginzburg visited him at his home in the 1950s to discuss his attitudes toward censorship. Sumner allowed him to take for photocopying a manuscript about his life.

5. S. J. Woolf, "A Vice Suppressor Looks at Our Morals," *NYT*, 9 Oct. 1932, sec. 7: 2.

6. John S. Sumner, "What Every Father Should Know," *Smart Set*, May 1928, 54, 115.

7. Boyer, *Purity in Print*, 5–9.

8. John D'Emilio and Estelle Freedman, *Intimate Matters: A History of Sexuality in America* (New York: Harper and Row, 1988), 159–67.

9. Boyer, *Purity in Print*, 23–30; Timothy J. Gilfoyle, *City of Eros: New York City, Prostitution, and the Commercialization of Sex, 1790–1920* (New York: Norton, 1992), 185–87.

10. Heywood Broun and Margaret Leech, *Anthony Comstock: Roundsman of the Lord* (New York: Boni, 1927), 87–88.

11. Gilfoyle, *City of Eros*, 187–91.

12. Broun and Leech, *Anthony Comstock*, 143.

13. Francis G. Couvares, "Hollywood, Main St., and the Church: Trying to Censor the Movies Before the Production Code," *American Quarterly* 44.4 (Dec. 1992): 586–90.

14. See *Who Was Who* and *The National Cyclopedia of American Biography*, 1975 ed., s. v. "Sumner, John Saxon"; and "John S. Sumner, Foe of Vice, Dies," *NYT*, 22 June 1971, 38.

15. Diana Rice, "Literary Booklegging," *NYT*, 6 Aug. 1922, Book Review section, 1; Boyer, *Purity in Print*, 5.

16. The WW Papers contain many letters to and from Sumner and Bodwell of the Watch and Ward, Yarrow of the Illinois Vigilance Association, and Pringle of the International Reform Federation regarding "book cases."

17. Much information about the NYSSV personnel and activities is contained in a transcript of testimony Sumner was forced to give on 9 and 10 Mar. 1931, in a pretrial examination insisted on by the defendants in a libel suit he filed against Bernarr Macfadden's *Evening Graphic*. The *Graphic* had claimed that Sumner improperly received 50 percent of all fines levied against defendants he had arrested. Much of Sumner's cross-examination was by Morris Ernst. The information about Sumner's consultations with his board is in NYS v. Mac, 5, 21, 78, 182–90.

18. "Druggist Bookseller Arrested," *PW*, 21 Oct. 1933, 1429; Rice, "Literary Booklegging," 1. See also Boyer, *Purity in Print*, 83, on Sumner's "shopping around" for convictions.

19. John S. Sumner to Charles Bodwell, 26 Feb. 1930, Paige box 3, WW Papers. See also "The Enforcement of Laws Against Censorship in New York," *Columbia Law Review* 28 (Nov. 1928): 950–57.

20. Ingram Bander, "Suppression a Modern Problem: An Interview with John S. Sumner," *Campus* (City College of New York magazine), 18 Apr. 1932, ACLU Archives, 508: 167. Sumner also explains his procedures in his "Truth About "Literary Lynching," *Dial*, July 1921, 63–68.

21. Joseph Lilly, "Books and Bookleggers No. 2," *New York Telegram*, 7 Mar. 1930, 13 (sec. 2:1). The article reproduces "Rotacidare's" letterhead. See also NYS v. Mac, 18.

22. Albert Fried, *The Rise and Fall of the Jewish Gangster in America*, rev. ed. (New York: Columbia University Press, 1993), 1–7, 78–80.

23. Sumner sent an unidentified financial agent to procure circulars from the Falstaff Press in 1935. *Annual Report of the Postmaster General* (Washington, D.C.: GPO, 1939), 139–49.

24. NYS v. Mac, 4, 53–54, 171–74. "Stool pigeons" was Morris Ernst's term, used in his pretrial examination of Sumner.

25. Mencken, *My Life as Author and Editor*, ed. Jonathan Yardley (New York: Knopf, 1993), 76–77.

26. John T. Slaymaker, the agent who cajoled the owner of the Dunster House bookshop to sell him a copy of *Lady Chatterley's Lover* in 1929, had to be fired four years later when his scheme, concocted with two known criminals, to "embarrass [the society's] President by making charges against the Secretary" was uncovered. "Record Made for Board of Directors," 10 Apr. 1933, Paige box 3, WW Papers.

27. Gardner Jackson, "My Brother's Peeper," *Nation*, 15 Jan. 1930, 64.

28. Milton Fairman, "Censorship in Chicago," *PW*, 11 Jan. 1930, 213–14. Fairman

wrote a series of articles on the Chicago situation, reprinted in *PW*, much as Joseph Lilly did for the *New York Telegram* the same year.

29. See especially Lilly, "Books and Bookleggers No. 2." The secondary headline reads "Charles J. Bamberger, Undercover Agent for Vice Suppression Society, Uses Tricks to Trap Unsuspecting Dealers." Harris's accusation surfaces in his "Sumner and His Satellites," *Pearson's Magazine*, Feb. 1918, 363.

30. Joseph Lilly, "Book Dealers Are Considering Own Censorship," *New York Telegram*, 13 Mar. 1930, 7. Scheiner Archive.

31. NYS v. Mac, 169–70.

32. Theodore Dreiser to Morris Ernst, 20 Mar. 1931, box 387, MLE Papers. Dreiser found many of the cuts Mencken and Sumner proposed to be "obnoxious," and "canceled the whole proceeding." The letter was one of many Ernst solicited before the New York Society v. Macfadden trial. See Mencken's *My Life as Author and Editor*, ed. Jonathan Yardley (New York: Knopf, 1993), 390–91.

33. Joseph M. March, *The Wild Party, The Setup, A Certain Wildness* (Freeport, Me.: Bond Wheelwright, 1968), 46. There is a more recent edition of *The Wild Party*, illustrated by Art Speigelman (New York: Pantheon, 1994). Covici's surprise at Sumner's confiscation is registered in a letter to the Gotham Book Mart, 9 July 1928, box 391, MLE Papers.

34. Sumner to Simon and Schuster Inc., 27 May 1930, file 386, MLE Papers.

35. Frances Steloff to John S. Sumner and Edward Greenbaum, both 21 Nov. 1930; Greenbaum to Sumner, 21 and 25 Nov. 1930, file 391, MLE Papers. The file also preserves a copy of catalog 31, "Modern First Editions," dated 1931, not 1930, describing what is obviously the copy Sumner alluded to. It was "Clara Tice's copy, containing her original etched bookplate. Also on first fly-leaf is an original crayon drawing by Miss Tice, signed." Greenbaum mentions this drawing in his letter of 21 Nov.

36. "Plans Laid to Censor All New Literature," *NYT*, 4 Aug. 1922, 1, 7.

37. Boyer, *Purity in Print*, 30. He quotes Pringle's comment in "Comstock the Less" that Sumner's smile "was as genial, if as synthetic, as that of a YMCA secretary meeting a squad of doughboys returning uproariously from a bordello."

38. Charles A. Madison, *Jewish Publishing in America: The Impact of Jewish Writing on American Culture* (New York: Sanhedrin, 1976), 253–60; Walker Gilmer, *Horace Liveright: Publisher of the Twenties* (New York: David Lewis, 1970), 8–11.

39. Tom Dardis, *Firebrand: The Life of Horace Liveright* (New York: Random House, 1995), 51.

40. Dardis, *Firebrand*, 164, quoting an "old guard" supporter of the Clean Books Bill (1923). Thomas Seltzer's wife, Adele, observed, "There really is a terribly strong feeling among the older firms against the three rising Jewish publishers — Knopf, Seltzer, Boni and Liveright" (Gerald M. Lacy, ed., *D. H. Lawrence: Letters to Thomas and Adele Seltzer* [Santa Barbara, Calif.: Black Sparrow, 1976], 258).

41. Geoffrey Perrett, *America in the Twenties: A History* (New York: Simon and

Schuster, 1983), 147–65, 424–28; Loren Baritz, *The Good Life: The Meaning of Success for the American Middle Class* (1982; New York: Harper and Row, 1990), 56–104.

42. Quoted in Mencken, *My Life as Author and Editor*, 163.

43. *U.S. v. Ben Rebhuhn, Anne Rebhuhn, and Ben Raeburn*, C97-410, U.S. District Ct., So. District of N.Y. (1939), trial transcript, 502–3.

44. "Red Poet Gets Thirteen Months," *NYT*, 11 June 1927, 34; "Six Reds Indicted for Misusing Mail," *NYT*, 30 June 1927, 30; "Young Poet Freed by Parole Board," *NYT*, 11 May 1928, 27.

45. "The Customs Censorship," *PW*, 22 Feb. 1930, 984–85; "Senators Debate Book Censorship," *NYT*, 18 Mar. 1930, 5.

46. This language forms part of the sentence that concludes sec. 334 in both the 1927 and 1940 editions.

47. Rochelle Gurstein, *The Repeal of Reticence: A History of America's Cultural and Legal Struggles over Free Speech, Obscenity, Sexual Liberation, and Modern Art* (New York: Hill and Wang, 1996), chaps. 1, 7.

48. John F. Noll, *Manual of the N[ational] O[rganization for] D[ecent] L[iterature]*, [Huntington, Ind.: Our Sunday Visitor], n.d.

49. The number of arrests in 1882, 1887, 1897, 1905, 1915, 1919, 1923, 1927, and 1930 total 225 Americans and 225 foreign-born. There are also a substantial number of offenders for whom nationality is not recorded. A chart in the annual report for 1931 (p. 17) also suggests that there was an equal number of arrests of citizens from the United States and from all other countries.

50. Committee of Fourteen Archives, box 37 (investigative reports of "Street Activities"), the New York Public Library, MS Division, New York, N.Y. The reports were prepared by numerous undercover agents employed by the committee.

51. Francesco Cordasco and T. M. Pitkin, *The White Slave Trade and the Immigrants* (Detroit, Mich.: Blaine Ethridge, 1981), 60–61, 86–87.

52. Gilfoyle, *City of Eros*, 303.

53. Boyer, *Purity in Print*, 44–45.

54. Frederick H. Whitin to John S. Sumner, 17 Mar. 1926, box 14, Committee of Fourteen Archives.

55. "Plans Laid to Censor All New Literature," *NYT*, 4 Aug. 1922, 7.

56. John S. Sumner to George E. Worthington, 20 Apr. 1927, box, 14, Committee of Fourteen Archives.

57. Frederick Whitin to A. DeSilver, 12 Apr. 1924, box 6, ibid.

58. Ibid.

59. The letters date from the fall and winter of 1925. Dickinson's flowcharts, titled "Agencies Concerned in Sex Problems" and "Genetics: Science Studies in Sex," are also in box 6, Committee of Fourteen Archives.

60. Quoted in Leonard Dinnerstein, *Anti-Semitism in America* (New York: Oxford

University Press, 1994), 65–66. Dinnerstein sees the 1920s as a period of "erecting barriers" to reinforce the domain of the Protestant establishment from Jewish presence, and the Depression period as one of unprecedented contempt, especially because of racist fears of an "international Jewish conspiracy."

61. Thomas Miller, *Immigrants and the American City* (New York: New York University Press, 1993), 36–43.

62. Paul Boyer, *Urban Masses and Moral Order in America, 1820–1920* (Cambridge, Mass.: Harvard University Press, 1978), 197–201.

63. For Sumner's characterizations of obscenity violators, see NYSSV, *Annual Reports* (1926), 10; (1928), 10; (1932), 10, 12; (1933), 12. For his comments restricting immigration, see (193), 17.

64. Esther Panitz, "In Defense of the Jewish Immigrant, 1891–1924," In *The Jewish Experience in America*, vol. 5, *At Home in America*, ed. Abraham J. Karp (Waltham, Mass.: American Jewish Historical Society, 1969), 23–28. See also Miller, *Immigrants*, 41; Gerald Sorin, *The Jewish People in America*, vol. 3, *A Time for Building: The Third Migration, 1880–1920*, ed. Henry Feingold (Baltimore, Md.: Johns Hopkins University Press, 1992), 62–64.

65. Panitz, "Defense," 59–61; Dinnerstein, *Anti-Semitism in America*, 96.

66. Walter Lippmann, "The Nature of the Battle over Censorship," in *Men of Destiny* (New York: Macmillan, 1928), 104.

67. Boyer, *Purity in Print*, 87.

68. President Roosevelt to William Schieffelin, 13 Apr. 1938. Reprinted in *Milestone 65: A Brief Survey of the New York Society* for the Suppression of Vice (New York, 1938), 11.

69. Richard Hofstadter, *The Age of Reform from Bryan to F.D.R.* (New York: Knopf, 1956), 78–86.

70. Arthur A. Goren, *New York Jews and the Quest for Community* (New York: Columbia University Press, 1970), 138–39; Dinnerstein, *Anti-Semitism in America*, 60–61.

71. Quoted in Boyer, *Urban Masses and Moral Order*, 209.

72. Fried, *Rise and Fall of the Jewish Gangster*, 59–67; Goren, *New York Jews*, 30–56.

73. Goren, *New York Jews*, 139–58; Sorin, *Jewish People*, 60–65.

74. Sorin, *Jewish People*, 86–92, 109–22.

75. Walter P. Zenner, *Minorities in the Middle: A Cross-Cultural Analysis* (Albany: State University of New York Press, 1991), 72.

76. Soren, *Jewish People*, 92, 214–18.

77. Joseph Lilly, "One Foe of Vice Spurns Tricks," *New York Telegram*, 11 Mar. 1930, 7. Scheiner Archive.

78. "W. J. Schieffelin of Drug Firm Dies," *NYT*, 1 May 1955, 88; *The National Cyclopedia of American Biography*, 1962 ed., s. v. "Schieffelin, William Jay."

79. Sumner, "What Every Father Should Know," 116.

80. Lilly, "One Foe."

81. Howard M. Sachar, *A History of the Jews in America* (New York: Vintage, 1992), 172; Sorin, *Jewish People*, 216–17.

82. Larry L. May and Elaine Tyler May, "Why Jewish Movie Moguls: An Exploration in American Culture," *American Jewish History* 72.1 (Sept. 1982): 16; Stephen Birmingham, *"The Rest of Us": The Rise of America's Eastern European Jews* (New York: Berkeley, 1985), 139–40, 176–78.

83. Ronald H. Bayor, *Neighbors in Conflict: The Irish, Germans, Jews, and Italians of New York City, 1929–1941* (Baltimore, Md.: Johns Hopkins University Press, 1978), 150–55, 157–60; Thomas Kessner, *The Golden Door: Italian and Jewish Immigrant Mobility in New York City, 1880–1915* (New York: Oxford University Press, 1977), 144–52.

84. John S. Sumner to Frederick H. Whitin, 10 June 1925, box 6; Committee of Fourteen Archives. This letter contains a copy of a letter of 8 June to the lessees, which states the terms of the agreement.

85. "Book Publishers Want No Pooh-bah," *NYT*, 6 Aug. 1922, 2: 1; "Plans Laid to Censor All New Literature," *NYT*, 4 Aug. 1922, 1, 7; Boyer, *Purity in Print*, 99–119.

86. "Roth's Magazine Accused," *NYT*, 10 Mar. 1927, 2.

87. John S. Sumner to Joseph B. Keenan (assistant attorney general), 24 Oct. 1934, U.S. Dept. of Justice, Central Files, file 97-51-7, NA.

88. John S. Sumner to Charles H. Bodwell, 25 June 1934, Paige box 3, WW Papers. The *Female* case is discussed in *People v. Irving Plotkin, Memorandum by American Civil Liberties Union*, Amicus Curiae, 20 Jan. 1934, 4, file 389, MLE Papers, which lists the reputable stores in which the book was sold.

89. "The Watch and Ward Society and Censorship," *Massachusetts Library Club Bulletin*, Oct. 1927, 70.

90. "Enforce All Existing Laws Against Unclean Literature," *New York American*, 11 Aug. 1927, JA Files.

91. Jackson, "My Brother's Peeper," 65, quoting E. Tallmadge Root, executive secretary of the Massachusetts Federation of Churches.

92. Hallam had sent Charles Bodwell a copy of a 16 June 1931 *Chicago Daily Tribune* article on the case, circling in crayon the paragraph about the book and writing his comment at the top of the clipping. Paige box 1, folder marked "H 1931," WW Papers.

93. Wirt W. Hallam to John S. Sumner, 1 May 1931, Paige box 3, WW Papers.

94. Clayton Spear to Roger Baldwin of the ACLU, 14 Nov. 1929, vol. 359 (microfilmed), ACLU Archives.

95. Hofstadter, *The Age of Reform*, 176–79; Joseph Gusfield, *Symbolic Crusade: Status Politics and the American Temperance Movement* (1963; Urbana, Ill.: University of Illinois Press, 1969), 99–100, 123, 155. See also Perrett, *America in the Twenties*, 155.

96. Michael Kazin, *The Populist Persuasion: An American History* (New York: Basic, 1995), 86–96.

97. Quoted in Boyer, *Purity in Print*, 142.

98. Gusfield, *Symbolic Crusade*, 3–9.

99. Adam Dingwall to ACLU, 24 Mar. 1931, ACLU Archives, 503: 101–4; "Three Publishers Held in 'Lewd' Book Sale," *NYT*, 24 July 1930, 8. In a letter to Charles Bodwell, 8 Aug. 1930, Sumner suggested Bodwell blacklist the *Stories*. Paige box 3, WW Papers.

100. Adam Dingwall to Morris Ernst, 16 July 1931, file 388, MLE Papers. Alexander Lindey reminded Clifton Read (5 July 1934, file 388) of Dingwall-Rock's decision not to pursue the matter when, in 1934, the firm asked for help in getting an edition of *The Memoirs of Casanova* through Customs. Lindey described Dingwall-Rock as "supplying classics of slight pornographic flavor."

101. The advertisement, headed "The Real Arabian Nights," appeared in *Scribner's Magazine*, Dec. 1930, 58.

102. Mae West, *Goodness Had Nothing to Do with It* (1959; New York: Macfadden-Bartel, 1970), 94.

103. Information about Boston can be found in Sidney S. Grant and S. E. Angoff, "Massachusetts and Censorship," *Boston University Law Review* 10 (Jan. 1930): 43–46; Boyer, *Purity in Print*, 171–73; "Censorship in Boston" (Boston: Civil Liberties Committee of Massachusetts, 1938), 8–10; Charles S. Bodwell to Lillian Block, 6 Mar. 1930, in Paige box 2, WW Papers; Felice Flannery Lewis, *Literature, Obscenity, and Law* (Carbondale: Southern Illinois University Press, 1976), 98–102.

104. Documents, including Mencken's journals about the case, are collected in Carl Bode, ed., *The Editor, the Bluenose and the Prostitute: H. L. Mencken's History of the "Hatrack" Censorship Case* (Boulder, Colo.: Roberts Rinehart, 1988).

105. "Censorship in Boston," 9.

106. "Investigative Reports," Paige box 5, WW Papers.

107. Ibid., 16 Mar. 1934.

108. Bernard De Voto, "Literary Censorship in Cambridge," *Harvard Graduates Magazine*, Sept. 1930, 32–33.

109. "Plans Laid to Censor All New Literature."

110. Boyer, *Purity in Print*, 184.

111. De Voto, "Literary Censorship in Cambridge," 32–33. De Voto says he received his unexpurgated copy of *Lady Chatterley's Lover* from a Boston store with which he had a standing order for Lawrence first editions, and that there were plenty of copies of the Orioli, Paris Popular, and American pirated editions to be had in the city from 1928 to 1930.

112. At least some of the *Chatterley* volumes sold by Dunster House were ordered from Samuel Roth, as Sumner learned when he raided Roth's Golden Hind Press in 1929. Several letters to and from Sumner and Bodwell of the Watch and Ward concern New York distributors of borderline mail-order erotica, readers, and Tijuana bibles; Sumner had exclusive information regarding their publishers.

113. Henry N. Pringle, "America's Burden of Commercialized Vice and Follies,"

Twentieth Century Progress (bimonthly of the International Reform Federation), Jan. 1937, 19.

114. Boyer, *Purity in Print*, 168–75, 181–84.

Chapter 4. "Fifth Avenue Has No More Rights Than the Bowery"

1. "Indict Seven for Obscene Books: Police Burn $150,000 Worth," *New York American*, 27 Nov. 1935; "Police Burn Literature They Seize as Indecent," *New York Tribune*, 13 Nov. 1936. Both in JA Files.

2. "Police to Burn $500,000 in Obscene Books," *NYT*, 14 Mar. 1935, 1; "Obscene Books Burned," *NYT*, 15 Mar. 1935, 44.

3. "Indict Seven for Obscene Books."

4. "Police to Burn."

5. One of the NYSSV periodical letters to its constituents, dated 26 Feb. 1930 and signed by Sumner, describes the burned books as the result of arrests of "Max Roth, Sam Roth, Malkin, Kallus, and Pesky." These letters, which appeared from 1925 to 1939, are in the collections of the New York Public Library (s.v. "Society to Maintain Public Decency, New York"). Usually the letters solicited contributions, badly needed by the society in the early 1930s. They were not all written by Sumner; others are by the society's president and treasurer.

6. Heywood Broun and Margaret Leech, *Anthony Comstock: Roundsman of the Lord* (New York: Boni, 1927), 223–24.

7. NYS v. Mac, 73. Sumner's two statements about his impartiality are found respectively, in his "Truth About Literary Lynching," *Dial*, July 1921, 66, and "New York Society for the Suppression of Vice," *PW*, 17 May 1930, 2518.

8. "Prelates Lay Plans to Fight Bad Books," *NYT*, 25 Feb. 1923, 1, 7.

9. "Plans Laid to Censor All New Literature," *NYT*, 4 Aug. 1922, 1, 7. Regarding the theater lease arrangement: John S. Sumner to Frederick H. Whitin, 10 June 1925, box 6, Committee of Fourteen Archives, New York Public Library, MS Division, New York, N.Y. Regarding the publishers' manuscripts: Patricia E. Robertus, "Postal Control of Obscene Literature, 1942–57" (Ph.D. diss., University of Washington, 1974), 71; G. Thomas Tanselle, "The Thomas Seltzer Imprint," *Papers of the Bibliographical Society of America* 58 (1964): 397, n. 45 (citing *PW*, 27 Jan. 1923, 221–23).

10. Paul Boyer, *Purity in Print: The Vice-Society Movement and Book Censorship in America* (New York: Scribner's, 1968), 99–109.

11. Boyer, *Purity in Print*, 108–10; John Tebbel, *A History of Book Publishing in the United States* (New York: Bowker, 1978), 3: 400; John D'Emilio and Estelle Freedman, *Intimate Matters: A History of Sexuality in America* (New York: Harper and Row, 1988), 172–73, 195–99.

12. "Amending Censorship Law," *PW*, 31 Mar. 1923, 1061.

13. "A Highly Moral Tale," *PW*, 15 July 1922, 118.

14. Walker Gilmer, *Horace Liveright: Publisher of the Twenties* (New York: David Lewis, 1970), 76, 78; Tom Dardis, *Firebrand: The Life of Horace Liveright* (New York: Random House, 1995), 161–70.

15. Gerald M. Lacy, ed., *D. H. Lawrence: Letters to Thomas and Adele Seltzer* (Santa Barbara, Calif.: Black Sparrow, 1976), 34–35; Claire Healey and Keith Cushman, eds., *The Letters of D. H. Lawrence and Amy Lowell, 1914–25* (Santa Barbara, Calif.: Black Sparrow, 1985), 105–6.

16. C. David Heyman, *American Aristocracy: The Lives and Times of James Russell, Amy, and Robert Lowell* (New York: Dodd, Mead, 1980), 261.

17. "Renewed Censorship Legislation," *PW*, 3 Mar. 1923, 627.

18. See Lacy, ed., *D. H. Lawrence*, 35, 41, 232.

19. Edward de Grazia, *Girls Lean Back Everywhere: The Law of Obscenity and the Assault on Genius* (New York: Random House, 1992), 76–78.

20. Gene Fowler, *Beau James* (1949; New York: Bantam, 1957), 57. Walker was New York State Senate Democratic (majority) leader at the time. According to Boyer (*Purity in Print*, 118), he led the floor debate against the bill. See "Clean Books Bill Dies in Senate," *NYT*, 3 May 1923, 1, 3.

21. "Clean Books Bill Draws More Foes," *NYT*, 22 Apr. 1923, 19.

22. Boyer, *Purity in Print*, 109–14.

23. See ibid., 111, 112, for both the Austin and Garland comments, and Dardis, *Firebrand*, 115.

24. See Boyer, *Purity in Print*, 35–36. Boyer remarks that Knopf "consistently yielded before Vice Society bluster" (135).

25. Lovat Dickson, *Radclyffe Hall at the Well of Loneliness* (New York: Scribner's, 1975), 168, quoting Blanche Knopf.

26. "Culture Burns Bright" (editorial), *NYT*, 18 Mar. 1935, 16.

27. Tebbel, *A History of Book Publishing*, 3: 419. There was a change of policy to some extent after 1930, as the bookseller Bernard G. Guerney pointed out in his satirical tabloid *Jack Ketch the Hangman*, July 1932, 4. He reproduced advertisements for sexology appearing in the *Times* Book Review section in 1932. The Book Review's 15 Jan. 1933 issue (p. 15) ran a notice for Esar Levine's Forum Librorum ("Facetious Curiosa, Unabridged Exotica").

28. "Renewed Censorship Legislation," *PW*, 3 Mar. 1923, 627.

29. *U.S. v. Levine*, 83 F2d 156, 2d Cir. (1936).

30. "Delicate Distinctions" (editorial), *New York World Telegram*, 16 Apr. 1936, ACLU Archives, 879: 172. The editorial followed by one day the newspaper's story " 'Tough Guy' Art to Sumner, Foe of Unarty Nude," ACLU Archives, 879: 171. "Tough Guy" was a popular sobriquet for a municipal statue.

31. Key decensorship decisions of the period are covered in Boyer, *Purity in Print*; Felice Flannery Lewis, *Literature, Obscenity, and Law* (Carbondale: Southern Illinois Uni-

versity Press, 1976); Morris Ernst and Alan U. Schwartz, *Censorship: The Search for the Obscene* (New York: Macmillan, 1964).

32. Tanselle, "The Thomas Seltzer Imprint," 397. Sumner pursued the case, as I discuss below.

33. "Sold Harvard Professors Banned Book," *Boston Herald*, 20 Dec. 1929[?], newspaper clipping preserved in box 21, file 22, Zechariah Chafee Papers, Special Collections Dept., Harvard University Law Library, Cambridge, Mass.

34. These headlines are from various clippings in the Chafee Papers.

35. "Sold Harvard Professors," col. 3.

36. "Lash Watch and Ward at Book Trial" (unidentified newspaper clipping), 20 Dec. 1929, Chafee Papers.

37. "Frank Harris," *Saturday Review of Literature*, 13 Feb. 1926, 553–54. This is a review of volume 2 of *My Life and Loves*.

38. "Sumner Makes Raid and Seizure," *NYT*, 4 July 1925, 6 (Ruze); "Raid Plant, Seize Book as Obscene," *NYT*, 27 June 1925, 3 (Mellstein, Mishkin, Pomerantz); "Sumner Charges Hold Three," *NYT*, 17 Jan. 1929, 14 (Lhevinne); "Female Found Obscene," *PW*, 2 Sept. 1933, 669 (Berg); "Library Operator Fined," *PW*, 9 Mar. 1935, 1068 (Plotkin); "Sumner Raids 2 Publishers," *PW*, 14 Apr. 1934 (Loewingers), "Book Scored, Seller Held," *NYT*, 5 Mar. 1930, 25 (Marks); "Indicted in Book Seizure," *NYT*, 23 Oct. 1931, 9 (Nussbaums and Costelito); "Raid Nets Two as Cops Seize Obscene Books," *Brooklyn Eagle*, 18 July 1939 (Reisberg, Brotman), JA Files.

39. Joseph Lilly, "Books and Bookleggers No. 3," *New York Telegram*, 8 Mar. 1930, 10. Jerome Britchey, in a letter to the *Saturday Review of Literature* about the value of the Bad Books Bill (which would hold publishers, not booksellers, responsible for charges of obscenity), describes the "the small book seller" as the NYSSV's most vulnerable and frequent target ("Letters to the Editor: Censorship and the Bad Books Bill," 18 July 1936, 9).

40. "'My Life' Leads to New Arrest," *New York American*, 14 Aug. 1925, JA Files.

41. "Detective as Poet Seizes Bookseller," *New York Sun*, 2 Apr. 1930; "Book Dealer Is Held," *NYT*, 3 Apr. 1930, JA Files.

42. "Bookseller to Leave Jail," *NYT*, 23 May 1930, 25.

43. John S. Sumner to Charles Bodwell, 25 June 1934, Paige box 3, WW Papers; "'Female' Found Obscene."

44. Sumner was very proud of this decision; it meant *Female* could no longer be sold in New York State. Sumner to Bodwell, 25 June 1934.

45. "Erotica Dealer Blames Sumner," *New York Evening Post*, 6 July 1934, JA Files.

46. Mrs. Lorraine Wilbur of Grammercy Books, Union Square, New York City, recalls the sign in Guerney's shop (personal interview, 21 July 1993).

47. I thank booksellers Jack Biblo and Chris Eckhoff of Brooklyn, New York, for copies of this hard-to-find publication (the masthead reads "Vol. 1 July 1932 No. 1").

48. "Clearing of Bookseller on Sumner Libel Charge Proves to Him That America Still Needs Kick in Pants," *New York Herald Tribune*, 10 Oct. 1932. The newspaper clipping

is preserved in the ACLU Archives, 503: 277. Morris Ernst and Alexander Lindey discuss Sumner's libel charge disparagingly in their *Hold Your Tongue! Adventures in Libel and Slander* (London: Methuen, 1936), 276–80.

49. "Communications. Guerney vs. Sumner," *PW*, 8 Apr. 1933, 1212.

50. "Gotham Book Mart Celebrates Twentieth Birthday," *PW*, 6 Jan. 1940, 42; "Ben Abramson in New Quarters," *PW*, 16 Mar. 1940, 1152–54; "Falstaff Officers Sentenced on Obscenity Conviction," *PW*, 15 July 1940, 162; "Conviction of Falstaff Press Officers Confirmed," *PW*, 9 Mar. 1940, 1084; "Falstaff Press Convictions Upheld by Supreme Court," *PW*, 22 June 1940, 2343.

51. Gershon Legman to the author, 4 Aug. 1985. Legman worked and wrote for Jack Brussel and Samuel Roth from approximately 1933 to 1953. Some of his reminiscences are contained in his introduction to Patrick Kearney's *Private Case* (London: Landesman, 1981); in the introduction to his *Art of Mahlon Blaine* (East Lansing, Mich.: Peregrine, 1982); and (presumably) in his unpublished autobiography, *Peregrine Penis: An Autobiography of Innocence*.

52. Edwin Wolf II and John Fleming, *Rosenbach: A Biography* (Cleveland: World, 1960), 585.

53. In 1951, Edwin Wolf II arranged for the Rosenbach Company a sale of some seven hundred items of French erotica to the Kinsey Institute. The books were once part of the Louis Olrey-Roederer collection; they had been stored in a garage. Wolf and Fleming, *Rosenbach*, 585.

54. Wolf and Fleming, *Rosenbach*, 304; file I:041:13 ("Clark, William Andrews, Jr."), Company Archives, Rosenbach Library and Museum, Philadelphia, Pa. Rosenbach wrote to Clark on 30 Oct. 1928: "As to 'Lady Chatterley,' it is almost impossible to obtain a copy here [in the United States], but I shall do my utmost to find a copy of it for you." Neither copy of the novel is inventoried in the archives. Rosenbach's statement is inconsistent with Bernard De Voto's regarding the ease with which one could get copies of *Chatterley* in Boston ("Literary Censorship in Cambridge," *Harvard Graduates Magazine*, Sept. 1930, 32–33). Rosenbach, however, must have been referring exclusively to the Orioli first edition, with the author's signature.

55. Purchase voucher B02089, Rosenbach Company Archives.

56. Rosenbach Company Rare Book Dept., *A Catalogue of Original MS, Presentation Copies, First Editions, and Autographed Letters of Modern Authors* (Philadelphia, 1933).

57. Rosenbach Archives, correspondence files I:082:13 ("Harris, Frank") and I:082:14 ("Harris, H. B."). The former contains a letter from Harris to Rosenbach dated 31 July 1928. See Wolff II and Fleming, *Rosenbach*, 304.

58. "Harry Marks, 78, Dealer in Books," *NYT*, 23 Aug. 1958, JA Files. In 1938, the Harry F. Marks Galleries and Bookshop moved to 280 Park Avenue. The 1935 *Directory of Booksellers in the United States* lists Marks's address as Rockefeller Center. The 1925 edition places him at 31 West 47th Street.

59. Harry T. Moore, ed., *The Collected Letters of D. H. Lawrence* (New York: Viking, 1962), 2: 1098.

60. I am indebted to Bernard Conwell Carlitz, retired Philadelphia bookseller, for this insight (interview of 15 July 1992).

61. The KI Files contain copies of circulars for the Nottingham edition and several catalogs of erotica issued by Abramson from the Argus Book Shop in Chicago. There are also a few letters and invoices for the notorious banned books of the era, apparently mailed to trusted clients.

62. D. B. Covington, *The Argus Book Shop: A Memoir* (West Cornwall, Conn.: Tarrydiddle, 1977), 26–27.

63. "Ben Abramson, 1899–1955," *PW*, 30 July 1955, 159–60.

64. "Bad Books Case Dropped," *New York Journal American*, 20 June 1947, JA Files.

65. Francis Russell, "Arty Crafty and the Beginnings of the Joyce Cult at Harvard," *The Great Interlude: Neglected Events and Persons from the First World War to the Depression* (New York: McGraw-Hill, 1964), 160–61.

66. Gershon Legman, "Erotic Folksongs and Ballads: An International Bibliography," *Journal of American Folklore* 103 (Oct.–Dec. 1990): 423.

67. The Copyright Office of the Library of Congress has on file a claim for *Hsi Men Ching* (translated by Chu Tsui-Jen) by Martin Kamin of New York City. The date is Jan. 1928 and there is a note to the effect that the claim for this title was contested.

Following Moss's divorce, he and Kamin operated the firm of Moss and Kamin: Booksellers and Publishers. According to W. G. Rogers (*Wise Men Fish Here: The Story of Frances Steloff and the Gotham Book Mart* [New York: Harcourt, Brace, World, 1965], 86, 105–6, 145–54), Moss and Kamin took with them a copy of the Gotham mailing list. After Moss died heroically in 1936, while saving two boys from drowning, Kamin founded a bookshop specializing in dance at 1423 Sixth Avenue. The 1938 edition of the *World Almanac and Book of Facts* carries a classified ad for the Kamin Bookshop at that address, specializing in "Art, Cinema, Dance, and Theatre." Kamin was an executive in the Book Trade Protective Association in 1930.

68. I possess a copy of Gautier's *Mademoiselle de Maupin* (n.p.: privately printed for the Pierre Louÿs Society, n.d.) that contains typed text pasted to the first page. The text extols the values of the edition and states, "For years Clara Tice has been regarded as the *bad girl of American Art.*" This was written by a bookseller, a lending-library operator, or a purchaser of the book.

69. Frances Steloff to Edward Greenbaum, 21 Nov. 1930, file 391, MLE Papers: "In as much as La Fontaine is illustrated by Clara Tice and our 'Friend' objects especially to her work, I would leave this item out" (of the catalog she was preparing). After Sumner's 1928 raid, he communicated with Steloff and her lawyers regarding return of some of the volumes taken.

70. Marie T. Keller, "Who Was Clara Tice?" introduction to *ABC Dogs*, by Clara Tice

344 ☞ Notes to Pages 155–58

(New York: Abrams, 1995), n.p.; Francis M. Naumann, *New York Dada, 1915–23* (New York: Abrams, 1994), 117; telephone interviews with Elizabeth Yoell, 20 Nov. 1998.

71. Rogers, *Wise Men*, 151.

72. Maurice Girodias, *The Frog Prince: An Autobiography* (New York: Crown, 1980), 202.

73. William Jackson Ltd. (Frederick Joiner and Alan Steele) acted as agents for Giuseppi Orioli, the printer of *Lady Chatterley's Lover*, and had extensive connections in the United States and Paris. See Frank Mumby and Ian Norrie, *Publishing and Bookselling*, 5th ed. (London: Cape, 1974), 371; and Michael Squires, *The Creation of Lady Chatterley's Lover* (Baltimore, Md.: Johns Hopkins University Press, 1983), 188–89.

74. Legman, introduction to Kearney, *The Private Case*, 55.

75. Legman told me this when I interviewed him on 17 June 1990. For the design of the Gotham sign, see Rogers, *Wise Men*, 69. Brown's comments are in a letter to author, 27 Aug. 1998.

76. *People v. David Moss*, trial transcript, 13 Sept. 1928, MLE Papers, folder titled "Gotham Book Mart vs. Sumner, legal papers and draft."

77. Gershon Legman, in his introduction to Kearney's *The Private Case*, refers to a bookseller, "Rudolph Bernays, though that was not his name," who was the "agent in New York" for the Oklahoma collector of erotica (54). "Rudolph Bernays" may be a kind of anagram for "Barnet Ruder," whose shop was at 20 East 49th Street. Ruder was acquainted with Anaïs Nin, one of the writers commissioned to produce stories for the collector. Robert Ferguson's *Henry Miller: A Life* (New York: Norton, 1991) identifies Ruder as an agent for collectors of pornography who got Miller, Caresse Crosby, Virginia Admiral, and others to write for them (276). Also identifying Ruder are Lawrence J. Shifreen and Roger Jackson (*Henry Miller: A Bibliography of Primary Sources* [n.p.: Shifreen and Jackson, 1993], 931), and Deirdre Bair (*Anaïs Nin: A Biography* [New York: Penguin, 1995], 261–63), who states that erotica writing for the collector came to an end when Ruder was drafted (282). A more extensive treatment of Ruder's involvement in this enterprise is by Noël Riley Fitch (*Anaïs: The Erotic Life of Anaïs Nin* [New York: Little, Brown, 1993], 231–33, 237, 248). She states that Nin "suppressed" Ruder's name from her published diaries. When I interviewed Mr. Ruder on 16 Mar. 1994, he was aware that Legman had made some kind of inference regarding his being an agent for the Oklahoma collector, and vigorously denied any involvement. He wanted to be remembered for his extensive catalog of American social thought, and for publishing an essay by Albert Einstein.

78. Tebbel, *A History of Book Publishing*, 3: 642; Nora Ephron, "Closeup: Storied Bookseller," *New York Post*, 2 July 1965. JA Files.

79. "*If It Die* Seized," *PW*, 21 Dec. 1935, 2229; Tebbel, *A History of Book Publishing*, 3: 648. Sumner's ledgers for 1935 record the arrest.

80. Sumner's statement is recorded in *People of the State of New York v. Gotham Book Mart*, defendant's brief, 18–19, bound vol. 95, MLE Papers.

81. "Picking On the Little Fellow," *PW*, 1 Feb. 1936, 604–5.

82. "Outdoor Sale Begun," *NYT*, 9 June 1932, 26.

83. "Picking," 104.

84. Quoted in Rogers, *Wise Men*, 153.

85. "Records of Censorship in New York," *PW*, 22 Mar. 1930, 1666; "Albany Hearings on Censorship," *PW*, 22 Feb. 1930, 983–84.

86. Sumner was manipulated by Hearst in 1920 when he prosecuted Clinton Brainard, a political enemy of Hearst, for publishing the anonymous *Madeleine* (Boyer, *Purity in Print*, 50), but the *Journal American* was regularly complimentary, especially of his attacks on pulp novels, salacious magazines, and under-the-counter readers in the 1930s, on *The First Lady Chatterley* (1944), and on Edmund Wilson's *Memoirs of Hecate County* (1946).

87. These headlines are from the *Post*, 26 Apr. 1935; *Post*, 8 May 1936; *Daily News*, 16 Apr. 1936 (all found in JA Files); *World Telegram*, 26 Apr. 1935 (found in bound vol. 95, MLE Papers); *Herald Tribune*, 14 Mar. 1929 (quoted in NYS v. Mac, 160). In his pretrial examination of Sumner on the occasion of the latter's libel suit against the *Daily Graphic*, Morris Ernst confronted him with many pejorative newspaper articles, most from the early 1920s. The "boy" who asked about Sumner's penality was not a defendant; he was observing a trial as part of a class field trip.

88. These quotations are from the *Herald Tribune*, 11 Aug. 1930; the *Daily News*, 16 Apr. 1936; and the *Daily Mirror*, 7 May 1938. The first source is in file 386, MLE Papers; the other two are in the JA Files.

89. See also journalist Henry Pringle's essay "The Genteel Crusader" in his *Big Frogs* (New York: Macy-Macius, 1928), 257–76.

90. Boyer, *Purity in Print*, 139. Boyer reports that by 1932 contributions had declined more than 50 percent from 1929 (138).

91. A clipping of this editorial, dated 14 Jan. 1930, is in the ACLU Archives, 630: n.p. [microfilm]).

92. Bernarr Macfadden's *New York Evening Graphic* on 9 Feb. 1927 published charges that Sumner received 50 percent of all fines "collected through its instrumentality." Martin Conboy, a counsel for the society, represented Sumner. Macfadden secured the services of Joseph Schultz. It was the right of the defense to examine the plaintiff before trial. The deposition took place in Conboy's offices on 9 and 10 Mar. 1931 and had "the same effect as if done before a [State] Supreme Court Justice." Morris Ernst conducted the interrogation. The issue of confiscated books is covered on pp. 28–38 of Sumner's pretrial deposition, NYS v. Mac. The files of district attorney cases in the New York City Municipal Archives contain a few communications between the district attorneys and Sumner, regarding which confiscated lots he could destroy (roll 152, p. 477, 23 July 1929; and roll 178, p. 788; 31 Jan. 1946) or must refrain from destroying (roll 151, p. 412, 10 May 1929, regarding Samuel Roth, who at the time had the right to appeal).

93. Gerald R. Scott, "Some Nudity Becomes Art to the 20-Year Vice Foe," 3 Feb. 1935, *New York Mirror*, Sunday magazine section, 5, JA Files.

94. *Gotham Book Mart, Inc. v. John S. Sumner and Joab H. Banton*, file 391, MLE

Papers. Although not many booksellers would risk the further loss of reputation involved in filing suit, publishers were more likely to do so. Covici-Friede sued in 1929, for the return of 865 copies of *The Well of Loneliness*. In 1922, the presiding judge in the vice-society suit against Liveright (for publishing Gautier's *Mademoiselle de Maupin*) ruled that the society might be countersued for false arrest (Tanselle, "The Thomas Seltzer Imprint," 396–97). That year, after Seltzer won the right to publish three books for which Sumner had prosecuted him, the publisher filed a thirty-thousand-dollar suit charging frivolous prosecution (Boyer, *Purity in Print*, 81).

95. Lilly, "Books and Bookleggers No. 3," *New York Telegram*, 8 Mar. 1930, 10.

96. Two sources for the existence of these rumors are the booksellers C. J. Scheiner of Brooklyn, New York, and Ivan Stormgart of San Francisco, California, both of whom specialize in books about censorship, erotica, and sexology. Gershon Legman stated in 1945: "There is gossip to the effect that Sumner does not burn the books he seizes with police help, but keeps part and turns the rest over to Harry Marks, a New York book-dealer; but this may be only gossip" ("Sex Censorship in the U.S.A.," *PLAN: Organization of the British Progressive League* [London], 2.1 [Jan. 1945], 3). Mr. Stormgart has as part of his research collection several of Marks's catalogs from the early 1920s, when his address was 187 Broadway.

97. Bernard Conwell Carlitz (Philadelphia bookseller), personal interview, 15 July 1992.

98. Tanselle, "The Thomas Seltzer Imprint," 400–406.

99. NYS v. Mac, 45–46.

100. That Sumner employed a staff member for the purpose of collecting contributions is specified in his deposition preceding his libel suit against Macfadden's *Evening Graphic*. NYS v. Mac, 4. The obscenity trial of the officers of the Falstaff Press in 1939 contains the testimony of one of these financial agents. See *U.S. v. Ben Rebhuhn, Anne Rebhuhn, and Ben Raeburn*, C97-410, U.S. District Ct., So. District of N.Y. (1939), trial transcript, 147.

101. NYS v. Mac, 76; Tebbel, *A History of Book Publishing*, 3: 636; Joseph Lilly, "Books and Bookleggers No. 1," *New York Telegram*, 6 Mar. 1930, 13 (sec. 2: 1).

102. NYS v. Mac, 76–77. The quotation reproduces the wording of Morris Ernst's question to Sumner.

103. Ernst's questions about Sumner's policy regarding "leading department stores" is recorded on pp. 74–75, NYS v. Mac. Bookseller Arnold Levy of New York City recalls colleagues' talk about one such raid. I could find no documentation for this. When Jake Brussel's Ortelius Book Shop was raided in the late afternoon of June 15, 1928 ("1500 Books Seized by Sumner in Raid," *NYT*, 16 June 1928, 36), the police activity caused a traffic jam around the nearby Wanamakers on 8th Street near Broadway, but it was not the department store that was raided, although someone might have gotten that impression.

104. A brochure announcing the council's formation is preserved in file 394, MLE Papers. A flyer titled "Repeal the Special Powers of the New York Vice Society" (c. 1932–33) exists in the Scheiner Archive. Samuel Walker's *In Defense of American Liberties: A*

History of the ACLU (New York: Oxford University Press, 1990) discusses the council (which he names "Committee"), on 85, 155, 228.

105. National Council on Freedom from Censorship, memorandum "on our present activities," 7 Jan. 1932, file 394, MLE Papers.

106. "Announcing the National Council on Freedom from Censorship" (pamphlet), [8], file 394, MLE Papers.

107. "Memorandum Submitted on Behalf of Defendant, the People of the State of New York v. Francis Steloff," 2–6, bound vol. 94, MLE Papers.

108. "People vs. Frances Steloff. Memo for People," 25 July 1931, 2, bound vol. 94, MLE Papers.

109. Briefs relevant to Sumner's complaint, and letters regarding Sumner's unsuccessful Jan. 1932 attempt to seek a grand jury indictment, are in bound vol. 94, MLE Papers.

110. "People vs. Frances Steloff," 2.

111. NYSSV periodical letter signed John S. Sumner, 15 Dec. 1931, file 391; MLE Papers.

112. John S. Sumner to Charles Boswell, 19 Dec. 1931, Paige box 3, WW Papers.

113. "Find Obscene Books on Increase Here," *NYT*, 6 Apr. 1932, JA Files.

114. Newman Levy to Thomas C. F. Crain, 1 Feb. 1932, bound vol. 94, MLE Papers.

115. Newman Levy to foreman of grand jury (Attn: Asst. Dist. Atty. Firestone), 18 Dec. 1931, 5 Jan. 1932, bound vol. 94, MLE Papers.

116. Levy to Crain, 1 Feb. 1932.

117. Morris L. Ernst to William McAdoo, 22 Oct. 1929, file 383, MLE Papers.

118. William McAdoo to Morris Ernst, 4 Nov. 1929, file 383, MLE Papers.

119. "McAdoo Admits Seized Books Have Vanished," *New York Telegram*, 14 Jan. 1930, 3. Article preserved in file 383, MLE Papers.

120. The information about *Pay Day* and *Casanova's Homecoming* is from a draft letter Ernst wrote to the editor of the *New York Telegram* in October 1930, file 386, MLE Papers. This letter was an intended response to an editorial of 6 Oct., criticizing Sumner's refusal to return books as an example of his placing himself above the law.

121. "People v. Miller . . . Summary of Facts," bound vol. 95, MLE Papers.

122. The MLE Papers ("Records of Censorship Cases," vol. 94) contain the following materials relevant to *People v. Benjamin Levine*, 18 Dec. 1931: Sumner's twelve-page typewritten brief, dated 8 Dec. 1931; a copy of the complaint and warrant, the printed brief of Greenbaum, Wolff, and Ernst on Panurge's behalf; a copy of the circular for *Flesh*; an interoffice memo signed by Alexander Lindey regarding the arrest and conviction of the bookseller Christian Gerhardt for possessing obscene literature; a copy of a circular advertising the book; letters from Ernst (20 Nov. 1931) and Lindey (5 Dec) to Judge Overton Harris regarding recent censorship decisions; reports of decisions in the cases of *People v. Boni and Liveright* (*Satyricon*, 1922), *People v. Seltzer et al.* (*Young Girl's Diary, Casanova's Homecoming*, 1922), *People v. Simon and Schuster* (*Casanova's Homecoming*, 1930), *People v. Steloff* (*Hsi Men Ching, From a Turkish Harem*, 1931), and *People v. Friede*

and Friede (*Well of Loneliness*, 1929); and "Memoranda: On Behalf of People" in "Reply to Defendant's Brief," dated 8 Dec. 1931 and (in reply to the latter) on behalf of defendant, dated 17 Dec. 1931.

123. "Memoranda on Behalf of People," 8.

124. Sumner twelve-page brief, MLE Papers, 7.

125. Defendant's brief, 10.

126. Two sources of information have been located regarding the disposition of this case: Sumner's ledgers, and a typed note in the index to the materials re *Flesh* (*People v. Benjamin Levine*), MLE Papers: "Complaint dismissed without Opinion, Dec. 18, 1931."

127. *U.S. v. Levine*, C97-165, U.S. District Ct., So. District of N.Y. (1935), trial transcript. The Appellate Court decision is *U.S. v. Levine* 83 F2d 156, 2d Cir. (1936).

128. Alexander Lindey to A. L. Wirin, Esq., 10 Jan. 1947, file 392, MLE Papers. Lindey was discussing an appeal of publisher Marcel Rodd's conviction for mailing an edition of *Call House Madam*: "[W]here the book in question is of dubious literary value and where it is difficult to get the court excited about the general value of its contents, it is futile to concentrate argument on the proposition that it is not obscene as a matter of law. The best path to take is to find some technical argument, quite aside from the question of obscenity." For the importance of the *U.S. v. Levine* appeal, see Frederick F. Schauer, *The Law of Obscenity* (Washington, D.C.: Bureau of National Affairs, 1976), 70–71.

129. Ernst and Schwartz, *Censorship*, 112.

130. de Grazia, *Girls*, 29. Letters relevant to this maneuvering are in file 270, MLE Papers: Alexander Lindey to Morris Ernst, 4 Jan. and 25 July 1933; Ernst to Jonas Shapiro, 15 and 25 Aug. 1933. See also Kenneth R. Stevens, "Ulysses on Trial," in *The United States of America v. One Book Entitled Ulysses by James Joyce*, ed. Michael Moscato and Leslie Le Blanc (Frederick, Md.: University Publications of America, 1984), 59–72.

131. Ernst to Lindey, 12 Aug. 1932 and Lindey to Ernst, 5 July 1932 and 4 Jan. 1933; Ernst to Coleman, 10 July 1933, File 270, MLE Papers, all concern the clear lines of communication and openness between Coleman, Medalie, and Ernst throughout the *Ulysses* deliberations.

132. Lindey to Louis Herman, 10 July 1936, file 269, MLE Papers. Herman had written an article in the *Book Collector's Journal* (July 1936) that cited Robert Kastor and Bennett Cerf but not Ernst as responsible for *Ulysses'* liberation.

133. Stevens, "*Ulysses* on Trial," 61.

134. Morris Ernst, "Reflections on the *Ulysses* Trial and Censorship," *James Joyce Quarterly* 3.1 (fall 1965): 4.

135. de Grazia, *Girls*, 27–28.

136. "Martin Conboy, 65, Noted Lawyer, Dies," *NYT*, 6 Mar. 1944, JA Files.

137. Stevens, "*Ulysses* on Trial," 63.

138. Paul Boyer, *Urban Masses and Moral Order in America, 1820–1920* (Cambridge, Mass.: Harvard University Press, 1978), 285–87.

139. "Sumner Condemns Rulings on Books," *NYT*, 5 May 1936, 8; "Purity at the Port," *Nation*, 22 Feb. 1933, 194.

140. NYSSV periodical letter signed John Sumner, 19 Nov. 1935.

141. As recorded in the NYSSV ledgers for 1935. For a description of the *Ladies in the Parlor* case, see Lewis, *Literature, Obscenity, and Law*, 136–39.

142. Francis X. Talbot, S.J., "Smut!" *America*, 11 Feb. 1933, 460–61; " 'Bad Books' Scanned by Geoghan and Police," *Brooklyn Eagle*, 1 March [?], 1933 (misdated by clipping service), ACLU Archives, 503: 64; "Campaign on Obscene Books Launched," *New York Journal*, 1 Mar. 1933, JA Files.

143. "Brooklyn to War on Obscene Books," *NYT*, 27 Feb. 1933, 17.

144. "Book Censorship by Licenses Urged," *NYT*, 14 Feb. 1933, 21. For McGoldrick's work with the IFCA's Motion Picture Bureau, see Gregory D. Black, *Hollywood Censored: Morality Codes, Catholics, and the Movies* (Cambridge: Cambridge University Press, 1994), 221–22.

145. "Fight on Obscene Books Hits Publishing World," *New York Journal*, 3 Mar. 1933, JA Files; "O'Ryan Details Police to Aid Moss Drive," *New York Journal*, 28 Feb. 1934, JA Files.

146. "Police to Help Hunt Sources of 'Bad' Books," *New York World Telegram*, 28 Feb. 1933, ACLU Archives, 503: 277.

147. " 'Bad Books' Scanned," ACLU Archives, 503: 64.

148. Francis G. Couvares, "Hollywood, Main St., and the Church: Trying to Censor the Movies Before the Production Code," *American Quarterly* 44.4 (Dec. 1992): 599–600, 607–8.

149. The relevant periodical letters are 2 May 1933 (signed Henry R. Dwight, Treasurer); 31 Oct. 1933 (signed Sumner), and 26 June 1934 (signed William H. Parsons, President).

150. Ingram Bander, "Suppression a Modern Problem: An Interview with John S. Sumner," *Campus* (City College of New York magazine), 18 Apr. 1932, ACLU Archives, 508: 167. "The Church," Sumner regretted, "has been rather diffident in supporting the Society's activities. It has too many activities of its own."

151. *Promoting Public Decency: 63rd Annual Report of the New York Society for the Suppression of Vice* (New York, 1936), 5.

152. Frances Steloff, "In Touch with Genius," *Journal of Modern Literature* 4.4 (Apr. 1975): 770.

153. Tebbel, *A History of Book Publishing*, 4: 95.

154. de Grazia, *Girls*, 209–29.

155. Joseph Lilly, "Book Dealers Are Considering Own Censorship," *New York Telegram*, Mar. 1930, 7, Scheiner Archive.

156. Reported in Gardner Jackson, "My Brother's Peeper," *Nation*, 15 Jan. 1930, 65.

Chapter 5. "Your *Casanova* Is Unmailable"

1. George Sylvester Viereck and Paul Eldridge, *My First Two Thousand Years* (New York: Macaulay, 1927), 500.

2. Documents concerning Sugar's edition of *The Memoirs of Casanova* exist in File 388, MLE Papers. These include Jerome Britchey to Harriet F. Pilpel, 4 May 1940; Albert Goldman to Martin Sugar, 10 May 1939; holograph notes headed "Reader Service"; file memo signed H.F.P., 6 May 1940; typed narrative by M. Sugar, undated. File 386 contains letters from Goldman to Sugar dated 24 Apr. (canceling the revocation of his mailing privileges) and 1 May 1939; letters from Sugar to Goldman of 24 and 25 Apr. 1939 (regarding the expurgations in the edition of the memoirs in question); and memoranda by Alexander Lindey and H. F. Pilpel, both 8 May 1940. It also preserves two of Sugar's order forms. The ACLU Archives (vol. 2158) contain a typed copy of a letter from Albert Goldman to the Library Guild (the corporation through which Sugar conducted his business) dated 28 Mar. 1939, and a copy of Sugar's circular.

3. U.S. Senate, Attorney General's Committee on Administrative Procedure, *Administrative Procedure in Government Agencies*, pt. 12: *The Post Office Department*, S. Doc. 186, 76th Cong., 1st sess. (Washington, D.C.: GPO, 1940), 38–40. "In cases involving lottery and unmailability questions . . . a major device of enforcing these statutes is through the medium of advance opinions. It is not at all uncommon for publishers and others to submit advertisements and other written materials" (39). See Patricia E. Robertus, "Postal Control of Obscene Literature, 1942–57" (Ph.D. diss., University of Washington, 1974), 71–72.

4. Attorney General's Committee on Administrative Procedure, 39: "The Department's officials do not consider that such advance opinions are in the nature of final judgements. . . . Nor are they considered binding upon the Department 'in the event that action becomes necessary under the postal laws and regulations'."

5. James N. Paul and Murray Schwartz, *Federal Censorship: Obscenity in the Mail* (Glencoe, Ill.: Free Press of Glencoe, 1961), 69.

6. Attorney General's Committee on Administrative Procedure, regarding foreign fraud order procedures: "The respondent normally knows nothing about the proceedings until suddenly he finds that no mail is arriving from the United States" (36). Obscene advertisements, the report goes on to say, are inherently fraudulent, since it is illegal to import the materials. The same procedure was applied to domestic unmailable determinations. The section of the report on fraud orders (15–41) deals with fraud and obscenity as related problems that the Post Office uses similar methods to combat.

7. "Publishers were given twenty-five days from the time of initial ruling to seek an Injunction against the Postmaster General" (Robertus, "Postal Control," 63). Regarding the improbability of courts overruling postal counsel decisions, see National Council on Freedom from Censorship, "An Outline History of Post Office Censorship" (New York, 1932), 182, 191, ACLU Archives, 509: 177–98 (typescript).

8. Attorney General's Committee on Administrative Procedure, 14.

9. Ibid., 42.

10. Harriet F. Pilpel to Morris Ernst, 15 and 21 Oct. 1940, file 386, MLE Papers. The 21 Oct. memo states, "we would be willing to take the case through the District Court for $1000 plus disbursements."

11. This information is recorded on a legal-size page of unsigned, undated holograph notes on the case in file 388, MLE Papers. The Nov. 1938 establishment of a book rate allowed booksellers to use the U.S. mails at a much cheaper tariff than that of Railway Express. This probably made the postal authorities suspect increasing use of the mails by those they considered smutmongers. However, mail-order booksellers wary of censorious postal inspectors would not have risked a carrier for their books other than Railway Express. See "President Reduces Postal Rates," *PW*, 5 Nov. 1938, 1664; "Important New Rulings on Postal Rates," *PW*, 12 Nov. 1938, 1757; "Postage on Books Is Cut by President to 1½ Cents," *NYT*, 2 Nov. 1938, 41; Richard B. Kielbowicz, "Mere Merchandise or Vessels of Culture: Books in the Mail, 1792–1942," *Papers of the Bibliographical Society of America* 82.2 (June 1988): 194–99.

12. "If a wary publisher of possible obscene publications decides to distribute them by express . . . so as to avoid trouble with the Post Office, he is still punishable under the federal criminal law. . . . However, there is no administrative censorship of interstate transportation outside the mails; and in the case of a border-line novel the publisher may think that the practical risks of a federal prosecution and conviction are small" (Zechariah Chafee Jr., *Government and Mass Communication* [Chicago: University of Chicago Press, 1947], 1: 290).

13. National Council for Freedom from Censorship, "Memorandum Regarding the Staff Report of the Attorney General's Committee on the Post Office Department," 10–11, ACLU Archives, 2158: 10–11; Boyer, *Purity in Print: The Vice-Society Movement and Book Censorship in America* (New York: Scribner's, 1968), 237–38; "Literary Expert Made Censor of Book Imports," *New York Herald Tribune*, 12 Oct. 1934, ACLU Archives, 687: 193.

14. Morris Ernst and William Seagle, *To the Pure: A Study of Obscenity and the Censor* (New York: Viking, 1928), 67–81, 149. See also Paul and Schwartz, *Federal Censorship*, 31–37, 91–94; National Council for Freedom from Censorship, "Memorandum Regarding the Staff Report," 2, 10.

15. Frederick F. Schauer, *The Law of Obscenity* (Washington, D.C.: Bureau of National Affairs, 1976), 14–15; Dorothy G. Fowler, *Unmailable: Congress and the Post Office* (Athens: University of Georgia Press, 1977), 65–66.

16. Fowler, *Unmailable*, 69–70; Rochelle Gurstein, *The Repeal of Reticence: A History of America's Cultural and Legal Struggles over Free Speech, Obscenity, Sexual Liberation, and Modern Art* (New York: Hill and Wang, 1996), 183.

17. Britchey to Pilpel, 4 May 1940.

18. U.S. House of Representatives, Subcommittee 8 of the Committee on the Post Office and Post Roads, *Hearings*, 74th Cong., 1st sess., H.R. 154, 3252, 5049, 5162, 5370 (Washington, D.C.: GPO, 1935), 92.

19. Morris L. Ernst and Alan U. Schwartz, *Censorship: The Search for the Obscene* (New York: Macmillan, 1964), 96–104; Felice Flannery Lewis, *Literature, Obscenity, and Law* (Carbondale: Southern Illinois University Press, 1976), 126–29.

20. See U.S. House of Representatives, Select Committee on Current Pornographic Materials, *Report*, 82nd Cong., 2d sess. H.R. 596 (Washington, D.C.: GPO, 1953), *Hearings*, 5–12, and the Minority Report, 122–23.

21. The function and methodology of the bureaucratic enforcer of a moral precept is analyzed in Donald T. Dickson, "Bureaucracy and Morality: An Organizational Perspective on a Moral Crusade," *Social Problems* 16 (fall 1968): 143–56; and in Richard Sennett, *Authority* (New York: Vintage, 1981), 93–104.

22. The concept of the layers or nests of authority that preserve conventional moral values is taken from Robert L. Peabody, *International Encyclopedia of the Social Sciences*, 1968 ed., s.v. "Authority." A discussion of "Autonomy, an Authority Without Love" appears in Sennett, *Authority*, 84–97, 100–104.

23. Lenny Bruce, *How to Talk Dirty and Influence People* (1972; New York: Fireside, 1992), 1.

24. See Paul Payne, "Another Con Job!" *Books Are Everything* (summer 1990): 26–27.

25. A. Heymoolen to National Council on Freedom from Censorship, 12 Aug. 1932, ACLU Archives, 503: 46–49; Alexander Lindey to H. C. Stewart, assistant collector, Customs, 17 May 1932, File 270, MLE Papers; Heymoolen v. U.S., 1 Aug. 1928, bound vol. 94, MLE Papers.

26. Courtney Ryley Cooper, *Designs in Scarlet* (New York: Little, Brown, 1939), 181–83, 196, 237.

27. One can find the papers, including indictments, relevant to these fraud orders in NA. Personnel in the Civil Reference Branch located these, using Arthur Hecht et al., comp., *Preliminary Inventories of the Post Office Department* (Washington, D.C.: National Archives and Records Service, 1967), and finding, relevant to archive 50, "Fraud Order Case Files." Docket books direct the reader (in some instances) to case files. I consulted cases 5815, 5885, 5896, 6171, 6667, 6688, 6694, and 6737, relevant to the "Tillie and Mac" fraud.

28. The following Post Office case files are fraud orders concerning the offers of Parisian erotic photos and booklets: 6536, 6565, and 6570 (preserved in NA).

29. Henry N. Pringle, memorandum, 19 Jan. 1932, Paige box 2, WW Papers.

30. "Bootleg Literature," *PW*, 28 Mar. 1931, 1689.

31. *Annual Report of the Postmaster General* (Washington, D.C.: GPO, 1937, 1938, 1939). There were 2,266 investigations in 1938 (141) and 2,380 in 1939 (92).

32. The society's president was Alfred C. Risdon. It shared an address with Dingwall-Rock Ltd., owned by Adam Dingwall, one of the best-established mail-order booksellers,

with many years of experience in finding and importing European classics. For Dingwall's obituary, see *NYT*, 9 Aug. 1935, 17.

33. Several Anthropological Library catalogs are in the vertical file at the library of the Kinsey Institute. The Jersey City address seems to be earlier than the New York one. Two names are mentioned: Alex Field and A[nthony] Engel. John Sumner, in a letter to Ellis Meyers of the American Booksellers Association dated 13 Mar. 1930, mentions a "Schwartzenfeld, alias Field." He was discussing the Post Bill and its provisions to make publishers corespondents with booksellers at obscenity trials, and objecting to the bill as not reaching underground distributors.

34. Shomer was called as a government witness at the May 1939 trial of Ben and Anne Rebhuhn of the Falstaff Press, and their business manager, Ben Raeburn. *U.S. v. Ben Rebhuhn, Anne Rebhuhn, and Ben Raeburn*, C-97-410, U.S. District Ct., So. District of N.Y., trial transcript, 194ff. The transcript is available at the library of the federal courthouse in Manhattan. Shomer's testimony concerned the sale of two editions of American Ethnological Press books to Rebhuhn.

35. Stated in the list of publishers appended to *The United States Catalogue*, 1 Jan. 1928.

36. *U.S. v. Esar Levine*, C97-165, U.S. District Ct., So. District of N.Y. (1935), trial transcript, 78.

37. *U.S. v. Ben Rebhuhn, Anne Rebhuhn, and Ben Raeburn*, 314; *U.S. v. Rebhuhn et al.* 109 F2d 512 (2d Cir. 1940), 515 (point 8); "Two Publishers Get Prison Sentences," *NYT*, 14 June 1939, 8. Ben Raeburn, a nephew of Rebhuhn, was office manager. He later became director of the Horizon Press. Raeburn's obituary ("Ben Raeburn, 86, Publisher of the Known and the Aspiring") appeared in *NYT*, 23 April 1997, D23.

38. The first advertisement for the press appeared in the 3 Dec. 1930 issue of the *Nation* (634). However, it did not describe the "scientific sexualia," "anthropological esoterica," or "unexpurgated classics exotically illustrated" that later notices did (for example, those in *Scribner's*, May 1934, 4, or the *Nation*, 30 May 1934, 621). The 1930 advertisement may have been written before Falstaff had developed its list or been incorporated. There is a two-volume edition of *The Tales and Novels of La Fontaine*, illustrated by Clara Tice, which was published in Holland and which has "Falstaff Press, 1929" on the spine and pastedown endpapers. I am grateful to Vytenis Babrauskas of Damascus, Maryland, who is compiling a list of Tice's illustrations, for sharing this information with me.

39. Duly recorded in the Library of Congress Copyright Office. For a checklist of the publications of the Panurge and Falstaff Presses, see my " 'Esoterica' and 'The Good of the Race': Mail-Order Distribution of Erotica in the 1930s," *Papers of the Bibliographical Society of America* 86.3 (1992): 333–40.

40. Jacob L. Chernofsky, "Sol. Malkin's Passion: The Best of All Possible Book Worlds," in *The 1987 Bookman's Yearbook* (New York: Bookman's Weekly, 1987), 3–9. A collection of Malkin's books and papers is preserved in the Pattee Library, Pennsylvania

State University, College Park, Pa. A checklist of the collection identifies him as translator or writer of several works.

41. Malkin was paid between $350 and $450 per assignment. He selected many of the illustrations from those he had collected during his Berlin studies; the rest were reproduced by permission from the magazine *Sexology*. The fact that these illustrations, although many reproduced classical erotic art, were generally unrelated to the text was noted at the 1939 trial of Rebhuhn, his wife, and Raeburn for mailing obscene matter. Malkin was responsible for the pamphlets *The Natural Method of Birth Control* and *Cultural and Scientific Pictorial Studies in Sex Anatomy and the Technique of Coitus*, both written under the pseudonym James Bruce. I am grateful to Mary Ann Malkin for sharing this information about her late husband with me.

42. The Copyright Office of the Library of Congress has claimant registration cards for the following Julian titles: Zola's *The Human Beast* (Mar. 1932), Bloch's *Marquis de Sade: The Man and His Age* (Sept. 1931), Moll's *Perversions of the Sex Instinct* (Apr. 1931), Hoddan's *Sex Life in Europe: A Biological and Sociological Survey* (Sept. 1933), Hirschfeld's *Sexual Pathology* (Aug. 1932), and Arnac's *Three of A Kind* (Dec. 1931). Copyright was applied for by Julia Brussel, Jacob's first wife. Addresses given were in Manhattan, Newark, and Brooklyn. There is one copyright claimed by Risus Press: Sade's *Justine, or the Misfortunes of Virtue*, with illustrations by Mahlon Blaine. The application was made in the name of I.R. Brussel, Jacob's brother.

43. "Government Acts to Stop Obscene Circulars," *PW*, 20 July 1935, 154–55. The KI Files contain circulars for Emerson, Allied, Abbey, and Parnassus. The Biblion Balzac, 15 Park Row, New York City, is cited in a letter by John Sumner to C. H. Bodwell, 17 May 1933, Paige box, 3, WW Papers. As Sumner conjectures, Biblion Balzac was dedicated to distributing remaindered copies of Panurge Press books, and was operated by two of Esar Levine's sisters (Susan Lane, letter to the author, 21 Nov. 1998). Emerson (Jacob Brussel, proprietor?) placed many advertisements in the *Nation* for 1934. The Allied Book Company may have been under the direction of Joseph Meyers of the Illustrated Editions Company.

44. Lamar Hardy to the Attorney General, 21 Apr. 1936, U.S. Dept. of Justice, Central Files, file 97-51-11, NA. John Sumner, when attempting to prosecute Levine in 1931 for Clement Wood's *Flesh*, assumed that twenty thousand were distributed per each limited edition of one thousand copies each (although he doubted the accuracy of the limitation statements); Panurge's office manager admitted to five thousand circulars. Testimony in 1935 established that between Jan. and May of that year, 219,163 were mailed, and for the previous four months, 62,765 had gone out (*U.S. v. Levine*, 83 F2d 156 (2d Cir. 1936), trial transcript, 74–75.

45. In 1935, the same Post Office campaign against obscene books and circulars that eventually brought about the conviction of Esar Levine and three Falstaff executives led to the arrest of Louis Shomer; one hundred copies of the American Ethnological Press's *Tender Bottoms* were confiscated ("Seven Book Sellers Indicted," *NYT*, 27 Nov. 1935, 19).

46. Eugenics had been under suspicion previously. In Nov. 1935, one of seven book-sellers indicted for mailing circulars for obscene literature was Mark Jacobs, then identified as president of the Book Collectors Association ("Seven Book Sellers Indicted," 19). In 1938, Jacobs was associated with the American Biological Society, from whom an FBI investigator purchased a pamphlet of nude photographs. With the order came circulars from Eugenics. The two firms shared a common address, and the agent assumed they were the same business (FBI Investigative Reports, 6 Oct. 1938 and 20 Oct. 1939; memorandum, 8 Mar. 1939; John J. Quinn to the Attorney General, 10 Oct. 1938; U.S. Dept. of Justice, Central Files, file 97-48-6, NA).

47. Levine discussed his admiration for Carrington in an interview with Brooklyn bookseller C. J. Scheiner, c. 1980.

48. That physicians and especially dentists were large consumers of mail-order erotica was volunteered to the present writer during personal interviews with the following: C. J. Scheiner, 5 June 1987 and 14 Nov. 1991; Adelaide Kugel, 3 July 1987; the New York bookseller and editor Arnold Levy, 3 June 1987; the erotic bibliographer, and one-time colleague of Jacob Brussel and Samuel Roth, Gershon Legman, 17 June 1990; and Mrs. Mina Brussel, Jacob's widow, 21 Dec. 1991.

49. "Government Acts," 154. See also "Obscene Book Ads Jail a Publisher," *NYT*, 21 Sept. 1935, 32.

50. See *U.S. v. Ben Rebhuhn, Anne Rebhuhn, and Ben Raeburn*, 179.

51. Ibid., 179. Testimony of F. F. Weiss of the J. A. Want Organization.

52. Ibid., 189. Testimony of J. D. Kisch of the Globe Mail Service.

53. Records of the Post Office, Office of the Postmaster General, Office of the Solicitor (archive 52 of the *Preliminary Inventories*), "Transcripts of Hearings on Fraud Cases, 1913–45," 9–26, box 2, in re Truth Publishing Company, NA, Hearing of 16 Dec. 1921. Most of the editors required a copy of the book before approving the advertising copy, but none turned it down.

54. Ibid., 161–71. Testimony of Paul Tomko of Roberts and Reimers.

55. Adelaide Kugel, personal interview, 3 July 1987.

56. "U.S. Starts War on Obscene Letter Clubs," *New York Herald Tribune*, 10 Dec. 1936, JA Files.

57. *U.S. v. Ben Rebhuhn, Anne Rebhuhn, and Ben Raeburn*, 183–90, 240–41.

58. Ibid., 183–91. Testimony of J. D. Kisch.

59. Ibid., 110–13. Testimony of William Fitzgibbon.

60. The docket books are in NA. See n. 27 above.

61. *Annual Report of the Postmaster General* (Washington, D.C.: GPO, 1939), 88.

62. Gershon Legman, "Sex Censorship in the U.S.A.," *PLAN: Organization of the British Progressive League* (London), 2.1 (Jan. 1945): 2–9.

63. Samuel Lubell, *The Future of American Politics* (New York: Harper's, 1951), 34–39; Richard Hofstadter, *The Age of Reform from Bryan to F.D.R.* (New York: Knopf, 1956), 298–301.

64. Francis G. Couvares, "Hollywood, Main St., and the Church: Trying to Censor the Movies Before the Production Code," *American Quarterly* 44.4 (Dec. 1992): 608.

65. Legman, "Sex Censorship," 5.

66. Samuel Roth, "The Women of Plentipunda, Part 3," *American Aphrodite* 4.15 (1954), 134.

67. Paul and Schwartz, *Federal Censorship*, 72. Paul Blanchard (*The Right to Read* [Boston: Beacon, 1955], 186) reports that the NODL was created by a "Bishop's Committee on decent literature. . . . It was headed for many years by Archbishop John F. Noll of Fort Wayne."

68. The council's passionate statement exists in its sixteen-page "Memorandum Regarding the Staff Report" prepared in June 1940 in response to the report of the Attorney General's Committee on the Post Office Department cited in note 3.

69. U.S. House of Representatives, Subcommittee 8 of the Committee on the Post Office and Post Roads, *Hearings*, 74th Cong., 1st sess., H.R. 154, 3252, 5049, 5162, 5370 (Washington, D.C.: GPO, 1935). The Subcommittee heard testimony regarding H.R. 5162 (mail fraud) from postal inspectors, and regarding H.R. 5370 (depositing obscene matter) from a Post Office inspector, representatives of physicians' organizations and citizens' groups, Monsignor John Ryan, Margaret Sanger, and Morris Ernst. See 59–60, 63–64, 86–89. H.R. 5370 was intended to allow prosecution in the jurisdiction to which, as well as from which, the material was sent; it was of special concern to those who advocated exempting information regarding birth control from antiobscenity laws.

In 1935, New York postmaster Albert Goldman informed the Eugenics Publishing Company that the pamphlet "The Natural Method of Birth Control" "should not be refused admission to the mails." Letter of 14 May, file 388, MLE Papers.

70. Blanchard's treatment of the NODL occurs in the first edition of his *American Freedom and Catholic Power* (Boston: Beacon, 1950), 188. In his introduction to the second edition, which appeared in 1958, Blanchard mentions the impossibility of publishing a paperback version because of Catholic threats of boycott.

71. John F. Noll, *Manual of the N[ational] O[rganization for] D[ecent] L[iterature]* ([Huntington, Ind.]: [Our Sunday Visitor], n.d.), 22, 116.

72. See note 3; Chafee, *Government and Mass Communication*, analyzes the report in detail (325–66). He describes it as the "[Dean] Acheson Monograph"; it was prepared under Acheson's supervision.

73. The quotation is in Alexander Lindey to Hazel Rice, 6 Apr. 1940, box 827, MLE Papers.

74. [Morris Ernst] to Dean Acheson, 10 July 1940, box 827, MLE Papers. Acheson was chairman of the Administrative Procedure Committee. As its director, Professor Walter Gellhorn of Columbia University was responsible for the language of the document (Dean Acheson to Morris Ernst, 22 Mar. 1940, box 827, MLE Papers).

75. Letters to John S. Sumner, 11 Nov. 1931 and 20 Dec. 1935, Paige box, 3, WW Papers.

76. Henry N. Pringle to Charles H. Bodwell, 2 Apr. 1935, Paige box 2, WW Papers.

77. "The Post Office Censor" (sixteen-page pamphlet) (New York: NCFC, 1936), file 827, MLE Papers.

78. All these names, except Cutting's, appear on the NCFC letterhead of a four-page communication dated 7 Jan. 1932, announcing the council's agenda (box 394, MLE Papers). Cutting spoke strongly against Customs' interdictions of books that its officers deemed obscene, and engaged in a famous debate on censorship with Senator Reed Smoot during the congressional debate on the tariff in 1930. See Chapter 3.

79. Samuel Walker, *In Defense of American Liberties: A History of the ACLU* (New York: Oxford University Press, 1990), 96.

80. Hazel Rice to Alexander Lindey, 15 Apr. 1940, box 827, MLE Papers.

81. Alexander Lindey to Joseph Mann, 9 Nov. 1932, file 388, MLE Papers. The reference to page numbers in the letter identifies the book as Carrington's edition; the Falstaff impression is a photolithographic reprint. Lindey describes the references to bestiality, rape, castration, etc., in the circular; it may be Panurge's advertisement for its Robin Hood House edition, which has similar language.

82. Clifton Read to Alexander Lindey, 13 Nov. 1933; Lindey to Read, 14 Nov. 1933, file 394, MLE Papers.

83. Walker, *In Defense of American Liberties*, 104.

84. NCFC, "Memorandum Submitted in Opposition to H.R. 9495" (fourteen-page brief), ACLU Archives, 1092: 209.

85. Walker, *In Defense of American Liberties*, 115–18.

86. Jane M. Friedman, "Erotica, Censorship, and the United States Post Office Department," *Michigan Academician* 4.1 (summer 1971): 12–14. The procedures for finding material unmailable are outlined in the section on the Post Office in the Attorney General's Committee on Administrative Procedure, 4–15 (regarding second-class mailing permits) and 15–38 (fraud orders). The decision to refuse second-class mailing privileges is discussed in relation to obscenity cases, and to situations where the periodical consists largely of advertisements. See also U.S. House of Representatives, Select Committee on Current Pornographic Materials, 117–19 (recommendation 2 of the committee), and the *Hearings* of the committee, 274–87 (testimony of the Post Office's director of mail fraud investigations, of a Post Office solicitor, and of one of its inspectors). This testimony and the 1940 report of the Attorney General's Committee on Administrative Procedures are the lengthiest primary-source explanations of postal methods of investigating and interdicting obscenity and fraud that I have found. The procedures apparently changed very little from the 1930s through the 1950s. See also Chafee, *Government and Mass Communication*, 1: 276–366; U.S. Post Office, *Postal Laws and Regulations of the United States of America* (Washington, D.C.: GPO, 1932), chap. 3 (Unmailable Matter).

87. U.S. House of Representatives, Subcommittee 8 of the Committee on the Post Office and Post Roads, *Hearings*, 74th Cong., 1st sess., 91.

88. *U.S. v. Rebhuhn et al.* point 9.

89. The legal term for guilty knowledge, "scienter," is used here, and often in fraud cases. When Rebhuhn filed an injunction to prevent District Attorney Cahill from prosecuting his case, one of the reasons given for denying the suit was that "Everyone who uses the mails . . . must take notice of what, in this enlightened age, is meant by decency, purity and chastity, in social life, and what must be deemed obscene, lewd, and suggestive" (*Rebhuhn et al. v. Cahill*, 31 F. Supp. 47 [1939]).

90. *U.S. v. Rebhuhn et al.*, 515 (point 9).

91. Decoy letters, inspection by a local postmaster of deposited packets, and the processing of citizens' complaints were the methods by which the Post Office solicitors prepared their cases. See the testimony before the Gathings Committee, *Hearings*, 274–81. First-class mail sent under seal could not be opened legally, but could be determined to be obscene when a postal inspector sent a decoy letter in response to an advertisement for the material. This was not held to be entrapment (Fowler, *Unmailable*, 76–78) but a legitimate way of determining if a crime had been committed. In contrast, for an inspector to place an advertisement himself was considered inducement and forbidden as of the 1890s. See *U.S. Code* title 18, sec. 334, n. 4 and 5 (1927 version). Apparently, however, a postal inspector could obtain a suspect's mailing list, and then write to one of the suspect's customers asking if he could suggest a distributor of "hot stuff." An inspector obtained a copy of *The Perfumed Garden* from Percy Shostak of Brooklyn in 1938 by this method (Roy Richards to Lamar Hardy, 3 Sept. 1938, U.S. Dept. of Justice, Central Files, file 33 S 251-1, NA).

FBI agents investigating the interstate transportation of obscene matter also wrote decoy letters. In one instance, having been informed of the whereabouts of a mail-order purchaser of Tillie and Mac spicy stories, the agent called upon the individual and requested that the package be opened in his presence. The embarrassed purchaser obliged and showed his inquisitor the short stories he had been sent, undoubtedly by first-class mail, which in this case were genuinely pornographic Tijuana bibles, not innocuous imitations (FBI Investigative Report, 4 Aug. 1936, U.S. Dept. of Justice, Central Files, file 97-0, NA).

92. Fowler, *Unmailable*, 171; Paul and Schwartz, *Federal Censorship*, 111–14; Edwin A. Roberts, *The Smut Rakers* (Silver Spring, Md.: National Observer, 1966), 66–69. See also Attorney General's Committee on Administrative Procedure, 32.

93. *Farley v. Simons*; 99 F2d 343 (1938); see point 9.

94. *U.S. v. Levine* 83 F2d 156 (2d Cir. 1936).

95. Gerald Gunther, *Learned Hand: The Man and the Judge* (New York: Knopf, 1994), 340–43. Gunther calls Hand's *Levine* statement "his best as well as his most authoritative writing on the subject of obscenity" (341).

96. "New York Publishers Convicted of Mailing Obscene Literature," *Mail Order Journal: The National Newspaper for Mail Advertisers*, July 1939, ACLU Archives, 2061: 84.

97. *Malinski v. New York*, 324 U.S. 410, 414 (1945). See Robertus, "Postal Control," 191.

98. U.S. Dept. of Justice, Central Files, file 97-51-14 (1939), NA; "Two Publishers Get Prison Sentences," *NYT*, 14 June 1939, 8.

99. *U.S. v. Ben Rebhuhn, Anne Rebhuhn, and Ben Raeburn*, 485.

100. FBI Investigative Report, 21 Nov. 1939, U.S. Dept. of Justice, Central Files, file 97-51-14, NA, 2–3.

101. Paul and Schwartz, *Federal Censorship*, 91.

102. Ibid., 139–49.

103. FBI Investigative Report, 21 Nov. 1939, 2–3.

104. Clifton Read to the members of the NCFC, 29 Apr. 1936, ACLU Archives, 2061: 82.

105. *U.S. v. Ben Rebhuhn, Anne Rebhuhn, and Ben Raeburn*, 4.

106. Book dealers suspected of obscenity apparently had to live with a Damocles' sword of possible legal action, postponed until a test case was adjudicated. In 1940, an assistant attorney general advised J. Edgar Hoover that since Customs considered Petronius's *Satyricon* a classic, the department would await the outcome of a case involving nudist books before attempting prosecution of Personal Books (another imprint of Eugenics), which the FBI had investigated (O. J. Rogge to J. Edgar Hoover, 26 Apr. 1940, U.S. Dept. of Justice, Central Files, file 97-0, NA).

107. U.S. Dept. of Justice, Central Files, file 97-51-11, NA, contains the following: John T. Cahill to the attorney general [Robert H. Jackson], 24 Feb. 1940 (see items 2, 11, 15); Lamar Hardy to the attorney general, 21 Apr. 1936, 2; Esar Levine to Hon. Adolph J. Sabath, [Jan.–Feb. 1940]; Adolph J. Sabath to the attorney general, 26 Feb. 1940.

108. See *U.S. v. Esar Levine*. The trial transcript records the verdict on pp. 10, 108–18. The result of the 1940 retrial is noted on back of "jacket" (form 235) for the indictment. These materials are filed in the Federal Records Center at Bayonne, N.J. (accession 44888).

109. Pretrial memos re *U.S. v. Levine* (Martin Manton, Learned Hand, Augustus Hand), box 197, file 1, Learned Hand Papers, Harvard Law School Library, Cambridge, Mass.

110. Alexander Lindey to A. L. Wirin, 10 Jan. 1947, file 392, MLE Papers. Ernst was discussing with the West Coast lawyer for his client, Marcel Rodd, their defense of a book entitled *Call House Madam*.

111. Advertised in the *Nation*, 11 Apr. 1934, 423, under the heading "An important contribution to the literature of that 'New Morality' which is growing up among thinking people."

112. The headlines are from the *American*, 22 Feb. 1936; *New York Evening Journal*, 10 Dec. 1934; and *New York Post*, 19 Oct. 1935. All found in JA Files.

113. Pretrial memo, *U.S. v. Rebhuhn et al.*, box 202, file 11, Learned Hand Papers.

114. Alexander Lindey to Jerome Britchey, 19 June 1939, ACLU Archives, 2061: 82. Lindey says he had not yet read the books closely, but would "write you again on this." There is no further correspondence in the archive on this matter.

115. *Ginzburg v. U.S.* 86 S. Ct. 942 (1966): "The decision in United States v. Rebhuhn, 109 F.2d 512, is persuasive authority for our conclusion."

116. See Schauer, *The Law of Obscenity*, 83–85; and Harry M. Clor, *Obscenity and Public Morality: Censorship in a Liberal Society* (Chicago: University of Chicago Press, 1969), 79–85, 275, for discussion of the legitimate place of the pandering concept in obscenity rulings, given the fact that it had never been part of the statutes.

117. Brennan cites Murray Schwartz, coauthor of *Federal Censorship: Obscenity in the Mail.*

118. Greenbaum, Wolff, and Ernst to Groff Conklin, 21 Apr. 1937, file 390, MLE Papers.

119. Greenbaum, Wolff, and Ernst to Joseph Brewer, 25 Sept. 1930, file 388, MLE Papers.

120. Greenbaum, Wolff, and Ernst to Joseph Mann, 9 Nov. 1932, file 388, MLE Papers. The letter from Egmont Arens to Morris Ernst, 14 Oct. 1932, is filed at the same location.

121. Arnold Levy (New York bookseller and editor), personal interview, 14 Nov. 1991.

122. The MLE Papers, File 388, contain a four-page memorandum, dated September 11, 1939, from Greenbaum, Wolff and Ernst to Eugenics ("Att: Mr. Mark Jacobs"), and a copy of the Eugenics' circular for the Chideckel title. The *Cumulative Book Index* for 1933–37 reports the book as published in 1935. The *National Union Catalogue* (pre-1956 imprints) lists two copyright dates, 1935 and 1938.

123. Alexander Lindey to Huntington Cairns, 5 Sept. 1939, file 388, MLE Papers. A letter from Mark Jacobs to Lindey (31 Aug. 1939) mentions the fee for this service as five hundred dollars.

124. Legman, *Love and Death: A Study in Censorship* (1949; New York: Hacker Art, 1963), 19–20.

125. Legman, "Sex Censorship," 8.

126. Legman, *Love and Death*, 20.

Chapter 6. The Two Worlds of Samuel Roth

1. James Joyce, *Finnegans Wake* (London: Penguin Books, 1976), 422–23. Leo Hamalian points out these references in "The Secret Careers of Samuel Roth," published in pamphlet form by Harry Barba (Saratoga Springs, N.Y.: Harian Press, 1969).

2. Bill Ryan and L. Horvitz, "Sam Roth," *Hustler,* Feb. 1977, 51; James R. Petersen, "The History of the Sexual Revolution," *Playboy,* Feb. 1998, 157.

3. Leo Hamalian, "Nobody Knows My Names: Samuel Roth and the Underside of Modern Letters," *Journal of Modern Literature* 3.4 (Apr. 1974): 889. This is the seminal treatment of Roth's career and is based on a personal interview with Roth conducted late in his life. There is an earlier version, with an added dimension of psychological analysis: "The Secret Careers of Samuel Roth." This is a revision of the article of the same title that

appeared in the *Journal of Popular Culture* 1.4 (summer 1968): 317–38. Another valuable and perceptive discussion covering Roth's career is Gay Talese, *Thy Neighbor's Wife* (New York: Dell, 1981), chap. 6.

4. This name appears on the verso of the title page of the anonymous *The Strange Confession of Monsieur Montcairn*, which both C. J. Scheiner (*Compendium. Being a List . . .* #1332) and Patrick Kearney (*The Private Case* [London: Landesman, 1981) item 1744) state to have been published by Roth. The title page border is especially distinctive of Roth publications. I am indebted to Scheiner for suggesting the "Jesus without a cross" implication.

5. Robert E. Park, "Human Migration and the Marginal Man (1928)," in *Race and Culture* (Glencoe, Ill.: Free Press, 1950), 356.

6. Maxwell Bodenheim [?], *My Life and Loves in Greenwich Village* (New York: Bridgehead, 1954), 239. The foreword states that "the editors" (Roth) gave Bodenheim office space with which to write this posthumously published volume. Jack B. Moore (*Maxwell Bodenheim* [N.Y.: Twayne, 1970], 171) doubts that Bodenheim wrote the book (he states that Roth did give the writer financial support and office space, and continues, "Roth helped Bodenheim when few could or would"). Roth credits David George Kin (real name Plotkin) with editing Bodenheim's manuscript.

7. See *My Life and Loves in Greenwich Village*, 252–54. I am indebted to Michael Sweeney of Holland, Mich. (letter of 14 May, 1997) for identifying Louis Grudin and for describing his career.

8. Samuel Roth to Milton Abernethy (editor of *Contempo*), 3 Dec. 1931, vertical file (s.v. *Contempo*), Humanities Research Center, University of Texas at Austin.

9. "We Nominate for Oblivion," *Vanity Fair*, June 1932, 42.

10. "Francis Page" edited *Casanova Jr.'s Tales*, a quarterly sold by subscription. "David Zorn" appeared in Roth's unpublished autobiography, one projected title of which was "The Natural History of David Zorn." "Daniel Quilter" is listed on the title page of the short-story collection *Body*. "Norman Lockridge" was used frequently as editor and writer, mostly in the 1940s and 1950s [*Bachelor's Quarters* (New York: Biltmore, 1944)], but beginning in 1935, as writer of the "imaginary dialogue" between Havelock Ellis and Olive Schreiner appended to the Black Hawk Press edition of Ellis's *Kanga Creek*). Roth used "Joseph Brownell" on the title page of his *Telephone Directory as a Guide to American Culture* (New York: Coventry House, 1929). "Eric Hammond" is listed as an alias in Roth's 1936 federal indictment.

11. "Books, Books, Books: William Faro, Inc.," *New Yorker*, 9 Jan. 1932, 76–77. Roth mentioned to Hamalian ("Nobody Knows My Names," 906) a *New Yorker* article by Dorothy Parker that contained "an imaginary conversation between Roth and his many pseudonyms." Perhaps he had in mind the piece cited here, although it is signed R.M.C.

12. Hamalian, "The Secret Careers of Samuel Roth," 110.

13. A letter from one John N. Price appearing in *Modern S4N Review*, Aug. 1926, states that three magazine publishers told him that Roth did not pay his advertising bills. The

issue is in box 129 of the Sylvia Beach Papers, Dept. of Rare Books and Special Collections, Firestone Library, Princeton University, Princeton, N.J.

14. Samuel Roth, "Count Me Among the Missing" (unpublished memoir; in possession of Adelaide Kugel), 297.

15. In *Stone Walls Do Not* (New York: Faro, 1931), 1: 103–4, Roth describes his concept of writing this history. A one-page transcript in the Clement Wood Papers at the Brown University Library, Providence, R.I., outlines the work, to be titled *The Imperial Motive in Contemporary American Poetry*. A 21 May 1921 letter from Roth to Wood (also at Brown) states that the book had been accepted by Dent. In *Stone Walls* Roth writes that Pound responded favorably to a 1921 letter in which he offered to share royalties with the poet if Pound would contribute the notes. *Stone Walls*, a two-volume memoir written during Roth's 1928 workhouse sentence, is an important source of information about his early career.

16. Hamalian, "Nobody Knows My Names," 903; William F. Ryan, "Samuel Roth: A Lion in a Den of Daniels" (unpublished essay, 1977[?]), 39–42. Ryan knew Roth personally for approximately the last two years of his life and admired him. His information regarding the underground classics Roth sold at his bookshop was no doubt based on what Roth told him.

17. Samuel Roth, *Now and Forever: A Conversation with Mr. Israel Zangwill on the Jew and the Future*, preface by Zangwill (New York: McBride, 1925), 9, 27.

18. Norman Lockridge [Samuel Roth], *Lese Majesty: The Private Lives of the Duke and Duchess of Windsor* (New York: Boar's Head, 1952), 42.

19. Roth, *Stone Walls*, 1: 106.

20. Roth calls his work a "novel" and attributes it to one of his aliases, David Zorn; *White Stains* was published under an alias in 1898.

21. A full-page advertisement for four Roth-edited magazines, including the first four numbers of *Two Worlds*, appeared in the *Saturday Review of Literature*, 13 Nov. 1926, 303. A copy of the advertisements may be found in box 129, Sylvia Beach Papers.

22. Samuel Roth to James Joyce, 10 May 1922, box 129, Sylvia Beach Papers.

23. Adelaide Kugel, in " 'Wroth-Rackt Joyce': Samuel Roth and the 'Not Quite Unauthorized' Edition of *Ulysses*," *Joyce Studies Annual* 3 (summer 1992): 242–48, cites several extant letters (some in her personal possession) from Pound to Roth and Joyce that corroborate Roth's own assertions that he had permission. See also R. F. Roberts, "Bibliographical Notes on James Joyce's *Ulysses*," *Colophon*, n.s., 1.4 (1936): 572–74; and Hamalian, "Nobody Knows My Names," 893–94.

24. Letter to the Editor, *New Statesman*, 16 Apr. 1927, 10.

25. The anti-Semitism implied here also surfaces in Joyce's references to Roth in *Finnegans Wake*. See Hamalian, "Nobody Knows My Names," 897–98.

26. Joyce filed suit, but never won any damages from Roth. He did gain an injunction (by that time *Two Worlds Monthly* had ceased publication) preventing the publisher from using his name for profit. Edward de Grazia (*Girls Lean Back Everywhere: The Law of Obscenity and the Assault on Genius* [New York: Random House, 1992], 277) states that

Joyce thus protected his literary property, which was not copyrightable as long as it was ruled obscene.

27. Regarding the *Little Review* expurgations, see Paul Vanderham, *James Joyce and Censorship: The Trials of Ulysses* (New York: New York University Press, 1998), 18–36. Gershon Legman, in a 14 May 1983 letter to Patrick Kearney, cites the Trechmann translation of Montaigne, published by the Modern Library until the United States signed the Berne Copyright Convention, as an example of the lack of U.S. copyright protection for literature published in Britain. I am indebted to Mr. Kearney for showing this letter to me. See de Grazia, *Girls*, 277; Walter Kendrick, *The Secret Museum: Pornography in Modern Culture* (New York: Viking, 1987), 197.

28. Root, "King of the Jews," *transition*, Dec. 1927, 180.

29. Hamalian, "Nobody Knows My Names," appended to his essay in the *Journal of Modern Literature* an excerpt from Roth's unpublished autobiography in which he recalls Freeman as a generous and helpful man (923). For Root's reference to "Joe Freeman" and his story about Roth, see "King of the Jews," 181. Freeman told Root that Roth had opined that "all the kings of the Jews had been literary men." This leads to Root's observation about Roth's "self-contentedness."

30. Joseph Freeman, *An American Testament: A Narrative of Rebels and Romantics* (New York: Farrar and Rhinehart, 1936), 207–09.

31. The *Nation*, 9 Dec. 1925, 681. The notice begins with the headline "On the Battlefield of the Ages without Mercy to Jew or Gentile," and quotes positive reviews from *The American Hebrew*, the *Rochester Herald*, the *Hartford Courant*, and *The Bookman*.

32. "Woman Acquitted in Sale of D. H. Lawrence Book," *New York Herald Tribune*, 10 Sept. 1931, ACLU Archives, 503: 188; "Denies Selling Banned Book," *NYT*, 10 Sept. 1931, 22.

33. "Sumner Drive Traps Five as Obscene Book Dealers," undated newspaper clipping, file 391, MLE Papers. Others arrested were Sol Malkin (then a clerk for Jake Brussel), Henry Klein (whom, according to Roth, Sumner had used to frame him), and David Moss of the Gotham Book Mart.

34. See H. Montgomery Hyde, *A History of Pornography* (New York: Dell, 1966), 190.

35. Hamalian, "Nobody Knows My Names," 901; also recorded in Roth's FBI files, in a list of arrests prepared under the heading NY 71-780. I am grateful to Patrick Kearney, of Santa Rosa, Calif., for sharing his copy of these documents with me.

The 1928 ledgers of the NYSSV state that Roth was also sentenced to six months in the House of Detention. However, another source, which seems more accurate since Roth would probably have been back at work in New York early in 1929, specifies "three months in the Work House." This is a letter marked "Confidential" from Harold Goldman, counselor at law, to George Barr Baker, 26 Oct. 1931, in HH-Misrep. These memos, letters, affidavits, and reports concern charges made against Hoover during his career as engineer, mine owner, and public servant. One-third of the material (containers 8–15) relate to the "smear books" of the early 1930s, including those Roth was involved in preparing.

36. Hamalian, "Nobody Knows My Names," 900–901; the book is also described in C. J. Scheiner's *Compendium* (Brooklyn, N.Y.: C. J. Scheiner, 1989), item 950. For the editions prepared by Burton, see Norman N. Penzer, *An Annotated Bibliography of Sir Richard Burton* (1923; rpt., London: Dawson's of Pall Mall, 1967), 173ff. Often, the Kama Shastra Society listed their place of publication as "Cosmopoli."

37. Roth, *Stone Walls*, 1: 104–9.

38. Ibid., 1: 117.

39. Ibid., 1: 115–18.

40. Goldman to Baker, 26 Oct. 1931, HH-Misrep.

41. "Summary of Report in the Case of Samuel Roth," 1, HH-Misrep. This is a three-page typescript prepared by Roth's probation officer, who states that Roth proposed substituting "legitimate books" for the interdicted one so that he would not lose the monies collected.

42. John Slocum and Herbert Cahoon, *A Bibliography of James Joyce* (New Haven, Conn.: Yale University Press, 1953), 28–29 (item A19). "This pirated edition of the ninth Shakespeare and Company *Ulysses* was printed by Adolph and Rudolph Loewinger, 230 West 17th St., for Samuel Roth, publisher of *Two Worlds* and *Two Worlds Monthly*, and his brother Max Roth. . . . Many copies of this piracy were seized by the Society for the Suppression of Vice, on October 5, 1929" (the press offices were raided 4 Oct. and the storeroom the next day). See also Roberts, "Bibliographical Notes on James Joyce's *Ulysses*," 574–75. The Random House edition, as Roberts shows, was based on Roth's piracy: "By some mischance a copy of the pirated edition, item I, was obtained instead of the intended Shakespeare and Company edition. . . . The publisher of I [Roth], if he has discovered these facts, has probably long since laughed himself into hopeless hysteria" (576–78).

43. [Publisher's] "Advertisement," *The Education of a French Model*, by Kiki (New York: Boar's Head, 1950), 7. He states, undoubtedly erroneously, that the conviction was because of that book.

44. *U.S. v. Samuel Roth*, C53-79, U.S. District Ct., So. District of N.Y. (1929), stenographer's minutes, 28–29.

45. Scheiner states this in his *Compendium*. Gershon Legman discusses Best in *The Horn Book: Studies in Erotic Folklore and Bibliography* (New Hyde Park, N.Y.: University Books, 1964), 34. In his introduction to Patrick Kearney's *Private Case* ([London: Landesman, 1981], 48), Legman states that Best was "Carrington's secret salesman in America."

46. The spine label, both in design, red border, and typeface, is very similar to that used on the backstrip of the second impression of Roth's expurgated edition of *Lady Chatterley's Lover* (New York: Faro, 1931) and his unexpurgated edition bound in black moiré cloth with red endpapers. The typographical border on the title page is similar to those in *Observations of an Old Man in Love* (Philadelphia, Pa.: privately published, 1929) and *The Telephone Directory as a Guide to American Culture*. The typeface is De Vinne, used in the expurgated Faro *Lady Chatterley* in Mirbeau's *Celestine* (New York: Faro, 1930), and in many other Roth productions of the late 1920s and early 1930s.

47. Adelaide Kugel to the author, 7 Sept. 1988; *U.S. v. Samuel Roth*, C53-79, "jacket" of indictment and p. 4 of Judge Knox's revocation statement; four-page memorandum, 12 Oct. 1931, p. 2, HH-Misrep. Three records indicate that the case against Roth for selling obscene books resulting from the 4 Oct. raid was "dismissed." One of these is part of an archive of materials about Roth compiled for Walter Winchell c. 1952, in the possession of the present author. A second is a two-page memorandum headed "Samuel Roth" in HH-Misrep, which states that the magistrate was the liberal, Tammany-connected Judge Brodsky, who infuriated Sumner in 1931 by clearing *Hsi Men Ching* (and *From a Turkish Harem*) on the grounds that the average contemporary adult would not be corrupted. A third is a record of all Roth's arrests compiled by Assistant District Attorney Mark F. Hughes, and made part of an affidavit (pp. 3–4) signed 1 May 1959. Hughes was in charge of the government's case when Roth appealed his sentence of five years in prison for distributing obscene literature. The document is part of *U.S. v. Samuel Roth*, Cr 148-9, U.S. District Ct., So. District of N.Y., 24030 (1959). Apparently, Roth could not be directly linked to the obscene books seized on 4 Oct. 1929, as could Henry Zolinsky (a store employee) and Max Roth. But his involvement in the operations of the Golden Hind Press (the preparation of mail advertisements for banned erotica; the presence of copies of *Lady Chatterley's Lover* at the office at which Roth was arrested) was indisputable and clearly violation of parole. Sumner's ledgers for 1929 state that Max Roth was sentenced to from six months to three years in the penitentiary.

48. *U.S. v. Samuel Roth*, C53-79, stenographer's minutes, 93. Sumner found this note on Roth's desk during the Oct. 1929 raid of the Golden Hind offices.

49. NYSSV periodical letter, signed John Sumner, 28 Oct. 1929. Since Sumner was most probably relying on the invoices he took from Roth's desk at the Golden Hind Press a few weeks earlier, the figures (even allowing for some exaggeration) should be reasonably accurate.

50. Leo Hamalian tells us that Roth "helped to finance [the] publication" of Means's book "and apparently shared in a percentage of the profits" ("Nobody Knows My Names," 905).

51. Fryefield's name does not appear on the title page of *The Strange Career*. Rather, the imprint reads "Guild Publishing." In her *Honesty or Politics*, Britton stated that Fryefield founded Guild at the suggestion of Means and May Dixon Thacker, a writer for Bernarr Macfadden's *True Confessions*. Thacker wrote that she and Means needed a substitute publisher for the latter's exposé, because the original one withdrew. See Nan Britton, *Honesty or Politics* (New York: Elizabeth Ann Guild, 1932), 312–22; Edwin P. Hoyt, *Spectacular Rogue: Gaston B. Means* (Indianapolis, Ind.: Bobbs Merrill, 1963), 283; May Dixon Thacker, "Debunking *The Strange Death of President Harding*," *Liberty*, 7 Nov. 1931, 12–13. The fact that Guild Publishing seems to have distributed some William Faro titles (Bell's *Memoirs and Mistresses* is another possibility) is evidence of a business agreement between Fryefield and Roth. In 1931 and 1932, Roth may have wanted orders to come to the Guild instead of the more common William Faro address to avoid Post Office investigations of his

books — either the Faros or suspected underground titles — and to hide his profits from government scrutiny. He was being investigated by Hoover operatives for a scandal book on the sitting president (see below).

52. We know that when Roth incorporated William Faro in August 1930, very soon after serving his Philadelphia sentence, he had twenty-five thousand dollars on hand: there is a two-page memorandum so stating headed "Samuel Roth," unsigned and undated, but prepared by one of the investigators sent by Herbert Hoover's secretary to investigate Roth after the publication of Hamill's *Strange Career of Mr. Hoover Under Two Flags*, HH-Misrep.

53. Samuel Roth, *Jews Must Live* (New York: Golden Hind, 1934), 190–92. Paro's criminal record is recorded on pp. 4–5 of a fifteen-page Post Office report prepared by C. H. Saffell for Hoover's smear-book investigators. It is titled "New York, NY: Publication and sale of a book entitled 'The Strange Career of Herbert Hoover Under Two Flags' " and is dated 28 Nov. 1931. This document is hereafter cited as Saffell, HH-Misrep.

54. This may be inferred from the criminal record of the city of Philadelphia, a copy of which was sent to C. H. Ebbets of the district attorney's office in Los Angeles, from John J. Kelly of the Philadelphia Police Dept. on 1 Mar. 1954. The record states that on 27 June 1930, Roth was arrested, pled guilty (to distributing *Ulysses* in that city) and was sentenced to sixty days in "County Prison." This record is part of a small archive of materials (in the possession of the present author) prepared for Walter Winchell c. 1954 after Roth published Lyle Stuart's *Secret Life of Walter Winchell*.

55. Roth, *Jews Must Live*, 190–92.

56. Samuel Roth, "By Way of Explanation," in *Lady Chatterley's Lover: A Dramatization*, Ardent Classics 2 (New York: Faro, 1931), 12.

57. Ibid., 9.

58. Roth, "Count Me Among the Missing," 298–99.

59. de Grazia, *Girls*, 174–76, 181–83; Lovat Dickson, *Radclyffe Hall at the Well of Loneliness* (New York: Scribner's, 1975), 167–69.

60. Roth, "Count Me Among the Missing," 303.

61. The letter, in response to Schwartz's discussion of the expurgated *Chatterley*, appeared in Schwartz's *This Book-Collecting Racket* (Chicago: Normandie House, 1937), 5–6.

62. So stated by Adelaide Kugel in an interview with the author, 3 July 1987.

63. Harry T. Moore and Dale B. Montague, eds., *Frieda Lawrence and Her Circle* (London: Macmillan, 1981), 34.

64. Ibid., 33.

65. Roth, "Count Me Among the Missing," 298.

66. Roth, *Jews Must Live*, 193.

67. For the preparation of the authorized edition of *Chatterley* and its distribution in England and America from 1932 to 1968, see my *Descriptive Bibliography of* Lady Chatterley's Lover (Westport, Conn.: Greenwood, 1989), 20–21, 59–64.

68. Review of the authorized [Knopf] edition of *Lady Chatterley's Lover*, *Nation*, 7 Sept. 1932, 214–15.

69. Schwartz, *This Book-Collecting Racket*, 6; Roth, "Count Me Among the Missing," 304.

70. Roth, "By Way of Explanation," 8–9. To warn customers may have been the idea of Arthur Brentano himself, or of Joseph A. Margolies, a buyer for Brentano's and later president of the American Booksellers Association (John Tebbel, *A History of Book Publishing in the United States* [New York: Bowker, 1978], 3: 149).

71. The relevant briefs, letters, memos, and lists of books confiscated can be found in file box 391, MLE Papers, in the folder titled "Gotham Book Mart vs. Sumner, Legal Papers and Draft." Dunster House's James A. Delacey's purchase of five copies of *Lady Chatterley's Lover* from the Golden Hind Press suggests an acquaintance with, and possibly previous orders, from Roth; Roth would not have sent those books without some sense of the proprietor's reliability.

72. Böske to Sylvia Beach, 9 June 1931, box 129, Sylvia Beach Papers.

73. Adelaide Kugel recalled this during an interview with the author, 3 July 1987.

74. Gudaitis preferred the shortened version of his name, Tony Gud, and used it in his letters and business dealings. But he published his novel *A Young Man About to Commit Suicide* (Faro, 1932) under his given name. For authorship of the sequels, see my *Descriptive Bibliography of* Lady Chatterley's Lover, 239–43.

75. Tony Gud, in a questionnaire returned to the present author, 7 July 1988.

76. There were illustrated and unillustrated impressions of this book, the priority of which is difficult to determine. Perhaps the second impression appeared without the illustrations (in the lubricious and decadent style of Rahnghild), out of deference to postal authorities.

77. Hamalian, "Nobody Knows My Names," 906; William F. Ryan, "Clement Wood" (unpublished essay, 1990), 5–7, 20–22. There is a well-researched summation of Wood's literary career to 1931 as part of the Greenbaum, Wolff, and Ernst brief prepared for *People v. Benjamin Levine*, 18 Dec. 1931; see bound vol. 94, MLE Papers, s.v. "Records of Censorship Cases."

78. Adelaide Kugel, in a letter to author of 27 Aug. 1987, identifies Wood as Dubois.

79. Hamalian, "Nobody Knows My Names," 906, states that Wood was in fact coauthor.

80. The dedication occurs in *Warren Gamaliel Harding: An American Comedy*, 30–31, published by Faro in 1932.

81. D. H. Lawrence, "Pornography and Obscenity," *Pornography and So On* (London: Faber and Faber, 1936), 23–24.

82. The index on file in the Archives of the Bankruptcy Court of the Southern District of New York lists William Faro Inc. as applying for bankruptcy on 5 June 1933 (vol. 122, case 57489). Records of cases for that period, however, are no longer available.

83. "Purity at the Port," *Nation*, 22 Feb. 1933, 194.

84. The 1933 impression, with a different title page than the 1930 one, states that it is the "Fourth Printing."

85. The Faro *Body* is another, possibly second impression of the work, which was also issued as "The First [and possibly the only] Publication of the Autographed Editions Club," a book club offering books autographed by their authors. John Tebbel's article "Main Trends in Twentieth Century," in *American Literary Publishing Houses, 1900–1980: Trade and Paperback*, ed. Peter Dzwonkoski (Detroit: Gale Research, 1986), 408, reproduces an advertisement for the club. That Daniel Quilter was really Roth was corroborated by his daughter, Adelaide Kugel, interview of 3 July 1987.

86. Harold Barber to Samuel Roth, 13 Oct. 1932; Roth to Barber, 15 Oct. 1932, box 2, Harris-Ross. "I need not add that I revised whatever work was submitted by my collaborator, so as to whip it, as much as possible, into the stream of my own narrative."

87. Barber to Roth, 4 Oct. 1932; Roth to Barber, 11 Oct. 1932, box 2, Harris-Ross.

88. Nellie Harris to A. L. Ross, 9 Dec. 1931, box 2, Harris-Ross.

89. A. L. Ross to Nellie Harris, 17 Mar. 1932; Harold Auer to Ross, 16 Mar. 1932; Auer to Elmer Gertz, 16 Mar. 1932, box 2, Harris-Ross. Roth's Coventry House imprint was reserved for books and authors he especially liked. The two-volume set of Voltaire's *Philosophical Dictionary* is a prime example, published with profits realized from his scandal book on Hoover. Roth expresses his admiration for Voltaire's work in *Jews Must Live*: "the chief literary and ethical guide of my boyhood" (201–2). Roth expected that reviewers and the general public would consider Coventry House books to be of consequence, and that they would have steady sales. None of them needed to be designated as "privately printed." These volumes, most of which appeared from 1929 to 1932, were higher priced than trade books (*My Friendship* cost four dollars). The Voltaire, however, "fell dead at my feet" because media would not review a book issued by someone with Roth's reputation for sensationalism.

90. "Scout Murder Hint in Gun Trap Death," *NYT*, 4 June 1931, 56: "Mr. Roth . . . said that he had known Dr. Bell for fourteen years."

91. "Burglar Gun Trap Kills Dr. R. H. Bell," *NYT*, 2 June 1931, 31.

92. Bell's statement about the title is on p. 288 of the first, longer Faro edition, and on p. 261 of the second. On p. 75 (p. 72 of the second edition), he talks about the possible misreading of his original title.

93. "Scout Murder Hint," 56; "Burglar Gun Trap," 31. Roth told police that he thought Bell was too careful to have accidentally triggered the gun, and that he suspected his friend had been murdered. There is no indication in the newspaper articles that Roth thought the crime was caused by what Bell wrote.

94. It is possible that a privately printed edition (which the present writer has not located), more explicit than either Faro version, existed. Roth may or not have been responsible. The copyright card for the title in the Library of Congress, submitted by Roth, gives his publication date as 24 Apr. Perhaps the second, shorter Faro (probably posthumous) version is the one Pringle mistakenly thought was privately printed. But the dust-jacket blurb on the second Faro version identifies the book as a "popular edition." To have people think there was a rare, expensive, *sub-rosa* edition would have stimulated sales of the popular edition.

95. The novel includes lurid but objectively described scenes of transvestism and homosexuality; twenty years later, Roth was still offering it by mail order.

96. Most of the Faro list were probably sold as Big Dollar books after the bankruptcy, some with altered title pages to bear the Big Dollar imprint.

97. John S. Sumner to Charles H. Bodwell, 28 Mar. 1931, Paige box 3, WW Papers.

98. "People v. Samuel Roth and People v. Julius Moss, Memorandum for People" (Magistrates' Court), file 90, MLE Papers, 2–4.

99. Gershon Legman, *The Horn Book: Studies in Erotic Folklore and Bibliography* (New Hyde Park, N.Y.: University Books, 1964), 24. In a letter to the author (4 Aug. 1985), Legman says that from 1936 to 1953 he was employed by Roth and that Roth "did a great deal by mail, both over- and under-cover."

100. For instance, *PW*, 16 May 1931, 2397.

101. Roth remaindered copies of his books to mail-order distributors such as the Union Library, the American Ethnological Press, and the Anthropological Library, which printed their own circulars. He also remaindered to a number of smaller-scale mail-order distributors who themselves placed small ads in newspapers and pulp magazines for Faro titles (e.g., *Bedtime Stories*, June 1933, 65; *Pep*, Feb. 1933, 60; *Spicy Stories*, Aug. 1933, 61).

102. In his testimony before the Kefauver Committee in 1955, Roth pointed proudly to a sign which had for a long time hung on his office door: "No books sold on the premises." U.S. Senate, Subcommittee to Investigate Juvenile Delinquency of the Committee on the Judiciary, *Hearings on Juvenile Delinquency (Obscene and Pornographic Materials)*, 84th Cong., 1st sess., S. Res. 62 (Washington, D.C.: GPO, 1955), 201.

103. Tony Gud to the author, 3 July 1987. "Often he would pay me in cash from a filing cabinet full of bills." Gud was himself a mail-order book dealer in the late 1920s and early 1930s, placing ads in the classified sections of New York newspapers and in the Books Wanted columns of *PW*. Lyle Stuart, who published his book on Walter Winchell with Roth in 1953, also recalls that Roth did a lot of direct cash sales, and that customers would often send him cash in the mail (telephone interview of 22 Mar. 1997).

104. "People v. Samuel Roth," 6–7.

105. "People v. Samuel Roth." Moss was represented by Greenbaum, Wolff, and Ernst; Roth by Bushel and Gottleib. Newman Levy and Alexander Lindey argued the case for Moss. These men did not respect prurient advertising methods. Apparently, the literary value of the two books outweighed the advertisements in importance.

106. "Clears Two on Indecent Book Charge," *NYT*, 8 May 1931, 4.

107. Roth, *Jews Must Live*, 194.

108. Ralph Cheyney, "Sex and Poetry," *Contempo*, July 1931, 1, 4.

109. Roth's correspondence with Milton Abernethy, the editor of *Contempo*, indicates that he carried ads and reviews for Roth's books and knew him personally.

110. Ryan, "Samuel Roth: A Lion in a Den of Daniels," 50, reports the incident. The *Vanity Fair* incident is also reported in Dante Cacici, "A Note on the Author," *Bumarap:*

The Story of a Male Virgin, by Samuel Roth (New York: Arrowhead, 1947), 248–49, indicating that Roth was fond of repeating the story.

111. "Books, Books, Books: William Faro, Inc."

112. Hamalian, "Nobody Knows My Names," 903.

113. "Samuel Roth, 79, Tested Obscenity," *New York Times Biographical Edition* (New York: The Times, 1974), 1031 (4 July 1974).

114. David Burner, *Herbert Hoover: A Public Life* (New York: Knopf, 1979), 317; Henry F. Pringle, "Throwing Mud at the White House," *Outlook and Independent*, 9 Dec. 1931, 462.

115. The following HH-Misrep documents concern sales of *Strange Career*. Copies sold: Samuel Roth to John Hamill, 30 Mar. 1932; three-page report headed "Post Office Investigation," 4 Dec. 1931, signed C. H. Saffell. Bank deposits Feb.–Mar. 1932: C. H. Saffell, three-page memorandum headed "Status of Bank Account," 29 Apr. 1932. Volume of mail: Saffell, HH-Misrep. Attempts to hide profits: Saffell three-page report, items 3–5. One of the shadow accounts was under the name of a company with the same address as Faro ("Norman Walters Associates," described by a Post Office inspector as a "cover up"), and the other used the name "Richard Ross." This latter concern was run by two confederates arrested with him at the Golden Hind Press in Oct. 1929, Julius Moss and Henry Zolinsky. Richard Ross also advertised the book.

116. Roth, *Jews Must Live*, 202.

117. Saffell, HH-Misrep, item 1.

118. Ibid., items 15–17 (pp. 5–7).

119. Ibid., items 21–23 (pp. 8–10).

120. The contract, in HH-Misrep, provides a generous allowance to Hamill for research purposes, and an advance of seventy-five dollars per week.

121. Dwight M. Miller, senior archivist, Herbert Hoover Library, to the author, 25 Apr. 1995. Miller states that there is evidence that Hoover did not want this kind of subterfuge to take place on his behalf.

122. Samuel Roth, "Seeing Mr. Hoover Through," *Plain English*, June 1932, 5–14. This magazine was "Copyright 1932 by William Faro, Inc." Its contributors included Rothian allies such as Clement Wood, his wife (Gloria Goddard), and Harold Auer.

123. Roth, *Jews Must Live*, 197.

124. Burner, *Herbert Hoover*, 317.

125. Saffell, HH-Misrep, items 6 and 7. Saffell states that O'Brien, as of the time he prepared his report, was a blackmailer. Part of a letter discussing the material Hamill researched, which Hamill wrote to O'Brien when he broke with him and which Arthur Train dates 4 Sept. 1930, was reproduced in Train, *The Strange Attacks on Herbert Hoover* (New York: John Day, 1932), 10–13. The complete four-page letter is part of HH-Misrep, as is Hamill's confessional affidavit. It documents the liaison between the two men, how it came about, and why it broke down.

126. So stated in Train, *Strange Attacks*, 14.

127. John Hamill, *The Strange Career of Mr. Hoover Under Two Flags* (New York: Faro, 1932), 81.

128. From Hoover's reports on the Kaiping mines, as quoted in Herbert Corey, *The Truth About Hoover* (Boston: Houghton Mifflin, 1932), 130. This is one of the two books published in 1932 defending Hoover against the smear books. The other was Train's *Strange Attacks*, which was largely a reprint of an article Train wrote for *Colliers'*.

129. As stated on p. 252, Hamill signed an affidavit in which he detailed the origins of the book, the sources he used, and why its conclusions were unsound. This document was summarized in several newspaper accounts when it was made public in Jan. 1933: "Author Repudiates Anti-Hoover Book," *NYT*, 5 Jan. 1932, 23. Hamill states that the British firm did not make a profit, and did not encourage importation of coolies (63, 64, and 71 of Hamill's affidavit). The document, with his signature at the bottom of every page, is in HH-Misrep.

130. Train, *Strange Attacks*, 19–22.

131. Corey, *Truth About Hoover*, 33; Clement Wood, *Herbert Clark Hoover: An American Tragedy* (New York: Michael Swain, 1932), 27.

132. "Court Bars Book on the President," *NYT*, 17 Dec. 1931, JA Files.

133. Roth repeats most of this account in *Jews Must Live*, 196–98.

134. Clement Wood was commissioned to rewrite Hamill's book. *Herbert Clark Hoover: An American Tragedy* contained a Prologue introducing Hoover as a "promoter" of various lucrative schemes and defending Roth as an honorable bookman. The injunction against *The Strange Career* was no longer in force when Wood's book was published, but Roth did not use the Faro imprint. He may have been anticipating that Cotillo would finally rule in favor of O'Brien. The publisher was identified as "Michael Swain." The work may have been issued as a refutation of Train and Pringle. It is also possible that Roth could have heard of Hamill's retraction. In any event, apparently both Wood's book, and O'Brien's, sold poorly. ("Status of [bank] account of Samuel Roth," 29 Mar. 1932, p. 3, HH-Misrep. The investigator learned that Macy's had sold only 10 copies of O'Brien in 6 weeks, and only 8 copies of Wood in 8 weeks.) As for the unsold copies of Hamill, Herbert Hoover, who thought many of his enemies were fellow-travelers, stated that for years they were sold in Communist bookstores. He also said, "the Communists brought out a cheap edition for wider circulation." There was a paperbound impression, which may have been the "tenth printing," the last one listed verso its title page (*Memoirs*, 3: 224).

135. The only detailed source for the events described in this section is *Jews Must Live* (204–19). Roth does not use real names, only deprecatory fictional ones. The narrative given here follows his account, with caution, and is supplemented in subsequent paragraphs by relevant, and partly corroborative, letters and Hamalian's article.

136. A search in WorldCat of the OCLC Online Union Catalog shows that the four titles listed here have Nesor as well as Faro imprints. *A Scarlet Pansy* and *Lady Chatterley's Lover* also have Royal imprints. The Royal text of *A Scarlet Pansy* is about half the length of the original edition. The Royal *Chatterley* is the same text as the Faro and Nesor.

137. Gershon Legman to the author, 4 Aug. 1985 and 6 Sept. 1988. The Rose Book-

binding Company at 200 West Street is listed in the *Phillips Business Directory* for New York City, 1928–29 ed.

138. See "Crown Publishers: The First Ten Years," *PW*, 11 Nov. 1946, 2806–10; Edwin McDowell, "Tight Grip on a Rich Empire," in *New York Times Biographical Service* (New York: Arno Press, 1981), 1448–49. We do not know for sure who Nesor was, but we know something about the kinds of binderies and printing concerns Roth used for some of his Faro titles. When Republican party investigators were looking into Roth's affairs in 1931, they found that the binder for *The Strange Career of Herbert Hoover Under Two Flags* was the Associated Binderies, a "consolidation of three small, unimportant binderies" (Uneeda [Max Rowan], Charlton [Samuel Berg], and Lafayette [Isidor Weisman]). Roth chose an obscure printer for the first twenty-six hundred copies but found some deficiencies, and so the bulk of the approximately fifteen thousand copies was entrusted to the Polytype Company and the Evolution Printing Company, the owner of which was L. Spiegel (a name mentioned elsewhere in connection with the Graphic Press, recommended to Esar Levine in 1925 as a possible printer for vols. 3 and 4 of Harris's *My Life*). Type was manufactured at the Appellate Press. Bloch Paper Company provided the sheets. All of these concerns were located in the lower Broadway or Varick Street area. Roth contracted with Uneeda Binderies for three early 1931 titles: *The Woman Who Was Pope, Moon over Broadway*, and *A Pregnant Woman in a Lean Age*. The relevant documents in HH-Misrep are a three-page memorandum headed "Post Office Investigation," 4 Dec. 1931, signed C. H. Saffell; and Saffell, HH-Misrep, item 4.

139. The information about the skywriting and the Nazi rallies is provided in a fascinating unpublished essay, "Samuel Roth," by Milton Hindus, whose important study of Céline, *The Crippled Giant*, was published by Roth in 1950.

140. *U.S. v. Pauline Roth and Samuel Roth* C99-114, U.S. District Ct., So. District of N.Y. (1936), Memorandum in Support of Application for Modification of Sentence (22 June 1937), 7.

141. Ryan, "Clement Wood," 27–28. Ryan interviewed Jack Brussel, who told him that Wood, not Roth, actually wrote the book, from notes provided by Roth. Brussel said Roth simply could not concentrate on such an intense writing task long enough to finish it. Roth had said something similar about himself in regard to *The Private Life of Frank Harris*, which Wood ghostwrote. Whoever wrote *Jews Must Live*, there is much of Roth's idiosyncratic character in it, and he must be held responsible.

142. Roth, *Jews Must Live*, 11.

143. "King of the Jews," *transition*, Dec. 1927, 181.

144. Hindus, "Samuel Roth," 4, 17–19, 27–28. *My Sister and I* was published under Roth's Boar's Head imprint in 1951. The title page credited Oscar Levy, editor of Nietzsche's complete works, with the translation. The book may be a hoax; Roth told Walter Kaufmann of Princeton that a manuscript of it had fallen into his hands. See Hamalian, "Nobody Knows My Names," 913–14.

145. Roth, *Stone Walls*, 2: 197–202. Roth states that Josephus surrendered at Masada, confusing that with Josephus's action at the city of Jotapata (198).

146. Zangwill, preface to *Now and Forever*, 27.

147. Roth, *Now and Forever*, 139–40.

148. Roth, *Stone Walls*, 1: 52–53.

149. On p. 50 of "Samuel Roth: A Lion in a Den of Daniels," William Ryan describes Roth's idiosyncratic dress. Milton Hindus, "Samuel Roth," 10, notes Roth's gloves, spats, well-tailored suits, and glasses. Gershon Legman, in a letter to Leo Hamalian and the present writer, 11 Nov. 1986, reminiscences about "the cane [Roth] always carried, à l'anglaise."

150. Lyle Stuart, telephone interview, 22 Mar. 1997.

151. These ideals and allegiances of Roth's are pointed out by Milton Hindus. They are stressed in one of the biographical essays Roth was wont to publish in his own books: "Public Bohemian No. 1," in Bodenheim[?], *My Life and Loves*, 237–46. The statement about man as beast is on p. 242.

152. Roth, *Jews Must Live*, 19–20.

153. Roth, *Jews Must Live*, 76–78. This incident is also described in *Stone Walls Do Not*, 2:264–66. For Yehoshea, spelled "Yehoash," at the Poetry Book Shop see *Stone Walls Do Not*, 1:90.

154. Roth, *Jews Must Live*, 107; writers present included Mina Loy, Karl Wisehart, John Gould Fletcher, and one "Herbert," whom Roth addresses at the beginning of the book. In *Stone Walls Do Not* (1:90), Roth lists other customers with whom he enjoyed discussing literary matters (E. A. Robinson, Edna St. Vincent Millay, Ralcy Bell, Herbert Gorman, Max Bodenheim) at his shop at 49 West 8th Street. The most comprehensive list of patrons of the Poetry Book Shop is in Cacici, "A Note on the Author," 233–56. This is one of several biographical essays Roth planted in books he published. The essays were written by friends, associates in his publishing business, or (possibly) by himself. Another is in Bodenheim[?], *My Life and Loves*.

155. Daniel Quilter [Samuel Roth], *Body: A New Study, in Narrative, of the Anatomy of Society* (New York: Autographed Editions Club, 1931), 33.

156. *U.S. v. Pauline Roth and Samuel Roth*. The terms of the sentence are inscribed on the "jacket" of the indictment. The sentences were recorded in a letter from FBI Special Agent Whitley to J. Edgar Hoover, 31 Dec. 1936 (the letter is part of Roth's FBI file). The bureau helped the U.S. attorney for the Southern District of New York, Lamar Hardy, by providing an expert to analyze a sample of Pauline Roth's handwriting. Another interesting group of three letters and memos relevant to this case document the request of Representative Emmanuel Celler of New York for Roth's criminal record. These are dated Jan. 1938 and may have been requested as part of an appeal by Roth for reduction of his prison sentence. Celler had liberal views on censorship and First Amendment issues, as his endorsement of the Minority Report of the Gathings Committee investigating pornographic materials (1952) indicates.

157. "U.S. Indicts Couple over 'Obscene' Mail," *New York American*, 2 Oct. 1936, ACLU Archives, 879: 164.

158. This minor conviction seems to have escaped some FBI and police listings of

Roth's arrest record. It is recorded in a letter from John S. Sumner to Charles H. Bodwell, 30 June 1934, Paige box 3, WW Papers, and Sumner records it in the NYSSV ledgers for 1934, stating thirteen books were involved and the sentence was a hundred dollars or twenty days. In the Walter Winchell Archive, there is a notation on an unsigned sheet indicating the arrest was on 19 Mar. 1934. An FBI record prepared in the mid-1950s, headed NY 71-780 (in Roth's FBI files) notes a 29 June 1934 conviction and combines it with the 1936 one in description of the offense: "possession of indecent books and mailing non-mailable matter." The affidavit of Assistant District Attorney Mark F. Hughes (*U.S. v. Samuel Roth*, Cr 148-9, U.S. District Ct., So. District of N.Y., 24030 [1959], 3–4) includes a thorough list of Roth's arrests and convictions. He states, "20 days or pay fine of $100; paid fine."

159. "Publisher Found Guilty," *NYT*, 10 Dec. 1936, 8.

160. "Roth and Wife Held Anew for Pornography," *New York Herald Tribune*, 4 Sept. 1936, ACLU Archives, 879: 164.

161. "Three Years for Samuel Roth," *NYT*, 17 Dec. 1936, 11.

162. *U.S. v. Pauline Roth and Samuel Roth*, affidavit for modification of sentence, 14 May 1937, 4: "The larger of my two bank accounts at the time of my arrest contained a balance of some Forty ($40) dollars." His lawyer's Memorandum in Support says that the two-thousand-dollar fine "will have to be paid despite a pauper's oath" (7).

163. The affidavit for modification of sentence is five pages, divided into nine parts. His lawyer's Memorandum in Support of Application for Modification of Sentence (22 June 1937) appends the letter from the prison physician dated 25 May 1937.

164. Hardy does say on p. 3 of his Memorandum in Opposition to Defendant Samuel Roth's Application for a Reduction in Sentence, 22 June 1937 (*U.S. v. Pauline Roth and Samuel Roth*) that Roth gave one name that led to the arrest of that person. I have been unable to determine the identity of this individual. A summary or transcript of Roth's statement would be especially interesting to uncover. It would not, of course, be part of a trial transcript, if one exists. Perhaps such a document has survived somewhere in the files of Chester Battles or Lamar Hardy.

165. Scheiner's *Compendium* is very helpful in describing these works. See also his *Essential Guide to Erotic Literature*, 2 vols. (Ware: Wordsworth, 1996). I thank Dr. Scheiner for his advice regarding the books listed in Roth's 1936 indictment.

166. The following are part of Roth's FBI files: R. Lindquist to E. A. Tamm, 17 and 20 July 1936; J. Edgar Hoover to agent in charge [R. Whitely], 2 Sept. 1936; E. A. Tamm, "Memorandum for the Director," 31 Aug. 1936; E. A. Tamm to Hoover, 17 Sept. 1936.

167. This unauthorized edition may have been Roth's way of insulting Lewisohn, coauthor of the international protest against him. Roth's negative opinion of Lewisohn as a Jewish-American writer and critic is expressed in *Jews Must Live*, 104. Roth's only positive comment on *Mr. Crump* was that it was "easy reading."

168. Chester Battles to Lamar Hardy, 9 Sept. 1938, U.S. Dept. of Justice, Central Files, file 33 S 251-1, NA. Battles, investigating the circularization of *The Secret Places of the Human Body* by the National Library, states that Maurice Fryefield purchased copies from

Pauline Roth in 1935, and that the latter was prosecuted for selling the book that year but was acquitted. Probably he refers to the 1935 trial of Samuel and Pauline, although he is mistaken on one point: Pauline was convicted and given a suspended sentence on that occasion. The National Library had been selling Roth's *Ananga Ranga* since the library's inception in 1932. Roth may have had business agreements with Fryefield prior to 1932, and may have helped finance Fryefield's publication of Gaston Means's *Strange Death of President Harding*. Fryefield and the National Library are discussed on p. 50 of *Transcripts of Hearings on Fraud Cases, 1913–45*, no. 443 (Knickerbocker Publishing), Records of the Post Office Dept., NA. Fryefield cofounded the concern with Michael Estrin.

169. The only lists the present writer has seen for such books are of this nature and were sent from Ben Abramson's Argus Book Shop in the late 1930s and early 1940s. Titles included *Fanny Hill*, *Child Love*, *My Life and Loves*, *Merry Muses of Caledonia*, *Abduction of Edith Martin*, *The Way of a Man with a Maid*, and *Nemesis Hunt*. These lists are located in "Erotica Dealers, United States, Twentieth Century" KI Files.

170. So stated in count 18 of the indictment.

171. Anton Holden, telephone conversation, 19 July 1993 and letter to author of 21 July 1993. For information on Nichols, see Peter Mendez, *Clandestine Erotic Fiction in English, 1800–1930: A Bibliographical Study* (Aldershot, Hants.: Scolar Press, 1993), 17–20 and 43–44, and Montgomery Hyde, *A History of Pornography* (New York: Dell, 1966), 185–88. Roth's own knowledge, not only of both borderline and under-the-counter erotica of the late twenties and early thirties, but also of customers for both kinds — which his mailing list clearly exemplified — lends plausibility to their association.

172. *U.S. v. Pauline Roth and Samuel Roth*, 1936, Memorandum in Support of Application for Modification of Sentence, 3. Roth's lawyer stated that Roth informed on the man who left the book in the subway locker. The statement from the district attorney is in the Memorandum in Opposition, 3.

173. This information is given by Lawrence J. Shifreen and Roger Jackson, *Henry Miller: A Bibliography of Primary Sources* (n.p.: Shifreen and Jackson, 1993), 11–12, using Legman as their source.

174. C. J. Scheiner, "An Annotated Anthology of Erotologically Significant Sexually Explicit Literature Published 1527–1969" (Ph.D. diss., McIlvenna Institute for the Advanced Study of Human Sexuality, 1995), 514–16, and his introduction to *White Stains* (London: Delectus, 1995), iii–v, ix–xi. Scheiner says in the latter that he once owned the copy of *White Stains* that Delectus used as copy-text; the book had the red endpapers that Roth (but also other erotica publishers of the 1920s) were fond of using.

175. *U.S. v. Pauline Roth and Samuel Roth*, count 8 of indictment. Other titles mentioned are *The Horn Book*, *Gamiani or Two Nights of Excesses*, *Memoirs of a Hotel Man*, as well as "Five Hollywood sex play photographs."

176. Name indecipherable (Post Office inspector) to John T. Cahill, U.S. district attorney, 17 Oct. 1940; *U.S. v. Pauline and Samuel Roth*, Petition for Revocation of Probation, 7 Apr. 1941.

177. Roth, "Count Me Among the Missing," 383; the estimate is recorded in U.S. Senate, Subcommittee to Investigate Juvenile Delinquency of the Committee on the Judiciary, *Hearings*, 191–96.

178. James N. Paul and Murray Schwartz, *Federal Censorship: Obscenity in the Mail* (New York: Free Press of Glencoe, 1961), 85; James Gilbert, *A Cycle of Outrage: America's Reaction to the Juvenile Delinquent in the 1950s* (New York: Oxford University Press, 1986), 143–61.

179. "SAC, New York," memorandum to J. Edgar Hoover, 30 Jan. 1956, in Roth's FBI files.

180. Circular from Coventry Books, advertising *Lèse Majesty: The Private Lives of the Duke and Duchess of Windsor*, KI Files, s.v. "Erotica Producers — 20th century — Roth, Samuel."

181. Transcript of Proceedings Before the Solicitor for the Post Office Dept., in the Matter of Arrowhead Books, 7 Nov. 1947, U.S. Dept. of Justice, Central Files, file 145-5-301, NA. This is the fraud order hearing for *Bumarap*. The document includes testimony of the postal inspector regarding the book, and Roth's defense of it.

182. The circular is included as Exhibit 6 in *Roth v. Goldman*, 172 F2d 788 (1949), U.S. Court of Appeals, 2d Cir., So. District of N.Y., *Transcript of Record*.

183. Ibid., 24–34.

184. John N. Makris, *The Silent Investigators: The Great Untold Story of the United States Postal Inspection Service* (New York: Dutton, 1959), 289–99.

185. The affidavit in *Roth v. Goldman*, Civ. 62-397, U.S. District Ct., So. District of N.Y. (filed 19 June 1951) contains a circular offering these pictures at $1.98 each.

186. Paul and Schwartz, *Federal Censorship*, 134. These photos were mentioned in one of the counts of the 1955 indictment.

187. Grand Jury Indictment, *U.S. v. Samuel Roth*, Cr 148-9, U.S. District Ct., So. District of N.Y. (1956), 1–27.

188. Paul and Schwartz, *Federal Censorship*, 134; de Grazia, *Girls*, 289.

189. *U.S. v. Samuel Roth*, Government's Summation, 52a–60a.

190. There are excellent treatments of the Roth case in de Grazia, *Girls*, chaps. 15 and 16; Paul and Schwartz, *Federal Censorship*, 143–51; and Felice Flannery Lewis, *Literature, Obscenity, and Law* (Carbondale: Southern Illinois University Press, 1976), 185–90.

191. Paul and Schwartz, *Federal Censorship*, 146.

192. Judge F. Van Pelt Bryan's language in *Grove Press and Reader's Subscription v. Christianberry*, 175. F. Supp. 488, as quoted in "Extracts from the United States District Court Decision," *Lady Chatterley's Lover*, by D. H. Lawrence (New York: Grove, [1959]), 380. The "Extracts" appeared in the paperback, not the cloth, impressions.

193. Samuel Roth, *My Friend Yeshea* (New York: Bridgehead, 1961), 588.

194. Ibid., 95.

195. Ibid., 628.

196. Hamalian, "Nobody Knows My Names," 921.

197. Ryan, epilogue to "Samuel Roth," 9–10; Robert Antrim, "Sam Roth, Prometheus of the Unprintable," *Eros*, Autumn 1962, 24.

Epilogue

1. Dr. Ronald Rebhuhn, personal interview, Westbury, N.Y., 12 Aug. 1992.

2. Lawrence Van Gelder, "Evan Esar, 96; Wrote Brooks on Jokes and Humor," *NYT*, 5 Jan. 1996, D21.

3. Dr. C. J. Scheiner, personal interview, New York City, 8 July 1993; "Link Brooklyn Man to Film So Lewd It Made Many Sick," *New York World Telegram Sun*, 26 May 1955, JA Files.

4. John Tebbel, *A History of Book Publishing in the United States* (New York: Bowker, 1981), 4: 311; Lyle Stuart to the author, 6 July 1998; "The Wild Genius of Merchandising the Bizarre: Lyle Stuart," *The Millionaire Pornographers* (*Adam* Special Report 12), Feb. 1977, 62–66.

5. Arnold Levy, personal interview, Secaucus, N.J., 3 June 1987.

6. Barney Rosset, personal interview, New York City, 23 July 1993.

7. The following summary of erotica dealers of the mid-twentieth century is based on the information in Edward de Grazia, *Girls Lean Back Everywhere: The Law of Obscenity and the Assault on Genius* (New York: Random House, 1992). For Brandon House, see Patrick Kearney, *A Bibliography of the Publications of the New York Olympia Press* (Santa Rosa, Calif.: Scissors and Paste Bibliographies, 1988), vi.

8. Gay Talese, *Thy Neighbor's Wife* (New York: Dell, 1981), 122–23.

9. Robert Antrim, "Sam Roth, Prometheus of the Unprintable," *Eros*, autumn 1962, 24–27.

10. See Bob Reitman, *Freedom on Trial: The Incredible Ordeal of Ralph Ginzburg* (San Diego, Calif.: PEC, 1966); and Ralph Ginzburg, *Castrated: My Eight Months in Prison* (New York: Avant Garde, 1973).

11. Reitman, *Freedom on Trial*, 73; "Immorality at All-Time High—Graham," *Philadelphia Daily News*, 20 June 1960, 22.

12. "Book Seller, Newsstand Owner Held for Court on Smut Charges," *Philadelphia Daily News*, 10 June 1960, 22; "Blanc Tactic Aimed at Extradition," *Philadelphia Inquirer*, 9 June 1960, Urban Archives, Paley Library, Temple University Libraries. Victor H. Blanc was the city district attorney; he planned to extradite and prosecute the publishers of the books taken and formulated the raid with this tactic in mind. Blanc's initiative occurred at the time Republicans were accusing him of vote fraud, and attempting impeachment ("House Unit Rejects Blanc Impeachment," *Philadelphia Daily News*, 14 June 1960, 3).

13. Allan Wilson, personal interview, New York City, 21 July 1994.

14. David Hebditch and Nick Anning, *Porn Gold: Inside the Pornography Business* (London: Faber and Faber, 1988), 368.

15. Jonathan Wallace and Mark Mangan, *Sex, Laws, and Cyberspace: Freedom and Censorship on the Frontiers of the Online Revolution* (New York: Holt, 1996), 1–40. The quotation about the family business is on p. 40.

16. Typically represented in two 1927 editorials in the *New York Journal American*: "Every State Should Ban the Peddling of Debased Books," 30 June; "Enforce All Existing Laws Against Obscene Literature," 11 Aug., JA Files.

17. On drugs, "Filthy Books and Plays Should Not Be Tolerated," *New York Journal American* (editorial), 13 Apr. 1940, JA Files. "There is another criminal industry, quite as depraved and dangerous as the 'dope' traffic. . . . Narcotics and pornographica are closely associated in their ultimate results." On dealers, "Dope and Smut Used by Reds, Senators Told," *New York Daily News*, 1 Mar. 1957, JA Files. The article stated that Narcotics Commissioner Harry Anslinger reported to the International Security Committee that mainland China was financing the distribution of pornography throughout Asia, using Russian equipment.

18. "N.J. Official Calls Dirty Books Red-like Attack on Morale," *New York Post*, 18 Dec. 1952, JA Files.

19. Inez Robb, "Smut Crackdown Encouraging; How About Using a Touch of the Lash?" *New York World Telegram Sun*, 15 Dec. 1959, JA Files.

20. "Some Voluntary 'Book-Burnings' Are Needed, Says Dr. Ayer, Assailing Filth in Literature," *NYT*, 22 May 1939, JA Files. Ayer was pastor of the Calvary Baptist Church.

21. Louis Sobol, "A Slap at Some Books," *New York Journal American*, 25 Feb. 1956, JA Files.

22. "Dewey Vetoes Bill on Written Obscenity, Holds It No Offense Unless Circulated," *NYT*, 8 Apr. 1947, JA Files. Dewey cited the "danger that the private writing of all persons, great or small, whether obscene or not, would be subject to the scrutiny and the opinion of some public official as to whether or not it is obscene."

23. "Obscene Book Penalty Lifted by High Court," *New York Journal American*, 14 Dec. 1959, JA Files.

24. William Claiborne, "Dole Scores Entertainment Industry for 'Debasing America'," *Washington Post*, 1 June 1995, A6; Bernard Weintraub, "Dole Attacks Hollywood Wares as Undermining Social Values," *NYT*, 1 June 1995, A1, B10; James Carney et al., "Violent Reaction," *Time*, 12 June 1995, 25–30.

25. "Lyrics from the Gutter," *NYT*, 2 June 1995, A29.

26. *Face the Nation*, Host Bob Scheiffer, CBS (Binghamton, N.Y.), 4 June 1995.

27. For the distinction between "primary" and "secondary or psychological harms," see Lloyd K. Stires, "Is It Time to Overturn the Miller Standard?" *Gauntlet* 2.14 (1997): 85–89.

28. Catherine Hancock, "Pornography," in *Encyclopedia of the American Constitution*, ed. Leonard Levy, Kenneth Karst, and Dennis Mahoney (New York: Macmillan, 1986), 3: 1429. She quotes Eva Feder Kittay.

29. Linda Williams, "Second Thoughts on *Hard Core*: American Obscenity Law and

the Scapegoating of Deviance," in *Dirty Looks: Women, Pornography, Power*, ed. Pamela Gibson and Roma Gibson (London: BFI, 1993), 48–55.

30. "State and Local Laws Attack Cyberspace Freedoms," *Newsletter on Intellectual Freedom* 45.3 (May 1996): 75.

31. Ibid.

32. Jonathan Wallace and Mark Mangan, ⟨markm@bway.net⟩, "Porn and the Liability of Internet Providers," 1 June 1997 ⟨jw@bway.net⟩ via ⟨http://www. spectacle.org/freespch/⟩.

33. Pamela Mendels, "Judge Rebukes Justice Department for CompuServe 'Decency' Inquiry," *NYT Cybertimes*, 17 May 1996 ⟨http://www.nytimes.com/library/cyber/week/0517decency.html⟩ (13 June 1996); Pamela Mendels, "Decency Act Hearing Erupts over FBI 'Review,' " *NYT Cybertimes*, 17 May 1996 ⟨http://www.nytimes.com/library/cyber/week/0511decency.html⟩ (13 June 1996).

34. Barbara Hoberock, "Suit Filed for 'The Tin Drum,' " *Tulsa World Online*, 4 July 1997 ⟨http://www.tulsaworld.com/cgi-ole/world.ARC.dsplyStory?970703_Ne_al3su⟩ (30 July 1997).

35. Pamela Mendels, "Newsgroup Smut Poses Campus Quandary," *NYT*, 29 Dec. 1996, *NYT Cybertimes*, 29 Dec. 1996 ⟨http://search.nytimes.com/search/daily/bi...David%29%26OR%26%Boren%29%26OR%26%28%29⟩(30 July 1997); Aesha Rasheed, "Boren Wins Lawsuit," *Oklahoma Daily Online*, 28 Jan. 1997 ⟨http://www.daily.ou. edu/issues/spring1997/jan-28/boren.html⟩ (30 July 1997).

36. "Five More States Assault Net Speech," *ACLU Cyberliberties Update* ⟨http://www.aclu.org/issues/cyber/upjulya.html⟩ (4 Sept. 1996).

37. "AOL Censors Gay Video Titles," 6 Dec. 1995 ⟨infoaclu@aclu.org⟩ (8 Dec. 1995); James Egelhof, "AOL's Culture of Censorship," *Cyberliberties* [June?] 1995 ⟨http://www.aclu.org/issues/cyber/arcl.html⟩ (June 1995).

38. "Focus on the Internet: White House Web Site Blocked," *Newsletter on Intellectual Freedom* 45.3 (May 1996): 77.

39. Lloyd K. Stires, "ACLU v. Reno: Looking Back, Looking Ahead," *Gauntlet* 2.12 (1996): 65.

40. People for the American Way, *Attacks on the Freedom to Learn, 1992–93 Report* (Washington, D.C., 1993), 5–25.

41. *Attorney General's Commission on Pornography: Final Report* (Washington, D.C.: GPO, 1986), 2: 323–48; John D'Emilio and Estelle Freedman, *Intimate Matters: A History of Sexuality in America* (New York: Harper and Row, 1988), 350–51.

42. *FCC v. Pacifica Foundation*, 438 U.S. 726 (1978). There is a great deal of information concerning indecency in sec. 3 and in nn. 14–17 and 23. A detailed review of this case and its effect on Internet censorship appears in Robert Corn-Revere, "New Age Comstockery: Exon vs. the Internet," *Policy Analysis* (Cato Institute), 28 June 1995 ⟨http://www. cato.org⟩ (July 1995).

43. "FCC Enforcement of Prohibition Against Obscene and Indecent Broadcasts," *Federal Communications Commission*, 16 Apr. 1996 ⟨http://www.fcc.gov/mmb/enf/forms/indecs.html⟩ (15 May 1998).

44. Dick Rolfe, "Wal-Mart Sells 'Sanitized' Music, Film — Censorship or Customer Service," *Hollywood and the Family*, Dec. 1996 ⟨http://www.dove.org/columns/1996/column9612.htm⟩ (31 July 1997).

45. "ACLU v. RENO: Trial Update," *ACLU Press Releases*, 15 Apr. 1996 ⟨http://www.aclu.org/news/n041596b.html⟩ (2 May 1996).

46. Alison Mitchell, "TV Executives Promise Clinton a Violence Rating System by '97," *NYT*, 1 Mar. 1996, A1, B14.

47. Ibid., B14.

48. Shabbir J. Safdar ⟨shabbir@vtw.org⟩ "The White House Casts Their Lot with Net Advocates," 16 July 1997 ⟨vtw-announce@vtw.org⟩ (28 July 1997).

49. Thomas Oliphant, "A Rush to Rate Television Shows," *Boston Globe*, 20 May 1997; reprinted in *Censorship News: A Newsletter of the National Coalition Against Censorship* 99 (summer 1997): [4]. For the rating system, see "About R[ecreational] S[oftware] A[dvisory] C[ouncil] [on the] I[nternet]," n.d. ⟨http://www.reac.org/fra_content.asp?onIndex=1⟩ (16 May 1998).

50. "Speech on the Line" (editorial), *Nation*, 21 July 1997, 3–4.

51. Gayle Rubin, "Thinking Sex: Notes for a Radical Theory of the Politics of Sexuality," in *Pleasure and Danger: Exploring Female Sexuality*, ed. Carole S. Vance (Boston: Routledge and Kegan Paul, 1984), 278.

52. Ira L. Reiss, *An End to Shame: Shaping Our Next Sexual Revolution* (Buffalo, N.Y.: Prometheus, 1990), 18–25.

53. Ellen Goodman, "Shame, Not Shamelessness, Generates 'Prom Moms,' " *Philadelphia Inquirer*, 20 July 1997, E7.

54. Lisa Duggan, Nan D. Hunter, and Carole S. Vance, "False Promises: Feminist Antipornography Legislation," in *Caught Looking: Feminism, Pornography, and Censorship* (New York: Caught Looking, 1986), 82. For the distinction between erotica and pornography, see David McCabe, "The Politics of Porn: Not So Strange Bedfellows," *In These Times*, 7 Mar. 1994; reprinted in *Censorship: Opposing Viewpoints*, ed. David Bender and Bruno Leone (San Diego, Calif.: Greenhaven, 1997), 136.

55. See two articles in Gibson and Gibson, *Dirty Looks*: Chris Straayer, "The Seduction of Boundaries: Feminist Fluidity in Annie Sprinkle's Art/Education/Sex" (156–75) and Linda Williams, "A Provoking Agent: The Pornography and Performance Art of Annie Sprinkle" (176–91).

56. Andrea Juno, "Holly Hughes," in *Angry Women*, ed. Andrea Juno and V. Vale (San Francisco, Calif.: Re/Search, 1991), 98.

57. John Heidenry, *What Wild Ecstasy: The Rise and Fall of the Sexual Revolution* (New York: Simon and Schuster, 1997), 331–32.

Selected Bibliography

Archival Sources

Archives of the American Civil Liberties Union, preserved at the Seeley G. Mudd Manuscript Library, Department of Rare Books and Special Collections, Princeton University, Princeton, N.J. (*ACLU Archives*)

Sylvia Beach Papers, Department of Rare Books and Special Collections, Firestone Library, Princeton University, Princeton, N.J.

Zechariah Chafee Papers, Special Collections Department, Harvard University Law Library, Cambridge, Mass.

Committee of Fourteen Archives, Manuscript Division, New York Public Library. Letters, clippings, and reports regarding social conditions in New York City during the earlier twentieth century.

Contempo letters (c. 1930), correspondence to and from Milton Abernethy, ed., vertical file, Harry Ransom Humanities Research Center, University of Texas at Austin.

Letters, trial transcripts, legal briefs, and personal papers of Morris L. Ernst, preserved at the Harry Ransom Humanities Research Center, University of Texas at Austin. (*MLE Papers*)

FBI files compiled during the lifetimes of Samuel Roth and Benjamin Rebhuhn, related to their careers as publishers of materials deemed obscene. In possession of the present author.

Papers of Elmer Gertz, including correspondence, clippings, and notes regarding Gertz's first book, a biography of Frank Harris. Manuscript Division, Library of Congress. (*Gertz*)

Archive of correspondence relevant to the works of Frank Harris, once in the possession of Harris's American lawyer, Arthur L. Ross. Harris-Ross Collection, Department of Special Collections, Syracuse University Library, Syracuse, N.Y. (*Harris-Ross*)

Frank Harris Papers in Fales Manuscript Collection, Fales Library, New York University. Includes correspondence with Arthur L. Ross, Harris's lawyer; scrapbooks of clippings relevant to Harris compiled by A. I. Tobin; and galley proofs of both volumes 3 and 4 of Harris's Niçois edition of *My Life* and of the first (pirated) American edition of these two works, published in one volume.

Harris Letters — HRC: a series of six letters, four telegrams, and one attorney's memorandum regarding the printing and publishing of *My Life and Loves*, preserved at the Harry Ransom Humanities Research Center, University of Texas at Austin.

Arthur Garfield Hayes Papers, preserved at the Seeley G. Mudd Manuscript Library, Department of Rare Books and Special Collections, Princeton University, Princeton, N.J.

"Misrepresentation Files" at the Herbert Hoover Presidential Library, West Branch, Iowa. Papers relevant to the smear books published 1930–32, denigrating Hoover and his work as engineer, administrator, and public servant. (*HH-Misrep*)

Vertical Files at the library of the Kinsey Institute for Sex Research at the University of Indiana, Bloomington. The files, especially "Erotica Producers (U.S.), Twentieth Century," hold many unpublished materials (letters, catalogs, brochures) relevant to the publishing of erotic literature in twentieth-century America. (*KI Files*)

Arnold Levy collection of manuscript writings and correspondence of Samuel Roth, related to his book *Lese Majesty* and other publishing activities during the 1950s.

Municipal Archives, Department of Records and Information Services, New York City.

National Archives, Washington, D.C. Important source of memoranda, correspondence, legal briefs, trial transcripts relevant to FBI, Post Office, and Justice Department actions against materials deemed obscene. (*NA*)

Research files (the "morgue") of the *New York Journal American*, preserved at the Harry Ransom Humanities Research Center, University of Texas at Austin. Clippings from a variety of New York newspapers from the 1920s through the 1950s. (The page numbers of most of the clippings are not referenced.) (*JA Files*)

Names and Records of Persons Arrested Under the Auspices of the New York Society for the Suppression of Vice. These are the ledgers of the society, recorded by Anthony Comstock and, after 1915, by John S. Sumner. They are now preserved on two microfilm reels (shelf 19,359) in the Manuscript Division of the Library of Congress. (*Ledgers*)

"New York Society [for the Suppression of Vice] v. Macfadden Publications, Inc. in the Offices of Martin Conboy." Pretrial transcript. File 387. MLE Papers. Preserved at the Harry Ransom Humanities Research Center, University of Texas at Austin. Transcript of an interrogation of John S. Sumner by Morris Ernst. Sumner had filed a libel suit against Macfadden; as plaintiff, he was subject to pretrial examination. (*NYS v. Mac*)

Archive of clippings, catalogs, and brochures related to the Panurge Press (1929–31), in the possession of antiquarian bookseller Dr. C. J. Scheiner, Brooklyn, N.Y. (*Scheiner Archive*)

Rebhuhn Archive. A sheaf of approximately seventy pieces of correspondence (mostly typed transcriptions of holograph originals) passing between Frank Harris, Esar Levine, and Benjamin Rebhuhn, dating from 1923 to 1929. Also contains a journal kept by the latter during the 1920s, several telegrams relevant to Harris's *My Life*, and a few brochures published by the Frank Harris Publishing Company. In the possession of Dr. Ronald Rebhuhn, Westbury, N.Y. (*RA*)

Rosenbach Company Archives, Rosenbach Library and Museum, Philadelphia.

Urban Archives (include "morgues" of Philadelphia newspapers), Paley Library, Temple University Libraries, Philadelphia, Pa.

Papers of the New England Watch and Ward Society, Special Collections Department, Harvard University Law Library, Cambridge, Mass. (*WW Papers*)

Winchell Archive. A collection of material about Samuel Roth (compiler unknown) for Walter Winchell, c. 1952. In possession of the present author.

Clement Wood Papers, Brown University Library, Providence, R.I.

Personal Communications

Biblo, Jack. Personal interview, Biblo Books, Brooklyn, N.Y., 8 Dec. 1991.

Brown, Andreas. Personal interview, New York City, 12 June 1998. Letter to the author, 27 Aug. 1998.

Brussel, Mina. Personal interview, New York City, 21 Dec. 1991.

Carlitz, Bernard Conwell. Personal interview, Bristol, Pa., 15 July 1992.

Chernovsky, Oscar. Telephone interviews, 6 Mar. and 1 Dec. 1992.

Eckhoff, Chris. Personal interviews (including also Arnold Levy and C. J. Scheiner), New York City, 14 Nov. 1991 and 8 July 1993.

Gertz, Elmer. Letter to the author, 26 Sept. 1993.

Gud, Tony. Letter to the author, 3 July 1987. Reply to questionnaire, 7 July 1987.

Holden, Anton. Telephone conversation, 19 July 1993. Letter to the author, 21 July 1993.

Kearney, Patrick. Letter to the author, 22 Sept. 1992.

Kugel, Adelaide Roth. Letters to the author, 14 July 1986 and 7 Sept. 1988. Personal interview, New York City, 24 July 1993.

Lane, Susan. Letter to the author, 21 Nov. 1998.

LeFevre, Karen Burke. Letter to the author, 11 July 1987.

Legman, Gershon. Letter to Leo Hamalian, "First Day of Spring, 1976." Letter to Patrick Kearney, 14 May 1983. Letter to the author, 4 Aug. 1985. Telephone conversation, 6 May 1987. Personal interview, La Clé des Champs, France, 17 June 1990.

Levy, Arnold. Personal interview, Carol Publishing Group, Secaucus, N.J., 3 June 1987.

Malkin, Mary Ann. Personal interviews, New York City, 6 Mar. and 30 Nov. 1992.

Miller, Dwight M. Letter to the author, 25 Apr. 1995.

Porter, Bern. Reply to questionnaire, 29 Sept. 1991.

Rebhuhn, Ronald. Personal interviews, Westbury, N.Y., 12 Aug. 1992 and 23 Dec. 1993.

Rosset, Barney. Personal interview, New York City, 23 July 1993.

Roth, Richard. Personal interview (including also Adelaide Roth Kugel), New York City, 3 July 1987.

Ruder, Barnet. Personal interview, New York City, 16 Mar. 1994.

Scheiner, C. J. Reply to questionnaire, 1 Mar. 1986. Personal interviews, C. J. Scheiner Books, Brooklyn, N.Y., 5 June 1987; New York City, 24 July 1992 and 8 July 1993. Telephone conversation, 8 May 1994.

Stuart, Lyle. Telephone conversation, 22 Mar. 1997. Letter to the author, 8 July 1998.

Sweeney, Michael. Letter to the author, 14 May 1997.

Tanselle, G. Thomas. Personal interview, New York City, 18 Mar. 1994.

Wilbur, Lorraine. Personal interview, Gramercy Book Shop, New York City, 21 July 1993.

Wilson, Allan. Reply to questionnaire, 27 July 1987. Personal interview, 21 July 1994.

Yoell, Elizabeth. Telephone interview, 20 Nov. 1998.

Books, Articles, and Other Sources

All *New York Times* and *Herald Tribune* articles are from late city edition.

Adelman, Bob. *Tijuana Bibles: Art and Wit in America's Forbidden Funnies, 1930–1950s.* New York: Simon and Schuster, 1997.

"Amending Censorship Law." *PW*, 31 Mar. 1923, 1061.

American Anthropological Society. *Catalogue and Review of Famous Books* (bookseller's catalog). [c. 1930]. Scheiner Archive.

American Book Trade Directory. New York: Bowker, 1935.

Annual Report of the Postmaster General. Washington, D.C.: GPO, 1937, 1938, 1939.

Antrim, Robert. "Sam Roth, Prometheus of the Unprintable." *Eros*, autumn 1962, 24–27.

Attorney General's Commission on Pornography: Final Report. 2 vols. Washington, D.C.: GPO, 1986.

Bander, Ingram. "Suppression a Modern Problem: An Interview with John S. Sumner." *Campus* (City College of New York magazine), 18 Apr. 1932. ACLU Archives, 508: 167.

Barnes, Harry Elmer. "The Liberal Viewpoint" (column). *New York World Telegram*, 14 Mar. 1932. ACLU Archives, 508: 152.

Bode, Carl, ed. *The Editor, the Bluenose and the Prostitute: H. L. Mencken's History of the "Hatrack" Censorship Case*. Boulder, Colo.: Roberts Rinehart, 1988.

Bodenheim, Maxwell [?]. *My Life and Loves in Greenwich Village*. New York: Bridgehead, 1954.

"Book Decadence Is Laid to Critics." *NYT*, 9 Jan. 1933, 24.

"Book Publishers Want No Pooh-bah." *NYT*, 6 Aug. 1922, 2: 1.

Britton, Nan. *Honesty or Politics*. New York: Elizabeth Ann Guild, 1932.

Broun, Heywood, and Margaret Leech. *Anthony Comstock: Roundsman of the Lord*. New York: Boni, 1927.

Brown, Bob [Robert Carlton]. *Gems: A Censored Anthology*. Cagnes-sur-Mer: Roving Eye, 1931.

Bruce, Lenny. *How to Talk Dirty and Influence People*. 1972. New York: Fireside, 1992.

Butler, Ellis Parker. *Dollarature or the Drug Store Book*. Boston: Houghton Mifflin, 1930.

Cabell, [James] Branch. "The Genteel Tradition in Sex." In *The American Spectator Year Book*, ed. George Jean Nathan et al., 219–21. New York: Stokes, 1934.

Cacici, Dante. "A Note on the Author." In *Bumarap: The Story of a Male Virgin*, by Samuel Roth, 233–56. New York: Arrowhead, 1947.

Canby, Henry S. *Definitions*. 2d series. New York: Harcourt Brace, 1924.

"Censorship in Boston." Boston: Civil Liberties Committee of Massachusetts, 1938.

Congressional Record, 18 Mar. 1930, 5509–10.

Conklin, Groff. *How to Run a Rental Library*. New York: Bowker, 1934.

Cooper, Courtney Ryley. *Designs in Scarlet*. Boston: Little, Brown, 1939.

"Court Denounces Harris' 'My Life.' " *NYT*, 21 Aug. 1925, 15.

"Court Holds Harris Book Not Obscene." *New York World*, 2 Apr. 1926, 3.

"Culture Burns Bright" (editorial). *NYT*, 18 Mar. 1935, 16.

Dennett, Mary Ware. *Who's Obscene*. New York: Vanguard, 1930.

De Voto, Bernard. "Literary Censorship in Cambridge." *Harvard Graduates Magazine*, Sept. 1930, 30–42.

Devoe, Alan. "Erotic Books and the Depression." *PW*, 5 Aug. 1933, 343–44.

"11,744 New Magazines Seized as Indecent." *NYT*, 10 Oct. 1934, 24.

"The Enforcement of Laws Against Censorship in New York." *Columbia Law Review* 28 (Nov. 1928): 950–57.

Ernst, Morris, and Alexander Lindey. *The Censor Marches On*. 1940. New York: Da Capo, 1971.

———. *Hold Your Tongue! Adventures in Libel and Slander*. London: Methuen, 1936.

Ernst, Morris, and William Seagle. *To the Pure: A Study of Obscenity and the Censor*. New York: Viking, 1928.

Fairman, Milton. "Censorship in Chicago." *PW*, 11 Jan. 1930, 213.

FCC Enforcement of Prohibition Against Obscene and Indecent Broadcasts. *Federal Communications Commission*. 16 Apr. 1996. ⟨http://www.fcc.gov/mmb/enf/forms/indecs.html⟩ (15 May 1998).

First Editions, Press Books and Finely Illustrated Editions: The Property of the Artist Miss

Clara Tice Including Selections from the Library of Mr. William Stanley Hall with a Few Additions (cover title; auction catalog). New York: American Art Association, 1929.

Ford, John. *Criminal Obscenity.* New York: Revell, 1926.

Fowler, Gene. *Beau James.* 1949. New York: Bantam, 1957.

Ginzburg, Ralph. *Castrated: My Eight Months in Prison.* New York: Avant Garde, 1973.

Gorer, Geoffrey. *Hot Strip Tease.* London, Cresset, 1937.

Haldeman-Julius, Emanuel. *The First Hundred Million.* New York: Simon and Schuster, 1928.

Hamill, John. *The Strange Career of Mr. Hoover Under Two Flags.* New York: William Faro, 1932.

Harris, Frank. "Sumner and His Satellites." *Pearson's Magazine*, Feb. 1918, 363.

"Harris Book Expurgated." *New York World*, 3 Apr. 1926, 3.

Hayes, Arthur Garfield. *Let Freedom Ring.* New York: Liveright, 1937.

Hecht, Arthur, et al. *Preliminary Inventories of the Post Office Department.* Washington, D.C.: National Archives and Records Service, 1967.

Hesnard, A. *Strange Lust: The Psychology of Homosexuality.* Trans. John Caxton Summers. New York: Amethnol, 1933.

Hygienic Book Company. *A Selection of the Best Books on Sex and Psychology* (bookseller's catalog). [c. 1925?]. KI Files.

Jackson, Gardner. "My Brother's Peeper." *Nation*, 15 Jan. 1930, 64–65.

"Jail for Selling Frank Harris." *PW*, 27 Mar. 1926, 1136.

Jenks, Anton Shrewsbury [Samuel Roth?]. *A Dead President Makes Answer to "The President's Daughter."* New York: Golden Hind, 1928.

"John S. Sumner, Foe of Vice, Dies." *NYT*, 22 June 1971, 38.

Kiki [Alice Prin]. *The Education of a French Model.* New York: Boar's Head, 1950; New York: Bridgehead, 1954.

Lawrence, D. H. *A Propos of Lady Chatterley's Lover.* London: Mandrake, 1930.

——. *The Letters of D. H. Lawrence.* Volume 6, *March 1927–November 1928.* Ed. James T. Boulton and Margaret Boulton. Cambridge: Cambridge University Press, 1991.

——. "Pornography and Obscenity." *Pornography and So On.* London: Faber and Faber, 1936.

"Lawrence Book 'Revision' Fought." *New York World*, 25 Oct. 1930, 7.

Leibling, A. J. "Clearing of Bookseller on Sumner Libel Charge Proves to Him That America Still Needs Kick in Pants." *New York Herald Tribune*, 10 Oct. 1932. ACLU Archives, 503: 277.

Lilly, Joseph. "Author Tells How Vice Man Seized Script." *New York Telegram*, 13 Mar. 1930, 7.

——. "Book Dealers Are Considering Own Censorship." *New York Telegram*, 13 Mar. 1930, 7. Scheiner Archive.

——. "Books and Bookleggers No. 1." *New York Telegram*, 6 Mar. 1930, 13 (sec. 2: 1).

——. "Books and Bookleggers No. 2." *New York Telegram*, 7 Mar. 1930, 13 (sec. 2: 1).

——. "Books and Bookleggers No. 3." *New York Telegram*, 8 Mar. 1930, 10.

——. "Ernst Asserts Sumner Has No Legal Support." *New York Telegram*, 15 Mar. 1930, 26.

——. "One Foe of Vice Spurns Tricks." *New York Telegram*, 11 Mar. 1930, 7. Scheiner Archive.

——. "Sumner Backs Agents' Ruses in Book Buying." *New York Telegram*, 10 Mar. 1930, 10.

Lindey, Alexander. "The Bad Book Bill" (letter to the editor). *Bowling Green*, 18 July 1936, 9–10. ACLU Archives, 878: 9–10.

——. "Thank the Censor!" *PW*, 21 Apr. 1934, 1508–10.

Lippmann, Walter. "The Nature of the Battle over Censorship." In *Men of Destiny*, 93–106. New York: Macmillan, 1928.

Lockridge, Norman [Samuel Roth]. *Lese Majesty: The Private Lives of the Duke and Duchess of Windsor*. New York: Boar's Head, 1952.

Mandeville, Ernest W. "Gutter Literature." *New Republic*, 17 Feb. 1926, 350–52.

March, Joseph M. *The Wild Party. The Set-Up. A Certain Wildness*. Freeport, Me.: Bond Wheelwright, 1968.

McMahon, Joseph H. "The Battle for Decency." *Commonweal*, 7 Sept. 1934, 441–43.

Meisel-Heiss, Grete. *The Sexual Crisis: A Critique of Our Sex Life*. Trans. Eden Paul and Cedar Paul. 4th ed. New York: Eugenics, 1933.

Mencken, H. L. *My Life as Author and Editor*. Ed. Jonathan Yardley. New York: Knopf, 1993.

Michelfelder, William. "Filth Dealers Openly Defy Raids by City." *New York World Telegram and Sun*, 5 Mar. 1956. JA Files.

National Council for Freedom from Censorship. "Memorandum Regarding the Staff Report of the Attorney General's Committee on the Post Office Department." ACLU Archives, 2158: 153–59.

——. "Memorandum Submitted in Opposition to H.R. 9495." ACLU Archives, 1092: 209.

"An Outline History of the Post Office Censorship." New York, 1932. ACLU Archives, 509: 177–98.

New England Watch and Ward Society. *Annual Reports*. Boston, 1923–39.

New York Society for the Suppression of Vice. *Annual Reports*. New York, 1928–1939.

——. Periodical Letters. New York, 1925–39.

Noll, John F. *Manual of the N[ational] O[rganization for] D[ecent] L[iterature]*. [Huntington, Ind.: Our Sunday Visitor], n.d.

Orwell, George. *Keep the Aspidistra Flying*. 1936. New York: Harcourt Brace Jovanovich, n.d.

Perry, Bliss. "Pernicious Books: Address." Boston: Watch and Ward Society, 1923.

"Picking on the Little Fellow." *PW*, 1 Feb. 1936, 604–5.

"Plans Laid to Censor All New Literature." *NYT*, 4 Aug. 1922, 1, 7.

"Police to Burn $500,000 in Obscene Books." *NYT*, 14 Mar. 1935, 1.

Pringle, Henry F. "Comstock the Less." *American Mercury*, Jan. 1927, 56–63.

——. "The Genteel Crusader." In *Big Frogs*, 257–76. New York: Macy-Macius, 1928.

——. "Throwing Mud at the White House." *Outlook and Independent*, 9 Dec. 1931, 462–63, 469.

Pringle, Henry N. "America's Burden of Commercialized Vice and Follies." *Twentieth Century Progress*, Jan. 1937, 19.

Promoting Public Decency: 63rd Annual Report of the New York Society for the Suppression of Vice. New York: The Society, 1936.

"Prosecutor Raids a Philadelphia Book Store." *NYT*, 25 Jan. 1930, 1.

"Purity at the Port." *Nation*, 22 Feb. 1933, 194.

"Records of Censorship in New York." *PW*, 22 Mar. 1930, 1666.

"Red Poet Gets Thirteen Months." *NYT*, 11 June 1927, 34.

Redman, Ben Ray. "Obscenity and Censorship." *Scribner's Magazine*, May 1934, 341–44.

Reitman, Bob. *Freedom on Trial: The Incredible Ordeal of Ralph Ginzburg*, San Diego, Calif.: PEC, 1966.

Rice, Diana. "Literary Booklegging." *NYT*, 6 Aug. 1922, Book Review section, 1, 24.

Roth, Samuel. Advertisement. *The Education of a French Model*, by Kiki. New York: Boar's Head, 1950.

———. "By Way of Explanation." In *Lady Chatterley's Lover: A Dramatization*. Ardent Classics 2, 5–13. New York: Faro, 1931.

———. "Count Me Among the Missing." Unpublished memoir.

———. *Europe: A Book for America*. New York: Boni and Liveright, 1919.

———. Introduction to *The Pastoral Loves of Daphnis and Chloe*. Trans. George Moore. New York: Boar's Head, 1954.

———. *Jews Must Live: An Account of the Persecution of the World by Israel on All the Frontiers of Civilization*. New York: Golden Hind, 1934.

———. "Mr. Sumner and *Beau*." *Beau*, Mar. 1927, 15.

———. *My Friend Yeshea*. New York: Bridgehead, 1961.

———. *Now and Forever: A Conversation with Mr. Israel Zangwill on the Jew and the Future*. New York: McBride, 1925.

———. "Publisher's Introduction." In *Men into Beasts*, by George Sylvester Viereck. New York: Bridgehead, 1955.

———. "Seeing Mr. Hoover Through." *Plain English*, June 1932, 5–14.

———. *Stone Walls Do Not: The Chronicle of a Captivity*. 2 vols. New York: Faro, 1931.

———. "The Women of Plentipunda, Part 3" (novella). *American Aphrodite* 4.15 (1954): 109–62.

Russell, Francis. "Arty Crafty and the Beginnings of the Joyce Cult at Harvard." In *The Great Interlude: Neglected Events and Persons from the First World War to the Depression*, 153–61. New York: McGraw-Hill, 1964.

"Samuel Roth, 79, Tested Obscenity." In *New York Times Biographical Edition*, 1031. New York: The Times, 1974. (4 July 1974).

Schwartz, Harry. *Fifty Years in My Bookstore, or A Life with Books*. Milwaukee, Wisc.: n.p., 1977.

———. *This Book-Collecting Racket: A Few Notes on the Abuses of Book Collecting*. Pt. 1. Milwaukee, Wisc.: Casanova, 1934.

———. *This Book Collecting Racket*. Chicago: Normandie House, 1937.

Scott, Gerald R. "Some Nudity Becomes Art to the 20-Year Vice Foe." *New York Mirror*, 3 Feb. 1935, Sunday magazine section, 5–6.

Scott, Temple. "Frank Harris." *Saturday Review of Literature*, 13 Feb. 1926, 553–54.

Shiffrin, A. B. *Mr. Pirate: A Romance*. New York: Mitchell Kennerley, 1937.

Steloff, Frances. "Censorship and the Gotham Book Mart," 181–83. In *Bookselling in America and the World*, ed. Charles B. Anderson, Quadrangle/New York Times, 1975.

———. "In Touch with Genius." *Journal of Modern Literature*, 4.4 (Apr. 1975): 749–82.

Sumner, John S. "The New York Society for the Suppression of Vice." *PW*, 17 May 1930, 2518.

———. "Something About Obscene Books and a City Magistrate" (periodical letter). New York, 15 Dec. 1931.

———. "The Truth About Literary Lynching." *Dial*, July 1921, 63–68.

———. "What Every Father Should Know." *Smart Set*, May 1928, 54–55, 114–16.

Talbot, Francis X., S.J. "The Failure of Contemporary Literature." *America*, 7 Jan. 1933, 338–39.

———. "More on Smut." *America*, 25 Feb. 1933, 500–501.

———. "Smut!" *America*, 11 Feb. 1933, 460–61.

Tarshish, Manuel B. "The 'Fourth Avenue' Book Trade." Pts. 1, 2, 3. *PW*, 20, 27 Oct., 3 Nov. 1969, 52–55; 50–53; 40–43.

Train, Arthur. *The Strange Attacks on Herbert Hoover*. New York: John Day, 1932.

U.S. House of Representatives. Select Committee on Current Pornographic Materials. *Hearings*. 82nd Cong., 2nd sess., H.Rs. 596 and 597. Washington, D.C.: GPO, 1953.

———. *Report*. 82nd Cong., 2nd sess., H.R. 596. Washington, D.C.: GPO, 1953.

U.S. House of Representatives. Subcommittee 8 of the Committee on the Post Office and Post Roads. *Hearings*. 74th Cong., 1st sess., H.R. 154, 3252, 5049, 5162, 5370. Washington, D.C.: GPO, 1935.

U.S. Post Office. *Postal Laws and Regulations of the United States of America*. 1932 ed. Washington, D.C.: GPO, 1932.

U.S. Senate. Attorney General's Committee on Administrative Procedure. *Administrative Procedure in Government Agencies*. Pt. 12, *The Post Office Department*. S. Doc. 186. 76th Cong., 1st sess. Washington, D.C.: GPO, 1940.

U.S. Senate. Subcommittee to Investigate Juvenile Delinquency of the Committee on the Judiciary. *Hearings on Juvenile Delinquency (Obscene and Pornographic Materials)*. 84th Cong., 1st sess., S. Res. 62. Washington, D.C.: GPO, 1955.

Wakem, Hugh [Samuel Roth?]. *The Diary of a Smuthound*. Philadelphia, Pa.: William Hodgson, 1930.

"The Watch and Ward Society and Censorship." *Massachusetts Library Club Bulletin*, Oct. 1927, 70–71.

"We Nominate for Oblivion." *Vanity Fair*, June 1932, 42.

"W. J. Schieffelin of Drug Firm Dies." *NYT*, 1 May 1955, 88.

Whitman, Alden. "Morris Ernst, 'Ulysses' Case Lawyer, Dies." *NYT*, 23 May 1976, 40.

"Why the Art Exhibit 'For Men Only' Upset the Vice Crusader." *New York Mirror*, 28 May 1933. JA Files.

"The Wild Genius of Merchandising the Bizarre: Lyle Stuart." *The Millionaire Pornographers (Adam* Special Report 12), Feb. 1977, 62–66.

Wolfe, Bernard. *Memoirs of a Not Altogether Shy Pornographer*. New York: Doubleday, 1972.

"Woman Acquitted in Sale of D. H. Lawrence Book." *New York Herald Tribune*, 10 Sept. 1931. ACLU Archives, 503: 188.

Wood, Clement. *Herbert Clark Hoover: An American Tragedy*. New York: Michael Swain, 1932.

———. *Lady Chatterley's Friends*. New York: Faro, 1932.

———. *Warren Gamaliel Harding: An American Comedy*. New York: William Faro, 1932.

Woolf, S. J. "A Vice Suppressor Looks at Our Morals." *NYT*, 9 Oct. 1932, sec. 7: 2.

Woolston, Howard. *Prostitution in the United States*. 1921. Montclair, N.J.: Patterson Smith, 1969.

Legal Citations and Reports

Farley v. Simons. 99 F2d 343 (1938).

Rebhuhn et al. v. Cahill. 31 F. Supp. 47 (1939).

Roth v. Goldman, 172 F2d 788 (1949). U.S. Ct. of Appeals, 2nd Cir., So. District of N.Y. *Transcript of Record*.

U.S. v. Esar Levine. C97-165. U.S. District Ct., So. District of N.Y. (1935; trial transcript)

U.S. v. Levine. 83 F2d 156 (2d Cir. 1936). (appellate court report)

U.S. v. Ben Rebhuhn, Anne Rebhuhn, and Ben Raeburn. C97-410. U.S. District Ct., So. District of N.Y. (1939; trial transcript)

U.S. v. Rebhuhn et al. 109 F2d 512 (2d Cir. 1940). (appellate court report)

U.S. v. Pauline Roth and Samuel Roth. C99-114. U.S. District Ct., So. District of N.Y. (1936; including stenographer's minutes)

U.S. v. Samuel Roth. C53-79. U.S. District Ct., So. District of N.Y. (1929; stenographer's minutes; indictment)

U.S. v. Samuel Roth. Cr 148-9. U.S. District Ct., So. District of N.Y. (1956; including briefs, affadavits, trial transcript)

U.S. v. Samuel Roth. Cr 148-9. U.S. District Ct., So. District of N.Y. 24030. (1959, On appeal from the U.S. District Ct. for So. District of N.Y.; including briefs, affadavits, trial transcript)

Recent Books, Articles, and Online Sources

Arendt, Hannah. *The Jew as Pariah: Jewish Identity and Politics in the Modern Age*. Ed. Ron H. Feldman. New York: Grove, 1968.

Attorney General's Report on Pornography: Final Report. Washington, D.C.: U.S. Department of Justice, 1986.

Bayor, Ronald H. *Neighbors in Conflict: The Irish, Germans, Jews, and Italians of New York City, 1929–1941*. Baltimore, Md.: Johns Hopkins University Press, 1978.

Becker, Howard S. *Man in Reciprocity*. New York: Praeger, 1956.

———. *Outsiders: Studies in the Sociology of Deviance*. New York: Free Press, 1963.

Birmingham, Stephen. *"The Rest of Us": The Rise of America's Eastern European Jews.* New York: Berkley, 1985.

Black, Gregory D. *Hollywood Censored: Morality Codes, Catholics, and the Movies.* Cambridge: Cambridge University Press, 1994.

Blanchard, Paul. *American Freedom and Catholic Power.* Boston: Beacon, 1950.

——. *The Right to Read.* Boston: Beacon, 1956.

Block, Alan. *East Side — West Side: Organizing Crime in New York, 1930–50.* New Brunswick, N.J.: Transaction, 1983.

Bogart, Max. "A Study of Certain Legally Banned Novels in the United States, 1900–1950." Ph.D. diss., New York University, 1956.

Bonacich, Edna. "A Theory of Middleman Minorities." *American Sociological Review* 38 (Oct. 1973): 583–94.

Bonacich, Edna, and Jonathan H. Turner. "Toward a Composite Theory of Middleman Minorities." *Ethnicity* 7 (1980): 144–58.

Boyer, Paul. *Purity in Print: The Vice-Society Movement and Book Censorship in America.* New York: Scribner's, 1968.

——. *Urban Masses and Moral Order in America, 1820–1920.* Cambridge, Mass.: Harvard University Press, 1978.

Burke, Redmond A. *What Is the Index?* Milwaukee, Wisc.: Bruce, 1952.

Chafee, Zechariah, Jr. *Government and Mass Communication.* Vol. 1. Chicago: University of Chicago Press, 1947.

"Charles Carrington: The Man and His Books." In *A Victorian Sampler*, ed. Richard Manton, 1–24. New York: Blue Moon, 1992.

Chernofsky, Jacob L. "*AB Bookman's Weekly*: The First 50 Years." *AB Bookman's Weekly*, 5 Jan. 1998, 4, 6, 10, 12, 14, 16.

——. "Sol. Malkin's Passion: The Best of All Possible Book Worlds." In *The 1987 Bookman's Yearbook*, 3–9. New York: Bookman's Weekly, 1987.

Cheyney, O. H. *Economic Survey of the Book Industry, 1930–31.* New York: Bowker, 1965.

Cochran, Thomas. *The Great Depression and World War II, 1929–1945.* New York: Scott Foresman, 1968.

Couvares, Francis G. "Hollywood, Main St., and the Church: Trying to Censor the Movies Before the Production Code." *American Quarterly* 44.4 (Dec. 1992): 584–615.

Covington, D. B. *The Argus Book Shop: A Memoir.* West Cornwall, Conn.: Tarrydiddle, 1977.

Dardis, Tom. *Firebrand: The Life of Horace Liveright.* New York: Random House, 1995.

Dearborn, Mary V. *The Happiest Man Alive: A Biography of Henry Miller.* N.Y.: Simon and Schuster, 1991.

de Grazia, Edward. *Censorship Landmarks.* New York: Bowker, 1969.

——. *Girls Lean Back Everywhere: The Law of Obscenity and the Assault on Genius.* New York: Random House, 1992.

——. "Obscenity, Censorship and the Mails I." *New Republic*, 23 Jan. 1956, 16–17.

D'Emilio, John, and Estelle Freedman. *Intimate Matters: A History of Sexuality in America.* New York: Harper and Row, 1988.

Dershowitz, Alan. *Chutzpah.* New York: Little, Brown, 1991.

Dickson, Donald. "Bureaucracy and Morality: An Organizational Perspective on a Moral Crusade." *Social Problems* 16 (fall 1968): 143–56.

Dinnerstein, Leonard. *Anti-Semitism in America*. New York: Oxford University Press, 1994.

Duggan, Lisa, Nan D. Hunter, and Carol S. Vance. "False Promises: Feminist Antipornography Legislation," 72–88. In *Caught Looking: Feminism, Pornography, and Censorship*, New York: Caught Looking, 1986.

Dzwonkoski, Peter, ed. *American Literary Publishing Houses, 1900–1980: Trade and Paperback*. Detroit, Mich.: Gale Research, 1986.

Ephron, Nora. "Closeup: Storied Bookseller." *New York Post*, 2 July 1965. JA Files.

Erenberg, Lewis. *Steppin Out: New York Nightlife and the Transformation of American Culture*. Westport, Conn.: Greenwood, 1981.

Ernst, Morris L. "Reflections on the *Ulysses* Trial and Censorship." *James Joyce Quarterly* 3.1 (fall 1965): 3–11.

Ernst, Morris L., and Alan U. Schwartz. *Censorship: The Search for the Obscene*. New York: Macmillan, 1964.

Facey, Paul W. *The Legion of Decency: A Sociological Analysis of the Emergence and Development of a Social Pressure Group*. New York: Arno, 1974.

Fishbein, Leslie. *Rebels in Bohemia: The Radicals of* The Masses, 1911–1917. Chapel Hill: University of North Carolina Press, 1982.

Ford, Hugh. *Published in Paris*. 1975. New York: Pushcart, 1981.

Fowler, Dorothy G. *Unmailable: Congress and the Post Office*. Athens: University of Georgia Press, 1977.

Fried, Albert. *The Rise and Fall of the Jewish Gangster in America*. Rev. ed. New York: Columbia University Press, 1993.

Friedman, Jane M. "Erotica, Censorship, and the United States Post Office Department." *Michigan Academician* 4.1 (summer 1971): 7–16.

Fryer, Peter. *The Birth Controllers*. New York: Stein and Day, 1966.

Gallagher, John F., ed. Introduction to *My Life and Loves*, by Frank Harris. New York: Grove, 1963.

Gamlin, Douglas H., ed. *The Tijuana Bible Reader*. San Diego, Calif.: Greenleaf, 1969.

Garrett, Charles. *The LaGuardia Years: Machine and Reform Politics in New York City*. New Brunswick, N.J.: Rutgers University Press, 1961.

Gertzman, Jay A. " 'Esoterica' and 'The Good of the Race': Mail-Order Distribution of Erotica in the 1930s." *Papers of the Bibliographical Society of America* 86.3 (1992): 295–340.

Gibson, Ian. *The English Vice: Beating, Sex and Shame in Victorian England and After*. London: Duckworth, 1978.

Gilfoyle, Timothy J. *City of Eros: New York City, Prostitution, and the Commercialization of Sex, 1790–1920*. New York: Norton, 1992.

Gilman, Sander L. *Jewish Self-Hatred: Anti-Semitism and the Hidden Language of the Jews*. Baltimore, Md.: Johns Hopkins University Press, 1986.

Gilmer, Walker. *Horace Liveright: Publisher of the Twenties*. New York: David Lewis, 1970.

Gilmore, Donald H. *Sex, Censorship and Pornography*. Vol. 1. San Diego, Calif.: Greenleaf, 1969.

Glazer, Nathan, and Daniel Patrick Moynihan. *Beyond the Melting Pot: The Negroes, Puerto Ricans, Jews, Italians, and Irish of New York City*. 2d ed. Cambridge, Mass.: MIT Press, 1970.

Goren, Arthur A. *New York Jews and the Quest for Community*. New York: Columbia University Press, 1970.

Grant, Sidney S., and S. E. Angoff. "Massachusetts and Censorship." *Boston University Law Review* 10 (Jan. 1930): 43–46.

——. "Massachusetts and Censorship (Continued)." *Boston University Law Review* 10 (Apr. 1930): 147–94.

——. "Recent Developments in Censorship." *Boston University Law Review* 10 (Nov. 1930): 488–509.

Gunther, Gerald. *Learned Hand: The Man and the Judge*. New York: Knopf, 1994.

Gurstein, Rochelle. *The Repeal of Reticence: A History of America's Cultural and Legal Struggles over Free Speech, Obscenity, Sexual Liberation, and Modern Art*. New York: Hill and Wang, 1996.

Gusfield, Joseph. *Symbolic Crusade: Status Politics and the American Temperance Movement*. 1963. Urbana: University of Illinois Press, 1969.

Hamalian, Leo. "Nobody Knows My Names: Samuel Roth and the Underside of Modern Letters." *Journal of Modern Literature* 3.4 (Apr. 1974): 889–921.

Hamilton, Gary. "Pariah Capitalism: A Paradox of Power and Dependence." *Ethnic Groups* 2 (1978): 1–25.

Hebditch, David, and Nick Anning. *Porn Gold: Inside the Pornography Business*. London: Faber and Faber, 1988.

Hendel, Charles W. "An Exploration of the Nature of Authority." In *Authority*, ed. Carl J. Friedrich, 3–27. 1956. Westport, Conn.: Greenwood, 1981.

Hertzberg, Arthur. *The Jews in America: Four Centuries of an Uneasy Encounter*. New York: Simon and Schuster, 1989.

Higham, John. "Social Discrimination Against Jews in America, 1830–1930." In *The Jewish Experience in America*, Vol. 5, "At Home in America," ed. Abraham J. Karp, 349–81. Waltham, Mass.: American Jewish Historical Society, 1969.

Hindus, Milton. "Samuel Roth." Unpublished essay.

Hoffman, Edwin D. "The Bookshops of New York City, 1743–1948." *New York History* 30 (Jan. 1949): 53–65.

Hofstadter, Richard. *The Age of Reform from Bryan to F.D.R*. New York: Knopf, 1956.

——. *Anti-Intellectualism in American Life*. 1962. New York: Vintage, n.d.

Holt, R. G. *Little "Dirty" Comics*. San Diego, Calif.: Socio Library, 1971.

Hoyt, Olga G., and Edwin P. *Censorship in Boston*. New York: Seabury, 1970.

Hyde, H. Montgomery. *A History of Pornography*. New York: Dell, 1966.

Joselit, Jenna W. *Our Gang: Jewish Crime and the New York Jewish Community, 1900–1940*. Bloomington: Indiana University Press, 1983.

Juno, Andrea. "Holly Hughes." In *Angry Women*, ed. Andrea Juno and V. Vale, 98–104. San Francisco, Calif.: Re/Search, 1991.

Kazin, Michael. *The Populist Persuasion: An American History*. New York: Basic, 1995.

Kearney, Patrick. *A Bibliography of the Publications of the New York Olympia Press*. Santa Rosa, Calif.: Scissors and Paste Bibliographies, 1988.

Kendrick, Walter. *The Secret Museum: Pornography in Modern Culture*. New York: Viking, 1987.

Kennedy, Jane. "United States Postal Rates, 1848–1951." Ph.D. diss., Columbia University, 1955.

Kessner, Thomas. *The Golden Door: Italian and Jewish Immigrant Mobility in New York City, 1880–1915*. New York: Oxford University Press, 1977.

Kielbowicz, Richard B. "Mere Merchandise or Vessels of Culture: Books in the Mail, 1792–1942." *Papers of the Bibliographical Society of America* 82.2 (1988): 169–200.

Kipnis, Laura. *Bound and Gagged: Pornography and the Politics of Fantasy in America*. New York: Grove, 1996.

Kirkpatrick, James J. *The Smut Peddlers*. New York: Avon, 1960.

Kligsberg, Moses. "Jewish Immigrants in Business: A Sociological Study." In Vol. 5, *At Home in America, The Jewish Experience in America*. ed. Abraham J. Karp, 249–84. Waltham, Mass.: American Jewish Historical Society, 1969.

Kugel, Adelaide. " 'Wroth-Rackt Joyce': Samuel Roth and the 'Not Quite Unauthorized' Edition of *Ulysses*." *Joyce Studies Annual* 3 (summer 1992): 242–48.

Lacy, Gerald M. *D. H. Lawrence: Letters to Thomas and Adele Seltzer*. Santa Barbara, Calif.: Black Sparrow, 1976.

Legman, Gershon. "Erotic Folksongs and Ballads: An International Bibliography." *Journal of American Folklore* 103 (Oct.–Dec. 1990): 417–501.

——. *The Horn Book: Studies in Erotic Folklore and Bibliography*. New Hyde Park, N.Y.: University Books, 1964.

——. Introduction to *The Private Case: An Annotated Bibliography of the . . . Erotica Collection* in the *British (Museum) Library*, by Patrick Kearney. London: Landesman, 1981.

——. *Love & Death: A Study in Censorship*. 1949. New York: Hacker Art, 1963.

——. "A Reminiscence." *The Art of Mahlon Blaine*. East Lansing, Mich.: Peregrine, 1982.

——. "Sex Censorship in the U.S.A." *PLAN: Organization of the British Progressive League* (London) 2.1 (Jan. 1945): 2–9.

Lestchinsky, Jacob. "The Position of the Jews in the Economic Life of America." In *Jews in a Gentile World*, ed. Isacque Graeber and Steuart H. Britt, 402–16. New York: Macmillan, 1942.

Lewis, Felice Flannery. *Literature, Obscenity, and Law*. Carbondale: Southern Illinois University Press, 1976.

Madison, Charles A. *Jewish Publishing in America: The Impact of Jewish Writing on American Culture*. New York: Sanhedrin, 1976.

Makris, John N. *The Silent Investigators: The Great Untold Story of the United States Postal Inspection Service*. New York: Dutton, 1959.

Maltby, Richard. " 'To Prevent the Prevalent Type of Book': Censorship and Adaptation in Hollywood, 1924–34." *American Quarterly* 44.4 (Dec. 1992): 554–83.

May, Elaine Tyler. *Great Expectations: Marriage and Divorce in Post-Victorian America.* Chicago: University of Chicago Press, 1980.

May, Larry L., and Elaine Tyler May. "Why Jewish Movie Moguls: An Exploration in American Culture." *American Jewish History* 72.1 (Sept. 1982): 6–25.

Mendes, Peter. *Clandestine Erotic Fiction in English, 1800–1930: A Bibliographical Study.* Aldershot: Scolar, 1993.

Michelson, Peter. *The Aesthetics of Pornography.* New York: Herder and Herder, 1971.

——. *Speaking the Unspeakable: A Poetics of Obscenity.* Albany: State University of New York Press, 1993.

Miller, Thomas. *Immigrants and the American City.* New York: New York University Press, 1993.

Moscato, Michael, and Leslie Le Blanc, eds. *The United States of America v. One Book Entitled Ulysses by James Joyce.* Frederick, Md.: University Publications of America, 1984.

Mumby, Frank, and Ian Norrie. *Publishing and Bookselling.* 5th ed. London: Cape, 1974.

New York (State). Supreme Court. Appellate Division. "In the Matter of the Investigation of the Magistrates' Courts in the First Judicial Department and the Magistrates Thereof, and of the Attorneys-At-Law Practicing in Said Courts." *Final Report of Samuel Seabury, Referee.* 1932. Reprint, New York: Arno, 1974.

Panitz, Esther. "In Defense of the Jewish Immigrant, 1891–1924." In *The Jewish Experience in America.* Vol. 5, *At Home in America,* ed. Abraham J. Karp, 23–63. Waltham, Mass.: American Jewish Historical Society, 1969.

Park, Robert E. *Race and Culture.* Glencoe, Ill.: Free Press, 1950.

Paul, James N., and Murray Schwartz. *Federal Censorship: Obscenity in the Mail.* New York: Free Press of Glencoe, 1961.

Penzer, Norman N. *An Annotated Bibliography of Sir Richard Burton.* 1923. Rpt., London: Dawson's of Pall Mall, 1967.

Perrett, Geoffrey. *America in the Twenties: A History.* New York: Simon and Schuster, 1983.

Polsky, Ned. "On the Sociology of Pornography." In *Hustlers, Beats and Others,* 183–200. New York: Doubleday, 1969.

Porter, Jack Nusan. "The Urban Middleman: A Comparative Analysis." *Comparative Social Research* 4 (1981): 199–215.

Posner, Richard A. *Sex and Reason.* Cambridge, Mass.: Harvard University Press, 1992.

Rembar, Charles. *The End of Obscenity: The Trials of* Lady Chatterley, Tropic of Cancer, *and* Fanny Hill. New York: Random House, 1968.

Rinder, Irwin. "Strangers in the Land: Social Relations in the Status Gap." *Social Problems* 6 (winter 1958–59): 253–60.

Roberts, Edwin A. *The Smut Rakers.* Silver Spring, Md.: National Observer, 1966.

Rogers, W. G. *Wise Men Fish Here: The Story of Frances Steloff and the Gotham Book Mart.* New York: Harcourt, Brace, World, 1965.

Rose, Alfred. *Register of Erotic Books.* 1935. 2 vols. New York: Jack Brussel, 1965.

Ryan, William F. "Clement Wood." Unpublished essay. 1990.

——. "Samuel Roth: A Lion in a Den of Daniels." Unpublished essay. 1977.

Sachar, Howard M. *A History of the Jews in America.* New York: Vintage, 1992.

Sagarin, Edward. "Sex Research and Sociology: Retrospective and Prospective." In *Studies in the Sociology of Sex*, ed. James M. Henslin, 377–408. New York: Appleton-Century-Crofts, 1971.

Schauer, Frederick F. *The Law of Obscenity*. Washington, D.C.: Bureau of National Affairs, 1976.

Scheiner, C. J. *Compendium: Being a List of All the Books (Erotica, Curiosa, and Sexology) Listed in Our Catalogs 1–6 (1978–88)*. Brooklyn, N.Y.: C. J. Scheiner, 1989.

——. *The Essential Guide to Erotic Literature*. 2 vols. Ware, Hants.: Wordsworth, 1996.

——. Introduction to *White Stains: by Anaïs Nin and Friends*. London: Delectus, 1995.

Sears, Hal D. *The Sex Radicals: Free Love in High Victorian America*. Lawrence, Kans.: Regents, 1977.

Sennett, Richard. *Authority*. New York: Vintage, 1981.

Shifreen, Lawrence J., and Roger Jackson. *Henry Miller: A Bibliography of Primary Sources*. N.p.: Shifreen and Jackson, 1993.

Simmel, Georg. "The Stranger." In *The Sociology of Georg Simmel*, ed. Kurt H. Wolff, 402–8. New York: Free Press of Glencoe, 1950.

Slade, Joseph W. "Pornography." In *Handbook of American Popular Culture*, 2: 957–1010. Rev. ed. Westport, Conn.: Greenwood, 1989.

Slocum, John, and Herbert Cahoon. *A Bibliography of James Joyce*. New Haven, Conn.: Yale University Press, 1953.

Sollors, Werner. *Beyond Ethnicity: Consent and Descent in American Culture*. New York: Oxford University Press, 1986.

Sorin, Gerald. *A Time for Building: The Third Migration, 1880–1920*. Vol. 3 of *The Jewish People in America*, ed. Henry Feingold. Baltimore: Johns Hopkins University Press, 1992.

Sorokin, Pitirim. *The American Sex Revolution*. Boston: F. Porter Sargent, 1956.

Squires, Michael. *D. H. Lawrence's Manuscripts: The Correspondence of Frieda Lawrence, Jake Zeitlin and Others*. New York: St. Martin's, 1991.

Steakley, James D. *The Writings of Magnus Hirschfeld*. Toronto: Canadian Gay Archives, 1985.

Stires, Lloyd K. "Is It Time to Overturn the Miller Standard?" *Gauntlet* 2.14 (1997): 85–89.

Stone, Helen E. "The Lost Ladies: The Marketing and Sale of the Florentine Editions of Lady Chatterley's Lover." Ph.D. diss. University of Nottingham, 1995.

Stonequist, Everett V. "The Marginal Character of the Jews." In *Jews in a Gentile World*, ed. Isacque Graeber and Steuart H. Britt, 296–310. New York: Macmillan, 1942.

Straayer, Chris. "The Seduction of Boundaries: Feminist Fluidity in Annie Sprinkle's Art/Education/Sex." In *Dirty Looks: Women, Pornography, Power*, ed. Pamela Gibson and Roma Gibson, 156–75. London: BFI, 1993.

Talese, Gay. *Thy Neighbor's Wife*. New York: Dell, 1981.

Tanselle, G. Thomas. "The Thomas Seltzer Imprint." *Papers of the Bibliographical Society of America* 58 (1964): 380–448.

Tebbel, John. *A History of Book Publishing in the United States*. Vols. 3 and 4. New York: Bowker, 1978, 1981.

Tobin, A. I., and Elmer Gertz. *Frank Harris: A Study in Black and White*. 1931. Rpt., New York: Haskell House, 1970.

Vanderham, Paul. *James Joyce and Censorship: The Trials of Ulysses*. New York: New York University Press, 1998.

von Weise, Leopold. *Systematic Sociology: On the Basis of the* Beziehungslehre *and* Gebildelehre. Adapted and amplified by Howard Becker. 1932. Rpt., New York: Arno, 1974.

Wallace, Jonathan, and Mark Mangan. *Sex, Laws, and Cyberspace: Freedom and Censorship on the Frontiers of the Online Revolution*. New York: Holt, 1996.

Weber, Max. "Judaism, Christianity, and the Socio-Economic Order." In *The Sociology of Religion*, 246–61. 1922. Boston: Beacon, 1963.

White, Kevin. *The First Sexual Revolution: The Emergence of Male Heterosexuality in Modern America*. New York: New York University Press, 1993.

Williams, Linda. "A Provoking Agent: The Pornography and Performance Art of Annie Sprinkle." In *Dirty Looks: Women, Pornography, Power*, ed. Pamela Gibson and Roma Gibson, 176–91. London: BFI, 1993.

———. "Second Thoughts on *Hard Core*: American Obscenity Law and the Scapegoating of Deviance." In *Dirty Looks: Women, Pornography, Power*, ed. Pamela Gibson and Roma Gibson, 46–61. London: BFI, 1993.

Woolf, Charlotte. *Magnus Hirschfeld: A Portrait of a Pioneer in Sexology*. London: Quartet, 1986.

Wyllie, Irvin G. *The Self-Made Man in America: The Myth of Rags to Riches*. 1954. New York: Free Press, 1966.

Yaffe, James. *The American Jews: Portrait of a Split Personality*. New York: Paperback Library, 1969.

Zenner, Walter P. "American Jewry in the Light of Middleman Minority Theories." *Contemporary Jewry* 5.1 (spring/summer 1980): 11–30.

———. "Middleman Minority Theories: A Critical Review." In *Sourcebook on the New Immigration*, ed. Roy S. Bryce-Laporte, 413–25. New Brunswick, N.J.: Transaction, 1980.

———. "Middleman Minority Theories and the Jews: Historical Survey and Assessment." *Working Papers in Yiddish and East European Jewish Studies 31*. New York: YIVO Institute for Jewish Research, 1978.

———. *Minorities in the Middle: A Cross-Cultural Analysis*. Albany: State University of New York Press, 1991.

Acknowledgments

I want to express special thanks to the following:

Chris Eckhoff, Arnold Levy, and C. J. Scheiner, for a bottomless well of advice and information, often delivered at dinner meetings of our "pornassian society" at Gus's Place in Greenwich Village (and thanks to Gus Theodoro, we could spend half the night talking). Cliff Scheiner's acquaintance with New York publishers and writers, whom he invited to our dinners, allowed me to contact and learn from a variety of people who knew personally the individuals I discuss in this book. He also shared his encyclopedic knowledge of erotic literature, and the books and papers in his unparalleled collection, including his archive of materials relating to the Panurge Press.

G. Thomas Tanselle, of Columbia University and the Guggenheim Foundation, for advice and information regarding bibliography and publishing history over a period of years. Dr. Tanselle's course in bibliography at Columbia University, which I attended in 1983, was a revelation without which I would not have begun to study publishing history.

Mary Dearborn, author of *The Happiest Man Alive: A Biography of Henry Miller*, for information about clandestine publishing and the New York book trade, for explanations of how to contact publishers and prepare manuscripts, and for helping me be patient and scholarly.

Jerry Singerman and Meryl Altman, for detailed and perceptive editing.

Patrick Kearney, for information about, and analysis of, erotic literature, and for his kindness in sharing with me the FBI files of Samuel Roth, which he obtained under the Freedom of Information Act.

Adelaide Kugel, for hospitality and generosity on several occasions, for helping me distinguish between fact and myth regarding the life and work of her father, Samuel Roth, and for helping me understand her father's motivations and intentions. I also want to thank her, and James Kugel, acting on his mother's behalf, for allowing me to quote a passage from Roth's unpublished autobiography, and to reproduce the illustrations that appear as Figures 39 and 41–48.

Gershon Legman, for invaluable information about the distributors of erotic books in America, their methods of manufacture, the ways to identify specific texts and editions, and the rationale for censorship of erotic materials. I learned of these facets of the American experience of sexually explicit books through a series of uniquely eloquent letters and during an interview at Mr. Legman's home near Nice, France, in June 1990.

Dr. Ronald Rebhuhn, for hospitality and generosity in allowing me access to his collection of papers, books, and letters relating to the publishing activities of his father, Benjamin Rebhuhn, which included invaluable copies of books published by the Falstaff Press, and correspondence with Frank Harris. I also thank Dr. Rebhuhn for allowing me to reproduce a photograph of his father and pages from his father's copy of volume 3 of *My Life and Loves*.

Elmer Gertz, for many letters of explanation and information regarding his papers, deposited in the Library of Congress, and for allowing me access to, and permission to quote from, the Elmer Gertz Papers, Library of Congress.

Anton Holden, for valuable information about his grandfather H. S. Nichols.

Bernard J. Koloski, for cogent advice regarding editing and publishing.

J. Richard Walker, for help with understanding consumer price indexes.

Vytenis Babrauskas, for extensive information about Clara Tice and her book illustrations.

The Harry Ransom Humanities Research Center, University of Texas at Austin, for an Andrew W. Mellon Foundation Fellowship in June–July 1994.

The Pennsylvania State System of Higher Education, for a research grant to travel to collections at the University of Texas, the National Archives, and the New York Public Library in the summer of 1993.

Mansfield University, for a research sabbatical for the 1991–92 school year, and summer research grants in 1989, 1990, and 1993.

Traci P. Allen, Nikki Kilgore, Erin Olenick, and Thomas Saveri, for help with indexing.

Finally, but certainly not least, to Mary Ann Malkin, not only for information about people in the New York book trade and the activities of her husband, the late Sol. Malkin, but for personal and financial encouragement, the latter in the form of a grant to help cover living expenses for January–August 1995, when I was on leave without pay for research purposes.

I also gratefully acknowledge the following individuals and institutions for granting me permission to discuss and reproduce unpublished material they own:

Arents Library, Harris-Ross Collection, Department of Special Collections, Syracuse University (correspondence relevant to the work of Frank Harris, once in the possession of his American lawyer, Arthur L. Ross).

Stephanie G. Begen (letters written by Morris Ernst and a photograph of Mr. Ernst).

Charles P. Chafee (newspaper clippings in the Zechariah Chafee Papers).

Jonathan Hand Churchill (pretrial memos regarding the *Ulysses*, Panurge Press, and Falstaff Press cases in the Learned Hand Papers).

The Crime and Justice Foundation (material from the papers of the Watch and Ward Society).

Fales Library, New York University (Frank Harris Papers in the Fales Manuscript Collection, including correspondence, clippings, and galley proofs).

General Research Division of the New York Public Library, Astor, Lenox and Tilden Foundations (Periodical letters from the New York Society for the Suppression of Vice) and the Manuscript and Archive Division (Committee of Fourteen records).

Harvard Law School Library (Watch and Ward Papers, the Zechariah Chafee Papers).

Professor Milton Hindus (unpublished essay titled "Samuel Roth").

Humanities Research Center, University of Texas at Austin (photographic images and text from the "morgue" of the *New York Journal American*, the photography collection, the *Contempo* files, the Morris Ernst Papers, and letters regarding the publication of Frank Harris's *My Life and Loves*).

Kinsey Institute (brochures in the vertical file labeled "Erotica Producers (U.S.), Twentieth Century" and for permission to reproduce one of the brochures).

McIlvenna Institute for the Advanced Study of Human Sexuality (brochures of the Panurge and Falstaff Presses).

Seeley G. Mudd Manuscript Library, Department of Rare Books and Special Collections, Princeton University (ACLU Archives, Arthur Garfield Hayes Papers).

National Archives and Records Administration, Washington, D.C. (information in the Post Office archives regarding nonmailable matter).

New-York Historical Society (reproduction of a photograph of a retail book outlet of the Trotskyites).

Rosenbach Museum and Library (Rosenbach Company Archives).

Edgar M. Ross (letters written by Frank Harris regarding the publication of *My Life and Loves*).

Urban Archives, Paley Library, Temple University (*Evening Bulletin* "morgue").

Elizabeth Yoell (reproductions of the drawings of Clara Tice).

The following individuals generously granted me interviews or answered questions by telephone or in questionnaires: Jack Biblo, Andreas Brown, Mina Brussel, Bernard Conwell Carlitz, Oscar Chernovsky, Chris Eckhoff, Elmer Gertz, Tony Gud, Anton Holden, Patrick Kearney, Adelaide Roth Kugel, Susan Lane, Karen Burke LeFevre, Gershon Legman, Arnold Levy, Mary Ann Malkin, Dwight M. Miller, Bern Porter, Ronald Rebhuhn, Barney Rosset, Richard Roth, Barnet Ruder, J. B. Rund, Lyle Stuart, C. J. Scheiner, Michael Sweeney, G. Thomas Tanselle, Lorraine Wilbur, Allan Wilson, and Elizabeth Yoell.

Earlier versions of portions of this book were previously published as follows. I thank the editors of these publications for permission to reprint: "A Trap for Young Book-leggers: The First American Printings of Frank Harris's *My Life*, Volumes Three and Four (1927)," *Papers of the Bibliographical Society of America* 89.3 (Sept. 1995): 316–38; "Erotic Novel, Liberal Lawyer, and 'Censor-Moron': 'Sex for Its Own Sake' and Some Literary Censorship Adjudications of the 1930s," *D. H. Lawrence Review* 24.3 (fall 1992): 217–27; " 'Esoterica' and 'The Good of the Race': Mail-Order Distribution of Erotica in the 1930s," *Papers of the Bibliographical Society of America* 86.3 (Sept. 1992): 295–340; "Postal Service Guardians of Public Morals and Erotica Mail Order Dealers of the Thirties: A Study in Administrative Authority in the United States," *Publishing History* 37 (1995): 83–110. By permission of Chadwyck-Healey Ltd.

Index